SEWN *and* PASTED
CLOTH *or* LEATHER

BOOK-
BINDING
FOR
BOOK
ARTISTS
REQUIRING
NO SPECIAL TOOLS
or EQUIPMENT

KEITH A. SMITH
and
FRED A. JORDAN

FIRST EDITION JUNE 1998

Published and distributed by keith smith *BOOKS*
22 Cayuga Street
Rochester, New York 14620–2153
Telephone or Fax: 716 473 6776
Email: ksbooks@netacc.net

Library of Congress Card Catalogue Number: 98–90543

ISBN: 0–9637682–5–5

SEWN *and* PASTED
CLOTH *or* LEATHER

BOOK-
BINDING
FOR
BOOK
ARTISTS

REQUIRING
NO SPECIAL TOOLS
or EQUIPMENT

BOOK NR 181

KEITH A. SMITH
and
FRED A. JORDAN

keith smith *BOOKS*   Rochester, New York

KE◉TH

For Scott & Ellie

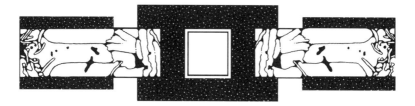

TABLE *of* CONTENTS

Marking the Stations, Sewing Stations Using a Knife, Ball Point Needle, Jogging for Sawing, Sawing the Stations, Sawing for Raised Cords, Sawing for Recessed Cords, Thread, Waxing the Thread, Threading the Needle, Knots, Procedure for Tying an Overhand K, Procedure for Tying a Square Knot, Weaver's Knot, Half Hitch, Kettle Stitch, True Kettle Stitch, Forward or Backward Drop, Preferred Backward Drop, Backward Drop, Link and Lock in One Maneuver, False Kettle Stitch, Sewing on the Bench, Tension in Sewing, Kettle Stations, Middle Stations

PRE*f*ACE

Fred Jordan came up with the approach for the leather bindings in this textbook, beginning on page 211. It eliminates equipment, substitutes household tools and cuts out elaborate techniques. The Tight Back, like the other bindings described in this book can be done by the beginner, yet they are lovely, even elegant. They are ideal for artists with no formal training in bookbinding.

Book artists want a fine looking binding which will show off their work. A lovely cloth or leather binding can be made, even if you are unskilled in binding techniques.

I wanted to show the Pamphlet Binding with Boards, as it has few pages, yet can be a nice looking hard cover binding. The Flat Back is a standard binding I find appropriate for many of my artists' books.

Fred wanted to devise a method of producing a leather bound book without a great deal of costly equipment and a minimal amount of training. He has gone through each step of making a Tight Back binding to find how to work without costly equipment. He has replaced bookbinding tools with those found around the house. Simplified procedures eliminate paring leather which requires great skill and practice. Hand sewn endbands are replaced with rolled core endbands. Instead of tooling leather, onlay lines of thread are embossed into the leather.

Fred would tell me his approach. I would go home and write for a week. Then, I would take it to Fred. He would tell me what he did not like. Sometimes I would defend how I had written something, but usually deferred to his knowledge. It is a good collaboration between Fred and me. We both thank Gail Ferris for her proofreading.

This manual is very different from the three books on *Non-Adhesive Binding*, which I have previously written. We are pleased to present a book on bindings: sewn and pasted, hard cover, with cloth or leather coverings. And, yet, they are accessible for anyone to bind.

Fred Jordan, full leather Tight Back. June 1998. 23.5 x 16 x 2.3 cm.
Blind tooling was done with a table knife and straight edge—an example of his approach to binding with no paring of leather or special
tools or equipment required.

PRE*f*ACE

Fred Jordan came up with the approach for the leather bindings in this textbook, beginning on page 211. It eliminates equipment, substitutes household tools and cuts out elaborate techniques. The Tight Back, like the other bindings described in this book can be done by the beginner, yet they are lovely, even elegant. They are ideal for artists with no formal training in bookbinding.

Book artists want a fine looking binding which will show off their work. A lovely cloth or leather binding can be made, even if you are unskilled in binding techniques.

I wanted to show the Pamphlet Binding with Boards, as it has few pages, yet can be a nice looking hard cover binding. The Flat Back is a standard binding I find appropriate for many of my artists' books.

Fred wanted to devise a method of producing a leather bound book without a great deal of costly equipment and a minimal amount of training. He has gone through each step of making a Tight Back binding to find how to work without costly equipment. He has replaced bookbinding tools with those found around the house. Simplified procedures eliminate paring leather which requires great skill and practice. Hand sewn endbands are replaced with rolled core endbands. Instead of tooling leather, onlay lines of thread are embossed into the leather.

Fred would tell me his approach. I would go home and write for a week. Then, I would take it to Fred. He would tell me what he did not like. Sometimes I would defend how I had written something, but usually deferred to his knowledge. It is a good collaboration between Fred and me. We both thank Gail Ferris for her proofreading.

This manual is very different from the three books on *Non-Adhesive Binding*, which I have previously written. We are pleased to present a book on bindings: sewn and pasted, hard cover, with cloth or leather coverings. And, yet, they are accessible for anyone to bind.

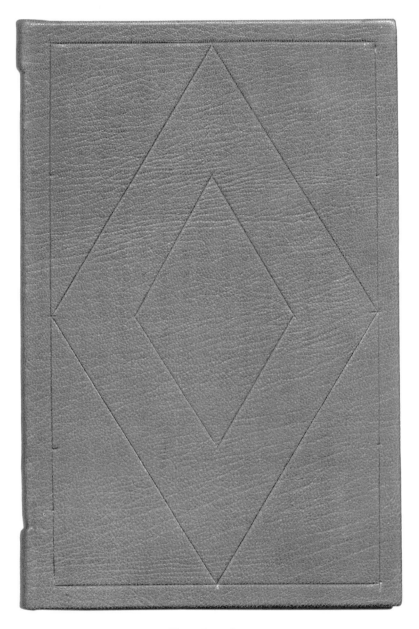

Fred Jordan, full leather Tight Back. June 1998. 23.5 x 16 x 2.3 cm. Blind tooling was done with a table knife and straight edge—an example of his approach to binding with no paring of leather or special tools or equipment required.

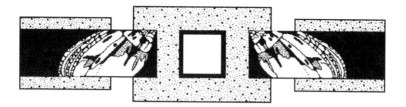

INTRODUCTION by FRED JORDAN

When Keith approached me to join him in writing a book on book-binding, my first thought was it has been done very well before by many people, including Douglas Cockerell, Laurence Town, Joseph Zaehnsdorf and others. His suggestion did, however, start me thinking of things that we could write and that led to this book.

I like working in leather. To me, and I think to most people, the finest bindings are done in leather. The leather bindings as described in this book are designed to be structurally sound, pleasant to look at and handle and, at the same time, not require the four or five years it takes to become a bookbinder with just a little knowledge and a lot to learn.

These pages are written for the book artist, art teachers and their students, craft's people, scouts and anyone who wants to make a book—for whatever reason.

What I have tried to do is show you, the reader, how to bind a book with leather and other materials using only the simplest equipment which can be obtained at a hardware store or found in your own kitchen and still have you produce a book you can be proud of.

I have never seen a book bound in this manner, nor have I run across an article or book describing it. Yet I cannot say that it has never been done before and, indeed, all I have done is put together things I have seen on other books I have worked on or examined. I have taken these ideas and blended them to develop the bindings we present here. The book structure itself is a compilation of many things. I started with an early book that had a leather spine and boards made of wood. The binding was crude, as the leather had not been pared and the book itself was not rounded.

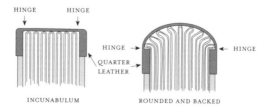

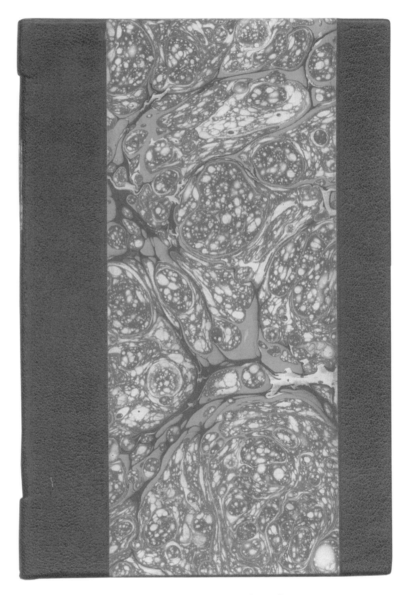

Fred Jordan, *Example 4*, half leather Tight Back. June 1998.
23.6 x 16.2 x 1.4 cm. Description of Fred's approach to binding the Tight
Back begins on page 211.

To see other examples of the bindings of which Fred speaks in his
introduction, refer to pages 14, 26, 213, 214, 215, 246, 300, 321 and 367.

The result was that the hinges were on the back of the book rather than on the sides, as they have been for the last few hundred years.

The advantage of this is you don't need to learn to pare leather, something that can take some time and lead to frustration as well as destroyed leather.

I rounded the book to give it a more durable hinge and, at the same time, a nice look and feel. Traditionally books have been rounded and backed with a bookbinding hammer. In this book I am doing the job with a bone folder. This is because an ordinary carpenter's hammer does not work well and bookbinding hammers are scarce. I learned the method of rounding and backing books with a bone folder in the 1950's when I was a student of Fleda Myers in Ithaca, N. Y. One summer Inez Pennybacker stayed with Fleda and showed all the students the "hammerless" method of rounding. I do not know where she learned it or when it was developed, but at that time Inez did most, if not all, her books in this way. It works very well. I still use it often and almost always on books that have delicate or tender paper, as I feel that it causes less stress to the paper.

Because the leather is not pared, the spine has a lump at the head and tail. I incorporated this into the design, just as raised cords have been incorporated into the design on some books. Rather than sewing endbands by hand I have chosen an 18th and 19th century method of wrapping cloth around cord, cutting to length, and gluing them to the spine at the head and tail of the book. This gives more substance to the endband than you can achieve with commercial endbands and also allows you to choose the color and pattern you want for your book. Filling in the board next to the leather on the inside and out gives the board a smooth look.

We have tried to do things requiring little special equipment and expense for you. If you do have some bookbinding equipment you will find that you can substitute it for what we have shown in this book.

One place where you should not cut corners is in choosing materials. Always use good acid-free paper and board. They may cost a little more but they are worth it and will last. The same is true of leather. Use a good leather that has been tanned for bookbinding from one of the suppliers we have listed.

There is no reason why you cannot make a fine book you can be proud of and will last.

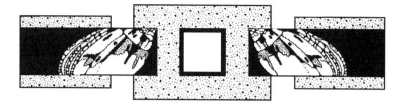

INTRODUCTION by KEITH SMITH

Fred Jordan, my binding teacher, and I have long discussed the idea of writing a book on traditional bookbinding. In writing my first three books on non-adhesive binding, it was always in the back of my head that I wanted to write on glued and pasted bindings. Friends, like Fred, would say that there are already enough books on the subject.[1] We would not wish to duplicate information.

As a book artist, I find all of the existing books on sewn and glued bindings geared towards the fine binder. As such, they are not as relevant to book artists who wish to hand bind their books. Fred and I came to feel there is a need to write a book eliminating equipment, substituting household tools and simplifying procedures for leather bindings.

This simplified method uses a bone folder, scissors, needle, straight edge and X-Acto™ knife. A common stainless steel table knife can double as a bone folder. Adhesives are limited to pastry flour and water, cooked or micro-waved and PVA glue. Two boards with *C*-clamps can be substituted for a book press.

With this manual in hand, those with little or no binding experience can make an attractive leather or cloth binding.

- *Pamphlet Sewn with Boards,* a 1-signature[2] book is pamphlet sewn, cased into boards, is described first.
- *Flat Back Cased-In Codex,* sewn onto tapes, follows.
- *Tight Back Casing,* sewn recessed cords, rounded and backed, which is a more substantial structure, is described next.
- *Hollow Back ,* sewn recessed cords, rounded and backed, is also referred to as the *Spring Back*. This is the final binding. The Tight Back and Hollow Back follow the procedures of which Fred speaks in his introduction.
- Finishing, inlays and various approaches to decorating edges of the book block are presented, as well as labels for the spine.

PASTING: Pasting is covered extensively. In the books on *Non-Adhesive Binding,* it seemed out of place to discuss pasting. Yet, even when the sewing is not glued, papers may be pasted on the boards of a non-adhesive binding. I have never explained the simple process of pasting I learned from Fred. I am happy this information is now available in one of my books.

Cooking flour is the traditional way of preparing wheat paste. In doing workshops I would meet people who are not cooks. One of them told me how they experimented with micro-waving wheat paste for a fail-safe batch. We will pass that on to you, as well.

Fred brings his knowledge of how to accomplish a task and, as I often hear about in my own work, what *not* to do. He shares many of these ideas with the reader.

This book is written in my voice. But in this manual, Fred is not only an adviser who suggests solutions, he is the force and the knowledge and the innovator of this simplified approach to hard cover, leather binding as a Tight Back or Hollow Back.

PURPOSE

This manual eliminates the need for any expensive equipment and even most of the tools. A book artist need not set up a full bindery in order to hand bind their books, even in leather.

Consequently, we use some different techniques than the traditional binder. This is not necessarily to simplify the process, but to eliminate equipment and the need to pare leather, plow the edges and to foil stamp. We try not to compromise on quality.

- *BACKING:* Since the book artist does not have access to a backing hammer, backing will be described using a bone folder. Actually, this is not a compromise. Many in fine binding back with a bone folder rather than a hammer, which could damage the paper.
- *ENDBANDS:* The book will have pasted-on commercial endbands, rather than hand-sewn. Sewn headbands are described in other books.[3] Fred suggests a simple rolled leather or fabric core-as-endband, which is described on page 238.

- *PARING LEATHER:* Paring is eliminated, as it requires practice and skill. Leather will be cut, not pared. The result is an attractive binding, which brings the possibility of leather bindings to the book artist. If, in time, the artist wishes to advance in skill in binding, they will study with a binder and learn to pare.
- *PLOWING THE EDGES:* Plowing the edges of the book block smooth gives a finished look. Practically, it makes it possible to dust the top edge of the book, referred to as the *head*. More importantly, a smooth edge prevents dust from working down into the pages. Rough edges are not as condensed. They act as a funnel, permitting dirt to enter the pages.

  I enjoy leaving the edges of my books irregular. It is part of my aesthetic—the uneven result looks hand made because a mechanical process cannot duplicate it. To Fred, even a book with hand made deckled edges should have the head of the book plowed. That edge looks bald to me. If I plowed the head, I would also plow the tail, leaving only the foredge with a deckle. Probably, I would leave all edges with the natural deckle and store the book in a clam shell. A slip case is not adequate protection; dust will still work into it. We cannot show plowing as it requires equipment.
- *LACING-IN:* The supports have been glued to the boards rather than laced-in.
- *FINISHING:* There will be no gold foil stamping described, but Fred has come up with ideas on decorating and on-laying paper to leather. In addition, coloring and cutting the edges will be described.

There should be *no compromise* on materials used. The added expense of using archival papers, book board, leather, cloth, paste and/or glue is minimal. It would be short-sighted to spend the time to make a hand-made book, only to have it deteriorate in a few years from scrimping on materials, or from ignorance of the need to buy superior materials.

CLOTH OR LEATHER COVERINGS

All the bindings described in this manual use paste. All have hard covers, using book board. The Flat Back has a third board on the depth of the spine.

We will describe how to attach the boards prior to adding the book block for each binding. Pasting the book block to the boards is referred to as *casing-in*.

Boards are attached to each other either with book cloth or leather. This acts as a hinge, permitting the covers to open and close. The remainder of the side-covers can be covered with decorative paper, cloth or leather.

QUARTER CLOTH OR LEATHER: If the cloth or leather covers the spine and extends onto the cover slightly at the spine-edge, it is referred to as *quarter leather*, or *quarter cloth*. See example on the facing page.

HALF LEATHER OR CLOTH: If the leather or cloth not only is used at the spine, but also protects the two corners of the board at the foredge, it is referred to as a *half cloth*, or a *half leather binding*.

Traditionally, half leather includes leather triangles at the foredge corners. See page 24. Half leather or cloth might also be a strip of leather, or cloth, along the entire foredge. See pages 16 and 26.

FULL CLOTH OR FULL LEATHER BINDING: If the cloth or leather covers both boards on the outside, it is referred to as *full cloth* or *full leather*. See examples on pages 14 and 25.

Proportion of cloth or leather to paper on the board is discussed on page 43.

Decorative papers supplement quarter and half coverings.[4]

FRED JORDAN, *BINDING TOOLS*, QUARTER LEATHER PAMPHLET BINDING WITH BOARDS. 24 X 16 X 1 CM.

A PAMPHLET SEWING CONTAINS A SINGLE SIGNATURE, WHICH CAN HAVE FROM 4, TO 32 PAGES. THIS PARTICULAR BOOK IS A 5-HOLE PAMPHLET SEWING. A JACONETTE HINGE IS SEWN ALONG WITH THE SIGNATURE, AND IS PASTED TO THE BOARDS IN CASING-IN AS THE HINGE. THIS IS TO GIVE STRENGTH TO THE HINGING ACTION.

THE ENDSHEET IS THEN PASTED TO THE BOARD, HIDING THE CLOTH HINGE. THE DETAIL ON THE LEFT SHOWS THE INSIDE OF THE BACK BOARD WITH THE ENDSHEET PASTED DOWN.

RAISED CORDS, HALF LEATHER FOUND BINDING, ALTERED.
TODD PATTISON, *THE LITTLE LIBRARY,* JULY 1995. 24.5 X 17 X 4.3 CM.

TIGHT BACK is a superior structure to the Flat Back Cased-In Codex. Along with Hollow Back, it is rounded and backed. There is no limit to the number of pages for this binding. It is described cased-in, rather than laced-in. The description begins on page 211.

Fred Jordan, full leather Tight Back, June 1997. The book is The Perfect tribute, by Mary Raymond Shipman Andrews, Charles Scribner's Sons, 1908. 19 X 12.4 X 1CM.

FLAT BACK CASED-IN CODEX: A THIRD BOARD USUALLY COVERS THE SPINE IN A
FLAT BACK BINDING. SINCE THE SPINE LACKS THE STRUCTURAL STRENGTH OF AN
ARCH IN A BOOK THAT HAS BEEN ROUNDED AND BACKED, THE FLAT BACK SHOULD BE
LIMITED TO 100 PAGES.

KEITH SMITH, *BOBBY*, BOOK NUMBER 100. COMPUTER DRAWINGS, OFFSET IN 3
COLORS. EDITION OF 50. HAND BOUND BY THE ARTIST. PUBLISHED BY NEXUS PRESS,
ATLANTA, 1985. HALF LEATHER BINDING WITH LEATHER HINGES. 29.2 X 23 CM.

HOLLOW BACK, or Spring Back, is rounded and backed and has a hollow back spine. The structure is superior to the Flat Back, in that there is no limit on the number of pages for this binding.

Scott McCarney, *ART: Search and Self Discovery*, 1993. full cloth found binding, altered. 28.4 x 40.6 x 43.2 cm.

PAMPHLET BINDING WITH BOARDS: Generally, a single signature booklet is paperback. A magazine is an example. Stapled in the centerfold, it is a single section or signature.

Book artists often make an offset edition which has a paper cover. The cover and the single signature are either stapled, or better, are sewn at once with a pamphlet sewing.

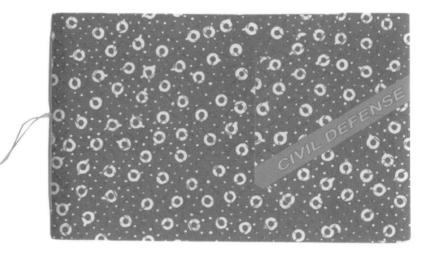

PHILIP ZIMMERMANN, *CIVIL DEFENSE*, PUBLISHED OFFSET BY SPACE HEATER MULTIPLES, 1983, 1984. PAMPHLET SEWING WITH PAPER COVER. THIS PARTICULAR SEWING STARTS ON THE OUTSIDE, SO THAT THE TIE-OFF IS ON THE SPINE. THREADS WERE NOT CLIPPED TO GIVE A TAIL AS DECORATION. 13 X 20.7 X .5 CM.

The single signature booklet we will describe has hard covers, endsheets, quarter cloth spine and cloth hinges inside. It has a good, substantial feel to it. It is described on page 125. Examples of the Pamphlet Binding with Boards can be seen on pages 23, 127, 128 and 132.

FLAT BACK CASED-IN CODEX: The Flat Back contains several signatures sewn onto tapes. The main characteristic is that it has a flat
spine. Since it lacks the structural arch of a spine that is rounded and
backed, this binding should be kept to less than 100 pages.

The Flat Back cased-in codex is not rounded and backed. Either
there are not enough signatures to round and back, or the structural
superiority of the arch has been omitted for speed in binding. It has
limited structural support without an arch from not backing, but it
has its place. It is structurally sound and it can even be exciting in
appearance. It is a work horse. It is probably the most suitable hard
cover solution for artists' books.

Backing is described with the Tight Back and Hollow Back bindings
on page 227. Those bindings are sewn recessed cords. See page 219.

CASING-IN: All the bindings described in this book are cased-in, not
laced-in: The tapes or cords are pasted to the boards. Casing-In is
less refined than lacing-in. On most fine bindings, *supports,* tapes or
cords, are laced, or pulled through the boards and glued in place.

LACING-IN: DETAIL OF THE OUTSIDE OF THE BOARD. CORDS HAVE BEEN
LACED-INTO BOARDS, PASTED AND DRIED UNDER PRESSURE. ENDS OF THE CORDS
WERE THEN TRIMMED OFF. SUEDE, RATHER THAN PAPER, IS PASTED OVER THE
BACKBONE.

LACING-IN: DETAIL OF THE INSIDE OF BOARD. THE FRONT BOARD IS OPEN
WITH THE BOOK BLOCK AT THE BOTTOM. CORDS, LACED-IN, WERE PASTED, THEN
DRIED UNDER PRESSURE. AN EXPOSED, PAPER-THIN LEATHER HINGE WAITS TO BE
PASTED ONTO THE BOARD. THE ENDSHEET WILL *NOT* BE PASTED DOWN.

PART I

PRELIMINARIES

MATERIALS AND TOOLS

There are surprisingly few tools and no equipment needed for these bindings. Fred devised his approach to leather bindings, rounded and backed, without the need for any tools except those found around the house. These are described on pages 36 and 37. A press is needed only for the Tight Back and Hollow Back books, although it is always helpful for casing-in any book. You can use C-clamps and boards, or dowel, boards and weight as a makeshift press. See page 38. Or, you can construct a fairly good press with not too much effort. See page 40.

These, as well as terminology for parts of the book are covered in this chapter.

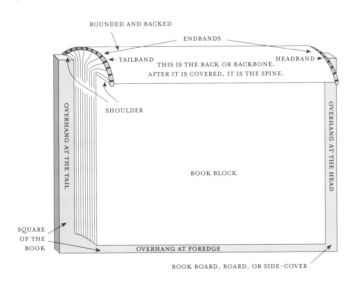

ROUNDED AND BACKED
ENDBANDS
TAILBAND
THIS IS THE BACK OR BACKBONE.
AFTER IT IS COVERED, IT IS THE SPINE.
HEADBAND
OVERHANG AT THE TAIL
SHOULDER
OVERHANG AT THE HEAD
BOOK BLOCK
SQUARE OF THE BOOK
OVERHANG AT FOREDGE
BOOK BOARD, BOARD, OR SIDE-COVER

THE TIGHT BACK AND HOLLOW BACK ARE SEWN, PASTED, THEN ROUNDED AND BACKED. THIS CREATES A BETTER STRUCTURE THAN A FLAT BACK. BACKING CREATES THE SHOULDER, WHICH THE BOARDS SIT AGAINST.

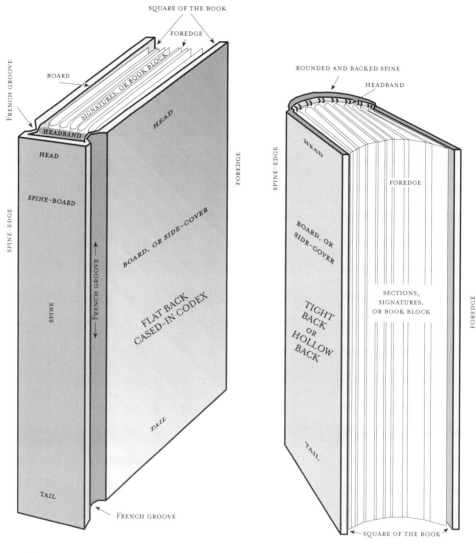

FLAT BACK CASED-IN CODEX   TIGHT BACK or HOLLOW BACK

ROUNDED AND BACKED

The Flat back Cased-In Codex on the left has 3 boards and a flat spine.
The drawing on the right is either a Tight Back, or a Hollow Back.
The Tight Back has leather or cloth pasted directly to the rounded
and backed spine. A Hollow Back pastes the fabric to a spine-paper,
which is not pasted to the spine. It is also referred to as a Spring Back.

DETAILS OF DECORATIVE AND MARBLED PAPERS FROM VARIOUS COUNTRIES.

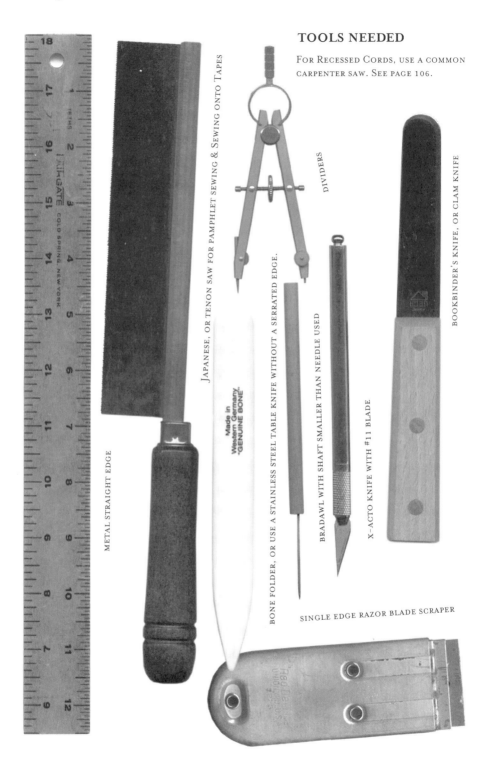

TOOLS NEEDED

FOR RECESSED CORDS, USE A COMMON CARPENTER SAW. SEE PAGE 106.

METAL STRAIGHT EDGE

JAPANESE, OR TENON SAW FOR PAMPHLET SEWING & SEWING ONTO TAPES

DIVIDERS

BONE FOLDER, OR USE A STAINLESS STEEL TABLE KNIFE WITHOUT A SERRATED EDGE.

BRADAWL WITH SHAFT SMALLER THAN NEEDLE USED

X-ACTO KNIFE WITH #11 BLADE

BOOKBINDER'S KNIFE, OR CLAM KNIFE

SINGLE EDGE RAZOR BLADE SCRAPER

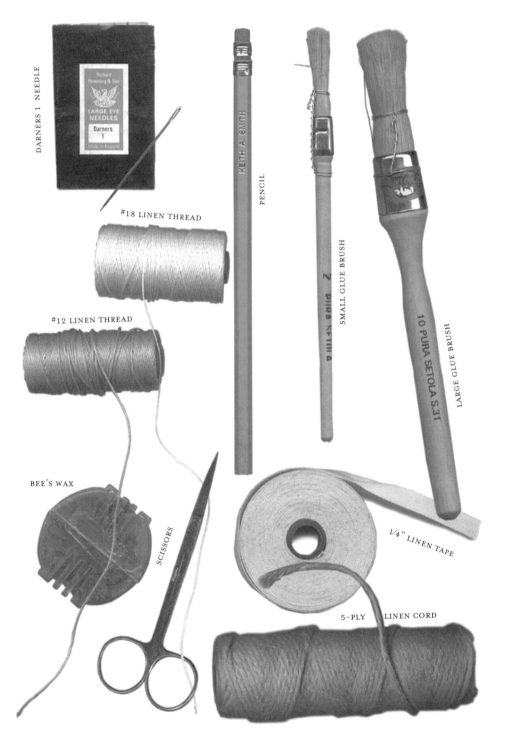

DARNERS 1 NEEDLE

#18 LINEN THREAD

#12 LINEN THREAD

BEE'S WAX

SCISSORS

PENCIL

SMALL GLUE BRUSH

LARGE GLUE BRUSH

1/4" LINEN TAPE

5-PLY LINEN CORD

SUBSTITUTES FOR A BOOK PRESS

C-CLAMPS AND BOARDS: Rather than drilling holes and using carriage bolts with butterfly nuts as on page 40, you can obtain pressure
by using two *C*-clamps. The clamps should have a 4" throat in order
to apply pressure in the middle of the book. Make sure the metal
never touches the book or any leather surface.

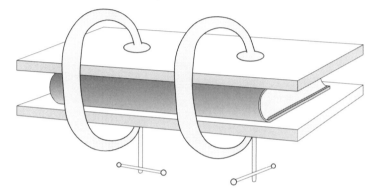

C-CLAMPS AND BOARDS AS A PRESS

*DOWELS, BOARDS AND
WEIGHT:* For casing-in, a
substitute for the press
described on page 40, is
to use weighted boards.
Two wooden, or acrylic
dowels are placed at the
hinge to indent the
French groove.

Acrylic dowels are pre-
ferred, since they can be
washed. Moist leather or
cloth will stain wooden
dowels, which then might
transfer that color stain
onto the cover of your
next book.

The *French groove* gives a
straight, indented fold
for the hinge.

WEIGHT ON TOP
MAKE SURE WOODEN BOARDS
AND THE WEIGHT EXTEND
BEYOND THE DOWELS, TO
MAINTAIN PRESSURE

WOODEN BOARD

WOODEN OR ACRYLIC DOWEL
FRENCH GROOVE

CASED-IN
CODEX

FRENCH GROOVE
WOODEN OR ACRYLIC DOWEL

WOODEN BOARD

DOWELS AND BOARDS: ACRYLIC OR WOODEN DOWELS,
ABOUT 1/8" IN DIAMETER, WITH A WEIGHT ON TOP, CAN BE
USED TO FORM THE FRENCH GROOVE IN CASING-IN A FLAT
BACK. HOWEVER, IT IS AN INFERIOR SUBSTITUTE FOR THE
COPPER-EDGE HARDWOOD BOARDS WITH A WEIGHT, PAGE
39, OR CLAMPING THE COPPER-EDGE BOARDS WITH CAR-
RIAGE BOLTS, SHOWN ON PAGE 40.

Otherwise, opening the cover the first time may result in an uneven crease. With the dowels in place, the hinge-fold is permanently creased, since the cloth or leather dries under pressure. One dowel is at the hinge-fold on the front board and one on the back board.

Dowels will give an inferior French groove, compared to the copper-edge boards described below. Sewing swells the spine. The spine-board will be thicker than the foredge, plus the two side-covers. The dowel method requires the book's spine-board be included sandwiched between the boards, resulting in uneven pressure. The dowels can shift. On the outside the French groove is not as pronounced. On the inside, the hinge is glued to the edge of the board side-cover only with the copper-edge board method.

COPPER-EDGE BOARDS WITH WEIGHT: Screw a copper strip along the edge of each pressing board. The copper protrudes above and below the surface of the board. On one side, it extends the depth of thin book board. On the other, the copper extends the depth of your thicker book board. This forms the French groove in the leather or cloth covering the side-boards.

The book's spine-board extends beyond the weighted sandwiched boards to give better pressure on the covers than the dowel method.

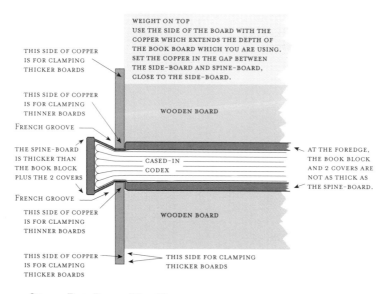

COPPER-EDGE BOARDS WITH WEIGHTS IS A GOOD SUBSTITUTE FOR A PRESS TO CASE-IN A FLAT BACK BINDING.

MAKING A PRESS

The press below is identical to the *Copper-Edge Boards and Weight* illustrated on the previous page. Here, there is no weight. Pressure is
obtained by screwing down the butterfly nuts on the carriage bolts.

Like the Copper-Edge Boards and Weight, this book press is ideal for
casing-in. Both approaches create a perfect French groove on the
outside of the covers. On the inside, the hinge that attaches the book
block to the boards will be attached on the edge of the board of the
side-covers, as well as on the surface. See illustration on the facing
page. Getting the hinge glued on the edge of the board is impossible
using dowels and a weight. The attachment is more secure and the
result is a finished look.

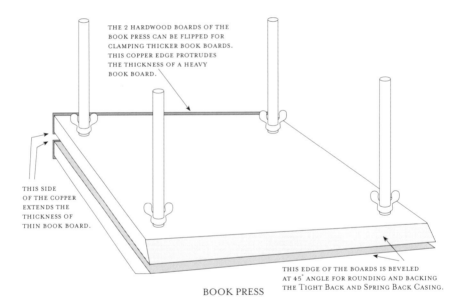

THE 2 HARDWOOD BOARDS OF THE
BOOK PRESS CAN BE FLIPPED FOR
CLAMPING THICKER BOOK BOARDS.
THIS COPPER EDGE PROTRUDES
THE THICKNESS OF A HEAVY
BOOK BOARD.

THIS SIDE
OF THE COPPER
EXTENDS THE
THICKNESS OF
THIN BOOK BOARD.

THIS EDGE OF THE BOARDS IS BEVELED
AT 45° ANGLE FOR ROUNDING AND BACKING
BOOK PRESS   THE TIGHT BACK AND SPRING BACK CASING.

BOOK PRESS: A BOOK PRESS CAN BE MADE WITH TWO HARDWOOD BOARDS AND
FOUR CARRIAGE BOLTS WITH BUTTERFLY NUTS. SPACE BETWEEN THE BOLTS
SHOULD NOT EXCEED 14". THIS WILL ACCOMMODATE ALL BUT LARGE BOOKS.
THIS TYPE OF MODEST PRESS IS ALSO AVAILABLE AT BINDERS' SUPPLY.

DEPTH OF THE BOARDS ILLUSTRATED IN THE FOREGROUND DO NOT HAVE COPPER
EDGING. THEY ARE CUT AT 45° FOR BACKING THE TIGHT BACK AND THE SPRING
BACK BINDINGS. THEY WILL BE BACKED WITH A BONE FOLDER, NOT A HAMMER.

This simple, fairly inexpensive book press is available from any binder's supply. Or it is easily made. You must use hardwood. To maintain even pressure in the center, space between the carriage bolts with wing-nuts cannot exceed about 14", using ¾" hardwood.

Buy copper strips to screw on one side of the depth of the boards. Saw the copper to proper length. Width of the copper is ¾" (the depth of your boards) plus the overhangs at top and bottom. One side overhangs the depth of a thin book board, which is about ⅛". The other, the depth of a thick book board, about 3⁄16". Measure the thickness of the book boards which you have on hand, prior to determining the width to cut the copper strips. Drill holes and screw into position.

The other edge of the boards, illustrated in the foreground on the facing page, should be cut at a 45° angle. This side is for the Tight Back and the Hollow Back. It is used for backing in those two bindings. The book block is clamped in, protruding the thickness of the cover. Backing is then done with a bone folder. This procedure is described on page 231.

INSIDE VIEW OF A FLAT BACK CASED-IN CODEX. THIS BOOK WAS CASED-IN WITH A PRESS LIKE THAT DESCRIBED ON THE FACING PAGE. THE HINGE THAT EXTENDS FROM THE BOOK BLOCK TO THE BOARD HAS BEEN GLUED TIGHTLY TO THE EDGE, AS WELL AS ON THE SURFACE, OF THE BOARD. THIS GIVES SECURE ATTACHMENT AND A FINISHED LOOK. IT IS IMPOSSIBLE TO ACHIEVE THIS WITH DOWELS AND A WEIGHT. THE HINGE WOULD GAP STRAIGHT FROM THE BOOK BLOCK TO THE SURFACE OF THE BOARD, RATHER THAN STAIR STEPPING UP THE EDGE.

KEITH SMITH, BOOK NUMBER 81, 1981. ONE-OF-A-KIND, QUARTER CLOTH FLAT
BACK BINDING. COVER HAS DECORATIVE PAPERS INLAID, WITH A PHOTOGRAPH OF
KEITH INLAID BY DEBORAH FLYNN POST. THE BOOK CONTAINS PHOTOGRAPHS,
ETCHINGS AND DRAWINGS. COLLECTION OF RICHARD AND RONAY MENSCHEL.
35.5 X 30.5 X 2.5 CM.

2

PROPORTION ON THE BOARD

Unless you are making a full leather or full cloth binding, your cover boards will have cloth or leather, supplemented by decorative paper. Proportion of leather to paper or cloth to paper must be considered.

QUARTER COVERING

Leather or cloth covers the spine and extends onto the boards. Width of quarter leather, or quarter cloth, onto the cover boards can be quite varied.

MEASURING THE WIDTH: The easiest way to measure is to set the boards in place on the book block. Take a scrap piece of paper. Hold the paper on the back cover at the point you wish the cloth or leather to extend. Bend the paper around the spine, onto the front board.

Mark the paper with a pencil the same distance onto the front board that the paper extends on the back. This measurement represents how much cloth or leather you want visible after the decorative paper is applied to the boards. Remember, decorative paper must overlap the leather on each board approximately 1/4". Therefore, add 1/2" to the measurement of the paper have the complete width of the quarter leather.

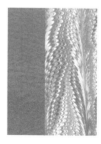

PAPER MUST OVERLAP THE LEATHER ON THIS EXAMPLE BY 1/2", SO THAT LEATHER IS SECURELY ATTACHED TO THE BOARDS.

NARROW STRIP OF LEATHER IS ELEGANT.

AVERAGE PROPORTION OF LEATHER TO PAPER.

RATHER WIDE AMOUNT OF LEATHER TO PAPER, BUT SOME PREFER THIS.

PROPORTION OF QUARTER CLOTH OR LEATHER TO PAPER ON THE BOARDS IS AN AESTHETIC DECISION.[4]

Decorative paper can overlap book cloth or butt against it. Measure width of the cloth accordingly.

Width of a quarter covering to paper depends upon your aesthetics. Some prefer the quarter leather to appear on the spine and just enough on the boards to form the hinge. It is important that the leather extend at least 1/2" onto the board so that the board is securely attached by the leather. Only a fraction of this leather need be seen, if you wish to overlap most of it with the decorative paper.

The boards will appear almost completely covered with paper, as in the example on the far left at the bottom of page 43. Actually, there will be more leather on the boards than is seen, since the paper overlaps the leather.

Others take the term *quarter leather* literally and extend it 1/4 the way across the boards. This often appears heavy, depending upon the color and texture of the leather and the colors and design of the paper.

Proportion of leather, or cloth, to paper on the board is a visual, not a mathematical decision. You do not have to read between the lines to know that I prefer a slight amount of leather showing, whereas Fred likes large proportions. Maybe it has something to do with our physical stature.

HALF COVERING

Traditionally, half covering includes triangles of cloth or leather at the foredge. See examples on pages 22, 25 and below. But it is difficult to design a cover with triangles on the corners without it looking like a ledger for posting debits and credits.

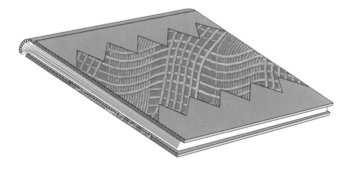

USE OF HALF LEATHER OR CLOTH CAN AND SHOULD BE, OPEN TO YOUR DESIGN.

LEFT: HALF LEATHER BINDING , KEEPING THE LEATHER TO JUST AN EDGE OF COLOR AND TEXTURE.

RIGHT: *MILLIMETER BINDING.* A MILLIMETER OF LEATHER BORDERS ALL EDGES FOR A REFINED LOOK AND DURABILITY. IN BOTH ILLUSTRATIONS, IT MUST BE STRESSED THE LEATHER COVERING THE SPINE AND BROUGHT ONTO THE SPINE-EDGE OF THE BOARDS MUST EXTEND ONTO THE BOARD FAR ENOUGH TO SECURE ATTACHMENT OF THE BOARDS. THE PAPER CAN OVERLAP TO GIVE THE APPEAR-ANCE OF A THIN EDGE OF LEATHER.

My favorite approach to half leather is to place a strip of leather com-pletely along the foredge. This protects the corners of the board and is easier to design. See pages 22 and 25, as well as above at the left.

This idea can be taken further. Bringing strips of leather in from the head and tail, with an island of paper on the outside of the board gives a millimeter of leather bordering the board. It is German cov-ering, a favorite of Betsy Palmer Eldridge.[5] See illustration above, on the right. However, it must be added that those German bindings were laced-in and what we are suggesting is to simply case-in, for a similar surface appearance to those bindings.

PROPORTION ON THE SPINE

For the Tight Back and Hollow Back only, the leather will be turned-in on the spine. See pages 257, 258. Since the leather is not pared, the turn-in creates a bulge. When we first discussed the idea of no equipment, no skill necessary in sewing endbands and paring leather, I saw the bulge on the spine as a necessary evil. With Fred's first protype, I fell in love with the turn-in bulge. It is not a "mistake," but form following function.

Light catches the bulges, which are anthropomorphic. The bulges fade as they approach the side-covers, which are totally flat. Finally, the bulges of this new approach to leather binding create a thicker spine at the head and the tail...a kind of border, an atavism of raised cord bindings.

The proportion on the spine which must be considered is how much turn-in of leather is desired at the head and tail. We prefer more at the tail, rather than an equal amount of turn-in at the head and the tail. It gives a sense of a base, just as in matting a print.

The size of the turns-in at the head and tail must be decided prior to measuring the super for the spine. See page 247.

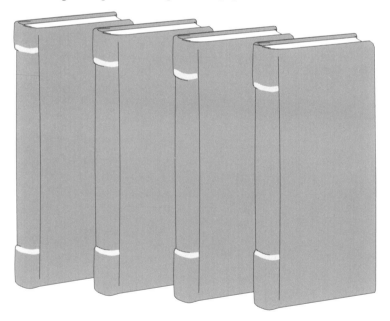

The height of the turn-in at the tail should be more than that at the head to give a sense of a base. Amount of each is an aesthetic decision.

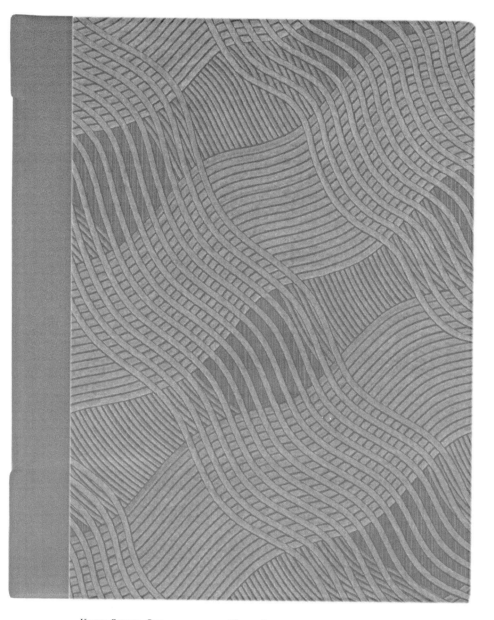

KEITH SMITH, QUARTER LEATHER TIGHT BACK ALBUM FOR PHOTOGRAPHS WITH PASTE PAPERS ON THE BOARDS. FEBRUARY 1998. 30.5 X 25.5 X 3.2 CM.

AN EXCESSIVE AMOUNT OF TURN-IN ON THE SPINE AT THE TAIL GIVES A MASSIVE PROPORTION TO THIS ALBUM. THE TIGHT BACK IS DESCRIBED ON PAGE 211.

3

ARCHIVAL MATERIALS

All materials should be acid-free.

The premise of this book is to present sewn and pasted, cloth or leather bindings, in a simplified manner. Equipment has been eliminated. Household items, such as a table knife, C-clamps and backsaw have been substituted for expensive binders' tools. But it must be very clearly stated that there should never be any compromise on materials. Again, we state, use only archival materials.

TESTS FOR ACIDITY

· One way to insure your materials are safe is to ask your binders supply if they handle only materials which they have tested and declared archival. Most fine suppliers meet this standard.

· You can perform your own tests for acidity on materials with an Abbey pH Pen.[6] Touch it to the surface. If the dot turns purple, the paper is neutral or alkaline (pH 6.8 or higher).

PAPERS: This is the main area of temptation, to not check that each paper you use is *pH* neutral, that is, chemically balanced and not acidic.

MARBLED PAPERS: Most marblers use safe pigments with lasting colors and archival paper. Ask before you buy.

BOOK BOARD

Very few boards are archival. Fred suggests using only Davey Red Board or museum quality 4-ply rag mat board. We use 4-ply rag mat board for our Pamphlet Bindings with Boards, as it is better proportioned to the thinner booklet. The Davey Red Board has to be tested; it is not guaranteed to be acid-free. However, Fred has never tested any that was not acid-free.

LEATHER

Use a good book binding leather. The leather should be 1 millimeter or less in thickness, preferably on the thinner side. Leather is available from binding suppliers that is tanned for book binding. Chrome-tanned leather will rot in a relatively short time just sitting on a shelf, without any use.

We would not recommend buying any leather from a craft store, but rather, from a book binding supplier.

GLUE

Hot glue will not be used in any bindings in this manual, as we are eliminating the expense of a glue pot. For centuries, this was considered the quintessential adhesive. (As I typed that word, I subconsciously left out the first letter *n*.) Hot glue does have its advantages. It adheres well, doesn't crack and in repairing bindings, it soaks off very easily for repairs, even after centuries.

The other glue is PVA, which has very limited use in this manual.

PVA: PVA, or *poly vinyl acetate,* has its admirers and conservators of books who despise it. There are two very fine instances to use PVA: One, is in box-making. No boxes or clam shells are described in this manual. The other is to attach the cloth hinge to the signature for a Flat Back. This is described on page 166. PVA will not be used in these bindings, neither on the spine, nor to attach leather, cloth, or paper to the boards.

I use *Jade 403* for box-making; Fred uses only paste. I do not use any generic hardware store type PVA glues. Even in art stores, there are very few PVA glues which are *pH*-neutral:

> "Jade [403 PVA] is one of only three brands of PVA which has been found to maintain a good *pH* level during natural aging tests, making it suitable for box-making and other book and paper uses." Cynthia Mowery, Bookmakers, Inc.[7]

Archival PVA glues can be purchased at a binders supply.

The term *archival* encompasses other elements besides whether the material is *pH*-neutral. Many conservators do not consider any PVA as "archival" because the process is not reversible. Once applied to paper, it is not easily removed. It is plastic, bonding to the surface.

For certain jobs, PVA is ideal, because it goes on easily, sets almost instantly and dries in 5 minutes. A good example is in gluing a book cloth hinge to a signature.

See *Gluing the Hinge To The Signature,* page 166. Only a thin bead can be used and the adhesive must bond.

Hot glue would be difficult. Paste would be impossible, as it does not have the viscosity to stick and requires saturating the surfaces to adhere. The signature would blister where the edge of the paper was moistened, next to the sheet, which remains dry.

One of the drawbacks of PVA is that the brush must be washed at once, or else the brush is ruined.

Hot glue and wheat paste are more forgiving. The brush is left in the glue pot when you are through. The glue pot is turned off. As the temperature lowers in the pot and the cooking smell lessens, the hot glue solidifies and the tip of the brush is laminated in the solid mass. Turning on the pot and heating it up for the next use, the brush is ready to use.

Paste causes no problems when accidentally allowed to dry in the brush. Soak it a minute or so and the wheat paste dissolves.

PVA will stain paper if it creeps around to the front surface. It will seep through un-sized fabric and leave stains. Wheat paste does not stain fabric or paper. It may, on occasion, change the tone of black paper if it is spilled on the surface.

CARE OF GLUE BRUSHES: Some place their glue brush in a glass of water when not pasting for a few minutes. The brush is stiff and will not curl and become misshapen like a water color brush. Still, it has to be dried before using PVA again. I think it better to simply clean it after each use. Even when I am continually gluing, I wash the brush periodically so that glue will not dry at the top of the bristles.

Always wash brushes in cold water. The bristles are attached with adhesive that could melt in hot water. Dry the brush, shape it and store it standing, bristles up, so there is no pressure from the bristles pressed against a surface. The brush would become misshapen.

Plan ahead. Suppliers do not ship PVA in winter, as it must be kept above freezing temperatures.

PASTE

We suggest using wheat paste. The only adhesive used in this manual, with one exception, is wheat paste. There are many pastes, of which wheat paste is one. Some binders make rice paste. We do not use methyl cellulose.

Many binders use methyl cellulose and it is considered archival. However, methyl cellulose has no long term record. No one can be certain how it will hold up in time, since it is has only been used for the past few years.

Wheat paste is centuries old and can be trusted.

TYPE OF FLOUR: Use only pastry flour. Flour and water form paste. What makes it stick is the gluten in the flour. An all-purpose flour has more gluten than pastry flour, so it has more viscosity. The reason it is not used to make wheat paste, is that gluten also attracts bugs while your book sits on the shelf. You want to use a flour with the least amount of gluten, yet enough to make the two surfaces adhere, but no more than necessary.

Pastry flour is not the same as cake flour nor bread flour. Pastry flour can be found in some supermarkets; it is available in almost all health food stores.

While doing a workshop in Hobart, Tasmania, our host, Penny Carey-Wells introduced us to tapioca flour. This makes a fine paste, clearer and more gelatin-like than pastry flour. We enjoyed using it.

NO COMMERCIAL PASTE MIXTURE: Never buy commercial wheat paste, even from an art supply store. The majority of it contains additives to keep the bugs away and to stop it from spoiling. You do not wish to purchase a wheat paste mixture that contains additives, when it serves no purpose in making paste and renders your work non-archival.

In addition, the commercial mixture will be marked up 10 to 100 times the price of pastry flour.

Do not use wallpaper paste. It is acidic.

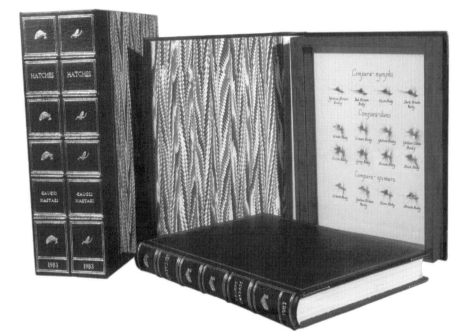

Fred Jordan, sewn Raised Cords, bound in full leather with gold tool-
ing. The book is *Hatches, A Complete Guide to Fishing the Hatches of
North American Trout Streams,* by Al Caucci/Bob Nastasi,
Comparahatch, Ltd., New York, 1983. 28.8 x 22.7 x 3.8 cm.

One volume, below, is the text. The second volume, to the right,
appears identical when closed. Opened, the back board contains a
wooden shadow box with glass which houses samples for fly fishing.
The front cover opens to show the color plates from the book.

To the left, both volumes are housed is a quarter leather clam shell
with gold tooling. The spine of the box has the same design as the spine
of the two books.

Neither Raised Cord sewing nor gold tooling of leather will be
described in this manual.

4

PASTE

MAKING PASTE

Wheat paste is one of those elements in a process that is a joy. Preparation of the paste is quick, it is simple to use, it doesn't stain fabric or papers, it doesn't smell, it cleans up easily and it isn't toxic. You could eat it if you like. In fact, if you would add an egg and a teaspoon of vanilla extract to the formula, you would have vanilla pudding.

The formula Fred uses and taught me to use, is from Bernard Middleton:

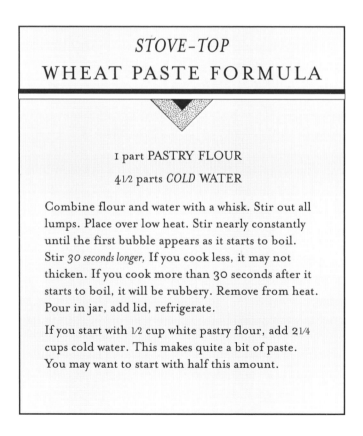

STOVE-TOP
WHEAT PASTE FORMULA

1 part PASTRY FLOUR

4 1/2 parts *COLD* WATER

Combine flour and water with a whisk. Stir out all lumps. Place over low heat. Stir nearly constantly until the first bubble appears as it starts to boil. Stir *30 seconds longer,* If you cook less, it may not thicken. If you cook more than 30 seconds after it starts to boil, it will be rubbery. Remove from heat. Pour in jar, add lid, refrigerate.

If you start with 1/2 cup white pastry flour, add 2 1/4 cups cold water. This makes quite a bit of paste. You may want to start with half this amount.

STOVE-TOP COOKING PASTE: The recipe on the facing page cooks on the stove. Use low to medium heat, watching carefully, so it does not burn on bottom. If you fail to stir constantly, or have too high heat, it will scorch. Best results, like any cooking, are easier with a good gourmet saucepan, which distributes the heat evenly. A good pan can cook the paste in half the time of a beat-up aluminum pan. Start to finish is about two minutes.

MICROWAVE PASTE: When Scott McCarney and I give workshops together, sometimes we find someone who has experimented with microwaving wheat paste. Many more times, people ask us if they can microwave rather than cook wheat paste. So Scott has played around with it. Below is his *no-cook for non-cooks* formula:

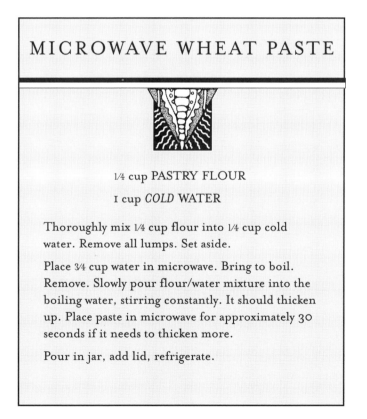

MICROWAVE WHEAT PASTE

¼ cup PASTRY FLOUR

1 cup *COLD* WATER

Thoroughly mix ¼ cup flour into ¼ cup cold water. Remove all lumps. Set aside.

Place ¾ cup water in microwave. Bring to boil. Remove. Slowly pour flour/water mixture into the boiling water, stirring constantly. It should thicken up. Place paste in microwave for approximately 30 seconds if it needs to thicken more.

Pour in jar, add lid, refrigerate.

PASTING TIPS

We are devoting a large amount of time to pasting, as I have found people have difficulty with the procedure. If it is explained in detail, it is easy to do and the results will be excellent.

Fred and I cook our paste. If we are going to paste that day, we can take out the pastry flour, measure, cook and within 3 minutes we are pasting paper. The paste will be warm, but it will stick. You do not have to wait until the paste is cold to use it.

SURFACE FOR PASTING: It always amazes me when I give a workshop at a book center and their general practice is to paste on scraps of paper. This is because that is the traditional way of doing it.

I find it is difficult to tell if the paper is clean. Some students invariably lay the book right in wet paste. Pasting on papers clutters and makes a disorderly work area. The practice is wasteful.

Pasting is so much easier when done on glass or formica surface and it does not waste paper. Clean up is easier too.

I paste on my light table. If I want to line up a patterned paper onto the board, I lay the board on the light table, after the paper is pasted. The light table is turned on and the pasted paper is held slightly above the board.

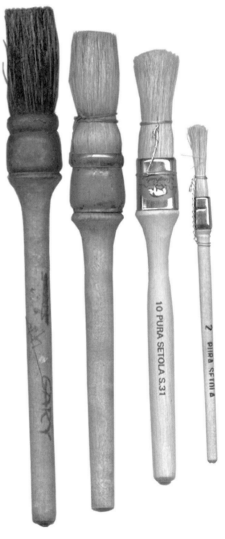

VARIOUS SIZE GLUE BRUSHES. IT WOULD BE GOOD TO HAVE A SMALL AND A LARGE BRUSH FOR PASTING.

Looking through the translucent paper allows the design to be lined up on the board beneath. The paper is lowered into position and tapped down with your fingers. Pick it up and you are ready to clip the corners and to make the turns-in on the inside of the board.

I keep a towel on my shoulder as I am pasting. I can quickly dry my hands to handle the decorative paper or answer the phone. I don't have to look for the towel after sponging the glass surface.

Immediately after pasting and covering the board, the glass or formica table top is sponged off and dried with a towel. It is immaculate, dry and ready to paste the next papers or leather. There are no scraps of paste-soaked papers laying around. There is no mess that encourages accidents to happen. It is orderly and makes the job of pasting so much more simple.

Fred pastes on his glass table top. He does not clean up with a sponge. He uses a scraper, which is a single edge blade in a handle. He uses it to scoop up excess paste to return it to the jar. If he does not get around to wiping up the paste right away, he scrapes the glass surface to remove the dried paste.

Adéle Outteridge, Helen Sanderson and Charlotte Drake-Brockman. Untitled collaboration, double concertina binding, one-of-a-kind. Brisbane, Queensland, Australia, 1997, 7 x 19 x 2.5 cm.

AMOUNT OF TIME TO PASTE

Pasting times vary with each paper. Newsprint would require 20 seconds of pasting. Typewriter paper would be about 30 seconds. The 80 lb. text weight paper used in printing this manual requires 90 to 120 seconds. Rives BFK heavyweight would require 4 to 5 minutes.

In workshops, I invariably find many students are too impatient. They will not paste the required time, even though it has been pointed out that each paper has a different thickness and absorbency rate determined by its density.

There is a simple test as to when you have pasted long enough: You start to paste, the paper will start to curl. As you continue to paste, the *curling will cease* and the paper has relaxed, *flat on the surface*. It is ready.

PASTING PROCEDURE

PASTING TWICE: Fred pastes twice. I paste continually. Both methods achieve the same results. Both allow the entire surface of the paper to become saturated with paste prior to covering the boards.

Fred applies a first coat of paste, until the curling action starts to subside. He leaves a rather thick coating of paste across the entire surface. He waits the required amount of time for the paste to saturate that particular thickness and density of paper.

Fred applies his second and final pasting. This time, his brush removes the excess of paste, leaving a thin even layer of paste across the surface of the paper.

PASTING CONTINUALLY: The surface of paper being pasted must be kept continuously wet, if not pasted continually. By continually pasting until the paper is saturated with paste, I insure no area of the paper goes dry. As paste is applied to the surface, it is drawn into the paper like a sponge. This could leave areas of the surface without paste, especially the thinner areas caused by brush strokes.

Even if you paste a second time prior to covering the board, those drier spots on the surface of the paper may not be saturated.

When you apply the paper to the board, it will continue to absorb the paste. The board will absorb even more of the paste, leaving little to no paste in these problem areas between the two surfaces. Blisters will occur where the paper has not stuck to the board.

I find it risky to paste the surface once, then wait for the suggested time to pass before applying the second coat.

Often I do not literally paste continually, but intermittently. Another reason for my method is that I prefer to apply thin coats rather than dollops. In this manner, I do not waste paste or have to scoop it up afterwards to return it to the paste jar.

PASTING LEATHER: Pasting leather requires several minutes. Test to see when the leather is ready to cover the board by lifting a corner to examine the good surface. If the leather is totally wet it has absorbed enough paste to saturate it. Apply the leather to the board.

Fred mists the good side of the leather *prior to pasting* to prevent capillary action from letting the paste come through mottled on light color leathers. The disadvantage is you cannot test when enough pasting has been done. You must rely upon experience.

After attaching let leather or cloth dry completely before pasting and adding decorative papers. Place scrap cardboard on each side of the book block and dry the leather or cloth under the weight of approximately three books.

PASTING PAPER: Hold down the center of the paper on a clean dry surface with a couple fingers, as you start to paste. Use a brush appropriate to the size of the paper, so you do not waste strokes.

Strokes should be from the center, out beyond the paper. Brush in a radiating manner. Lift your fingers to finish pasting the paper. Do not brush from the surface onto the paper, or you may push paste under, to the front side of the paper. As soon as the paper stops curling it will start to relax to a flat sheet.

Do not over-compensate with excessive application of paste. It is not how much you pile up paste on the surface, but an even and very thin layer of paste on the surface. If the paste was over-cooked and is too thick and rubbery, thin out the paste by misting the jar of paste with water; do not mist directly onto the paper.

WEIGHTING DOWN A PASTED OBJECT: A blotter should go between the surface which was pasted and the weight. This will absorb moisture. Before adding a weight, a smooth wooden board should be placed down. Fred recommends using masonite. This will insure the weight is distributed evenly across the pasted surface. After half an hour, Fred usually changes the blotter between the pasted surface and the masonite. For cloth and paper, place a sheet of wax paper on the outside of the boards, prior to adding the blotter. The blotter can stick to cloth, as well as to some papers.

APPROACHES TO PASTING

Here, again, Fred and I have different ways of working. This time it is based on the necessities of *what* we teach and therefore *how* we cover the boards. Fred teaches leather binding and the steps require the leather to dry totally between steps. The binding is completed over a period of several sessions.

Even if you are using quarter cloth, this approach is far better than covering both sides of the boards at once, if you are binding an edition. An edition is always done in steps, working in assembly-line fashion. All the boards can be cut. All the leather or cloth attached to the edition, then all the books are cased-in. Later, the decorative papers are pasted to the board. If you were to bind an edition by completing one book at a time, it would take far longer.

COVERING THE BOARDS OVER A PERIOD OF TIME: If the binding is quarter or half leather, the leather is pasted and applied to the board. Leather must dry completely before the remainder of that side and the other side of the board can be covered. The cover is sandwiched between two scraps of book board. A weight is placed on top to keep the board from warping. The weight is not removed when the leather is dry, until you are ready to continue covering the board. Humidity can cause the partially covered board to warp.

The next session, the remainder of the outside of the board is covered with leather, cloth or paper. If no leather is used in this session, the inside of the board is covered also. If only one side is completed, again, the cover is sandwiched between two scraps of book board. A slight weight is placed on top to keep the board from warping.

The third session, the inside of the board is covered.

COVERING THE BOARDS IN A SINGLE SESSION: My teaching is done solely in workshops which last a day, two days, or two weeks at the longest. Several bindings are completed and covering the boards must be done in a single session. This does not allow for the use of leather, which must dry totally on the board before the remainder of that side of the board, or the other side can be covered. This limits covering of boards to book cloth and decorative papers. I have evolved my working method, with no delays, no weighting down of the boards and no need for a press.

No weight is required if there is no wait.

WARPAGE FROM GRAIN

With either approach, it is important to keep the grain of the papers, blotters, as well as the grain of the board, parallel to the spine. See *Grain of Paper,* page 67.

WARPAGE FROM COVERING ONE SIDE ONLY

Warpage is caused by partially covered boards drying without being in a press or under weight, until both sides of the boards are covered.

WARPAGE FROM TENSION

There must be a counter-balance of tension on each side of a pasted board. Tension is caused by the *pull factor:* Paper, leather and some cloth will pull when they dry. When they are pasted, they expand in one direction, perpendicular to the grain. When they dry, they contract. This is the pull factor.

PERPENDICULAR TO THE GRAIN: Paper expands perpendicular to the grain: When it is pasted to the board with the grain parallel with the spine, it will expand side to side, not top to bottom.

The pull factor requires the same weight of paper must be used on each side of the board to counter-balance the pull, in order to prevent the board from warping. This is not always true. Handmade paper has no grain and thus, no pull factor. If a handmade paper covers the outside of the board and a commercial paper is used on the inside, the pull from the commercial paper will warp the board. Even if the handmade paper is thick and the commercial paper is thin, the tension is not counter-balanced.

However, if you are using only commercial papers and no paper is extremely low in pull factor, weight of the paper is the main way to determine how much each will pull. A heavier paper *usually* pulls more than a thinner one.

If one side of the board is covered with a heavier paper, usually it will warp the board in that direction. To prevent this, first paste an additional thin sheet of paper on the other side of the board. This additional sheet is white and pasted down first. The additional sheet of paper is the size of the bare board to be covered, but does not extend around to other side of the board. Then proceed with the instructions for covering boards. The *Steps in Pasting Papers* are described in the chapter, *Covering,* page 279.

The two thin sheets should equal and thus counter-balance the pull of the one heavier sheet on the other side of the board.

With experience you will find some heavier papers which have surprisingly little pull.

The other side of the board must be covered with the same paper, or a thinner paper, which will have the same amount of pull. No amount of time leaving the board in a press will prevent the board from warping later on if you have covered the two sides of the boards with material which has a different pull factor. The cover will come out of the press flat. As soon as the humidity rises, the boards will warp.

WARPAGE FROM DELAYS

If you are covering both sides of the boards in a single session you must work quickly, but not in a rush. You cannot be interrupted by the telephone or doorbell.

FINISH ONE BOARD BEFORE STARTING THE SECOND: If you are using *an island paste-down,* described on page 351, both sides of one board are completed before covering the second. You will not have to wait a moment to complete the covering of both sides of one board.

Do not paste and attach the front paper to both boards, then paste and attach the paste-down on the inside of both boards. By the time you get around to attaching the pastes-down, moisture from the paper on one side only will cause the board to start warping. If you are using thin book board, this warpage will be an extreme arc. See example on page 288. You will have to add the paste-down on the other side of the board, which will have an extreme arcing curve to it. This will stretch the paste-down over the arc. As the paste-down starts to counter-balance warpage, the board will flatten, distorting the paste-down with wrinkles or blistering.

Unlike pasting down the endsheets, the boards can be dried closed using an island paste-down. Covering both sides of the board in a single session requires all the papers to be pre-cut. You will not be able to interrupt the process of pasting and applying the papers to the board.

If you are using *the endsheet as paste-down,* you cannot cover both sides at once. This is because in pasting down the endsheet the boards must dry in a fully open position. See *Pasting Down the Endsheets for a Tight Back,* page 296.

Lay out the papers needed to cover both sides of one board on your pasting surface. Be sure you have the board, scissors, bone folder, paste, towel and water mister on hand prior to wetting the paper.

AIR DRY BOTH SIDES EVENLY: If you cover both sides of a board at once, then cover the remaining board, you can slip wax paper between the boards and book block and dry closed under weight. That is the traditional method.

However, here is a faster drying method. After both boards are completed, stand the book up to air dry. Open the book slightly, so the inside of the damp boards does not touch the book block. This also allows air to get to both sides of the boards so they will to dry evenly. Counter-balance of tension will prevent warpage.

The boards may warp while drying, but as the papers dry on each side, the board should be pulled back to straight again. Covers on a 1-signature booklet are proportionally rather thin. If you cover both sides of 2-ply mat board at once, the board will warp to an extreme while drying. However, by the end of drying, warpage is counter-balanced and the boards will be flat, or near flat.

Once dry, if there is a slight amount of warpage, you can carefully bend the board to straight. Be very careful not to crack the board in half. This is also a critical test of whether you waited long enough in pasting. If you did not, the paper will blister, as you are straightening the board.

BOARDS ARE RARELY PASTED: Rarely is paste applied directly to book board. Paste goes on the leather, which is placed onto the board. Paste goes on paper or book cloth and each is applied to the board.

Oriental paper often has little wet strength. Lace-like papers can fall apart during pasting. The board is brushed with a *very thin* coating of PVA glue. The dry, delicate paper is laid onto the glued board.

The same approach is used for silk and fine cloth. A thin coat of PVA is applied to the board. This time, wait until the glue is almost dry. It will be tacky. Place the fabric on the board. Cover with a blotter and iron it on a low to medium heat. The results are not always favorable.

REPAIRS
EASY REMOVAL OF SOILED PASTED PAPERS: Restoration work is made easy when the papers are pasted, rather than glued to the boards. If a paper is soiled, the surrounding papers or leather can be covered with wax paper. The soiled paper is then misted with water.

When the paper is fairly well soaked, about one minute, it can be peeled off the board. The board will not be scarred and all of the soiled paper will lift in one piece.

MIXING PASTE WITH GLUE: Some students form a mixture of half wheat paste, half PVA to paste papers to boards. We advise against this. The reason for pasting is so that the paper can be removed easily for repairs. PVA bonds the paper to the board. Second, it is easier to handle papers wet with wheat paste. They can be slid into position; it is not tacky like PVA. PVA is harder to handle and offers no advantage being mixed into the wheat paste.

If for some reason you do mix the two, never dip your brush containing wheat paste into your supply of PVA. The next time you open the PVA, it will have mold growing in it. Obviously, I have done that.

CARE OF BRUSHES

Pasting can be done with a glue brush. Oil painting brushes are a good substitute if large enough, but an actual glue brush, is far cheaper than oil brushes.

Unlike gluing, if the brush dries with paste in it, the brush can be soaked in cold water, dissolving the paste. The brush is washed and stood with the bristles up, not to misshape the bristles.

Do not sit a brush in water for a long period of time. It will misshape the brush.

Do not use hot water to clean any brush. It will dissolve the glue which is holding the bristles in place.

ADÉLE OUTTERIDGE, TEA BAG BOOK II, APPROXIMATELY 600 USED TEA BAGS,
LINEN THREAD, ONE-OF-A-KIND, 1994—95, 8 X 15 X 8 CM.

5

PAPER TRAITS

Part I, *Preliminaries,* discusses paper, grain, signatures, thread, knots and sewing. These are basic to all sewings. Books which are rounded and backed have specific requirements. Those will be elaborated in Part IV, beginning on page 211.

There are many factors to consider in the seemingly simple act of folding paper.

GRAIN OF PAPER: Machine-made paper can be folded more easily in one direction than the other. In commercially making paper, water runs across the surface. More of the fibers settle in this direction. That direction is referred to as the *grain* of the paper. It is easier to fold with the grain than against it.

It is critical to have the grain parallel with the spine. This allows the pages to roll open. The paper will naturally curl open. If some of your signatures are grained incorrectly, the pages will bow from head to tail, rather than from foredge to spine-edge.

If you are folding down a signature, keep in mind how many folds are needed. See diagrams on pages 86–89. The final fold creates the spine, so the final fold must be with the grain.

Book board has a grain also. Again, cut the side-covers so the grain is parallel to the spine.

Hand-made paper and certain commercial papers have multi-directional fibers, so there is no strong direction of grain. These papers can be folded in either direction with no concern for grain.

TESTING FOR GRAIN: Rolling a sheet first in one direction, then the other, is a test for direction of the grain. There will be less resistance rolling the paper when the grain is parallel with the curve of, and potential fold of, the roll.

If it is difficult to determine the direction, moisten the edge of the sheet. It will naturally curl with the grain. That is, the curl is determined by the grain, by not bending the grain.

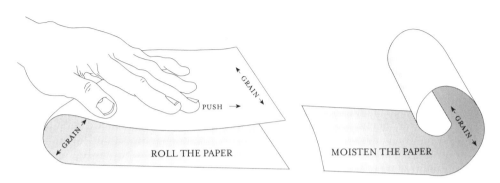

ROLL THE PAPER   MOISTEN THE PAPER

TESTS FOR GRAIN DIRECTION: ROLL A SHEET OF PAPER WITHOUT CREASING
IT, FIRST IN ONE DIRECTION, THEN THE OTHER. THE DIRECTION IN WHICH THE
ROLLING IS LESS RESISTANT, THE GRAIN RUNS PARALLEL WITH THE FOLD.
IF YOU CANNOT TELL, MOISTEN A SCRAP PIECE. IT WILL CURL WITH THE GRAIN.

Book board is easy to test. Bending a full sheet, the board will flex
more easily in the direction that is parallel with the grain. It is difficult to test a scrap of board. Therefore, before you cut a new board,
run several light pencil lines across the board to indicate the direction of the grain. Later on, when you have a small portion of the
board, you will know which direction to turn the board so that the
pencil line is parallel with the spine of your book.

SPECIFYING THE DIRECTION OF THE GRAIN: Paper is usually grain
long. Paper companies generally list the direction of the grain as the
second dimension: 32 x 48".

Other companies will point out
the direction of the grain by
underlining that dimension: 48 x
32". The *same* paper stock can be
long or short grain, depending on
the size of the sheet the store han-
dles. The diagram to the right
shows a full sheet as grain long.
The identical paper, if offered in
half sheets, would be grain short:

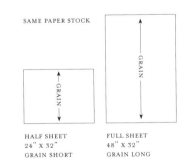

SAME PAPER STOCK

HALF SHEET
24" X 32"
GRAIN SHORT

FULL SHEET
48" X 32"
GRAIN LONG

SPECIFYING THE DIMENSIONS OF A FINISHED WORK: The dimensions
of a book, signatures or a photograph are usually listed with the
height first, then the width. If the work has a third dimension, it is
listed third. This book is 9 x 6 x 1 13⁄32".

MARKING THE MEASUREMENT: Indicate the measurement to be folded on the sheet. Never use ink or ball-point. An unsharpened pencil mark can be erased, but is inaccurate because of its width, leaving to chance whether the fold is on the left, right or center of the mark.

A light pencil dot with a sharpened pencil is better. More accuracy is gained by a pin prick, or indentation. An ideal tool is the edge of your thumbnail. The indentation along the top edge of the sheet is the start of the fold. Use the top edge as a guide.

MAKING A SINGLE FOLD: The following is to make one fold in a sheet, such as to fold a sheet in half, constructing a folio. For directions on several folds in a sheet, folding down a sheet to form a signature, see *Folding Down Signatures,* page 77 and *Folding Down a Sheet,* page 86.

Other than folding in half
For a single fold, other than folding the sheet in half, mark the point of the fold along the top edge of the sheet.

· Start a loose fold with the mark on the outside of the fold.

· Crease the paper down an inch at the mark of the pencil dot or indentation.

· Line up the two top edges of the sheet and firmly hold in place with one hand, while completing a soft crease lightly with the palm of your other hand.

This single stroke should go downward and outward, away from the point where the two top edges are being held aligned. This insures the fold is at a right angle to the top edge.

Give the fold a permanent crease with a bone folder. Do not use several strokes with the bone folder as this will cause the paper to shine. A substitute for a bone folder is a common stainless steel table knife. Make sure the knife is stainless steel and has a non-serrated edge.

A COMMON STAINLESS STEEL TABLE KNIFE WITH A NON-SERRATED EDGE IS A GOOD SUBSTITUTE FOR A BONE FOLDER. IF THE END OF THE HANDLE IS SMOOTH AND ROUNDED, IT CAN ALSO BE USED FOR BACKING. SEE PAGE 231.

Dark color paper can be scuffed and shine from a single stroke with a bone folder. If the paper is dark, lay a scrap sheet of white paper over it. Crease with the bone folder on the waste sheet to crease the dark paper without marring it.

Folding in half
To fold a sheet in half, make a loose fold, lining up the top corner with the top corner beneath it. This lines up the top edge. Holding the two corners in place and stroking away from them with your hand towards the loose fold will find the exact center. Stroke downward and outward, away from the point where the two top corners are being held aligned. Give the fold a permanent crease with a bone folder.

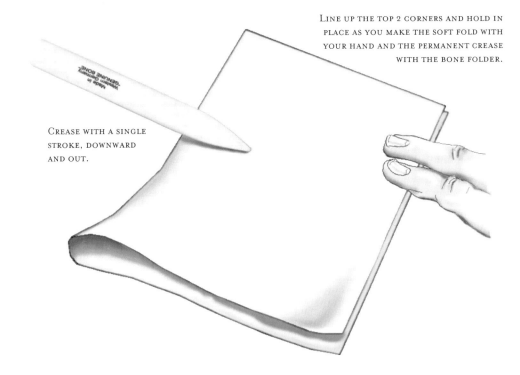

LINE UP THE TOP 2 CORNERS AND HOLD IN PLACE AS YOU MAKE THE SOFT FOLD WITH YOUR HAND AND THE PERMANENT CREASE WITH THE BONE FOLDER.

CREASE WITH A SINGLE STROKE, DOWNWARD AND OUT.

FOLDING A SHEET IN HALF: THE FOLD IS PARALLEL WITH THE GRAIN OF THE PAPER. LINE UP THE TOP EDGE WITH ITSELF IN THE UPPER RIGHT. HOLDING THIS IN PLACE FOR A 90° ANGLE, MAKE A SOFT FOLD WITH YOUR HAND. MAKE A PERMANENT CREASE WITH A BONE FOLDER, OR STAINLESS STEEL NON-SERRATED TABLE KNIFE.

TO SCORE WITH A BONE FOLDER: Keeping the straight edge held firmly in position, score with a pointed bone folder. Hold the straight edge with one hand and fold paper back against the straight edge, along the indentation. This can help in the process of creasing to obtain a clean fold. A bone folder indents to score, whereas a knife incises to form a score on heavier stock paper or book board.

TO SCORE THICK PAPER OR BOARD WITH A KNIFE: Cut 1/8 the way down through the thickness of the paper or board with an X-Acto™ knife. Heavy stock used for covers or a fold book should give a clean fold when it is parallel with the grain of the paper.

If it tends to crack at the crease, the paper will first have to be scored, that is, slightly incised where it is to be folded.

Position a right angle lining up with the bottom edge of the cover paper. Cut lightly along the edge of the right angle. If you cut too deeply, you will weaken the paper. Make the fold with the cut on the mountain peak.

Alternate the cuts with the other side of the sheet. Be consistent in lining up the right angle either with the top or the bottom edge. If the paper has been cut slightly off from 90°, the top and bottom edges will not be parallel and neither will the resulting folds.

TO TEAR PAPER: Torn paper edges are often attractive in a hand-bound book. They are impossible in a commercially-made production book, which makes them all the more desirable in small edition hand-bound and one-of-a-kind books. Sometimes the deckled-edge is incorporated in the binding but the sheet is larger than the page. The other edges must be either machine cut or torn. Tearing paper can imitate the deckled-edge. Instead of placing all deckled-edges at the head and your torn edges at the tail, alternate the deckled-edge with the torn to offer less comparison between the two. Each method of tearing gives a different edge:

- Lay a straight edge where the paper is to be torn. Firmly hold it in place with one hand, while you tear against the straight edge.
- For a more exaggerated torn edge, use a wooden ruler which has a metal edge inserted. Since the metal is raised above where the paper is held down to the surface of the table, the tear will peel as it frays. The higher the metal edge is from the surface, the more exaggerated the tear. You can increase the height of the metal by placing masking or duct tape on the bottom of the ruler.

- The most extreme and perhaps the best imitation of the deckled- edge by tearing is accomplished by a different approach. Fold and crease the paper where it is to be torn. Reverse the fold and crease. With a damp sponge, stroke the folded edge. Do not run the sponge on the surface of the paper, only across the edge of the fold. Reverse the fold and stroke it with the sponge. Open the paper and gently pull it in two at the weakened fold. The paper will fray more than tear, leaving an edge of hairy fibers.
- Run a Rapidograph™ filled with water along a ruler for Eastern papers with long fibers. Hold ruler in place and gently pull. If an area resists, scrape the fiber with an X-Acto™ blade, but don't cut.

TO CUT PAPER: Cutting and trimming paper by hand should be done with a sharp blade using a metal straight edge as a guide. Slits are made in the same manner. An X–Acto™ knife with a #11 blade is recommended as it has a narrow point which is easily positioned and is thin so it does not throw a burr on the paper.

Whenever possible, lay the straight edge on the material to be saved. If the knife wanders, it will veer into the excess which is being trimmed, rather than into the good material.

CUTTING WET PAPER: Sometimes moisture expands paper more than allotted for. It may become necessary to trim the pasted paper before it can be applied to the board. The paper can be laid on a self-seal cutting mat, paste side up. A straight edge and X–Acto™ blade will probably tear as it cuts. Lowering the angle and using a new blade helps. Better, is to cut with a rotary-blade knife.

ROTARY KNIFE

Never cut directly on the table, not only to protect the furniture, but to avoid a ragged cut. Always use a self-sealing cutting mat under the sheet to be cut. Scrap book board is a poor substitute. Your cut will be imperfect if it extends over an area where the book board is incised from a previous cut. Only use #11 blades with a self-sealing mat. Heavy-duty blades will shorten the life span of the mat. A cutting mat may seem expensive, but it is a valuable tool and a pleasure to use, and they last for years even when used daily.

PAPER CUTTERS: An ideal paper cutter has a clamp-bar close to the blade to hold the paper in position so the paper does not creep as the blade slices through. The clamp-bar should come down parallel with the plate, so it must be hinged at both ends. A cutter with a clamp-bar having a single hinge located near the fulcrum of the blade is to be avoided.

The right angle bar may be located along the top or bottom edge. It should be adjustable and all paper cutters should be checked monthly with a large metal right angle to determine if the angle bar needs adjusting. Do not take it for granted that all paper cutters cut at a right angle. Few do. Only those capable of being adjusted and which are serviced regularly will give you an accurate cut. In folding, especially concertinas, it is impossible to achieve acceptable folds if you do not start with a sheet with 90° corners.

Never try to cut several sheets of paper at once. The bottom sheets will be ragged and probably not cut at 90°. The practice abuses the hinge of the blade.

Never cut book board or card on a paper cutter; you will destroy the potential for precision cutting of paper. If you do not have a board shear, cut by hand using a heavy-duty mat knife and straight edge. Place scrap book board underneath.

Rather than plowing the book block, one option is to carefully cut sheets. Fold into folios and compile your signatures.

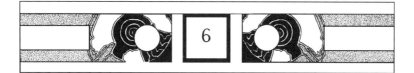

6

SIGNATURES
(SECTIONS)

COMPILING SIGNATURES

Signatures can be assembled by *compiling* 2 or more folios, to be sewn at once, as a sewing unit:

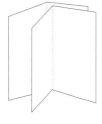

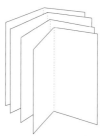

2 FOLIOS COMPILED AS A
QUARTO

3 FOLIOS COMPILED AS A
SEXTO

4 FOLIOS COMPILED AS AN
OCTAVO

Signatures also can be constructed by *folding down* a sheet.
Folding down a sheet will be described. See page 86.

A SHEET FOLDS IN HALF TO BECOME A FOLIO WHICH FOLDS TO A QUARTO WHICH FOLDS TO AN OCTAVO

Generally, the approach of the artist is to compile folios. In this manner, they can design and image folios rather than imaging a huge sheet which would be folded down to a signature of 4 to 32 pages. If they make a mistake, they have only wrecked 4 pages, instead of up to 32 pages of a folded down sheet.

Whether compiled or folded down, it is faster to sew several pages grouped as a signature than to sew individual folios. The main reason quartos or sextos are sewn is not for speed, but to keep the spine from bulking up. See *Choosing the Thread,* page 217 and *Swell,* page 382. Octavos, or larger signatures, will not be needed in the bindings described.

Binders do not compile signatures. They always fold down sheets to form a signature. It is quicker and they are dealing with blank sheets for a blank book.

Commercially, publishing houses must fold down sheets. The equipment to mechanically fold down paper is costly. In the long run, the costs are far cheaper than hand folding and hand assembly of compiled folios and the machinery is far faster and more accurate.

SECTIONS vs SIGNATURES: Signature is a printer's term; *section* is a binder's term. It is important to define terms to avoid confusion. Most binders refer to *section* and never use the term *signature.* Many graphic arts book designers speak of *signatures.* They do not use the term *sections.*

Section
1. A sheet *folded down* to yield four or more pages, such as a folio, quarto, sexto or duodecimo. 2. Two or more loose folios *compiled* to form a quarto, sexto or duodecimo.

A section can be blank paper or printed. If printed, then it is specifically a *signature.*

Signature
A specific type of section, differing from the general term *section,* in that a signature is a sheet that has been printed, then folded down.

A signature is a section, but a section is not necessarily a signature. That said, in this manual, the term *section* will never be used. Instead I will always refer to sections as "signatures," in deference to Fred Jordan's preference for that term.

FOLDING DOWN
A SIGNATURE

SHEET

FOLIO

QUARTO

OCTAVO

FOLDING DOWN SIGNATURES

As a book artist, I tend to compile signatures. As a binder, Fred always folds down a sheet to become a signature.

Sheet
A sheet is a piece of paper consisting of a front and a back. It is not a signature; it has no fold as a hinge.

Folio aka *fo*
A folio is a sheet folded in half to yield 2 leaves and 4 pages. The fold is with the grain. The resulting folio has the grain parallel with the spine.

Quarto aka *4to*
FOLDED DOWN: A sheet folded in half twice, to yield a signature of 4 leaves or 8 pages. The first fold is against the grain; the second is with the grain. The resulting signature will have the grain parallel with the spine.

COMPILED: Two folios compiled.

Octavo aka *8vo*
FOLDED DOWN: A sheet folded in half three times, to yield a signature of 16 pages with 8 leaves.

COMPILED: Four folios, each slipped inside the other, to form a unit of sewing.

COMPILING
A SIGNATURE

SHEET

FOLIO

QUARTO

OCTAVO

- Folding a sheet in half not only sets up facing pages, the fold becomes a hinge, facilitating turning pages.
- The fold-as-hinge allows the pages to open and lie flat.
- The fold creates an ideal location for the sewing path. The sewing will not obstruct the hinging action of the fold.
- The fold allows pages to be sewn at once as a signature.
- Size of the signatures, along with the thickness of thread, allow controlling the amount of swell on the spine.
- Numerical order of the sheet, or the folios to be compiled is not serial. Only the constructed signatures have the page numbers in serial order. See *Imposition of Signatures,* page95.

FOLDING DOWN
A SIGNATURE

SHEET

FOLIO

QUARTO

OCTAVO

USABLE FOLIOS AND OCTAVOS

FOLDING DOWN SHORT GRAIN PAPER: Choosing the proportion of your book is done *prior* to folding down the sheet. It is done when you purchase the paper.

For example, two different papers may be offered in the identical size, 24" x 32". However, one is grain long, the other is grain short.

The following diagrams show the different proportions from folding a sheet of paper proportioned 6:8, such as a sheet measuring 24" x 32". Grain must be considered. The sheet may be grain short:

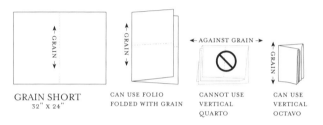

GRAIN SHORT
32" X 24"

CAN USE FOLIO
FOLDED WITH GRAIN

CANNOT USE
VERTICAL
QUARTO

CAN USE
VERTICAL
OCTAVO

If grain short, the manufacturer would list the grain dimension last: 32" x 24". Or, the grain direction may be underlined: 24" x 32". This often is the case, because the sheet may have been cut from a larger sheet, twice as large, or 32" x 48". The larger version of the sheet is grain long. See diagram at the bottom of page 68.

Folding down short grain paper making the first fold with the direction of the grain will yield a folio. The next fold gives a quarto, but it cannot be used. The major fold, or spine, is against the grain. Folded again, as shown above, creates an octavo. It can be used, because the major fold, or spine-fold is parallel with the grain.

FOLDING DOWN LONG GRAIN PAPER: Another sheet of paper is also 24" x 32". This sheet is grain long:

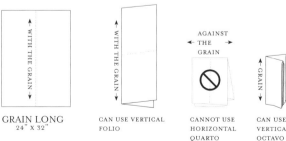

GRAIN LONG
24" X 32"

CAN USE VERTICAL
FOLIO

CANNOT USE
HORIZONTAL
QUARTO

CAN USE
VERTICAL
OCTAVO

Folding down the first fold of a grain long paper with the direction of the grain will yield a folio, as illustrated at the bottom of the facing page. The next fold gives a quarto, but it cannot be used. The major fold, or spine, is against the grain. Folded again, creates an octavo. It can be used, because the major fold, or spine-fold is parallel with the grain.

USABLE QUARTOS

FOLDING DOWN SHORT GRAIN PAPER: A sheet of paper, 24" x 32" can be folded down to make a usable quarto:

GRAIN SHORT
32" X 24"

CANNOT USE VERTICAL FOLIO
FOLD IS AGAINST THE GRAIN

CAN USE HORIZONTAL
QUARTO

Folding down short grain paper, make the first fold against the direction of the grain. This will give an un-usable folio. Folding the paper in half again gives an un-useable and *horizontal* quarto. The major fold, or spine, is with the grain.

FOLDING DOWN LONG GRAIN PAPER: Another sheet of paper is also 24" x 32". This sheet is grain long:

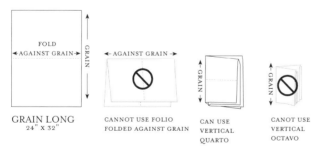

GRAIN LONG
24" X 32"

CANNOT USE FOLIO
FOLDED AGAINST GRAIN

CAN USE
VERTICAL
QUARTO

CANOT USE
VERTICAL
OCTAVO

Folding down grain long paper with the first fold against the direction of the grain will give an un-usable folio. Folding the paper in half again gives an useable and *vertical* quarto. The major fold, or spine, is with the grain.

NOTE: In folding down a sheet, folds alternate in direction. The first fold is *with* the grain if you want a usable *folio* or *octavo*. The first fold is *against* the grain if you want a usable *quarto*.

PROPORTION OF THE PAGE: Proportion of the page requires planning ahead if you are folding down a signature. If you are compiling folios to make quartos or octavos, there is less problem. Simply fold all the folios with the grain.

Size of the book is in relation to the size of sheet with which you start.

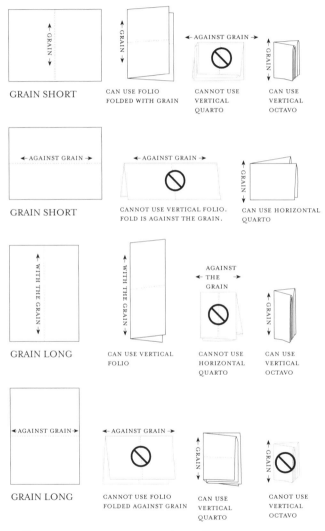

PROPORTION OF A SHEET FOLDED DOWN. FOLDING DOWN A SHEET, EVERY OTHER FOLD IS IN THE OPPOSITE DIRECTION. EVERY OTHER FOLD CREATES A SIGNATURE THAT CANNOT BE USED, SINCE IT IS FOLDED AGAINST THE GRAIN.

NUMBER OF PAGES IN A SIGNATURE FOR A FLAT BACK: For a Flat Back cased-in codex, you can use any number of pages as a sewing unit: folios, quartos, sextos or octavos, if there are no insertions.

Number of pages in a signature, along with the thickness of thread and how much the paper absorbs the thread determine how much the spine will be expanded. This is referred to as *swell.* Compiling 2, 3 or 4 folios as a signature is not done primarily for speed in sewing, but to control the thickness, or the swelling of the spine. See *Choosing the Thread,* page 217 and pages 282, 283.

INSERTS FOR A FLAT BACK: If you are going to tip in inserts after the book is bound, compile folios with *spacers.* Sew with thin thread, in order to swell the spine larger than the foredge. Once the inserts are added to the scrapbook or album, the boards should be parallel. To heavily swell the spine, compile folios with spacers and sew with thicker thread to increase the swell of the spine even more. Failure to expand the spine and then add inserts would spread the foredge of the book.

NUMBER OF PAGES IN A SIGNATURE FOR A TIGHT BACK: For a relatively thin (40 to 100 pages) Tight Back or Hollow Back, you should use only folios or quartos. Octavos or larger signatures cannot be used. An octavo is a 16-page signature. A minimum of 10 signatures are needed to round and back a book with a bone folder.

- Sewing 10 signatures with octavos would give a 160 page book. Since you will probably need a book of fewer pages, you should sew with a sextos, quartos or folios.

- Sewing 10 signatures with sextos would give a 120 page book.

- Sewing 10 signatures with quartos would give an 80 page book.

- Sewing 10 signatures with folios would give a 40 page book.

INSERTS FOR A TIGHT BACK: If you are going to have inserts in a Tight Back or a Hollow Back binding, *stubs* should be used: After the book is sewn, rounded and backed, a sheet will be cut out close to the gutter. If the insert is twice as thick as the paper in the binding, two sheets will be removed.

DETAIL ROUNDED AND BACKED BOOK WITH 10 SIGNATURES. FEWER THAN 10 SIGNATURES IS DIFFICULT TO ROUND AND BACK.

The Tight Back and the Hollow Back will not need any signature larger than a quarto, because a minimum of 10 signatures are needed. But the Flat Back can easily use a 12 page sexto, 16 page octavo, or 24 page duodecimo as signatures. Use of these larger size signatures are rare, however.

Z-FOLD: A sheet can be folded down to yield 12 or 24 pages. A 12 page signature is a *sexto*. A 24 page signature is a *duodecimo*.

Both of these signatures start by folding the sheet in thirds. This is called a Z-fold. The first fold of a Z-fold is always against the grain.

Sexto aka *6to*

A *sexto* is a signature folded down to give 6 leaves and 12 pages. A sexto can also be compiled by placing 3 folios within each other as a sewing unit.

To fold down a sexto, mark a sheet with 2 dots along one edge of the sheet that is parallel with the grain, which will divide the sheet into 3 equal parts. The sheet is folded against the grain, into 3 equal parts. This is referred to as the Z-*fold*.

Fold in half in the other direction, perpendicular to the Z-fold. This makes the final fold, which is the spine-fold, parallel with the grain.

The sexto makes the Z-fold against the grain, so that the final fold is with the grain:

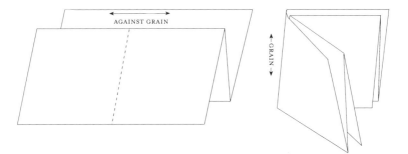

SEXTO: FOLDING DOWN A SHEET TO FORM A SEXTO. THIS SIGNATURE HAS 6 LEAVES AND 12 PAGES. THE SHEET IS FOLDED INTO THIRDS, AGAINST THE GRAIN. THIS IS REFERRED TO AS A Z-FOLD. THE FINAL FOLD IS PERPENDICULAR TO THIS AND THE FOLD IS WITH THE GRAIN.

Duodecimo aka *12mo*

A *duodecimo* is a signature folded down to give 12 leaves and 24 pages. A duodecimo can be created by compiling 6 folios within each other as a sewing unit.

A sheet folded down with a Z-fold, against the grain. Then, fold in half the other direction perpendicular to the Z-fold. Fold in half, again, in the *same* direction:

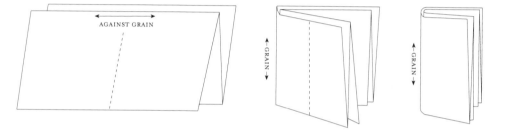

DUODECIMO: Folding down a sheet to form a duodecimo. This signature has 12 leaves and 24 pages. The sheet is folded into thirds, against the grain. This is referred to as a Z-fold. The second and the third folds are both perpendicular to the first fold. The last two folds are in the same direction, with the grain.

DECKLED-EDGE SIGNATURES: In folding down a sheet with deckled edges, there is no problem to create a folio, as it still retains the deckled-edge at the head, tail and foredge.

Other signatures can be folded down only if you wish to plow or cut the final fold at the head. If you wish to tear the final fold as a fake deckle, do not fold down the signature. Compile folios to form your signatures. This will allow you to alternate the true deckled edges with the torn, imitation deckle.

There are various ways to tear and fray paper. Each method gives a different irregular edge. Make tests and choose the method which most resembles the deckled-edge of the paper you are using. To tear a fake deckle, see *To Tear Paper*, page 71.

CREASING PROBLEMS IN FOLDING DOWN A SHEET: Folding a folio presents no problem in creasing. Folding the paper a second time to form a quarto is more difficult. A third fold to create an octavo is even more difficult. The folds become less defined and tend to wrinkle at the top edge where the folding begins. These wrinkles are called *crow's feet* in bookbinding jargon.

If the book is to be rounded and backed, the crow's feet may disappear. With a Pamphlet Binding with Boards or a Flat Back, the wrinkles will always show. Crow's feet never happen in compiling folios, but you do not have to resort to assembling signatures to avoid crow's feet. The quarto or larger signature can be folded down in such a way as to avoid this wrinkling, as described on page 86.

KNIFE: There is a trick in folding down a sheet that will avoid crow's feet every time. First, you will need a binders knife. A good substitute is a clam knife. You can use a table knife, if the edge is thin. Do not use a sharpened paring knife. The purpose is not to cut the paper, but to tear it.

A clam knife makes a good substitute for a bookbinder's knife and often at a lesser price. The blade is thin, but dull. The process requires the paper to be ripped cleanly, but not cut.

Judith Haswell, *Sing Weaving,*

"Designed and constructed by Elizabeth Steiner, Auckland, New Zealand, 1996. Two small books in a clam box, 150 mm. x 110 mm. x 23 mm. covered in hand made paper from NZ flax (Phormium tenax) and red Elephanthide paper.

Sing Weaving is printed on flax paper from Centrepoint Paper Mill. The construction of *Sing Weaving* is a non-adhesive binding using interlocking strips of Elephanthide paper, that also catch in additional decorative papers. An edition of 25 copies signed and numbered."

1. FOLD THE SHEET IN HALF, WITH THE GRAIN FOR A
FOLIO OR OCTAVO, AGAINST THE GRAIN FOR A QUARTO.

2. SLICE THE FOLD JUST BEYOND THE HALFWAY POINT.
(DO NOT SLICE IF YOU WANT A FOLIO; IT IS COMPLETED).

3. MAKE THE SECOND FOLD, KEEPING LAYERS OF PAPER
TIGHT AS YOU START THE FOLD. THIS IS A QUARTO.

STEPS
IN FOLDING DOWN
A SHEET

1. Decide how many pages you desire in your signatures. If you want 4 or 16 pages, you will fold down to a folio or an octavo. With either of these 2 signatures, your first fold is with the grain. The final fold will be with the grain.

If you want 8 pages, you will fold down to a quarto. The first fold must be against the grain, so that the final fold of the signature is with the grain.

Fold the sheet in half. Make the fold permanent by creasing with a bone folder. This is a folio.

2. Close the signature. Use the knife to rip the fold, slicing just beyond the halfway point. This will relieve the pressure at the start of the next fold, avoiding any crow's feet.

3. For a quarto, fold in half again. Keep the layers of paper tight, as you start to slice.

If you want quartos, the steps are completed.

Create as many quartos as needed to form the book block. Continue with Step 4 for a signature of more pages.

4. If you want octavos, keep the signature closed. Slice the fold just beyond halfway.

5. Fold the signature in half. Keep the layers of paper tight, as you start to slice. The signature is now an octavo.

The octavo is completed. Create as many as needed to form the book block.

6. Assemble your book block. Pre-pierce your sewing stations and sew.

After the spine is glued, the partially cut folds at the head can be plowed or cut.

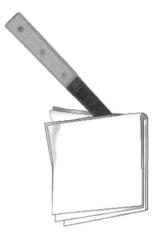

4. FOR AN OCTAVO, SLICE THE FOLD OF THE CLOSED QUARTO, JUST BEYOND HALFWAY.

5. MAKE THE THIRD FOLD, KEEPING LAYERS OF PAPER TIGHT AS YOU START THE FOLD. THIS IS AN OCTAVO.

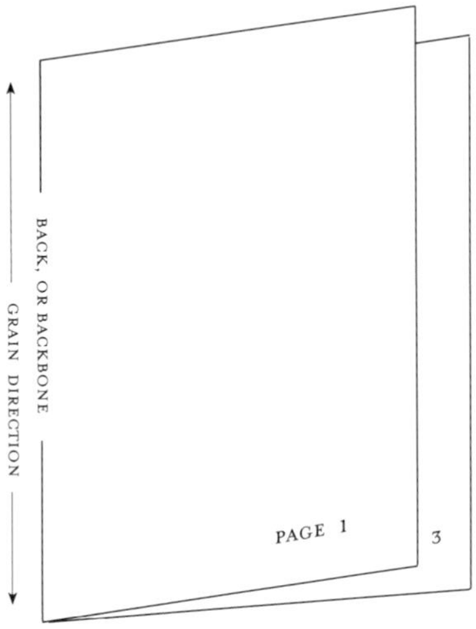

BACK, OR BACKBONE

GRAIN DIRECTION

PAGE 1   3

FOLIO 18" X 12"

GRAIN DIRECTION

PAGE 1   3

QUARTO 18" X 6"
BOTH FOLDS WITH THE GRAIN

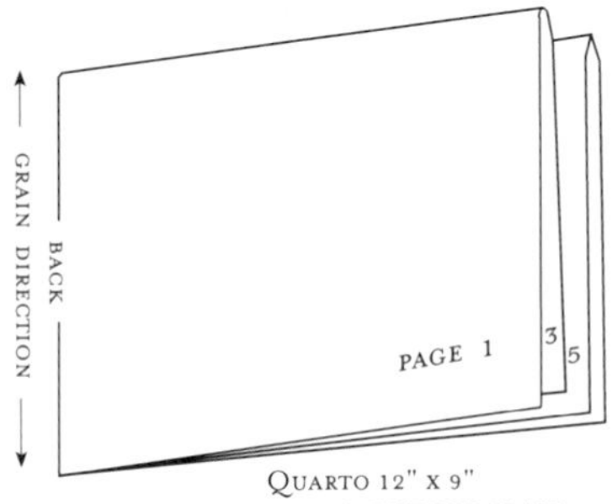

GRAIN DIRECTION

BACK

PAGE 1   3 5

QUARTO 12" X 9"
FIRST FOLD AGAINST THE GRAIN
SECOND FOLD WITH THE GRAIN

GRAIN DIRECTION

BACKBONE

PAGE 1   3 9 13

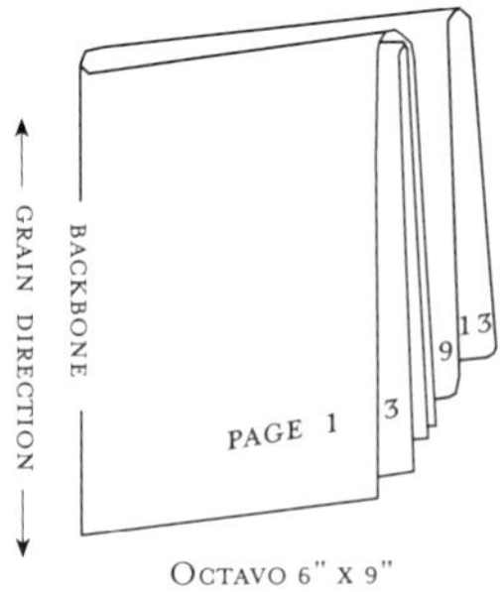

OCTAVO 6" X 9"
FIRST FOLD WITH THE GRAIN
SECOND FOLD AGAINST THE GRAIN
THIRD FOLD WITH THE GRAIN

GRAIN DIRECTION

BACKBONE

PAGE 1   3 9

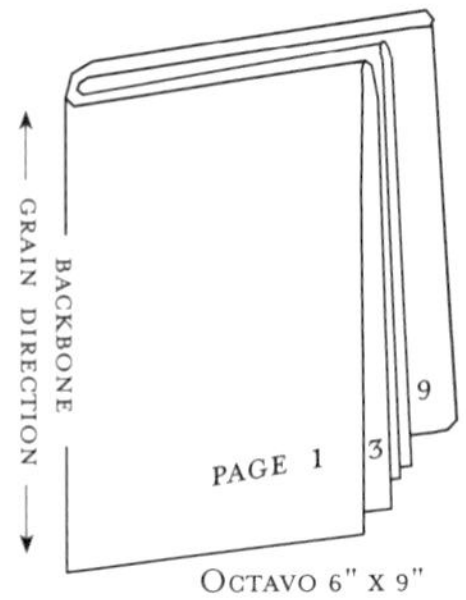

OCTAVO 6" X 9"
FIRST FOLD AGAINST THE GRAIN
SECOND FOLD WITH THE GRAIN
THIRD FOLD WITH THE GRAIN

GRAIN

PAGE 1

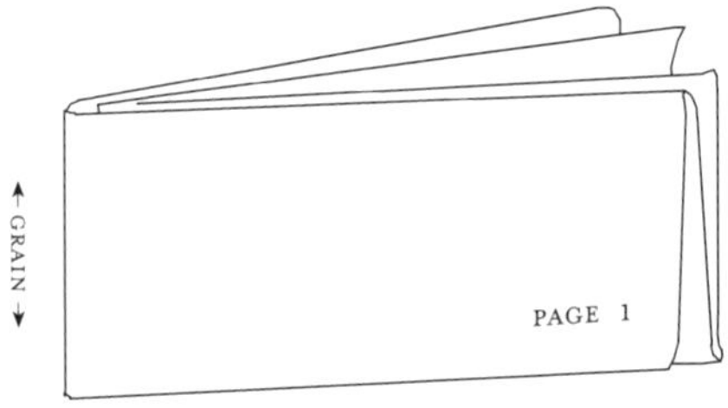

SEXTO 6" X 12"
Z-FOLD IS AGAINST THE GRAIN
FINAL FOLD IS WITH THE GRAIN

SHORT GRAIN: FOLDING DOWN AN 24" X 18" SHEET TO FORM A SIGNATURE.
GRAIN SHORT GIVES A MORE STANDARD PROPORTION, EXCEPT FOR THE SEXTO.

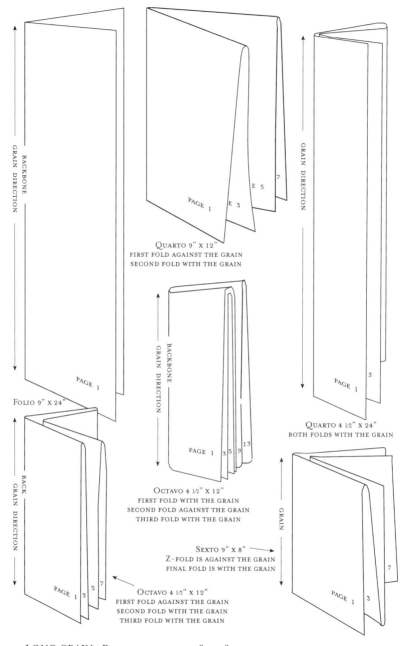

QUARTO 9" X 12"
FIRST FOLD AGAINST THE GRAIN
SECOND FOLD WITH THE GRAIN

FOLIO 9" X 24"

QUARTO 4 ½" X 24"
BOTH FOLDS WITH THE GRAIN

OCTAVO 4 ½" X 12"
FIRST FOLD WITH THE GRAIN
SECOND FOLD AGAINST THE GRAIN
THIRD FOLD WITH THE GRAIN

SEXTO 9" X 8"
Z-FOLD IS AGAINST THE GRAIN
FINAL FOLD IS WITH THE GRAIN

OCTAVO 4 ½" X 12"
FIRST FOLD AGAINST THE GRAIN
SECOND FOLD WITH THE GRAIN
THIRD FOLD WITH THE GRAIN

LONG GRAIN: FOLDING DOWN AN 18" X 24" SHEET TO FORM A SIGNATURE.
GRAIN LONG IS GOOD FOR A TALL, VERTICAL SIGNATURE.

FOLDS-OUT

For the artist making books, the *fold-out,* or *throw-out,* offers great potential. Visually, they are exciting. They offer the opportunity for a drawing which is wider or taller than a two page spread. They can be a thrown-down, or thrown-up, as well as thrown-out.

THROW—OUT   THROW—UP

THROWS—UP   THROWS—DOWN AND UP

Structurally, they offer protection for prints, with a built-in mat, eliminating the need to insert a tissue over a print. See example 5A, page 92.

Design-wise, they free the one-of-a-kind book from the rigidity of dry-mounting photographs onto a heavy page. The result is not only bulky, the emphasis is on the photograph, not on the composition of the page, the 2-page spread, or the book. This is discussed in *Structure of the Visual Book.*

Whether your signatures are folded down or compiled, you may wish to have an occasional fold-out. You can add a fold-out to be sewn between any two signatures, not within a signature. Or, your entire book may consist of compiled folds-out.

The most typical fold-out opens to an extra page beyond the foredge of the book. See example 2, page 91. Look at old books for an example that can suggest visual possibilities. For instance, an old geography book may have a map of the region as the final page, a right hand fold-out, at the end of a chapter. The first page of the chapter directs the reader to fold out the map, then return to the beginning of the chapter to read. The entire chapter is read with the map to the right of all the opened 2-page spreads.

Each chapter could be so designed. The fold-out may be a picture or text, seen in context with each 2-page spread of that chapter. Or, the fold-out may be part of a drawing. Each 2-page spread of that chapter may contain a partial picture, which is augmented or completed by the throw-out. There are endless possibilities for the fold-out, rather than the obvious—to house a big picture. The fold-out lends itself to the artists' book, to children's books, or even to poetry.

SEWING FOLDS-OUT: During sewing, each fold-out is opened *only* while it is sewn. It is closed before sewing the next fold-out or signature. This insures the spine will be swollen to the thickness needed, when the book is shelved. If a book of folds-out were bound with the folds-out extended, the spine would be a third to a half the required thickness. When the folds-out would be closed, the foredge would bulge. See examples 3 and 4 below.

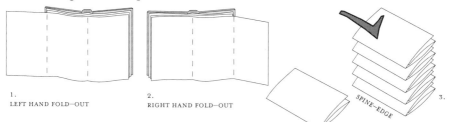

1.
LEFT HAND FOLD—OUT

2.
RIGHT HAND FOLD—OUT

3.
SPINE—EDGE

1-2.
THE SINGLE PAGE FOLD—OUT IS FOLDED INTO THIRDS, THE SIZE OF A PAGE. THE THIRD WHICH IS THE FOLD—OUT IS TRIMMED SLIGHTLY LESS WIDE TO AVOID RISK OF CREASING WHEN FOLDING—IN WITH EACH READING.

1-2.
THE FOLD—OUT IS A SINGLE SEWING UNIT. THE BOOK BLOCK CAN BE SIGNATURES, WITH ONE OR MORE FOLDS—OUT, OR, THE ENTIRE BOOK CAN BE SEWN WITH FOLDS—OUT.
3. CLOSE EACH FOLD—OUT AFTER SEWING, BEFORE SEWING THE NEXT. THIS WILL MAKE THE SPINE THE SAME THICKNESS AS THE FOREDGE. IF SEWN OPEN, AND FOLDED—IN AFTER THE BOOK IS BOUND, THE FOREDGE WOULD BULGE.

1A.
VARIATION ON THE LEFT HAND FOLD—OUT
WINDOW OPENINGS ARE CUT IN THE LEFT AND CENTER PANELS. THE UNIT IS CLOSED AND SEWN. A PRINT IS TIPPED IN ON EACH SIDE OF THE THIRD PANEL. THE UNIT IS CLOSED AND GLUED SHUT WITH A THIN BEAD OF PVA.

1A.
VARIATION ON THE LEFT HAND FOLD—OUT
THE UNIT IS CLOSED AND SEWN. A PRINT IS TIPPED IN ON EACH SIDE OF THE THIRD PANEL. THE UNIT IS CLOSED AND GLUED SHUT WITH A THIN BEAD OF PVA. THE RESULT IS A PAGE WITH A MATTED PRINT ON THE RECTO AS WELL AS THE VERSO. THIS STRUCTURE WAS DESIGNED BY SCOTT McCARNEY.

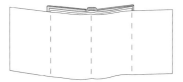

4.
GATE FOLD
THE GATE FOLD THROWS—OUT LEFT AND RIGHT. THE FOLDS—OUT MUST BE TRIMMED SLIGHTLY LESS WIDE THAN THE PAGES, TO AVOID THE RISK OF CREASING.

4.
GATE FOLD
OPEN EACH GATE FOLD ONLY WHILE IT IS BEING SEWN. CLOSE EACH BEFORE THE NEXT FOLD—OUT OR SIGNATURE IS SEWN. IF IT WERE LEFT OPEN, AND CLOSED AFTER BEING BOUND, THE FOREDGE WOULD BE TWICE AS THICK AS THE SPINE.

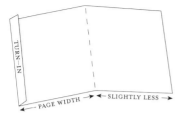

5.
FOLD—OUT WITH TURN—IN
THE FOLD—OUT WITH TURN—IN DOES NOT REMAIN A FOLD—OUT. AFTER IT IS SEWN AND CLOSED, PVA IS APPLIED TO THE TURN—IN, AND THE UNIT IS GLUED SHUT.

5.
FOLD—OUT WITH TURN—IN
THE FOLD—OUT WITH TURN—IN IS SEWN AND CLOSED BEFORE SEWING THE NEXT TO KEEP THE FOREDGE THE SAME THICKNESS AS THE SPINE. AFTER THE BOOK IS BOUND, PVA IS APPLIED TO THE TURN—IN, AND THE UNIT IS GLUED SHUT.

5A.

5A.
FOLD—OUT WITH TURN—IN MAY BE USED TO PROTECT A PRINT. A WINDOW IS CUT. THE UNIT IS SEWN, CLOSED. THE TURN—IN SWELLS THE SPINE, ADDING THICKNESS, SO THE ADDITION OF THE PRINT WILL NOT BULGE THE FOREDGE.

5A.
AFTER BOOK IS SEWN AND GLUED, A PICTURE IS TIPPED IN. THE WINDOW IS GLUED SHUT. IT IS NO LONGER A FOLD—OUT, BUT A 2—PLY PAGE, PROTECTING THE PRINT, WITHOUT AN AWKWARD TISSUE LAID OVER.

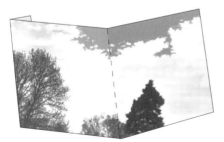

5B.
FOLD—OUT WITH TURN—IN CAN BE PRINTED ON "N" SURFACE PHOTOGRAPHIC PAPER, WHICH FOLDS WITHOUT CRACKING, AND, ACCEPTS PENCIL. THIS IS IDEAL PAPER FOR BLEEDS, AND PRINTING AROUND THE FOREDGE, FROM RECTO TO VERSO.

5B.
PHOTOS MOUNTED ONTO PAPER PAGES MAKE STIFF PAGES. GRAPHIC DESIGN IS ALWAYS CONFINED TO HAVING A PAPER BORDER. THE RESULT IS THE PHOTO IS COMPOSED, BUT THE PAGE, AND 2—PAGE SPREADS, ARE NOT. THE FOLD—OUT WITH TURN—IN RESOLVES THAT PROBLEM.

GATE FOLD: The *gate fold* is a fold-out with two facing folds-out. See Example 4, page 91. Each fold-out is hinged on a foredge of an opened folio. When the gate fold is opened, or thrown-out, there are four facing pages, the two at each extreme extend beyond the book block.

The gate fold is the height of a page and four times as wide. After it is folded, open the page flat. Trim the extended pages 1/8" less wide than the book block. When they are folded shut, the turns-in will not quite meet in the gutter. This will prevent them being accidentally creased with each viewing.

FOLD-OUT WITH TURN-IN: The fold-out with window protects prints, as in Example 1A, page 91 and 5A, page 92. In both instances, a thinner paper than normally used for the book block can be used since the fold-out will be glued shut along the gutter after the book is bound, creating a 2-ply page. Use a bead of PVA glue on the turn-in after the book is bound and any prints are tipped in. Do not laminate the entire foldout, but keep the glue limited to the small turn-in at the spine-edge.

The small turn-in has two purposes:

· It gives a fold, into which to sew.
· It is a *spacer,* adding thickness to the spine, to accommodate the print which later will be tipped in.

The fold-out with turn-in can be photographic paper. A few photo papers, such as *A Surface* and *N Surface,* as well as some photo mural papers, can take a crease without cracking the emulsion. The photographically printed fold-out is also glued shut along the turn-in after the book is bound. The result is a 2-ply page with a photo on each side, or, one photo which continues around the foredge, from recto to verso. This solves graphic design problems of making a one-of-a-kind photo book that is not bulky.

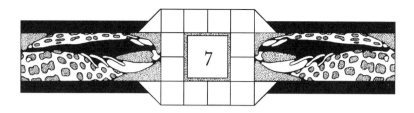

7

IMPOSITION

The *imposition* of a sheet is the laying out of page numbers on a sheet, so that they will be in numerical order when the sheet is folded down into a signature.

FRONT AND BACK, OR SIDE *A* AND *B* OF THE SAME SHEET, FOLDED TO A FOLIO.

FOLIO: Imposing a folio is simple. The right hand side of Side *A* is page 1, while the left is page 4. Side *B* is page 2 on the left, 3 on the right.

QUARTO: Imposing the numbers on a sheet to be folded down into 8 pages or more is difficult on a flat sheet. The easiest method is to take a scrap sheet. Fold it down to whatever number of pages desired. In this instance, 8 pages. Start at the front of the signature and number the pages in numerical order, 1 through 8.

Open the signature to a flat sheet. Examine it:

One side, Side *A,* is page 1, as well as the final page, 8. Notice that pages 4 and 5 on this side of the sheet are upside down.

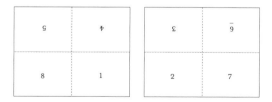

IMPOSED QUARTO SIDE *A* AND SIDE *B*

Side *B* is not a separate sheet, but the back side of the same sheet. Notice that page 2 backs up with page 1. Page 2 is across the gutter from page 7. They are not in numerical order, but they are definitely in an order: The numbers are in their *imposed* order.

If you were designing a flat sheet that later would be folded down, you would lay out the pages in their imposition, as in the illustration, above.

IMPOSING A COMPILED QUARTO: Rather than folding down a sheet to 8 pages, you might compile 2 folios as a quarto.

Folio I would not be numbered as a folio, diagrammed at the top of the previous page. It would be numbered as part of a quarto.

Instead, on Side *A* of Folio I would be page I on the left, but page 8 on the right.

Side *B* would be pages 2 and 7.

Folio 2 would be slipped inside the first to form a quarto.

Side *A* would be pages 6 and 3. The other side of the second folio would be sides 4 and 5.

FOLIO 1

First Sheet, Side *A*   First Sheet, Side *B*

FOLIO 2

Second Sheet, Side *A*   Second Sheet, Side *B*

FOLIOS 1 & 2
COMPILED AS
A QUARTO

Imposition of two folios compiled as a quarto.

SIDE A IS THE PEAK: It is important to remember in compiling folios to form a signatures, that Side *A* always represents the mountain *peak* of the fold. Side *B* is the *valley* of that same fold. "Front" and "back" are irrelevant terms. Each page of the signature *is* a front when opened to it. The same page becomes a back as that page is turned. Thus, the sheet is referred to as Side *A* and Side *B*.

side *A*   side *B*

facing page: CHART OF IMPOSITIONS

One sheet, 4 pages and 2 sides are shown imposed, at the top, as a folio. Next, the same size sheet is imposed as a quarto. Thirdly, if the sheet is folded down into an octavo, the page numbers would be imposed as shown. At the bottom, a sheet would be folded against the grain with a Z-fold, then in half to form a sexto. The sheet is imposed as a sexto.

FOLIO   SIDE A   SIDE B

4	1

2	3

QUARTO   SIDE A   SIDE B

5	4
8	1

3	9
2	7

OCTAVO   SIDE A   SIDE B

5	12	9	8
4	13	16	1

7	10	11	9
2	15	14	3

SEXTO   SIDE A   SIDE B

8	5
9	4
12	1

6	7
3	10
2	11

SEWING PREPARATION

Although the type and pattern of stitches vary with different bindings, all codex bindings have certain preparations and procedures in
common.

SEWING STATIONS

The holes through which you sew are called *sewing stations* or *stations*.[8] All
binding starts with pre-piercing or sawing the sewing stations.
Piercing is done with a *bradawl, bodkin* or a pointed needle.

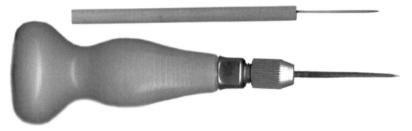

TOP: BRADAWL OR BODKIN. THIS IS A CERAMIC TOOL, AVAILABLE IN AN ART SUP-
PLY STORE FOR UNDER $2. IT CAN BE MADE USING A 1/4" WOODEN DOWEL AND
INSERTING A NEEDLE IN THE END, AFTER REMOVING THE EYE OF THE NEEDLE.

MIDDLE: A BINDER'S AWL HAS A REMOVABLE POINT. A VARIETY OF POINTS COME
WITH THE WOODEN HANDLE. EACH POINT HAS A SHAFT, DIFFERENT IN DIAMETER.
THE POINT IS CHOSEN DEPENDING UPON WHICH SIZE THREAD IS USED. THE
SEWING STATION SHOULD BE SMALLER IN DIAMETER THAN THE NEEDLE USED IN
SEWING. THE NEEDLE SHOULD SLIGHTLY ENLARGE THE STATION AS YOU SEW.

Do not use an awl designed for leather, as shown below. The shaft
increases in diameter farther up from the point whereas a bradawl,
bodkin and some binder's awls have a shaft constant in diameter.

NEVER USE A LEATHER AWL TO PIERCE SEWING STATIONS. YOU CANNOT CONTROL
THE SIZE OF THE HOLE, OR SEWING STATION BECAUSE OF THE GRADUATED SHAFT.

PIERCING THE STATIONS FROM THE INSIDE TO THE OUTSIDE

For production work, stations are pierced from the middle of the inside to the outside of the signatures, that is, from the *valley to the mountain peak*. Piercing is done with a bodkin or bradawl, not an awl. A bodkin, or bradawl, is a special kind of awl which has a narrow shaft. Thickness of the shaft is uniform, whereas an awl has a shaft that is graduated from a small diameter to a much larger one. An awl is designed to pierce leather or book board for lacing-in cords. The small diameter at the tip permits an easy start. The farther down you push, the deeper hole is made for the cord.

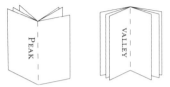

MOUNTAIN PEAK AND VALLEY OF A SIGNATURE

Piercing sewing stations, there is no need for a larger wound; in fact, it is undesirable. The bradawl should be chosen in conjunction with the needle. The diameter of the bradawl should be less than that of the needle. In sewing, the needle forces a slightly larger opening of the wound, just enough to pull the needle through. If your bradawl were thicker than the needle, you would have excessively large wounds in the paper. An awl would cause even more damage.

If hand-holding the signatures when piercing, you must place your thumb and forefinger very close to the mark, so that the paper is supported close to the piercing. Otherwise, you will kink the paper.

Far better results are obtained by not holding the signature in the air, but piercing with the signature supported by a surface. This can be a table top, a board with a slot, or better, in a cradle.

TABLE TOP PIERCING: In piercing, it is easier to pierce from the valley of the signature to the mountain peak. However, almost always, it is the mountain peak which has been marked for the stations. Piercing with a support, such as a table surface, a board with a slot or a cradle, permits easy piercing from the valley to the peak.

The table top method of piercing is a substitute for the cradle method. Using a table that accepts a leaf, open the crack slightly. Place the signature flat on the table, with the fold aligned with the crack. As you pierce, the point of the bradawl enters the crack of the table. The table provides good support, right up to the point of piercing. Related to this method is constructing a board with a slot.

BOARD WITH SLOT: You could construct a board with a slot in the middle, a foot long and a quarter inch wide. Screw a ruler as guard at the bottom to center the signature.

The signature is laid flat on the surface with the fold aligned with the slot and ruler. One hand firmly holds the signature in position, while the sewing stations are easily pierced with no fear of kinking the paper causing a dimple.

BOARD WITH SLOT is not as accurate as a cradle, which centers the signature.

PIERCING THE STATIONS USING A CRADLE: Piercing several signatures is easier by setting up some sort of a jig. The best is a cradle, into which opened signatures are individually laid. Stations are pierced from the inside to the outside, valley to peak, making sure the angle is bifurcated. This will insure that the bradawl pierces all the layers of the signature precisely on the fold.

The cradle method of piercing is good, because the paper does not have to be marked; it is also faster. A sheet of stiff paper, the exact height of the signatures, is marked as a guide for the locations of the sewing stations. After a signature is set into the cradle, the piece of paper is placed in the signature, next to the fold. The paper guide eliminates the need to mark the stations on any of the signatures.

The cradle might be constructed out of book board and can be used time and again. The bradawl will pierce the seam of the scored and folded diagonal boards.

A permanent cradle can be constructed out of wood. In this instance, a small slot is left between the two diagonal boards to allow the needle to pass through the gap between the boards.

The cradle is a production method and provides access to quick, accurate piercing and it saves your dining room table.

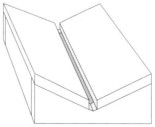

WOODEN CRADLE with slot

PIERCING FROM THE OUTSIDE TO THE INSIDE

Stations in a multiple signature binding generally are marked and pierced from the outside through to the inside of the signature, that is, from the *mountain peak* to the *valley*. Use the marks on the first signature as a guide. With a right angle, mark all the dots down through the stack across the folds of all the signatures.

NUMBER AND POSITION OF STATIONS: For the Flat Back, see page 170. For the Tight Back, the kettle stations are 3/8" in from the head and tail, since you will not plow. Use five cords evenly spaced across the *backbone,* or back of the book block. For a larger book, use more cords. Space between sewing stations should not be more than 11/2".

Open each signature separately and saw the holes. Place the signatures back in their correct order.

MARKING THE STATIONS: Only one closed signature of the book block is measured and marked on the fold of the peak. Mark the stations on one signature with a sharp, #2 pencil. Never use ink. It can bleed to the inside of the pages. Place this signature back on the book block. It will be used as a guide to mark the remaining signatures.

Jog the book block for marking. Always jog on the backbone and the head, not the tail. The head must be positioned as smoothly as possible, as it will not be plowed. A smooth head resists dust filtering into the book block as it is stored on the shelf.

Without disturbing the alignment of the jog, the book block is carefully laid on the table in order to mark the position of the holes on the remainder of the signatures.

A small right angle is stood on the table against the backbone. It is positioned at one station. A pencil is drawn down across the folds of the remaining signatures, marking all the signatures at once, across the edge of the folds. The remaining stations are so marked.

Mark lightly with a sharp, #2 pencil to achieve the precise location to be pierced. Mark the signatures on the fold, not onto the surface of the page, as it would be seen in the book. Do not use ink or ball point pen. It might smear or bleed.

If the stations were marked on the *inside* of each signature, each would have to be measured and marked individually. Since it is faster to mark the outside of the signatures, piercing must be from the outside to the inside, peak to valley. Open each signature to pierce.

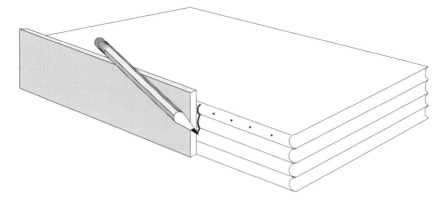

MARKING THE STATIONS USING A RIGHT ANGLE: Measure and mark the top signature, only. Jog the book block. Place a right angle against the backbone at each dot. Use a sharp pencil to make a precise line down across each signature. Never use ink; it can bleed. Kettle stations are ⅜" in from the head and tail. Middle stations for tapes or cords are never more than 1½" apart.

If it is not a blank book, take care to keep the signatures in their proper order. Hold the bradawl erect, to pierce perpendicular to the fold. This will insure the point will pass through each successive fold and not veer onto the page. Use a bradawl which will leave a hole slightly smaller than the needle which will be used for the sewing. This will allow the sewing procedure to leave as small a hole as necessary, wounding the paper as little as possible.

SEWING STATIONS USING A KNIFE: With practice, some prefer to extend the book block off the edge of the table. Use a thin bladed sharp knife, such as an X-Acto™ or a knife with break-off blades. Slice the stations, similar to sawing.

BALL POINT NEEDLE: Sewing is with a binder's needle which is also called a ball-point needle, as it has no sharp point. A substitute is to use sand paper on a sharp needle to dull it.

A ball point needle cannot be used for piercing the paper. Pre-piercing the sewing stations, then sewing with a ball point needle permits speedy sewing, without the risk of accidentally scarring the paper, piercing an unwanted hole, or stabbing your finger. That said, I do not sew with a ball-point needle; I use a pointed darners needle.

JOGGING FOR SAWING: Place a scrap piece of book board on
each side of the book block. Care must be taken not to allow the book
block to go askew after being jogged.

- If the book block is blank paper, jog on the head, then on the backbone.
- If the sheet is printed, then folded down into a signature, proceed
  as follows: Place a scrap piece of board on each side of the book
  block. The book board is the same height, or slightly taller than the
  book block. The width of the scrap boards should be about half the
  width of the book block. This is because in sawing, the book block
  and boards extend above the jaws of the press. There must be
  enough board within the press to be held securely. If you do not
  have a press, use two wooden boards and C-clamps as a substitute
  press, as described on page 38.

  Set the scrap boards flush with the spine-edge, aligned with the
  head. If the scrap boards are longer than the book, allow them to
  extend at the tail.

  Jog on backbone and head. That is, strike the spine of the book
  block, sandwiched with the scrap boards, on a flat surface to level it.
  Then, strike the head of the book block on the table to align all the
  signatures at the head, as opposed to the tail. This is important, as
  the registration of the text is at the head. It is also to keep the head
  flush, since this manual does not employ a tool for plowing.

  Jog the book block again on the backbone, keeping the alignment at
  the head, as well. Lay the book on the table carefully, not to disturb
  the alignment. Mark the stations, so the stations at 90° to the
  spine-edge.
- If folios are compiled into signatures, or, if re-binding an old
  book: The jogging procedure is the same, although you cannot rely
  upon the alignment of the registration. You have to go through and
  line up the text block. Each signature must be examined, to check
  the registration. The old book being rebound will not be sawed,
  but jogged and sewn.

SAWING THE STATIONS: Place in a laying press, with the spine extending approximately ⅜", but not more than ½". Otherwise, there is not sufficient support at the spine when sawing. If you do not have a press, you can place the book block between two boards. Use *C*-clamps to hold the signatures tight.

Instead of individually piercing each hole and each signature, sawing creates *kerf stations*. *Kerf* is a term which means cuts made with a back-saw across the signature folds of an unsewn text. If the sewing stations are sawed rather than pierced, they are *kerf stations*.

Sawing kerf stations is a commercial short-cut discouraged by many because of the risk of cutting too deeply. Other binders, such as Fred, argue that these stations are more precisely aligned. Practice will tell you how deeply you should saw.

Practice on some scrap signatures, if you wish. You might not saw deeply enough, in which case, the outer folds of the signature will be cut, but the inner ones may have to be pierced by hand. Sawing is quicker than piercing each signature individually.

SAW FOR PAMPHLET SEWING : Since the Pamphlet Sewing has only a single signature, it should be pierced, rather than sawed. If you were making an edition, you could place a dozen of the book blocks together to be jogged and sawed at the same time. Use a thin bladed Japanese saw or tenon saw illustrated on page 36. These saws work on the back stroke. The blade is very thin, making a narrow width wound.

SAW FOR SEWING ON TAPES (FLAT BACK): Stations for the Flat Back can be pierced or sawed. If you saw the sewing stations, use a Japanese saw or tenon saw illustrated on page 36.

Since this binding is described with a cloth hinge attached to the first and last signature, the sawing may not cut the inside paper of these two signatures. You may have to finish by piercing these signatures.

SAWING FOR RAISED CORDS: Use a thin bladed tenon saw. Hold the saw at a 90° angle, perpendicular to the plane of the backbone. With one or two strokes, saw only deep enough to cut through the inner-most folio of the signature. Saw all stations, including the kettle stations. The sawing is complete if you are sewing for raised cords.

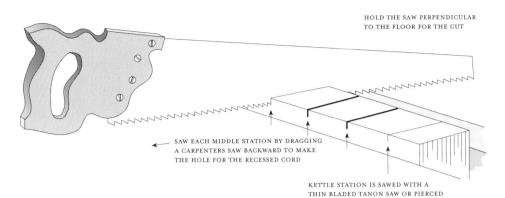

HOLD THE SAW PERPENDICULAR
TO THE FLOOR FOR THE CUT

SAW EACH MIDDLE STATION BY DRAGGING
A CARPENTERS SAW BACKWARD TO MAKE
THE HOLE FOR THE RECESSED CORD

KETTLE STATION IS SAWED WITH A
THIN BLADED TANON SAW OR PIERCED

SAWING THE STATIONS FOR RECESSED CORDS: Saw the middle stations with a carpenters saw perpendicular to the spine. Draw the blade
back to create a hole for the cords to be pulled into the signature.
The kettle stations need a smaller hole for the thread, only. Pierce or
saw with a thin bladed tenon saw. See page 36.

SAW FOR RECESSED CORD SEWING: The middle sewing stations (all
stations except for the kettle stations at the head and tail) must be
sawed for recessed cord sewing; they cannot be pierced. Fred suggests
a common carpenters saw. Instead of a forward stroke, he says drag
the saw towards you to make the cut. The larger hole from this saw
will be ideal for recessed cord sewing.

This will open space within the signature. As you are sewing, the cord will be
pulled inside the signature, as you pull
on the thread when you proceed to the
next station. Do not use the carpenters
saw for the kettle stations; use a tenon
saw, or pierce with a bradawl.

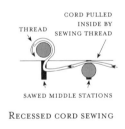

CORD PULLED
INSIDE BY
THREAD   SEWING THREAD

SAWED MIDDLE STATIONS

RECESSED CORD SEWING

NOTE: Never saw stations if you are going to span from one signature
to the next. The span will creep inside the signature and not be seen.
Spanning is used in Coptic sewings and The Butterfly, also known as
the *Double Span-Span Span-Span.* These bindings are described in *Exposed
Spine Sewings,* Volume III, *Non-Adhesive Binding.*

THREAD

Archival materials should be used. Linen thread is generally considered to have more strength and longevity than cotton.

Non-traditional sewings might use copper wire or some other linear substance. Plastic fishing line is strong and will last, but risks ripping the paper. After knots are tied, they would have to be fused with a match. Although these substitutes have a nice unusual appearance, they do not function as well as cotton or linen thread.

Binding suppliers sell unbleached and unwaxed linen thread. It is important that the thread be unbleached, so that it will not rot. Craft stores often handle spools of pre-waxed linen thread in various colors. A list of suppliers is in the *Source Section,* page 417. A longer list is available on my web site.[9]

WAXING THE THREAD: Thread should be waxed prior to sewing. Waxed thread is stiffer and will become less tangled as you sew. Stitches will tend to cling in position, remaining tighter during sewing. The main reason for waxing the thread is not for convenience, but archival. After sewing, turning pages will have less friction and the book will wear better.

To wax the thread, run an arm's length of thread across the edge of a cake of beeswax. Speed is more important than pressure. It will create friction, melting the wax onto the thread. Run the length of cut thread two or three times across the wax until it is a little stiff.

THREADING THE NEEDLE: Use as small a needle as you are able to thread. Too large a needle will create larger holes in the paper than the thread can fill.

Sewing is usually done with a single thread, rather than centering the needle on the length of thread and making double threads as the stitches. Cut about an arm's length of thread. Less requires too many knots during the sewing. More is difficult to handle.

It would be awkward and time consuming pulling this entire length through the sewing stations. Thread the needle, pulling a little more than a third of the thread through the needle. This will cut the distance the thread must be pulled through the sewing stations almost in half, without giving a double thread stitch. As more and more thread is used up in the sewing, adjust the needle closer to the loose end of the thread, so that the stitches are not of double thread.

KNOTS

If you are clipping a thread after a knot is tied, clip the loose ends to about ¾". Do not clip close to the knot to get rid of the loose ends, thinking they are unsightly. The knot might work itself loose and the sewing will come untied. Do not be ashamed of hand-tied knots. They are evidence of the individual and should not be down-played. Such irregularities are part of the craft of hand-binding.

There are several knots used in binding: the *Overhand K, Square Knot* or *Reef Knot, Slip Knot*, also known as a *Running K and* the *Weaver's Knot.*

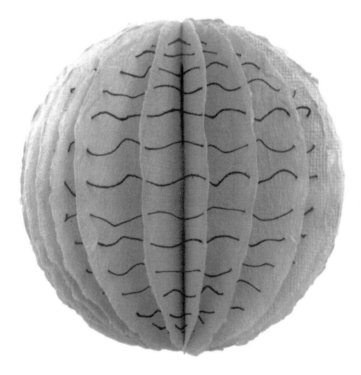

ADÈLE OUTTERIDGE, *THREADED SPHERE*, ONE-OF-A-KIND. HANDMADE PAPER, LINEN THREAD, 1995. 20 CM. DIAMETER. ADÈLE IS AN ARTIST/TEACHER IN BRISBANE, AUSTRALIA.

PROCEDURE FOR TYING AN OVERHAND K: Grasp one loose end of the thread with your left hand with an inch of thread extended from your grip. This will be referred to as the left thread. Grasp the other end with your right hand in the same manner. Lay the left thread over the top of the right. Hold this into position with your left thumb and forefinger. Take your right forefinger and push the left thread under and around the right, through the loop. Both loose ends are now pointing upwards. Tighten the knot. This configuration is known as the *Overhand Knot.*

PROCEDURE FOR TYING A SQUARE KNOT: The *Square Knot* is also known as the *reef* and as the *Flat* K.

First, form an Overhand K by laying the left thread over the top of the right. Take your right forefinger and push the left thread under and around the right thread, through the loop. Tighten.

OVERHAND *K*

LOOSELY TIED SQUARE KNOT

TIGHTENING THE SQUARE KNOT

TIGHTENING THE SQUARE KNOT

TIGHTENED SQUARE KNOT

REEF, SQUARE KNOT, OR FLAT *K*

THIS KNOT IS COMMONLY CALLED A *square knot* IN THE STATES. IN AUSTRALIA, IT IS KNOWN AS THE *Reef Knot.*

Second, go through this procedure for a second time, but this time in reverse, or symmetrically:

Lay the right thread over the top of the left. Take your left forefinger and push the right thread under and around the left thread, through the loop. Tighten. When it is tied, this is a single *Square Knot.* It looks square, also, when it is tightened as shown above.

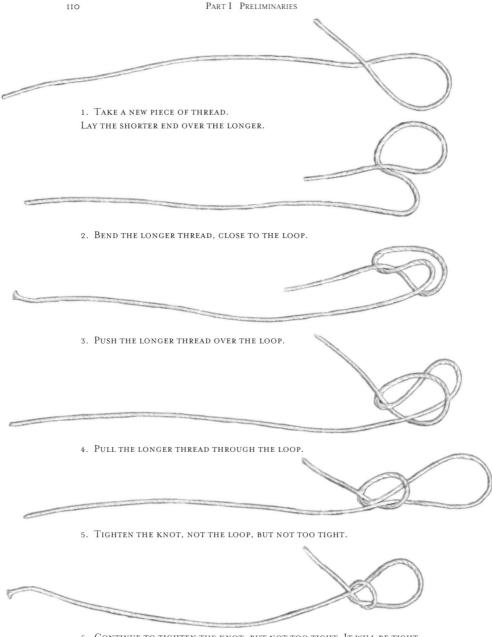

1. Take a new piece of thread.
Lay the shorter end over the longer.

2. Bend the longer thread, close to the loop.

3. Push the longer thread over the loop.

4. Pull the longer thread through the loop.

5. Tighten the knot, not the loop, but not too tight.

6. Continue to tighten the knot, but not too tight. It will be tightened completely when forming the *Weaver's Knot*.
Adjust the size of the loop to about the diameter of a pencil.

SLIP KNOT: Above are the steps in tying a *Slip Knot*. It is used to form a *Weaver's Knot*, described on pages 111–114. Scale: 1:1, #12 thread.

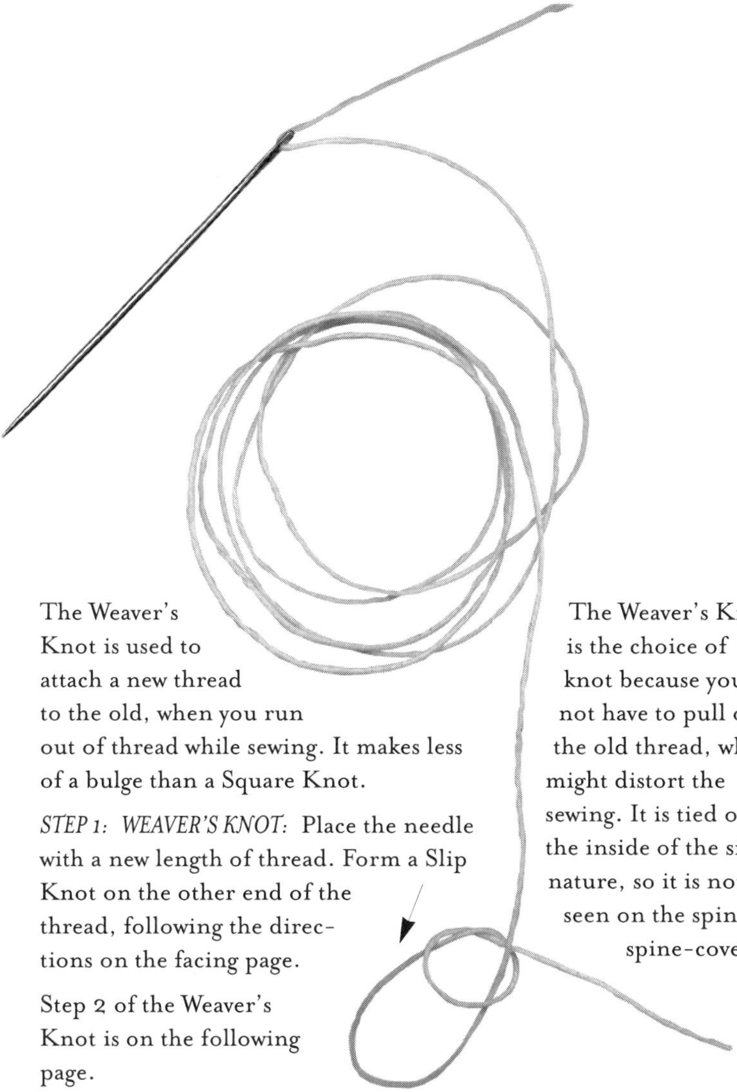

The Weaver's Knot is used to attach a new thread to the old, when you run out of thread while sewing. It makes less of a bulge than a Square Knot.

STEP 1: WEAVER'S KNOT: Place the needle with a new length of thread. Form a Slip Knot on the other end of the thread, following the directions on the facing page.

Step 2 of the Weaver's Knot is on the following page.

The Weaver's Knot is the choice of knot because you do not have to pull on the old thread, which might distort the sewing. It is tied on the inside of the signature, so it is not seen on the spine or spine-cover.

STEP 1 TO FORM THE WEAVER'S KNOT: THREAD THE NEEDLE. ON THE OTHER END, FORM A SLIP KNOT, SHOWN ABOVE AND DESCRIBED ON THE FACING PAGE.

STEP 2: In tying the Weaver's Knot, it is important to slip the *loop* of the new thread over the old thread. Do not slip the old thread though the knot of the Slip Knot.

The loop and the knot will probably be a little smaller than shown in Step 2.

STEP 3: Pull the new thread until the knot is very small, but not tight. Adjust the loop until it, too, is small.

Move the Slip Knot onto the old thread, illustrated as darker for clarity, to the precise position you wish to tie the Weaver's Knot.

STEP 4: Tighten the knot by pulling on both ends of the *new* thread. Pull in opposite directions to tighten. When you have tightened suffi-ciently, you will feel a slight click when it locks.

Do not pull on the *old* thread. This will loosen the loop and the new thread will slip off.

Pull on the old thread only to untie the Weaver's Knot.

To test if the knot is secure, tug on the *new* thread. If it slips off, you did not tighten enough in Step 4.

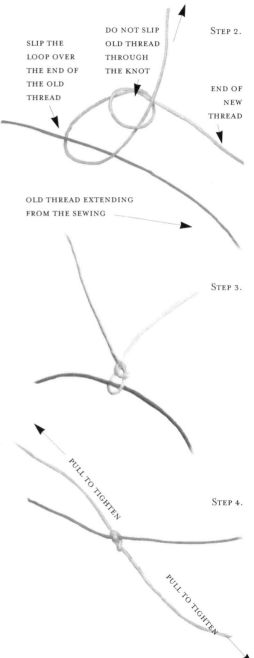

THREAD CONTINUES TO THE ATTACHED NEEDLE

SLIP THE
LOOP OVER
THE END OF
THE OLD
THREAD

DO NOT SLIP
OLD THREAD
THROUGH
THE KNOT

STEP 2.

END OF
NEW
THREAD

OLD THREAD EXTENDING
FROM THE SEWING

STEP 3.

PULL TO TIGHTEN

STEP 4.

PULL TO TIGHTEN

NOTE: THE TWO VIEWS OF THE WEAVER'S KNOT SHOWN ON THIS PAGE HAVE NOT YET BEEN TIGHTENED, SO THAT YOU CAN SEE THE FORMATION. IF YOU LEFT THE KNOT LIKE THIS, WITHOUT TIGHTENING IT, THE NEW THREAD WOULD SLIP OFF.

WEAVER'S KNOT, SHOWN HERE, NOT TIGHTENED, AS THE FRONT AND BACK VIEWS, MAGNIFIED 500%.

A DARKER THREAD WAS USED AS THE OLD THREAD, IN THE ILLUSTRATIONS ON THIS AND THE FACING PAGE, TO DIFFERENTIATE IT FROM THE NEW THREAD.

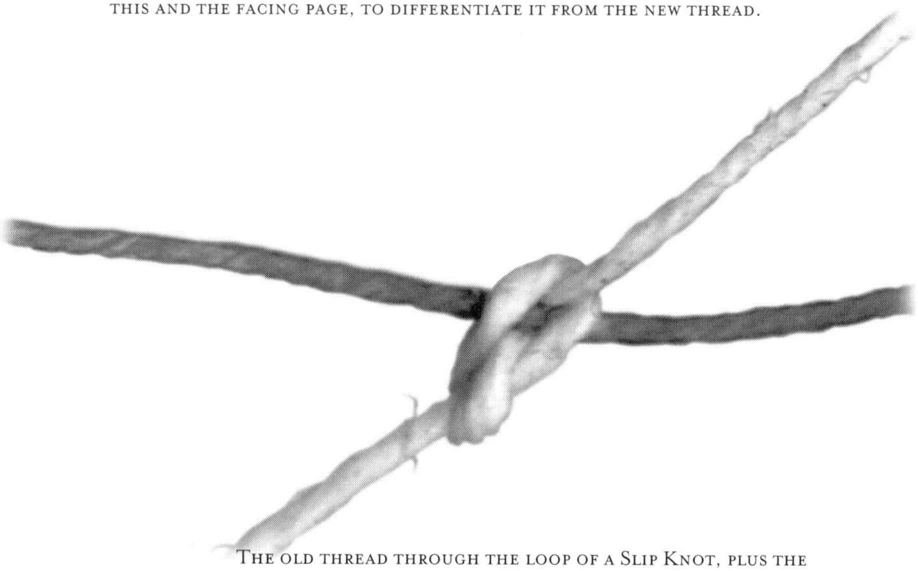

THE OLD THREAD THROUGH THE LOOP OF A SLIP KNOT, PLUS THE SLIP KNOT, ONCE TIGHTENED, FORMS THE WEAVER'S KNOT.

TIGHTENED WEAVER'S KNOT SHOWN ON THE FOLLOWING PAGE.

WEAVER'S KNOT, TIGHTENED, FRONT AND BACK VIEWS, AT 500%. THE NEW
THREAD IS THE LIGHTER COLOR. THE DARKER THREAD IS THE OLD THREAD.

HALF HITCH: The final knot needed is the half hitch. In completing a
sewing, you cannot always tie a square knot, because you have only
one loose end of thread. You can tie the half hitch on the spine,
looping around the final kettle stitch. If you don't want the bump of
a knot on the spine, tie the half hitch inside the final signature,
looping the thread between the final two holes:

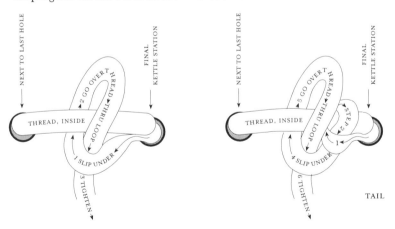

HALF HITCH, SHOWN TIED-OFF INSIDE THE SIGNATURE, AT THE TAIL. AT THE
LEFT ARE THE FIRST STEPS. THESE ARE REPEATED, AS SHOWN ON THE RIGHT. THE
HALF HITCH IS THE BEST WAY TO TIE-OFF WITH ONLY ONE LOOSE END OF THREAD.

KETTLE STITCH

All the multi-signature sewings in this manual utilize the kettle stitch as the means to end the sewing of a signature and the method of locking it to the previously sewn signatures, as well as the means to climb and enter the next signature to be sewn.

TRUE KETTLE STITCH: In order to form a true kettle stitch, there must be three actions:

· drops and links under the two previously connected signatures. This ties the signatures just sewn to the book block.

· slips under to lock the kettle.

· climbs and enters the next signature to be sewn.[10]

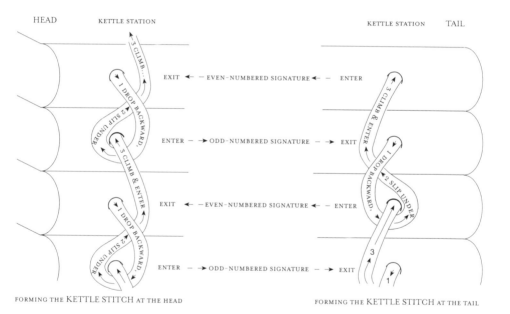

FORMING THE KETTLE STITCH AT THE HEAD   FORMING THE KETTLE STITCH AT THE TAIL

KETTLE STITCH DETAIL OF THE HEAD AND TAIL OF A SEWING ALONG THE SPINE. THE KETTLE DROPS, LINKS UNDER THE PREVIOUSLY TWO CONNECTED SIGNATURES, SLIPS UNDER THE THREAD TO LOCK, CLIMBS AND ENTERS THE NEXT SIGNATURE TO BE SEWN.

IN THE ABOVE ILLUSTRATION, THE THREAD DROPS BACKWARD, THAT IS, IN THE OPPOSITE DIRECTION OF THE SEWING FOR THAT SIGNATURE. A TRUE KETTLE STITCH COULD DROP FORWARD, AS ILLUSTRATED ON THE TOP OF THE FOLLOWING PAGE. HOWEVER, THIS IS A DIFFICULT MANEUVER. IT IS FAR EASIER TO DROP BACKWARD, LINK AND LOCK, ALL IN A SINGLE ACTION, AS ILLUSTRATED ON THE BOTTOM OF PAGE 117.

FORWARD OR BACKWARD DROP: As long as it links, locks and climbs, the true kettle can drop forward or backward.

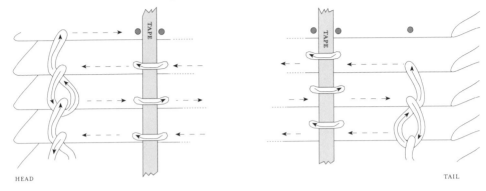

FORWARD DROP: This true kettle stitch links, locks and climbs. Dropping forward is difficult to sew and is not recommended.

PREFERRED BACKWARD DROP: Dropping backward to the inside is preferred, because it is easier to enter from the inside, rather than the outside, as illustrated below. Without opening the book, the needle is slipped between the last two connected signatures at a diagonal until the point of the needle extends beyond the head (or tail). This forms the link. The thread is looped over the point of the needle. When the needle is pulled to adjust the tension, this forms the lock as well as the link, all in one motion. See bottom of facing page.

The kettle is the turn-around, or *change-over:* It marks the change in the direction of sewing, either towards the head, or towards the tail.

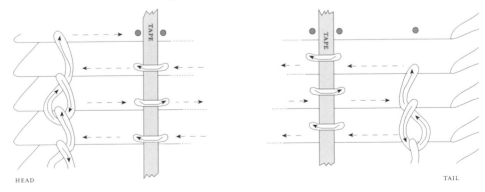

BACKWARD DROP: This ideal true kettle stitch drops *BACKWARD,* links, locks and climbs. This is preferred over dropping forward.

In dropping *backward,* direction of the sewing shifts. The kettle drops in the direction of the following signature, not the current. The middle sewing stations in the signature are for sewing onto tapes or cords. The kettle stitch is only at the head and the tail.

Notice that the ideal kettle stitch at the tail is formed in the same manner as that at the head, but it is the mirror image. This is because in both instances the kettle drops to the inside, or drops backward.

Below is a true kettle, because it links under, locks and climbs. However, it is extremely difficult to sew and offers no other advantage. It is too much trouble:

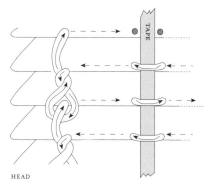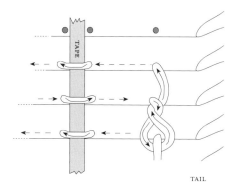

HEAD   TAIL

AN IMPRACTICAL TRUE KETTLE STITCH.

BACKWARD DROP, LINK AND LOCK IN ONE MANEUVER:
As shown on the right, as well as on the bottom of the facing page, the kettle drops backward, because it is far easier to take the needle from the inside to the out-side than vice versa.

This can be achieved in a single maneuver, as shown on the right:

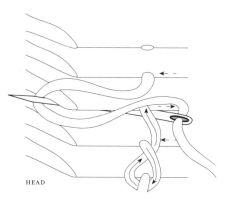

HEAD

DROPPING BACKWARD TO THE INSIDE, LINKING AND LOCKING THE KETTLE STITCH. PULL THE NEEDLE THROUGH, CLIMB AND ENTER THE NEXT SIGNATURE.

FALSE KETTLE STITCH

It is also important to show what should not be done. This is what the Germans refer to as a "false", that is, incomplete kettle stitch:

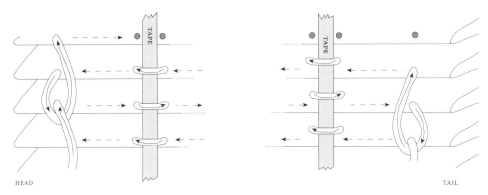

HEAD   TAIL

FALSE KETTLE STITCH AFTER LINKING, THE KETTLE FAILS TO SLIP UNDER TO LOCK, BEFORE CLIMBING AND ENTERING THE NEXT SIGNATURE.

AFTER EXITING THE SIGNATURE, THE KETTLE DROPS FORWARD TO LINK UNDER. THIS IS CORRECT, BUT IMPRACTICAL.

Sewing onto tapes, the middle stations, is correct, but the kettle stitches are not. At the tail, the kettle drops to the outside, links and climbs to the next signature. It is a "false" kettle because it does not lock. It is correct inasmuch as the kettle drops forward, but impractical, making it difficult to link under.

This is another false kettle:

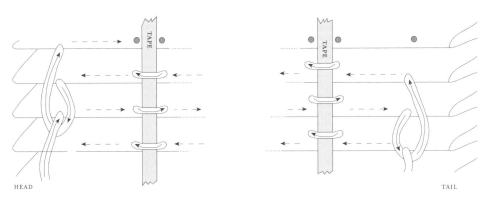

HEAD   TAIL

FALSE KETTLE STITCH AFTER LINKING, THE KETTLE FAILS TO SLIP UNDER TO LOCK, BEFORE CLIMBING AND ENTERING THE NEXT SIGNATURE.

AFTER EXITING THE SIGNATURE, THE KETTLE DROPS BACKWARD TO LINK UNDER. THIS IS CORRECT, AS FAR AS IT GOES, BUT IT FAILS TO LOCK.

At the tail and at the head, this kettle stitch drops to the inside, links and climbs. This kettle is practical in that it drops backward to the inside, making it easier to link under. It is a false kettle because it does not lock.

NOTE: In forming your kettles, be careful not to tighten too much; it is very easy to over-tighten. See *Tension in Sewing,* page 121.

SEWING ON THE BENCH
Placing the book on a table, or on a sewing frame to sew, is referred to as sewing *on the bench.* This leaves both hands free to sew.

All the instructions and illustrations herein are described for sewing back and forth along the signatures on the bench. None require the use of a sewing frame.

FACE UP: Some binders sew in the order from the last signature in the book to the first.

· The advantage is that you do not have to flip over the signature.
· The disadvantage is that you have to remember to always take from the bottom of the stack when you select the next signature to be sewn. This order of sewing is referred to as *face up.*

Sewing face up, the head is to the left. It is referred to as the *German style.* If you choose to sew face up, just remember when the instructions say to sew the "first" signature, for you, means the signature adjacent to the back cover.

FACE DOWN: If you wish to sew from the front to the back of the book, sew face down, head to the right. This is in the manner of the English.

· The advantage is you don't have to pick up each signature to be sewn from the bottom of the stack.
· The disadvantage is that you have to flip each signature upside down when you pick it up from the stack to lay it in position to sew.

If you pierce your sewing stations symmetrically, the pierced holes will line up, even if the signature is incorrectly laid down. As a fail-safe, if you sew face down, pierce the stations asymmetrically. The holes won't line up if you make a mistake in positioning it to be sewn.

BACK TO FRONT, OR FRONT TO BACK: It makes no difference whether you sew from back to front, or front to back (face up or face down).

Fred has a good method of solving the problem of not sewing a signature on upside down. Also, his method is good if you sew from front to back or back to front:

Place the signatures in order. Set the book block at arm's length, with the spine facing away from you. It does not matter if the first or last signature is facing up. As you sew, pick up the top signature. Flip it 180° towards you, so the spine-edge is facing you. Sew that signature. Each time, pick up the top signature. Flip it over, set it on top of the sewn signatures, ready to sew.

In this manual, for uniformity, all sewings will be described sewing from the head to the tail. The "first" signature refers to the *first to be sewn,* not whether it is the first in the book, or the final signature—it does not matter.

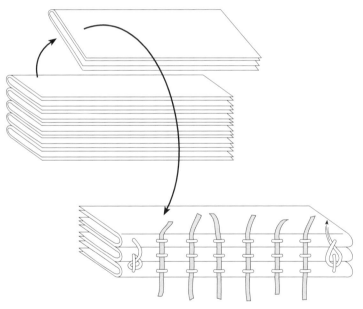

SEWING FACE DOWN: BE CAREFUL TO SEW EACH SIGNATURE IN PROPER ORDER, WITH NONE UPSIDE DOWN. FRED PREFERS THE ENGLISH METHOD: THE FOREDGE OF THE UNSEWN SIGNATURES FACE YOU. FLIP EACH TO BE SEWN 180° AS YOU SEW THE NEXT SIGNATURE. IT DOES NOT MATTER IF YOU START THE SEWING FROM THE FRONT OR BACK OF THE BOOK BLOCK. I PREFER THE GERMAN STYLE, WHICH IS ALSO DESCRIBED ON PAGE 119.

TENSION IN SEWING

Tension must be correct in degree and uniform throughout. Sewing must not be too loose or too tight. Stitches should be uniform in size and shape. To achieve this, it is best to sew the book at one sitting, without a break.

KETTLE STATIONS: Beginners often sew the kettle stitches too tightly. Too tight a sewing is usually at the kettle stations, since it is easy to apply extreme pressure in forming the kettle stitch. This results in two errors:

- Tightening the kettle stitches too much will pull every other signature in from the head and the tail. Each signature will jog back and forth with a corduroy effect on the head and the tail.
- Forming the kettles to an extreme will pinch the head and tail. The result is a spine that is not parallel, but bows in at each end. It is far more difficult to tighten the sewing at the middle stations.

Form your kettle stitches carefully. Pull to lock only enough to make the thread taut, so that you do not bow the signature. When the kettle is too tight, the mistake is to think the sewing at the middle stations is too loose.

MIDDLE STATIONS: In sewing, do not use a bone folder to compress each signature between the supports as it is sewn. It is very easy to get too tight a sewing compressing with a bone folder. The result is a book that is difficult, if not impossible to round and back. Excessive compression will actually bow the spine to a concave on the sewing frame. The spine should remain flat and backing will form a convex spine.

Knocking down after the sewing is completed gives a good compression. See page 228.

Adéle Outteridge, *Gaia,* one-of-a-kind, engraved perspex (plexiglass),
linen thread, 1997, 14 x 8 x 3 cm.

Single sheet binding poses problems of how to sew, rather than to stab
the page. Adéle's book is an excellent example of problem solving. The
pages open flat, while the sewing thread creates a spherical display.

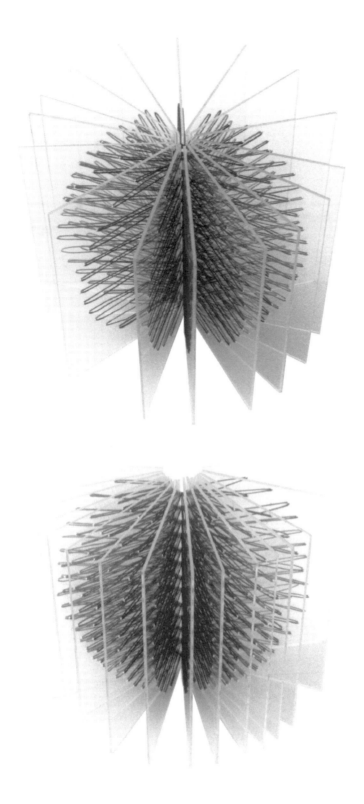

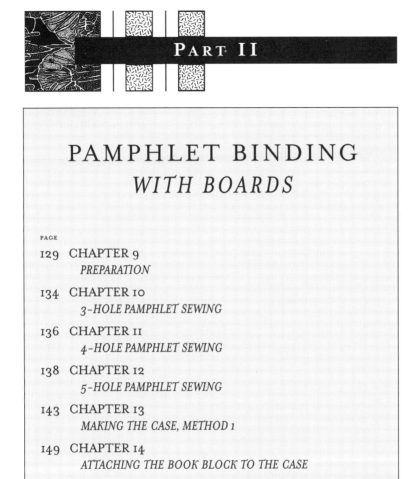

PART II

PAMPHLET BINDING
WITH BOARDS

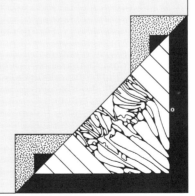

Keith Smith, *Back and Forth,*
Book Number 108. Pamphlet
Binding with Boards, quarter
leather with gold foil stamping and leather hinges.
Offset in edition of 200, self-
published, and hand bound by
the artist, 1985. Also illustrated on pages 127 and 128.

INTRODUCTION

When we think of a single signature format, we generally think of a magazine—a single signature and cover stapled as a unit. A disposable book. Maybe we think of a hand sewn pamphlet sewing with paper cover and foredge turn-in.[11] But a single signature can be quite a substantial hardcover book. It can even have quarter leather spine and leather hinges. Fred taught me this construction.

The Pamphlet Binding with Boards is ideal for books of few pages, under 9 x 12". However, artists often desire to bind large prints into a book. A variation of the Pamphlet Binding with Boards can be used. If the pages are over 17", the binding is called a *Portfolio Book*. The structural variation is described in the *Notes*.[12]

```
                    I      P  O  N  D  E  R      I  F
            I      C  A  N      H  E  A  D      B  A  C  K
    O  N      T  H  E      R  O  A  D      N  O  R  T  H
    T  O      F  O  R  T      W  A  Y  N  E
    5  0  0      M  I  L  E      D  A  S  H
    B  O  R  E  D
       M  E  M  O  R  I  E  S      E  X  T  E  N  D
    T  H  E  N      E  R  O  D  E
    I      K  N  O  C  K      O  N      H  E  R
    D  O  O  R      A  N  D      P  A  U  S  E
                   W  I  L  L      I  T
                   G  O      U  N  H  E  A  R  D

       W  I  L  L      T  H  I  S      B  E
```

KEITH SMITH, *BACK AND FORTH,* BOOK NUMBER 108. A BOOK-LENGTH POEM WITH VARIABLE PAGE SIZE. EACH PAGE IS WIDER BY ONE LETTER. FOR EACH TWO PAGE SPREAD, THE TEXT IS COMPOSED OF LETTERS FROM ALL THE PAGE EDGES ON THE RIGHT. THE ON-GOING POEM MUST MAKE USE OF ALL THE LINE ENDINGS FROM ALL THE PAGES. OFFSET IN EDITION OF 200, SELF-PUBLISHED, AND HAND BOUND BY THE ARTIST, 1985. 20.3 X 15.3 X .6 CM.

KEITH SMITH, *BACK AND FORTH*, BOOK NUMBER 108. 1985. INSIDE, THE BACK COVER SHOWS INLAID
PAPERS. THE ISLAND PASTES-DOWN HAS BORDER DRAWN WITH PEN AND INK. GOLD FOIL BINDER'S
STAMP IS AT THE TAIL. FOR ISLAND PASTES-DOWN AND EXPOSED HINGES, SEE PAGE 351.

PREPARATION

The Pamphlet Binding with Boards is a very special format. Being only one signature in size, it can have from 4 to 32 pages. That would be 1, or up to 8 folios compiled. Within this amount of compiled folios, there can be quite a variety of display possibilities. For instance, if the Pamphlet Binding with Boards is four folios com‑piled, it could contain from four to sixteen pages of text, depending upon how many of the folios are used as endsheets:

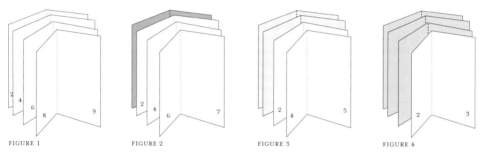

FIGURE 1   FIGURE 2   FIGURE 3   FIGURE 4

PAMPHLET BINDING WITH BOARDS , 4 FOLIOS COMPLIED, 16 PAGES:

1. IF 4 FOLIOS ARE USED, THE BOOK COULD BE 16 PAGES OF TEXT.

2. THERE COULD BE 3 FOLIOS, OR 12 PAGES AS THE TEXT, PLUS 1 FOLIO AS END‑SHEET. THIS WOULD GIVE 2 PAGES OF ENDSHEETS AT THE FRONT AND 2 PAGES OF ENDSHEETS AS THE FINAL PAGES OF THE BOOK.

3. IF 2 FOLIOS, OR 8 PAGES ARE TEXT, THERE WOULD BE 2 FOLIOS OF ENDSHEETS WITH 4 PAGES OF ENDSHEETS AT THE FRONT AND BACK.

4. IF 1 FOLIO, OR 4 PAGES ARE TEXT, THERE WOULD BE 3 FOLIOS OF ENDSHEETS WITH 6 PAGES OF ENDSHEETS AT THE FRONT AND BACK.

ALL FOUR EXAMPLES ARE SEWN AS A SINGLE SIGNATURE, ALONG WITH THE HINGE.

Compiling more than four or five folios may cause the book to gap open to the center folio, where it is sewn. Thinner paper can accom‑modate more folios compiled without gapping open. Thicker paper is more resistant.

3-PLY HINGE

The hinging action of opening and closing the book is made up of three layers pasted together. The book cloth that connects the two boards is one layer and this spine-cloth is on the outside of the boards. See *Making the Case*, page 143.

The other two layers of the hinge are on the inside. They attach the book block to the boards: the cloth hinge and endsheet as paste-down. If a paper island is pasted down instead of the endsheet, the hinge is 2-ply. See *Exposed Hinges & Islands as Pastes-Down*, page 351.

In the following description, the endsheets will be pasted to the inside of the boards, attaching the book block to the boards. With production books, the endsheet is all that attaches the book block to the boards and this is why it often rips away from the covers.

In this binding, we will reinforce the paper hinge with a strip of cloth, folded in half. It is treated as if another compiled folio and sewn as part of the signature It will not be seen as the endsheet will be pasted down over it. This reinforcement can be book cloth, super, or airplane linen. We suggest jaconette, which is available from most binders' supply.

Jaconette is "a thin coated fabric recommended by Bernard Middleton".[13]

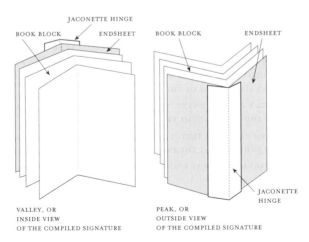

JACONETTE HINGE
BOOK BLOCK   ENDSHEET   BOOK BLOCK   ENDSHEET

JACONETTE HINGE

VALLEY, OR   PEAK, OR
INSIDE VIEW   OUTSIDE VIEW
OF THE COMPILED SIGNATURE   OF THE COMPILED SIGNATURE

TWO VIEWS OF THE SIGNATURE, WITH THE TEXT BLOCK, ENDSHEET AND JACONETTE READY TO PIERCE THE SEWING STATIONS AND SEW AS A SINGLE UNIT. JACONETTE OR AIRPLANE LINEN OR SUPER REINFORCES THE ENDSHEET AS HINGE. IT IS PASTED TO THE BOARDS PRIOR TO PASTING DOWN THE ENDSHEETS.

NO LEATHER HINGE: We do not discuss paring leather. A leather hinge would have to be pared very thin. It does not make a strong hinge and would be reinforced by jaconette pasted down first, slightly smaller in dimensions than the leather hinge which covers it.

EXPOSED BOOK CLOTH HINGE: The inside hinge can be exposed book cloth sewn with the signature in place of jaconette. In addition, the endsheet would *not* be pasted down. The cloth hinge would be seen, with a paper paste-down on the remainder of the inside of the board. See *Exposed Hinges & Islands as Pastes-Down,* page 351. as well as *Case for the Pamphlet Binding, Method 2,* page 343.

DIMENSIONS OF THE JACONETTE

Width of the jaconette is approximately 2" wide to allow 1" to attach to each board.

Height of the jaconette hinge is cut slightly smaller than the height of the signature. This is so that it will not show at the head and the tail on the inside of the boards, but will be covered by the endsheet which is pasted down over it. When piercing jaconette with the signature, center the jaconette on the mountain peak, so that it will not protrude at the head or the tail.

The binding edge of a text prior to sewing is referred to as the *back* or *backbone.* It differs from the *spine,* which includes the sewing, adhesive and spine-covering.

TYPE OF SEWING

The Pamphlet Binding with Boards is a pamphlet sewing. After the book is sewn, the boards are measured and the quarter cloth is applied with paste. The book block is cased-in by pasting or gluing the hinge to the boards. This is described on page 149 for the hinge and 292 for the endsheet.

In pamphlet sewing, you can start either on the peak or in the valley. The side you start on, is where you will end up, at the same sewing station. I suggest for this binding always starting in the valley. In this manner, the knot will not bulge the backbone which would be noticeable on the outside of the book on the quarter cloth covering the spine.

The book block, endsheets and hinge are assembled, in order to pierce the sewing stations through all three at once. For information of grain of paper, folding and sewing stations, see *Part 1, Preliminaries.*

Fred Jordan, full leather Pamphlet Binding with Boards. The booklet is *The Edward and Catherine O'Donnell Collection of Modern Literature*, an exhibition at the University of Rochester, Fall 1979. 23 x 14.5 x 1 cm.

DETAIL: On the right is the inside of the back cover. Marbled paper has been pasted to the final page of the booklet, and over onto the board as the paste-down.

At the tail on the spine-edge of the board is *F. Jordan* in a blind stamping.

SEWING STATIONS

Minimum number of sewing stations is three. If the book is taller than 12", there should be four or five stations pierced. Each requires a different sewing pattern. The first to be described is the *3-Hole Pamphlet Sewing*, on page 134.

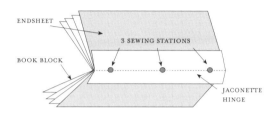

ENDSHEET

3 SEWING STATIONS

BOOK BLOCK

JACONETTE HINGE

PRE-PIERCING THE SEWING STATIONS. USE EITHER 3, 4 OR 5 STATIONS. EACH REQUIRES A DIFFERENT SEWING PATH.

SEWING PATH

The following pages describe the 3-Hole, 4-Hole and 5-Hole Pamphlet Sewings. Keeping in mind the path of the sewing helps to understand pamphlet sewing. The path of the 3-Hole Pamphlet Sewing creates the letter *"B"*. This is referred to as a *B stitch*. All pamphlet sewings utilize the *B stitch*, although the path does not literally form the letter *B,* as with the 3-Hole, but a variation of the letter:

- Since you are starting on the inside, the needle exits the middle station forming one of the curved shapes of the capital letter *B.*

- The needle enters to the inside, at either the head or the tail. Skip the middle station and exit the station at the other end of the fold. This forms the long stitch, which is the straight, vertical of the letter *B.* (If you were to exit the middle station, the sewing path would form the shape of the number *8.* This is wrong. This is not a *figure 8* sewing.)

- Exit and enter to the middle of the signature at the middle station. This forms the second curved shape of the letter *B.* Tie-off.

3-HOLE PAMPHLET SEWING

PREPARATION

POSITION OF SEWING STATIONS: Three sewing stations are to be pierced along the fold. Position of the holes is important. The two end stations should be close enough to the head and tail for the sewing to provide support. But they should not be positioned any closer to the edge than 3/8", or the sewing will weaken the paper between the hole and the edge. It could rip.

The middle station should be centered from head to tail, on the fold. Station 1 is at the tail. Pierce the three stations with a bradawl or bodkin. The hinge and signature are pierced at the same time.

THREAD: Cut a length of unbleached linen thread, 2 1/2 times the height of your book block. Wax the thread. Thread the needle.

SEWING PROCEDURE

1. Start at sewing station 2, on the inside. Take the needle from the valley, through the signature and the hinge to the outside, leaving about 4" of loose thread hanging on the inside.

2. Proceed on the outside to station 3. Take the needle through the hinge cloth and signature, pulling the stitch taut. Do not pull so hard that the thread is pulled out of the middle station, but hard enough to reduce the length of loose thread dangling on the inside until it is 1 1/2". This will be enough to tie a square knot when the sewing is completed. If you had tried to leave only the desired shorter amount of loose thread as you exited the initial station, it might have accidentally slipped through the hole. However, once you have passed through two of the sewing stations, the thread is less apt to accidentally fall out of the station and can be pulled to a desired length.

3. Proceed along the inside fold, to station 1. Insert the point of the needle through the signature. Lift the hinge to position the point of the needle onto the sewing station of the hinge. Pull the needle and thread through to the outside of the signature and hinge.

Carefully pull the sewing taut without reducing the 1 1/2" length of loose thread at the center sewing station. You are now on the outside of the signature.

4. Proceed on the outside to the center station. Take the needle through station 2 to the inside, back to where you started.

Examine the sewing before you tie the knot. On the inside, there is one long stitch, extending from station 1 to station 3. Flipping the book over, the other side has two stitches, each half the size of the single longer stitch.

Look at the longer stitch. At the center station is the 1½" loose thread, as well as the opposite end of the thread where the needle is threaded. One thread should be on one side of the long stitch, the other thread on the other side, so they they straddle the stitch. If they are on the same side, place the needle under the stitch and pull that thread to the other side, so that the two ends of the thread straddle the stitch.

5. Tie a square knot. The long stitch will be tied down at its center point. See *Square Knot*, page 109.

In the future, when you take the needle through the final sewing station of the pamphlet sewing, make sure the needle comes through the hole on the opposite side of the loose thread, to straddle the stitch. It will then be ready to tie the knot and clip the loose ends. Notice the sewing path creates the *B* stitch.

The book block is completed and ready to case-in. Wrap a sleeve of wax paper around the book block and tape it shut. See page 139. Pull the hinges to the outside of the wax paper sleeve. The covers will be made next. Proceed to *Boards for the Pamphlet Binding*, page 140.

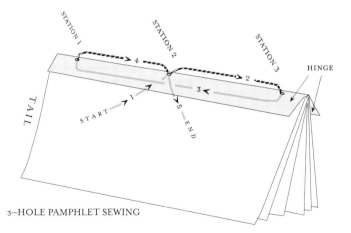

3–HOLE PAMPHLET SEWING

4-HOLE PAMPHLET SEWING

Booklets larger than 12" in height, but less than 16", should be sewn with 4 sewing stations.

PREPARATION

SEWING STATIONS: Prepare the signature and hinge. Mark the first and fourth sewing stations on the hinge at the head and the tail. These should be no closer to the edge than ⅜", no farther from the edge than 1".

Measure the distance between these two extreme sewing stations and divide it by three. This will be the distance between each of the four sewing stations, so that they are spaced equidistantly across the spine. Mark the remaining two sewing stations and pierce the four stations.

THREAD: Wax a length of the thread which is 2½ times the height of the spine. Start at sewing station 2, on the inside the signature.

SEWING PROCEDURE

Start on the inside of the signature. Take the needle through the signature and the hinge at the second sewing station to the outside.

1. Pull all but 4" of the thread through the hole.

2. Proceed on the outside, along the spine to station 3. Take the needle through the hinge and signature, pulling the stitch taut.

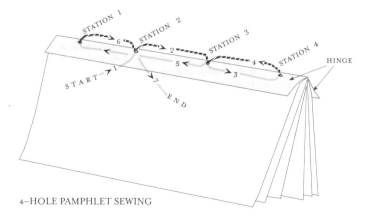

4–HOLE PAMPHLET SEWING

Do not pull so hard that the thread is pulled out of the station 2 but enough to reduce the length of loose thread dangling inside the signature until it is only 1l/2" in length.

3. Proceed on the inside to sewing station 4. Take the needle through the signature and the hinge at station 4, to the outside. Since you have reached the other extreme of the spine, you will proceed back in the other direction.

4. Proceed on the outside of the signature to sewing station 3. Take the needle through the hinge and signature to the inside.

5. Proceed on the inside of the signature to station 1. Take the needle through to the outside.

6. Proceed on the outside to station 2 and take the needle through to the inside. You are now back where you started. Make sure the two ends of the thread straddle the long stitch which crosses over the initial sewing station. Tie a square knot, described on page 109.

The book block is completed and ready to case-in. Wrap a sleeve of wax paper around the book block and tape it shut. See page 139. Pull the hinges to the outside of the wax paper sleeve. The covers will be made next. Proceed to *Boards for the Pamphlet Binding,* page 140.

GARY FROST, *THREE BOOKBINDINGS,* SEWN BOARDS BINDING, 1993.[1] 21.5 CM. X 14 CM. X 9 MM.

ALTHOUGH THIS IS *NOT* A PAMPHLET BINDING, IT DOES ILLUSTRATE THE ELEGANCE OF BOARDS FLUSH WITH THE BOOK BLOCK AND AN ECONOMY IN LABELING: A SINGLE LABEL FOR THE SPINE EXTENDS ONTO THE FRONT COVER.

5-HOLE PAMPHLET SEWING

Books taller than 16" should be sewn with 5 sewing stations.

PREPARATION

SEWING STATIONS: Prepare the signature and the hinge. Mark the two end positions first, stations 1 and 5. They should be no closer to the edge than 3/8" and no farther from the edge than 1". Mark station 3, which is in the center of the spine.

Mark station 2 which is centered between stations 1 and 3. Mark station 4, which is centered between stations 3 and 5. Pierce the five stations.

THREAD: Length of the thread is 2 1/2 times the height of the spine. Wax the length of unbleached linen thread. Thread the needle.

SEWING PROCEDURE

The illustration will start on the inside of the signature.

1. Take the needle through the signature and the hinge at station 3. Pull all but 4" of the thread through the hole.

2. Proceed on the outside to station 4. Take the needle through the hinge and the signature, pulling the stitch taut. Pull to reduce the length of loose thread dangling inside the signature to 1 1/2".

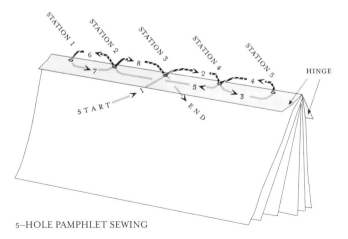

5–HOLE PAMPHLET SEWING

3. Proceed on inside to station 5. Take the needle through the signature and the hinge to the outside.

4. Proceed on the outside back to sewing station 4. Take the needle through the hinge and signature to the inside.

5. Proceed on the inside to station 2, by-passing sewing station 3. Take the needle through the signature and the hinge.

6. Proceed on the outside to station 1. Take the needle through to the inside. Since you have reached the other extreme of the spine, you will proceed back in the other direction.

7. Proceed on the inside to station 2. Take the needle through the signature and the hinge to the outside.

8. Proceed on the outside to station 3. Take the needle through the hinge and signature to the inside. Make sure the two ends of the thread straddle the long stitch which crosses over the initial sewing station. Tie-off with a square knot, which is described on page 109.

SLEEVE OF WAX PAPER: Wrap the book block in an envelope of wax paper, slightly wider than the book block and 2½ times the height. This is a moisture barrier for casing-in and will keep it from getting soiled. Make sure the hinge is on the outside of the wax paper. Start the wrapping on the front of the book block. Tape the wax paper shut. The masking tape will be on the front. Lightly mark an arrow pointing up on the masking tape. This is so when you case-in, you will not attach the book block upside down.

SLEEVE OF
WAX PAPER
TO PROTECT
BOOK BLOCK

JACONETTE
HINGE IS
ON THE
OUTSIDE OF
THE SLEEVE

MASKING TAPE

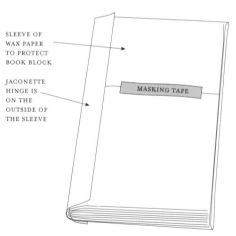

BOARDS FOR THE PAMPHLET BINDING

After you have sewn the book block of a single signature with either a 3-, 4-, or 5-Hole Pamphlet Sewing, you are ready to prepare the boards. There are two boards in this binding, the front and back cover. The spine is book cloth reinforced by pasting a strip of paper on the inside, in the gap between the boards. This is described on page 147.

BOARD PROPORTION: Thickness of the boards should be proportional to the height and width of the book. The spine of single signature Pamphlet Binding with Boards is not very thick. If it is 6" x 9" or smaller, the book will look better with rather thin boards. I use 2-ply museum mat board; Fred uses 4-ply. Any thicker board will make your book look stubby unless you desire a heavy proportion. Likewise, sew with a thinner thread for a smaller book. All materials, size of type, borders, should be kept to scale.

If your book is approximately 8" in height, we suggest using 4-ply museum mat board. Any larger size book, use binder's board.

BOARD OVERHANG: Boards usually overhang the book block on three sides, the head, tail and foredge. This is to protect the book block. Traditionally, the board overhangs a distance that is 1½ times the thickness of the board you are using. This is referred to as the *square of the book.*

On this particular binding, Fred prefers an overhang that is 2 to 3 times the thickness of the board.

DIMENSIONS OF BOARDS: The board starts exactly at the spine-edge of the book block. (This is not true for the Flat Back, Tight Back or Hollow Back.)

Width of the board is the width of the book block plus the foredge overhang. Generally, add 1½ thickness of the board or more for the amount of overhang on the foredge.

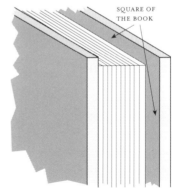

SQUARE OF THE BOOK

THE SQUARE OF THE BOOK IS USU-ALLY 1½ TIMES THE THICKNESS OF THE BOARD. SOMETIMES THERE IS NO OVER-HANG. SEE ILLUSTRATION ON PAGE 137.

Height of the board is the height of the book block plus 3 thicknesses of the book board. Centered, this gives 1½ thickness of board as the overhang at the head and the tail.

CUTTING AND SANDING THE BOARDS: If you do not have access to a board shear, mark the dimensions with a pencil, making sure the grain is parallel with the spine. On a cutting surface, cut the board with a mat knife, using a metal straight edge. Lightly sand the boards with fine sand paper. Thin boards cannot be sanded very much.

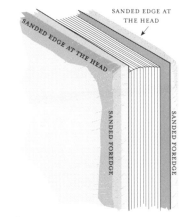

SANDED EDGE AT THE HEAD

SANDED EDGE AT THE HEAD

SANDED FOREDGE

SANDED FOREDGE

The head, tail and foredge will look and feel better if it tapers slightly, rather than leaving the board a block. Place medium sandpaper around a sanding block. Sand the edges to a bevel, but not so thin as to weaken the edge.

SANDING THE EDGES IS JUST ENOUGH TO REMOVE THE SHARP CORNERS.

BOOK CLOTH: Use a fairly thin book cloth. There are some as thick as kitchen table cloths. That is too bulky to cover well. In addition, the hinge must be paper thin, as it will be attached to the depth of the board. A good binders supply will have a variety of brands, thickness, as well as colors and textures.

TWO METHODS FOR MAKING THE CASE

When the cloth on the spine is attached to the outside of the two cover boards, this is referred to as the *case*.

Fred and I have quite different approaches to applying the pasted quarter cloth to the boards. His is more simplified with no marking the position of the cloth on the boards. However, it requires cutting the cloth after it is wet and on the boards, which I find more difficult. In his approach, the first endsheet is pasted down over the cloth hinge. This will be described first, as *Making the Case*, page 143.

My approach is more frugal use of cloth, but requires aligning the cloth on the board. This will be described as *Making the Case, Method 2*. See page 343. The endsheet is not pasted over the cloth hinge, which is left exposed as a design element.

Use the approach that best suits your style of working.

Sample 3-Hole Pamphlet Sewing has been cased-in. The two boards are connected with quarter cloth across the spine, which is referred to as the *case*. Later, two marbled papers were inlaid onto the outside of the boards. See *Inlaid Papers*, page 359. 18.3 x 11.6 x .5 cm.

13

MAKING THE CASE

1. Place a scrap piece of card temporarily on each side of the book block. Place the boards on the outside of the card. The card is to increase the space between the closed boards and the book block. This will allow plenty of room for the thickness of the papers which will be pasted down on the inside. Jog on the tail and spine-edge, so that the boards, card and book block are flush on these two edges.

2. Cut a piece of book cloth to be used on the spine.

Height should be 1½" taller than the boards. Center top to bottom, giving a ¾" turn-in at the head and tail.

Width should be approximately 2 to 3" *wider* than the distance you want the cloth to extend onto each board, plus the thickness of the book block, card and boards assembled in Step 1. It will be trimmed to exact width in Step 5.

Remember, the final width must extend at least ½" onto the spine-edge of the covers to securely attach the boards. It will bear tension, as it acts as a hinge in conjunction with the inside hinge. See *Proportion of the Board,* page 43.

3. Wheat paste the quarter cloth. With one hand, pick up the book block, card and boards, careful not to allow them to slip from alignment, after being jogged. With the other hand, center the pasted cloth head to tail, side to side across the spine, onto the boards. Lightly stroke the cloth from the spine-edge towards the foredge of the boards to adhere the cloth to the boards.

4. Lay the book on the table, with the back cover down.

Carefully open the front board and lay it on the table, keeping the spine cloth flat.

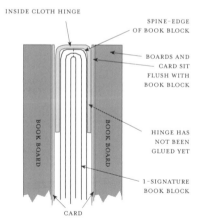

STEP 1:
DETAIL OF CROSS-SECTION
ASSEMBLE THE BOOK BLOCK AND
BOARDS, WITH CARD TEMPORARILY
BETWEEN TO INCREASE THE GAP.
THE GAP BETWEEN THE BOARDS DOES
NOT HAVE TO BE MEASURED.

Remove the book block and throw away the two pieces of card.

5. Make the turn-in at the head. Press the cloth against the depth of the front board with a table knife or a thin bone folder. Keep that bone folder in place, while using a second bone folder to press the cloth against the depth of the remaining board. Using one bone folder, only, the cloth will come off the edge of the first board, while you are pressing against the edge of the next.

Make the turn-in at the tail in the same manner.

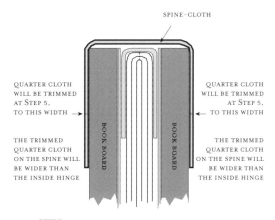

SPINE-CLOTH

QUARTER CLOTH WILL BE TRIMMED AT STEP 5, TO THIS WIDTH →

QUARTER CLOTH WILL BE TRIMMED AT STEP 5, ← TO THIS WIDTH

THE TRIMMED QUARTER CLOTH ON THE SPINE WILL BE WIDER THAN THE INSIDE HINGE

BOOK BOARD

BOOK BOARD

THE TRIMMED QUARTER CLOTH ON THE SPINE WILL BE WIDER THAN THE INSIDE HINGE

STEP 3:

CENTER THE PASTED QUARTER CLOTH OVER THE SPINE AND ATTACH TO THE BOARDS.

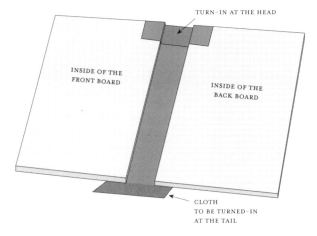

TURN-IN AT THE HEAD

INSIDE OF THE FRONT BOARD

INSIDE OF THE BACK BOARD

CLOTH TO BE TURNED-IN AT THE TAIL

STEP 5:

TURNING-IN THE CLOTH AT THE HEAD AND TAIL. USE TWO BONE FOLDERS. HOLD ONE AGAINST THE EDGE OF ONE BOARD, WHILE THE OTHER CREASES THE CLOTH AGAINST THE EDGE OF THE OTHER. THE PROCEDURE IS REFERRED TO AS *WALKING THE BONE FOLDERS*. SEE PAGE 156.

TRIMMING THE OUTSIDE WIDTH OF CLOTH: Turn the boards over, so the quarter cloth on the spine is facing you. Width of the cloth on the boards will now be trimmed. If you are going to overlap the cloth with the paper, leave the width a little wider than will show once the paper overlaps. See *Overlapping vs Butting the Paper to the Spine-Covering,* page 356.

Lay a straight edge on the good part of the book cloth on the back cover. Line it up with where you wish to trim off the excess. If the knife veers, it will cut into the area of cloth to be trimmed off rather than into the good part of the cloth. With a thin bladed sharp knife, trim the excess width of cloth from each board. After you make the cut on the outside of the board, you must cut the cloth on the edge of the board, then on the inside of the board. Peel away the excess cloth. Proceed to Step 6.

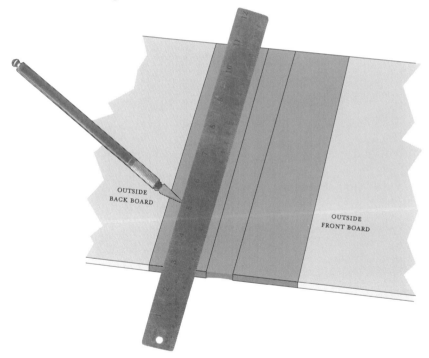

OUTSIDE
BACK BOARD

OUTSIDE
FRONT BOARD

STEP 5: After making the turn-in at the head and tail, turn the board over. With a straight edge and knife, trim off the excess width on each board. Continue the cut down the edge of the board. Turn the board over and trim off the excess width of the turns-in. Peel away excess cloth.

Alternate Step 5. Trimming the width of the cloth on the spine can be done another way, although it is rather awkward. A variation would be to apply the pasted cloth to the boards, but do not make the turns-in.

Carefully turn the two boards over, with the outside of the boards facing up. Be careful that the boards do not slip from their attached position from the cloth. Lift the overhang of cloth at the head. Slide a scrap of book board in from the head to butt against the two boards. Do the same at the tail. Trim the excess cloth from the two boards. Turn the boards over. Apply more paste on the turns-in at the head and the tail. Make your turns-in at the head and the tail.

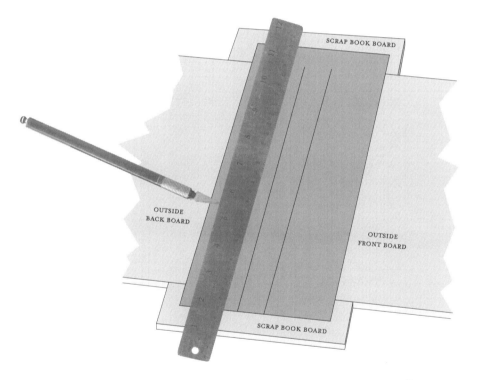

Alternate STEP 5: Do not make the turns-in at the head and tail. Turn the board over. Lay scrap board under the excess cloth at the head, butted to the two covers. Do the same at the tail. With a straight edge and knife, trim off the excess width along the entire cloth on each board. Turn the boards over. Paste the turns-in again. Make the turns-in at the head and tail. Peel away excess cloth.

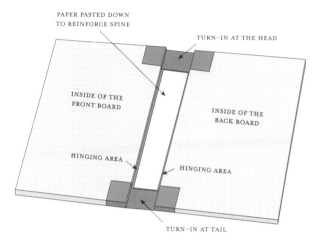

PAPER PASTED DOWN
TO REINFORCE SPINE

TURN-IN AT THE HEAD

INSIDE OF THE
FRONT BOARD

INSIDE OF THE
BACK BOARD

HINGING AREA

HINGING AREA

TURN-IN AT TAIL

STEP 6: REINFORCE THE SPINE BY PASTING PAPER INSIDE.

HEIGHT OF THE PAPER SHOULD BUTT UP TO THE TURNS-IN.

WIDTH IS SLIGHTLY LESS THAN THE GAP BETWEEN THE BOARDS. THIS PERMITS THE CLOTH ALONE TO ACT AS THE HINGE.

6. Place the boards on the table with the inside of the boards facing up. Reinforce the spine by pasting on a piece of stiff paper:

Height of the paper must be cut precisely, so that it does not overlap the turns-in at the head and the tail. Otherwise it will cause a bulge on the outside of the spine-cloth.

Width of the paper does not extend to the boards, but is fairly close. This will leave a thin vertical column of cloth only between the boards and the paper, permitting easy hinging action.

The 1-signature book block with jaconette hinge has been sewn. The *case* (the two connected side-covers) is now completed. You are ready to case-in.

14

ATTACHING THE BOOK BLOCK TO THE CASE

Attaching the book block to the boards is referred to as *casing-in.* This is done in two steps:
· pasting the jaconette hinge onto the inside of the boards and then
· pasting down the endsheets over the jaconette.

The jaconette will reinforce the endsheet-as-hinge. However, when the endsheet is pasted down over the jaconette, there will be a bulge showing through, revealing the shape of the jaconette. If you wish to avoid this, you can cut out the shape of the jaconette hinge on the book board to the depth of the jaconette. Simply incise the shape and peel off a layer. Check to see if another layer needs to be peeled so the hinge will be flush with the board. This will inlay the hinge flush with the inside of the board. When the endsheet is pasted down, you will not see any bulge from the jaconette.

If you are going to have an exposed book cloth hinge, do not inlay the hinge in the board, as the hinge must be trimmed.

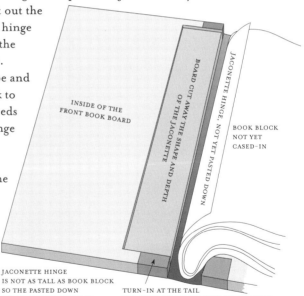

INSIDE OF THE FRONT BOOK BOARD

BOARD CUT AWAY THE SHAPE AND DEPTH OF THE JACONETTE

JACONETTE HINGE, NOT YET PASTED DOWN

BOOK BLOCK NOT YET CASED-IN

JACONETTE HINGE IS NOT AS TALL AS BOOK BLOCK SO THE PASTED DOWN ENDSHEET WILL COVER IT.

TURN-IN AT THE TAIL PARTIALLY CUT AWAY TO INLAY THE HINGE

CUTTING AWAY A LAYER OF THE BOOK BOARD IN THE SHAPE OF THE JACONETTE ALLOWS IT TO BE INLAID FLUSH WITH THE BOARD.

JACONETTE HINGE

When the pasted quarter cloth on the boards is dry, place the boards on a clean surface, with the inside of the boards facing up.

CHOOSING PASTE OR GLUE: The jaconette hinge is wheat pasted, or you can use PVA glue. If you use wheat paste, the jaconette may curl causing problems in applying. Let it sit for a few moments and it will flatten. The advantage is you can work with it longer and move it around on the board. The advantage of PVA is it sets up quickly, but you cannot move it around after a minute or so.

Measure the height of the hinge and the amount the hinge extends from the fold towards the foredge. Cut 2 pieces of wax paper slightly larger than these measurements.

Set one piece of wax paper between the front hinge and the wax paper sleeve around the book block. Make sure scrap wax paper slides in all the way to the fold, in order to keep paste or glue from touching the wax paper sleeve. Set the second piece of wax paper under the back hinge.

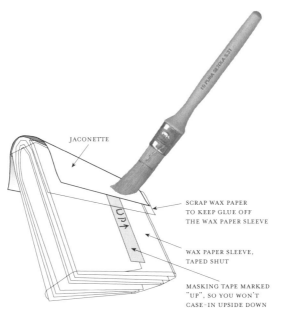

JACONETTE

SCRAP WAX PAPER
TO KEEP GLUE OFF
THE WAX PAPER SLEEVE

WAX PAPER SLEEVE,
TAPED SHUT

MASKING TAPE MARKED
"UP", SO YOU WON'T
CASE-IN UPSIDE DOWN

HAND-HOLD THE BOOK BLOCK. PLACE SCRAP WAX PAPER UNDER THE HINGE TO CATCH EXCESS GLUE. BRUSH HINGE WITH PASTE OR PVA GLUE. REMOVE SCRAP WAX PAPER. DO THE SAME ON THE OTHER SIDE OF THE HINGE.

GLUING THE JACONETTE HINGE: Choose a proper size glue brush which will allow you to glue the hinges in a quick manner. Using too small a brush will take so long that the hinge will start to curl in on itself. This will let the PVA touch the other surface of the hinge.

Hold the book block in one hand and glue the hinge with the other. Do not let the scraps of wax paper behind the hinges fall out. Quickly glue the front hinge. Remove the scrap wax paper and discard. Turn the book block around so that you can glue the back hinge, including the fold and the thread on the back. This must be done while holding the book block in the air to keep the wet hinge off any surface. Discard the scrap wax paper after gluing.

ATTACHING THE JACONETTE TO THE BOARDS:
Two methods will be described. Fred's method is on page 154.

I place the case open with the inside of the boards up. Set the book block onto the inside of the quarter cloth, centered up and down and left to right. Hold the book block upright with one hand.

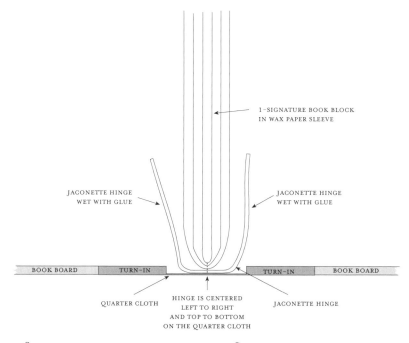

1-SIGNATURE BOOK BLOCK
IN WAX PAPER SLEEVE

JACONETTE HINGE
WET WITH GLUE

JACONETTE HINGE
WET WITH GLUE

BOOK BOARD   TURN-IN   TURN-IN   BOOK BOARD

QUARTER CLOTH

HINGE IS CENTERED
LEFT TO RIGHT
AND TOP TO BOTTOM
ON THE QUARTER CLOTH

JACONETTE HINGE

SET THE BOOK BLOCK ONTO THE SPINE-CLOTH. CENTER IT FROM LEFT TO RIGHT AND FROM TOP TO BOTTOM. MAKE SURE THE BOOK BLOCK IS PARALLEL TO THE BOARDS. IF YOU ARE USING PVA, YOU CANNOT DALLY.

1. With your hand which is not holding the book block, use the point of a table knife or a sharp bone folder, press the hinge against the quarter cloth on both sides of the book block. This is the gap between the boards.

2. Run the point of the bone folder against the edge of the back board to securely glue the hinge to the edge of the board.

3. Holding the book block upright, use the palm of your other hand to lightly brush the hinge against the surface of the back board. Brush from the book block towards the foredge of the board. Use light strokes, or you will pull the hinge away from the edge of the board. Once the hinge is on the board, then you can apply pressure straight down, but do not pull towards the foredge.

4. Set a light object on the back board to prop the book block, to free both hands. Prop must not be too near the spine-edge, or the book block will fall to the front board.

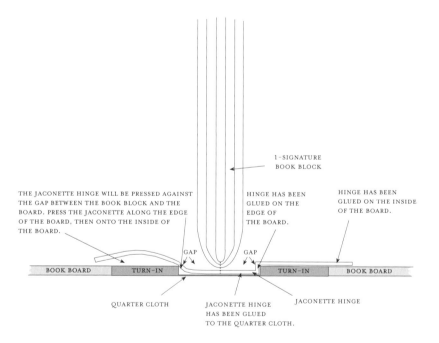

STEPS 2–3: CROSS-SECTION, SHOWING THE START OF IN CASING-IN. THE
HINGE IS PRESSED AGAINST THE EDGE OF THE BACK BOARD WITH A BONE FOLDER,
THEN ONTO THE SURFACE OF THE BACK BOARD, FORMING SHARP, RIGHT ANGLES.

Allow the book block to lean against the prop on the back board in a nearly vertical position.

5. With a bone folder in each hand, use one to hold against the edge of the back board from the head to the tail while simultaneously pressing the hinge against the edge of the front board with the second bone folder. It is easier if you use several short strokes. Both bone folders must be level, perpendicular to the spine. This will apply pressure at the same point along the edge of the front and back boards. This is similar to *Walking the Bone Folder,* page 156.

If you used only one bone folder, pressing against the edge of the front board, the tension would pull the hinge away from the edge of the back board.

6. Lightly brush the second hinge against the surface of the front board. Apply pressure straight down, but do not pull towards the foredge. Place a prop on the front board as well, adjusting both props so that the book block is vertical.

If you use PVA glue, allow 30 minutes before removing the props and closing the covers. It will dry in 5 to 10 minutes, but it is better to wait and be safe. If you use wheat paste, allow the hinges to dry overnight before closing the book.

7. Remove the props. Close the boards.

When the glue is dry the book can be closed. When the boards are in the closed position, the jaconette hinge on the edge of the board will rest against the area of the jaconette that is pasted to the quarter cloth. See illustration on the right.

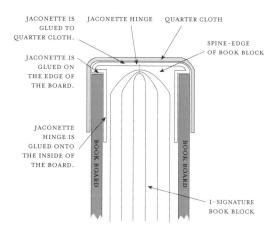

CROSS-SECTION SHOWING THE BOOK CLOSED AFTER CASING-IN.

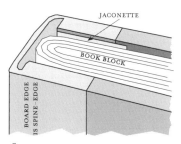

SPINE-EDGES OF THE BOARDS SIT FLUSH WITH THE BACKBONE.

When the book is opened, this area is the gap between the board and the book block. See illustration below. This is why the gap must be wide enough to accommodate the thickness of the board, plus the inside paste-down, when the book is shut. Otherwise, your cover will not fully close with the boards parallel.

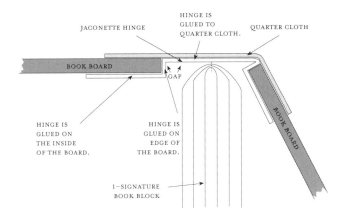

CROSS-SECTION SHOWING THE BOOK PARTIALLY OPEN, AFTER CASING-IN.

ALTERNATE METHOD OF ATTACHING THE BOARDS: The reason I use the first method is I can carefully center the book block onto the spine. Also, I can inlay the hinge into the board, if I have cut and peeled an indentation described on page 149. If you are not indenting the hinge, you can follow Fred's method:

1. Lay the book block on the table. Slide in a scrap of wax paper under the hinge. Paste the hinge with strokes away from the spine towards the foredge.

2. Turn book block over, with the wet hinge dangling over the edge of the table. Remove the scrap wax paper. Insert a new scrap of wax paper under the hinge to be pasted. Paste.

3. Slide book block into partially closed case, centering it top to bottom. Close and press along the quarter cloth front and back with fingers and thumb to adhere the hinges. Open one board and bone the hinge on the edge of the board. Insert a scrap of wax paper between hinge and sleeved book block. Close. Open the other board and do the same. Insert a scrap of wax paper. Dry with the book closed.

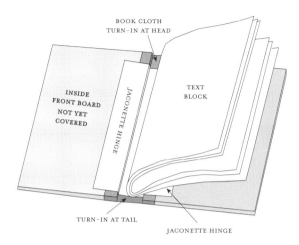

BOOK CLOTH
TURN-IN AT HEAD

INSIDE
FRONT BOARD
NOT YET
COVERED

JACONETTE HINGE

TEXT
BLOCK

TURN-IN AT TAIL

JACONETTE HINGE

WITH EITHER METHOD, THE BOOK BLOCK IS ATTACHED TO THE BOARDS WITH THE JACONETTE HINGE. NEXT THE OUTSIDE OF THE BOARDS ARE COVERED BEFORE PASTING DOWN THE ENDSHEETS.

I find when the book is opened, this method has the hinge going directly from the book block onto the board. The hinge is not glued to the edge of the board. I prefer the apperance of the hinges up the edge and onto the board. It also holds the book block tight against the spine-cloth.

COVERING BOTH SIDES OF THE BOARDS: Paper is pasted to the outside of the boards and turned-in. This is described in Chapter 24, *Covering*, page 279. The inside of the board is then covered. Usually this is by pasting down the endsheets which cover the jaconette hinge, as well as the inside of the board. See page 292.

If you use an exposed book cloth hinge, an island of paper is pasted to the inside of the board. This variation is described on page 351.

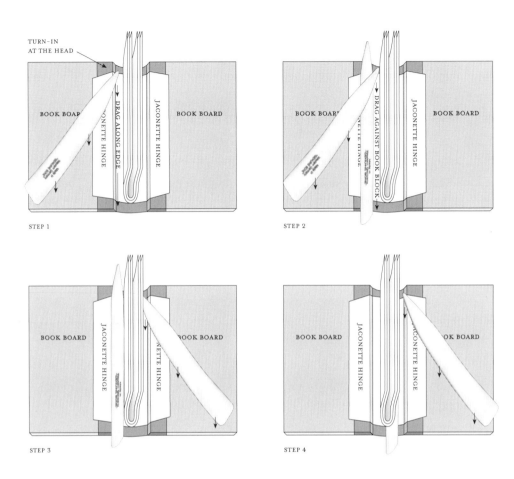

Walking the Bone Folders requires two bone folders:

1. Press with the tip of the bone folder along the edge of the left board.

2. Lay that bone folder down against the edge of that board to hold the pasted hinge tight against the board. Use the tip of your second bone folder to press the hinge flat against the quarter cloth, along the edge of the book block, while holding the first bone folder in place.

3. Move the first bone folder over against the left edge of the book block to hold the hinge in place. Use the tip of the second bone folder to press the hinge down along the right side of the book block, while holding the first bone folder tightly in place.

4. Move the first bone folder over against the right side of the book block to hold the hinge in place. Take the second bone folder and crease the hinge tight against the edge of the right board, while holding the first bone folder tightly in place.

Holding the previous crease in place insures the next does not pull the hinge away from your previously creased edge.

FLAT BACK
CASED-IN CODEX

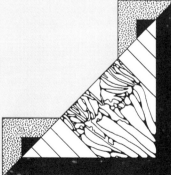

INTRODUCTION

The Flat Back is a long time favorite of mine. When I started making one-of-a-kind books in the 1960's, I did not know how to bind. I spent several hundred hours on *A Change in Dimension, Book Number 2.* Then I took the sheets to AA Bindery on South Dearborn in Chicago. The gracious owner said she could bind it and that I should bring her the fabric I wanted for the cover.

When I picked up the completed binding, I asked her how much the binding would cost me. She asked if I were a student. I said, "Yes." She said there was no charge. She said that if I made another book, to fold the paper in half. It would be easier for her to sew.

As I completed each of the following ones-of-a-kind, I would take it to her. Each time she would not charge me to bind them. I was very poor and I am indebted to her.

For the first five years of making my books, I did not know how to bind. Gary Frost invited me to Newberry Library. There, he took me through the steps of making a cased-in codex, which is described here. For the next ten years, each book I made I bound as a Flat Back—the only binding I knew.

In 1982, embarrassed by the nice bindings my students were doing in a class on the structure of the visual book, I decided it was time I learned to bind.

Book Arts is such a large field. Many are drawn to it through calligraphy, printmaking, binding, graphic design. I was drawn to books as a format that allowed me to say more than I could in a single picture. Structure and movement were my concerns. It took me many years to build up my ideas of structure. Only then, 15 years after I started, could I turn my attention to binding. I started taking classes with Fred Jordan.

Although I have learned dozens of bindings and devised close to 150, the Flat Back is an old friend. It is a work horse and I recommend it to you highly.

For exposed cloth hinges, the good side of the cloth faces the book block. The side of the material to be pasted down faces out, as seen below. This book is shown cased-in on the following page. Cover for the book below appears on page 337. Its paste-down is on page 340.

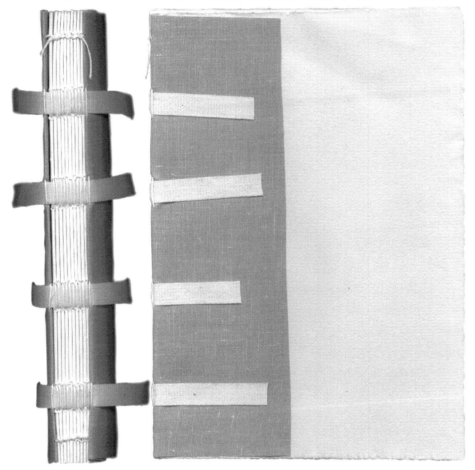

The Pamphlet Binding with Boards has a single hinge across the backbone. The Flat Back, above, has *two* separate inside hinges, one attached to the first signature, the other to the final signature, prior to sewing.

The signatures are sewn onto tapes. Tapes, as well as the hinges will be glued to the case. Generally the hinge material is jaconette and is hidden when the endsheet is pasted down to the inside of the board.

The hinges of the above book are book cloth and will be exposed. See pages 192 and 351. They are made wider than needed and will be trimmed to the width of the outside cloth after casing-in. See page 160. The endsheet will not be pasted over them. Instead, an island of paper will be pasted down on the inside of the board. See page 340, 352 and 355.

Compare this book-in-
progress with the earlier
stage on the previous page,
as well as finished, on
pages 337 and 340.

This Flat Back will have exposed book cloth hinges, with quarter cloth on
the spine. After it was cased-in, a straight edge was placed on the inside of
the board. The hinge was trimmed at the point of the cloth on the outside
of the board and the excess was peeled off. See page 194. Next is *Covering
the Outside of the Boards*, page 279. Since the endsheet is not pasted down,
an island paste-down will butt against the inside hinge. See page 351.

PREPARATION

RATING THE VARIOUS HINGES

The Flat Back Cased-In Codex will be described by sewing onto tapes. Tapes are the supports for the sewing. In addition, they are the means of attaching the book block to the boards in conjunction with a jaconette or an exposed book cloth hinge. The tapes give the attachment *tensile* strength;the hinge, glued completely along the spine-edge of the board, gives *lateral* strength.

• *SUPPORTS:* Tapes and cords make a poor hinge in and of themselves. Tapes or cords are superb as supports and excellent as the means to attach the sewn book block to the boards by lacing-in. They are a good means of attaching the book block to the boards even when the supports are merely glued to the boards.

Tapes or cords give tensile strength in the attachment. However, cords and tapes do not give lateral strength. The boards can shift from top to bottom.

• *PAPER:* Paper is a poor hinge. Often, the tapes are pasted to the first page and the page is pasted to the board. But this is relies upon a sheet of paper for the lateral strength for hinging action. Paper is a weak material and a poor choice as hinge. Even if the paper has been reinforced by super (gauze), the paper will eventually tear, revealing the super. This binding will be described with an exposed, book cloth hinge. An ideal hinge is described on page 162.

• *PAPER ALONE:* The worst possible hinge is to rely solely upon gluing the first page to the front board and the last page to the back board. Commercially, this is done often. The book block can rip loose and fall out of the covers.

• *PAPER WITH SUPER:* A better way is to glue super across the spine, between the tapes. The super is the height of the spine and 3" wider. It is glued centered on the spine.

Later, the amount that hangs over is glued to the boards as a hinge. I
will not elaborate this method, as there is a superior way of hinging
the book block to the boards, which is described next.

· *THE IDEAL HINGE:* The best hinge is a jaconette hinge covered by
the endsheet paste-down or an exposed book cloth hinge with an
island paste-down butted to it.

The jaconette hinge would be sewn the same as the book cloth hinge illustrated on page 159. With the jaconette hinge, the outside of the
board is covered and dried under weight. When dry, the jaconette
hinge is pasted and the endsheet is also pasted at the same time with a
sheet of wax paper under it. The sheet of wax paper would be replaced
with a clean one. The same pasting would be done on the other hinge
and endsheet. The book would be placed in the press. Pasting down
the hinge with the endsheet is a variation of pasting down the endsheet described on page 294.

Casing-In has the advantage that you can dry the boards closed. It is
fast. However, pasting the endsheet can cause it to stretch. You must
check to see. This can be an awkward process, unlike the exposed
hinge and island paste-down.

The exposed book cloth hinge can be pasted or glued. I glue it. This is done
before the boards are covered. Once it is dry, both sides of the
boards are covered at once. An island paste-down is butted to
exposed hinge. See *Exposed Hinges & Islands Pastes-Down,* page 351.

The jaconette and exposed book cloth hinge both provide lateral
strength all along the length of the spine. This creates a sturdy hinging action. However, this hinge must be combined with the tensile
strength of the supports. The tapes are glued to the boards in addition to the cloth hinge. Together, the supports for tensile strength
and the cloth hinge for lateral strength create an ideal structure. I
will described the exposed book cloth hinge in this sewing. If you
prefer to use the endsheet as paste-down, substitute jaconette wher-
ever a book cloth hinge is described in this sewing.

· *CLOTH HINGE WITHOUT TAPES:* A cloth hinge without tapes is a bad
hinge. It is a mistake to sew with tapes, then cut off the supports,
rather than attaching them to the boards. Neither should the supports be turned back and glued to the spine. They need to be glued
to the boards, if not laced-in.

Sewing in the hinges is not enough in itself. Without the additional attachment of the tapes, tremendous stress is placed between the first and second signature where the hinge is attached. The same stress is between the next to last and the final signature. The book will rip at these points. It is important to remember that the supports must be glued to, or laced into the boards for tensile strength. Likewise, the hinge wears from opening and closing. A flimsy sheet of paper will not suffice. The hinge must be a thin book cloth.

The ideal exposed cloth hinge adds another texture and element of design to the opened book, stemming from function, not mere decoration. It is especially nice looking with a quarter cloth binding. See pages 340, 351, 352, 354, 355.

2-PLY HINGING

The ideal exposed cloth hinge described on the facing page is actually half the hinge. The hinge that is attached to the signatures is referred to as the *inside hinge*. The case is the other ply of the hinge:

The quarter cloth extends from the back cover, across the gap to the spine-board, across the gap to the front cover. This spine-cloth is the *outside hinge*.

In casing-in, the inside hinge will be glued to the outside hinge, making a 2-ply cloth hinge reinforced by the tapes. This is apparent in the drawings on pages 191–193. The gaps between the boards consists of only this 2-ply hinge of the outside cloth glued to the inside hinge. This permits the hinging action.

PREPARING THE INSIDE HINGES

For the inside hinge, sized book cloth is cut square with a sharp knife or rotary knife and straight edge, or with a paper cutter. It is critical that the edge of the cloth be clean and straight. This is because you will fold over a scant 1/16" of cloth. The other edge will be seen on the inside of the book board.

Width of the inside hinge will line up vertically with the width of the quarter cloth on the boards. It is impossible to cut the inside hinge to fit precisely. The inside of the board will look bad if that hinge is short and does not meet the turn-in. The inside hinge will be made 1/2" longer than necessary and be trimmed after is is glued. The illustration at the bottom of page 160 shows the scuffed area on the inside of the board where the trimmed hinge has been peeled off.

Determine how far you wish the cloth to extend on the outside of the side-cover. Measure from that point to the spine-edge of the board. Add 1/2". The inside hinge is easily trimmed to meet the edge of the quarter cloth later. It is the same as for the Pamphlet Binding. See *Exposed Hinges* page 343 and illustrations on pages 347, 348.

Opening and closing the book, the same amount of material is seen on both sides of the board at the spine-edge.

Height of the inside hinge is 1/2"taller than the signatures. This allows some leeway in attaching the hinge to the signature, rather than trying to line it up precisely. Once it is glued, the hinge will be trimmed even with the head and tail of the signature.

A separate hinge will be glued to the first and to the last signature of the book block. The two hinges are cut after the signatures are prepared, but prior to sewing. Since one hinge is folded around the first signature, it will be sewn with that signature. The same is true with the last signature and the other book cloth hinge.

After the book block is sewn and the covers are prepared, the tapes will be glued to the hinges and the hinges will be glued to the inside of the boards. This approach to hinging creates a strong attachment between the book block and case. This is because the hinge is not only glued, it is sewn into the book block.

FOLDING THE HINGES: There are two methods. I have always done it as taught to me by Gary Frost. In writing this, Fred says it is too difficult and offers his quicker method. I will describe his method first and the way I do it will be called *Method 2*.

Folding Method 1
· Cut the hinges on a paper cutter with more width than you need.
· Lay the hinge extended over the edge of the table surface of the paper cutter about 1/4" or more The good side of the cloth must face down.
· Press with your finger on the cloth to make a sharp crease. Be careful not to run your finger off the cloth onto the metal, or you might cut your finger.
· Crease with a bone folder. Open the hinge flat. On the shorter side of the fold, trim the cloth to 1/16" with a thin bladed sharp knife and straight edge.

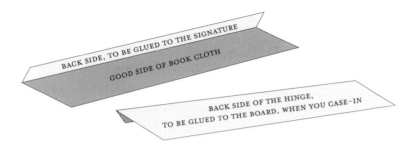

TWO VIEWS OF AN INSIDE HINGE: IF YOU USE BOOK CLOTH FOR AN
EXPOSED HINGE IN METHOD 2 THE GOOD SIDE OF THE CLOTH FACES THE BOOK
BLOCK. THE BACK OF THE BOOK CLOTH FACES OUT, TO BE PASTED TO THE
BOARDS.

WHETHER YOU FOLLOW METHOD 1 WITH A HIDDEN JACONETTE HINGE, OR
METHOD 2 WITH AN EXPOSED HINGE, CUTTING AND FOLDING THE HINGE MUST
ACCOMPLISH THREE THINGS:

THE BOOK CLOTH BE CUT CLEANLY, SO THE CLOTH IS NOT FRAYED.

ONLY A SCANT 1/16" MUST BE FOLDED OVER.

WIDTH OF THE HINGE MUST BE 1/2" WIDER THAN THE AMOUNT THE QUARTER
CLOTH EXTENDS ONTO THE BOARD. IT WILL BE TRIMMED TO MEET THE QUARTER
CLOTH.

Folding Method 2

· Lay the hinge on the table with the good side of the cloth facing up.
· Make a small fold, a scant 1/16", along the height of the hinge, turning in towards the good side of the cloth. This smaller side of the
fold is where the front hinge will be glued to the first signature.
Likewise, the other hinge will be glued to the last signature.

In making the fold, start at one edge, turning in as small an amount
as possible. This must be done in stages, using your fingers, then a
bone folder over a short distance. Continue to fold over a small
amount, creasing it with a bone folder. Do not try to run the bone
folder along the entire length of the fold, or the amount turned it
will vary. It must be done in stages. It is critical that the fold be
straight and only about 1/16" be turned in. The turn-in will be glued
to the signature on one side of the fold of the spine-edge. If more
than a scant amount is folded over, it will be visible in the gutter
when the pages are turned.

GLUING THE INSIDE HINGE TO THE SIGNATURE: Here, again, Fred says my method is painstaking. I will show his method first, then describe how I do it as *Method 2*.

Gluing Method 1

Fred's method eliminates folding the hinge, as described on the previous page. It could be folded, but it is not necessary:

· Lay the hinge on the table, good side facing up.

· Lay a piece of wax paper over the hinge, except for the small amount beyond the fold. If you choose not to fold the hinge, lay the wax paper over the hinge, except for 1/16" of cloth along the height of the hinge.

· Apply a thin coat of PVA onto the exposed part of the hinge. The strokes must be from the wax paper out, beyond the cloth. Do not brush in the opposite direction, or you will force glue under the wax paper. You cannot use strokes along the hinge, parallel with the edge of the wax paper. This, too may cause capillary action.

· Discard the wax paper.

· Move the hinge to a clean, dry surface. Lay the signature beside the hinge so that the fold of the signature is parallel with and almost tangent to, the glued edge of the hinge. Page 1 of the signature should be facing up.

· Pick up the signature and move it onto the hinge, in 1/16". The signature will overlap the hinge only the amount that has been glued.

· Press down. Fred says there should be no oozing out of the glue. Allow to dry for 10 minutes.

· Pick up the signature. Fold the hinge around to page 1 of the signature. Use a bone folder to place a crease in the hinge at the fold of the signature.

Gluing Method 2

In my approach, I have found it far easier to glue the signature than to glue the hinge. This sounds strange, but this is the reason: Only the small turn-in of the hinge is attached to the signature. It is not attached to the first page at the front of the book, but the last page of the first signature. In making the hinge for the back of the book, the hinge is not attached to the last page of the book, but to the first page of that signature.

The hinge must be attached only on the side of the paper, next to the spine-fold of the inside page of that signature. No glue is on the first page of the book or the last page of the book.

Gluing does not take place on the fold of the hinge or on the fold of
the signature. This is because the glue could easily creep to the other
side of the signature to the page which faces the board.

Later, when you would open the book, the opening hinge would tear
away from the first page to the spine-edge.

You could use a tiny brush to glue only the 1/16" turn-in of the hinge,
but you would have to open the hinge to glue it.

Then you would have to fold it over the fold of the signature. It
would be almost impossible to line up and get an even amount of the
turn-in beyond the fold.

This problem is avoided when the paper, not the hinge is glued. The
hinge is folded and laid on the table. The good side of the book cloth
faces upward for the larger part of the cloth. The turn-in is away
from you. The backside of the cloth shows on the turn-in. There is a
sharp crease on the book cloth. You will hand hold the signature to
apply the glue, then slip the signature into the hinge, which remains
on the table.

· A bead of PVA glue is run across the first signature (often the endsheet) on the sheet which will be bound towards the second signature,
the last page of the first signature. The bead of glue should fall along
the edge of the page, not on the fold, or oozed around onto the first
page. It is critical that the bead of glue have no breaks, otherwise the
hinge will not be attached completely along the edge of the paper.

You could use a brush to apply the glue along the edge of the signature. I have found you can get a thin bead of consistent small width
with no breaks by using your thumb rather than a brush. It is quicker
too and speed is important. It sounds crude compared to using a
brush, but it is not. Practice on a scrap of folded paper and a neatly
prepared hinge.

Use a brush or a scrap of paper to place a dot of PVA onto your thumb.
Hold the signature with your other hand with the fold facing you.
Start at one edge and run your thumb onto the page, next to the
fold, but do not glue the fold of the signature.

On your test, vary the angle of your thumb. You will see that a sharp
angle gives a small bead of glue on the surface of the paper.

Lowering the angle of your thumb increases the width of the bead of glue. You want a thin, consistent width bead. When the bead ends as you run out of glue, apply another small dot of glue to your thumb and continue the application of the bead of glue until you have one, continuous thin bead of glue on the edge of the paper.

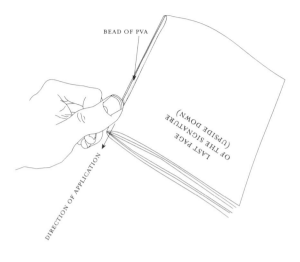

BEAD OF PVA

LAST PAGE
OF THE SIGNATURE
(UPSIDE DOWN)

DIRECTION OF APPLICATION

APPLYING A BEAD OF PVA GLUE
METHOD 2 APPLIES THE PVA TO THE SIG-
NATURE, NOT THE HINGE. ANGLE OF THE
THUMB CONTROLS WIDTH OF THE BEAD.

· Quickly, but carefully slide the signature, centered, into the hinge, which remains on the table. This is where you will be glad the hinge is taller than the signature. You will not have to take time to carefully line it up from top to bottom.

· Make sure the fold of the signature makes contact with the fold of the hinge. Have a tissue handy.

· Press down with the tissue, on the small folded over part of the hinge to apply pressure. Pressing should start from beyond the fold of the hinge, inward, towards and onto the top page of the signature. This will help insure the hinge makes good contact with the fold on the signature.

Pressing is done in short strokes. If any glue oozes onto the signature, the tissue will immediately absorb it. No glue should ooze onto the surface of the page if you have applied a thin bead of glue.

· Five minutes after the hinge is attached, trim the hinge even with the head and tail of the signature.

· Repeat these steps for the last signature, attaching that hinge so the small fold is glued to the first page of the final signature. The process is symmetrical, with the larger flap of the hinges on the top and the bottom of the book block.

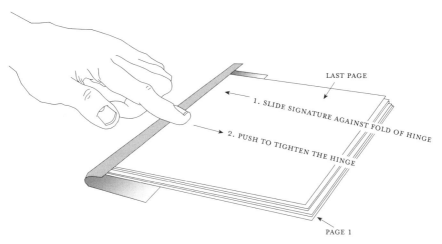

1. SLIDE SIGNATURE AGAINST FOLD OF HINGE

2. PUSH TO TIGHTEN THE HINGE

LAST PAGE

PAGE 1

1. SLIDE SIGNATURE INTO THE HINGE.

2. PRESS INWARD ON THE SMALL FOLD OF THE HINGE CLOTH TO INSURE THE FOLD
BUTTS AGAINST THE FOLD OF THE SIGNATURE. HAVE A TISSUE HANDY TO BLOT
ANY POSSIBLE OOZE OF GLUE FROM THE CLOTH. TRIM THE HINGE TO THE HEIGHT
OF THE SIGNATURE.

TAPE SUPPORTS

For the Flat Back Cased-In
Codex, the signatures are sewn
onto 1/4" linen tape. This is not
adhesive tape, but sewing tape.
A reel of tape can be purchased
from a binder's supply.

A minimum of three tapes
across the spine are used for
stability of the book block. Use
four for a book 8" to 10" high
and five tapes for a book 11" to
14". Make the tapes longer,
rather than shorter. You can
always cut off the excess.

If you are not attaching the
tapes to a sewing frame, the
length of the tapes is determined by adding the thickness
of the book block plus 3".

1/4" LINEN TAPE IS USED AS THE
SUPPORTS IN THIS SEWING.

This will allow 1½" of tape to temporarily hang over towards the first and last page of the book block, over the hinges. *Example:* A book block which is ½" thick would need tapes cut 3½" long. After the sewing is completed, the tapes will be glued to the hinges prior to the hinges being glued to the boards.

SEWING STATIONS

The positions of the kettle stitch at the head and the tail are called *kettle stations,* or *sewing stations.* A single hole will be pierced ⅜" in from at the head and the tail of each signature for the kettle stations.

Positions of the tapes are called *sewing stations.* A tape requires a 2-hole station. If you use 3 tapes, there will be 3 stations for the tapes, with a total of 6 holes.

Cords and kettle stitches use 1 hole at each station. However, a tape requires 2 holes at each station, one located on each side of and tangent to, the tape. One hole is to exit to the outside and one hole to enter the signature.

Example: If your book to be sewn uses 3 tapes, you will have 5 sewing stations—the 2 kettle stations and 3 tape stations. This will require piercing 8 holes to do the sewing.

Signatures are pre-pierced for all sewings.

NUMBER OF TAPES REQUIRED: To determine the number of tapes necessary, tapes are laid across the spine, spaced along the spine of the book. Exact position of the tape supports is not critical, since they will be hidden by the spine board.

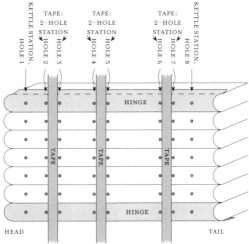

POSITIONING THE HOLES FOR THE TAPES FOR A BOOK 8 TO 10" TALL. TAPES ARE NOT LAID OUT SYMMETRICALLY. THAT WAY, YOU CANNOT SEW A SIGNATURE IN UPSIDE DOWN.

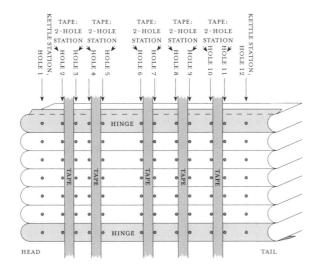

Positioning for a book 11 to 14" tall.

Placing the tapes asymmetrically prevents sewing a signature upside down. Each tape requires 2 pierced holes.

When sewing raised cord, position of the supports must be considered because the bulge of the cords will show on the spine. There is a traditional formula for positioning the cords. This is irrelevant for the flat back binding, since a third board covers the spine.

For structural purposes, all that matters in positioning the tapes for sewing is not have a gap of more than 2" between two tapes, or between the kettle station and a tape station.

For purpose of a reminder, I do not position my tapes symmetrically. With symmetrically pierced stations, the holes line up, when the signature is laid on upside down, as well as right side up. By positioning the tapes and stations asymmetrically, the signature can only fit if it is placed right side up. This acts as a reminder, or fail-safe.

MARKING AND PIERCING THE HOLES

Pick up the first signature to be sewn. Lay it on the table with the hinge up. Lay the number of tapes required for this size book along this first signature. The tapes should be perpendicular to the fold of the signature. Spread the tapes out, positioning them along the fold.

Use a sharp pencil to mark a dot on each side of the tapes on the top signature only. Since you have added the hinges, the pencil marks will be on hinge material rather than on the paper. A sharp pencil is critical so that you will know the precise location of each hole.

KETTLE STATION: This first station, in from the head about ⅜", is a *kettle station.* See diagram on the previous page. It requires one pierced hole. Kettle stations are used to form a kettle stitch in order to end the sewing along that signature and attach the head or tail to the following signature. See *Kettle Stitch,* pages 109–112.

The distance of the hole from the head would be greater if the top edge of the book were to be plowed. Plowing creates a smooth surface, allowing the book block to be dusted. Plowing requires equipment and will not be described in this manual, which is relegated to the bare necessities of binding.

Mark the position of this first hole with a pencil.

TAPE STATIONS: The middle holes are for the tapes. Each tape will require two pierced holes, one on either side and tangent to the tape. See diagram on the previous page. Make a dot with the pencil on each side of each tape for the middle holes.

NOTE: In diagramming the sewing path of sewing onto tapes, I will label the holes, not the stations, in order to simplify the directions.

KETTLE STATION: The final station along the spine is a kettle station. Like the station at the head, it is in from the tail about ⅜". Make a dot on the fold in from the tail for the final hole.

All the sewing stations are now marked on the top signature, only. Place this marked top signature back on the stack of signatures. Pick up the book block. Jog on the head and spine to even up the stack.

Without disturbing the alignment, the book block is carefully laid on the table in order to mark the position of the holes on the remainder of the signatures.

Use the marks on the first signature as a guide. With a right angle, mark all the dots down through the stack across the folds of all the signatures. See diagram on page 103.

Open each signature separately and pierce the holes. Place the signatures back in their correct order. You are ready to sew. For more information, see *Sewing Stations,* page 93 and *Piercing from the Outside to the Inside,* page 94.

KEITH SMITH, BOOK 53, ONE-OF-A-KIND, 1974. FLAT BACK, QUARTER CLOTH. THE
BLANK BOOK WAS "IMAGED" AFTER IT WAS BOUND BY TEARING PAGES. OVERSIZED
BOARDS OFFER A HALF INCH BORDER OF INLAID MARBLED PAPER AROUND THE
OPENED BOOK, SUGGESTING A FULL SHEET OF MARBLED PAPER IS ON THE INSIDE OF
THE BOARDS. COMPARE TO THE BOOKS ON PAGES 354, 355. 27 X 21.5 X 1.5 CM.

THREAD

Cut a length of linen thread that is easy to handle. It should not be
more than two arm's length. See *Thread,* page 97. You can add more
with a *Weaver's Knot,* as described on page 101. Wax the thread. See
Waxing the Thread, page 97. Sewing is with a single, rather than a double
thread.[14] See *Threading the Needle,* page 97.

Top and lower left: Barbara Mauriello, *Laced Book/Box*, 1997.
Sewn onto tapes. 14.5 x 12.7 x 3.7 cm.

Bottom right: Barbara Mauriello, *Amen, The thirteenth Day*, box
cover, 1997. 16 x 12 x 7 cm.

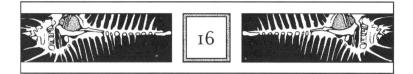

16

SEWING ONTO TAPES

SEWING FRAME: None of the bindings in this manual need to be sewn on a frame. Since we are eliminating the need for equipment in this manual, no sewing frame is described. If you wish to know how to use one, or wish to have plans for an easy-to-build frame, they are described and illustrated in my book *Exposed Spine Sewings,* Volume III, *Non-Adhesive Binding,* on pages 18–23.[9]

FACE UP OR FACE DOWN: It makes no difference whether you sew from back to front or front to back. See *Sewing on the Bench,* page 109 and *Back to Front, or Front to Back,* page 114.

In this manual, for uniformity, all sewings will be described sewing from the head to the tail. The head will always be on the left. The "first" signature refers to the *first to be sewn,* not whether it is the first in the book, or the final signature.

SEWING
FIRST SIGNATURE: Place the hinge side of the signature down on the table and open to the center, keeping the bottom half on the table. This is referred to as sewing *on the bench*.

1. Start sewing from the outside of the signature through the hinge and paper to the inside, through the sewing station at the head. Allow about 6" of thread to remain on the outside.

2. Proceed on the inside along the fold towards the tail to the next hole. Exit hole 2 to the outside of the signature. Now that the needle has gone through two holes, you can adjust the amount of thread dangling from the first hole. Pull in the direction of the backbone, until only about 2" of thread remain hanging from the first station.

If you were to start with such a small amount extending, you might accidentally pull the entire thread to the inside when exiting the second hole.

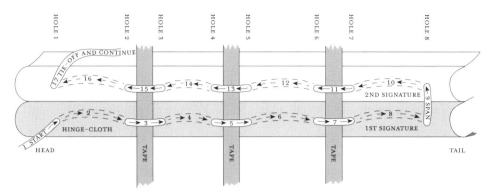

SEWING ONTO TAPES, sewing the first two signatures

3–4. Enter the third hole to the inside. Proceed on the inside towards the tail. Exit hole 4.

5–8. Exit on the back side of the tape, *lap* (proceed over the tape support) and enter on the forward side. Proceed until you come out of the station at the tail, which is hole 8.

Close this signature. Insert all the tapes on the back of the fold through the loops of thread created by sewing the first signature. Hold onto each end of the thread and tighten the loops by pulling parallel with the spine-fold.

Center the overhang of the tapes on each side of this first signature. The bottom part of the overhanging tapes can be slipped under the first signature, against the hinge and table. Or, place the fold of the signature along the edge of the table, allowing the tapes to hang down the edge of the table.

Tighten the sewing at the end of each unit sewn by pulling the thread in the *same* direction as you're sewing, parallel with the fold. Never pull the thread perpendicular to the fold, as this will tear the paper of any signature which does not have a hinge.

Sewing each additional signature, you will come out the hole on the back side of the tape *(exit backward)* and enter on the forward side of the tape. See illustration on the facing page.

Be careful not to pierce the tapes. They must be able to be adjusted. As the sewing proceeds, you will periodically adjust the tapes, keeping an even amount overhanging each end of the sewn signatures.

SECOND SIGNATURE: Place the second signature on top of the one just sewn and carefully align the two. Open the top half of the new signature to continue sewing. Never insert the needle into a closed signature, as you can scar the paper.

9. Start sewing the second signature at the tail, where the thread and needle have last exited the first signature. This is not a kettle stitch, but merely a *span* from the first to the second signature.

10–17. After entering the second signature, continue sewing in and out as before, exiting on the back side of the tape. Lap the tape and enter on the forward side of the tape. Exit the station at the head, which is hole 1. Close the second signature.

Tighten the sewing by pulling the thread parallel with the backbone, in the same direction as you were sewing. Do not pull perpendicular to the back to avoid tearing the paper. As each signature is sewn, press down firmly on the top signature and gently tug on the tapes, making sure there are no gaps in the tapes. Be careful not to accidentally pull a tape completely from the sewing.

DETAIL OF THE SEWING

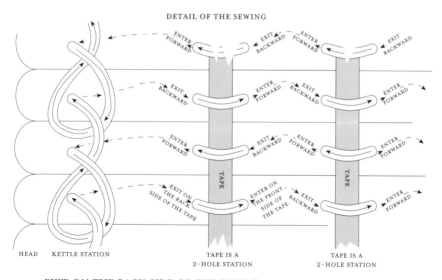

EXIT ON THE BACK SIDE OF THE TAPE THE TERMS *LEFT* AND *RIGHT* ARE IRRELEVANT. IN SEWING THE ODD-NUMBERED SIGNATURES, THE HOLE ON THE BACK SIDE OF THE TAPE IS ON THE LEFT. IN SEWING THE EVEN-NUMBERED SIGNATURES, THE HOLE ON THE BACK SIDE OF THE TAPE IS ON THE RIGHT. JUST REMEMBER TO EXIT BACK OF THE TAPE AND ENTER ON THE FORWARD SIDE IN THE DIRECTION IN WHICH YOU ARE SEWING THAT PARTICULAR SIGNATURE.

Tie a square knot with the loose end of thread at the head of the first signature. Do not clip the thread. See *Square Knot,* page 108. This is the only knot in the binding until either you run out of thread and must add more using a Weaver's Knot, or you complete sewing all signatures, when a final tie-off is needed using a half hitch.

CAUTION: Open the top signature, only, to check the tension on the inside. Do not look through the remainder of the book until back has been glued, or you will stretch the sewing.

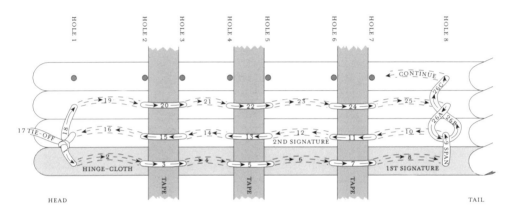

SEWING ONTO TAPES, SEWING THE THIRD SIGNATURE WITHOUT LOCKING THEM TOGETHER. FOR GROUPING AND LOCKING, SEE CHAPTER 18, PAGE 199.

THIRD SIGNATURE: The third signature can be sewn without grouping and locking the stitches, as illustrated above. Or, better, the first three signatures and the final three, can be grouped and locked, as you exit at the tape stations, as illustrated on the top of the facing page. That sewing will be elaborated on page 202. First I will describe the procedure without locking the signatures:

Not locking

18. Place the third signature on top of the second. Open the third signature to the middle. Climb. Enter the third signature at hole 1.

19. Proceed inside towards the tail. Exit hole 2.

20. Lap and enter on the forward side at hole 3.

21–25. Exit the tape stations on the back side. Lap and enter on the forward side of the tapes.

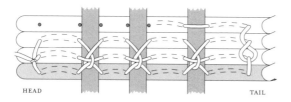

ALTERNATIVE: SEWING THE THIRD SIGNATURE CAN GROUP AND LOCK THE FIRST 3 TOGETHER. THIS APPROACH IS CALLED *GROUPED GATHERED LAP-GROUP.* IT IS DESCRIBED ON PAGE 202.

26A. Exit backward. Link.
26B. Slip under to lock.
26C. Climb.

Set on the next (fourth) signature. Open to the middle. Enter the new signature at the tail. To review, see *Kettle Stitch,* pages 109–112.

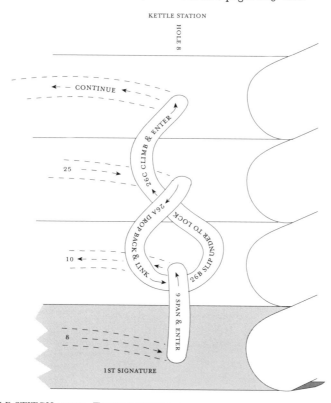

KETTLE STITCH DETAIL. THE FIRST KETTLE IS AT THE END OF THE THIRD SIGNATURE. SHOWN HERE AS STEP 26A, B AND C.

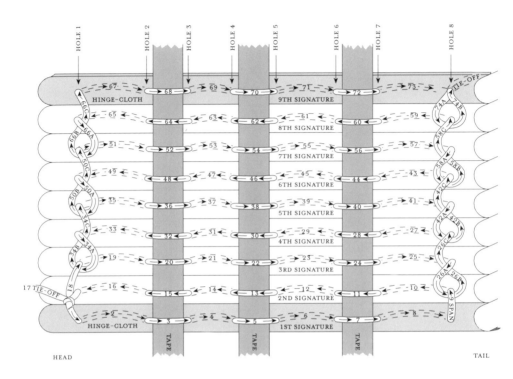

SEWING ONTO TAPES, without grouping and locking Step 74 is a partial kettle stitch: Drop backward, link, re-enter the final signature.
Tie—Off on the inside with a half hitch, described on page 108.

FOURTH SIGNATURE:

27–32. Proceed towards the head. Exit on the back side of the tapes,
lap and enter on the forward side, sewing in the manner of the second signature, as illustrated on page 176.

33. Exit at the kettle station. Tighten the sewing by pulling in the
direction of the sewing and parallel with the fold. Tighten the tapes
to remove any gap between the signatures. Close this signature. Form
the kettle at the head.

34A. Drop backward, link between the the last two connected signatures, (Step 18).

34B. Slip under Step 34A to lock.

34C. Set on the next signature and open. Climb and enter at hole 1.

REMAINING SIGNATURES: Sew the remaining signatures the same as the third and fourth. At the end of each row, form a kettle stitch. Link under the last two connected signatures. Slip under to lock, climb and enter the next signature.

FINAL TIE-OFF: If you have an odd number of signatures, the tie-off will be at the tail. With an even number, the tie-off will be at the head. After exiting the final station of the last signature, drop and link. Re-enter the final kettle station to the inside of the signature. This will form a partial kettle stitch, since you do not slip under to lock, or climb to a new signature.

Tie-off the kettle stitch on the inside with a half hitch. This is described on page 108. The sewing is complete.

SLEEVE OF WAX PAPER: Wrap the book block in an envelope of wax paper, slightly wider than the book block and 2½ times the height. This is a moisture barrier for casing-in and will keep it from getting soiled. Pull the hinge and tapes to the outside of the wax paper. Start the wrapping on the front of the book block. Tape the wax paper shut. The masking tape will be on the front. Lightly mark an arrow pointing up on the masking tape. This is so when you case-in, you will not attach the book block upside down.

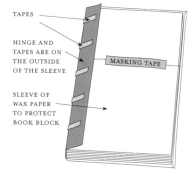

TAPES

HINGE AND TAPES ARE ON THE OUTSIDE OF THE SLEEVE

MASKING TAPE

SLEEVE OF WAX PAPER TO PROTECT BOOK BLOCK

SLEEVE OF WAX PAPER

GLUING THE BACK

Jog the book at the head, then against the back. Set the book block on the table with the spine-edge extending about ¼" beyond the edge. The bottom hinge and tapes should extend along the depth of the table edge. The top hinge and tapes lay on top of the book block. Lay a scrap of book board over the book block, about ¼" in from the spine-edge. Any closer to the edge would cause the backbone to distort, since it is wider from *swell*. Place a weight on top. The weight should extend to the edge of the cardboard, close to the spine-edge. The weight should not be so heavy as to distort the back to a concave or convex curve. The weight must be sufficient to keep the glue in the crevices from creeping onto the pages. A tight sewing is important.

Paste or glue the back, applying a *thin* coat. Fred uses wheat paste; I use PVA glue.

The important thing is not to put on a thick coat, but to push the glue into the crevices between the signatures. This is the point at which you glue one signature to the next. Glue on the remainder of the backbone is not structural, only the glue in the crevices adheres one signature to the next.

Do not try to fill all the cracks of the crevices in one thick application of glue. Apply a second thin coat to the back, concentrating on the crevices. Some wipe the paste or glue from the back so that all that remains is in the crevices.

Be sure the glue gets in the crevices. Allow to dry. PVA will turn clear when dry in about ten minutes. Paste must dry 2 hours.

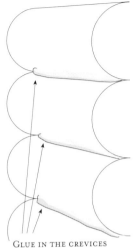

GLUE IN THE CREVICES
OF THE SIGNATURES

Only when the second coat of glue dries can the book be opened. If you examine the book block, replace the sleeve of wax paper. Pull the hinges to the outside of the wax paper. Tape the wax paper shut. This will protect the book block from becoming soiled or bent until covers have been attached. This is especially critical if you intend to leave the hinges exposed. The first and last pages will not be glued to the board, but will be visible.

ROLLED CORE ENDBANDS: Headbands and tailbands dress up the book block. It is strongly advised. They are added at this point. You can buy commercial faux endbands or make your own. For descriptions, see *Endbands,* page 238.

Other methods of sewing onto flat supports are described in Chapter 18, beginning on page 199. For your next book sewn onto tapes, you might wish to try one of these variations.

Before adding the boards, you may wish to color the edges of the book block. See *Edge Decoration,* page 369. If there is no edge decoration, proceed to *Boards for the Flat Back,* in the following chapter.

17

BOARDS AND CASING-IN
THE FLAT BACK

MEASURING THE BOARDS

NUMBER OF BOARDS: There are three boards: the front cover, back cover and spine-board. Binders board is recommended, but 4-ply mat board may be substituted. Binders board comes in several thicknesses and should be chosen in proportion to the dimensions of the book.

OVERHANG: Generally, the overhang of board on the head, tail and foredge are the same. Many binders have a rule that the overhang, or *square of the book,* is $1\frac{1}{2}$ times the thickness of the board for any size book.

Fred prefers a small book about 4" tall to have an overhang of about $\frac{1}{16}$", whereas if the book is about 16" tall, he would leave an overhang of at least $\frac{1}{4}$". He does not go by the general rule of $1\frac{1}{2}$ times the thickness of the board.

The overhang is something you can decorate. Since it is always visible on the inside, at every opened page, it can be imaged with text or an inlay. Possibilities are presented in Part V, *Finishing,* page 335.

COVER-BOARD MEASUREMENTS: Height of the cover-boards, or *side-covers,* is the height of the book block plus three thicknesses of book board (3T). When these boards are centered on the spine, there will be $1\frac{1}{2}$ T overhanging at the head and the tail.

The finished width of the side-covers will be determined later. For now, temporarily measure them $\frac{1}{2}$" wider than the book block.

SPINE-BOARD MEASUREMENTS: Width of the spine-board measures the same as the thickness of the backbone plus the thickness of the two side-covers (2T) or slightly wider, ($2\frac{1}{2}$T).

Height of the spine-board is the same in height as the side-covers.

ORDER OF CUTTING: Since all the boards are the same height, this measurement should be cut first from a sheet of book board. Make sure the grain of the board is parallel to the spine of the book. When the three boards have been cut, sand the cover-boards along the head, foredge and tail. See *Sanding the Boards,* page 195.

Lay the boards side by side on the table with the spine-board in the middle.

GAP BETWEEN THE BOARDS: The gap between the spine-board and the side-cover allows for hinging action for the covers to open and close. The gap between the spine-board and side-cover is a minimum of 3½ times the thickness of the book board.

To fix the gap between the boards, lay them on a table. Place a straight edge on the table. Line up the tail of each board against a straight edge. Spread the boards apart to the desired gap. A larger gap means the side-covers will start farther in from the spine-edge.

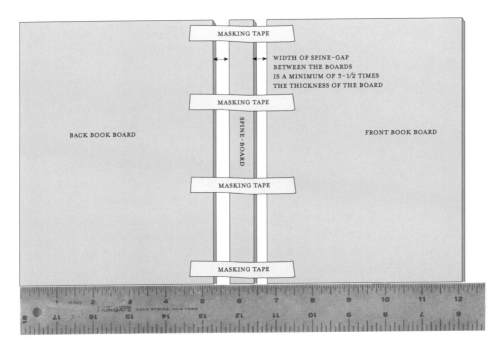

FIXING THE GAP BETWEEN THE BOARDS. LINE UP BOTTOM EDGES OF ALL 3 BOARDS AGAINST A STRAIGHT EDGE. CENTER THE SPINE-BOARD. ADJUST THE GAP TO 3½ TIMES THE THICKNESS OF THE BOARD. USE MASKING TAPE TO HOLD THE BOARDS IN POSITION.

Use masking tape to secure the gap between the boards. Don't extend the tape to the edge of the boards. Start the masking tape at the head below where the turn-in at the head will extend. The strips of masking tape at the tail should be above where the turn-in at the tail will extend. In this manner, you will not have to remove the masking tape until after you make the turns-in. There will be no risk that the spine-board will be pulled out of alignment when you remove the masking tape, since the turns-in at the head and tail will secure it.

DETERMINING THE FINAL WIDTH OF THE SIDE-COVERS: Slip the sewn book block into the covers with the masking tape on the outside of the boards. Make sure the back of the book block rests against the spine-board.

1. Mark where the foredge of the book block ends on the side-covers.

2. From this pencil mark, add the amount of overhang you desire on the foredge with a second pencil mark at the head and tail, and connects the dots with a pencil line. The overhang, or *square of the book,* is traditionally 1 1/2 times the thickness of the board along the head, foredge and tail.

With a straight edge and knife, trim the foredge of both side-covers to the finished width.

Note in the drawing to the right, the side-board does not extend back to the spine of the book block. When the covers are closed, the gap between the boards extends from the spine, towards the foredge. This is why the finished cut of the width of the boards is determined at this stage.

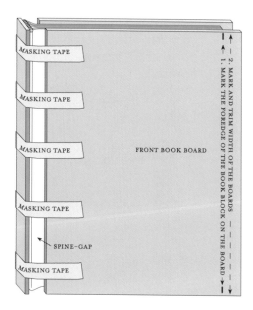

SET THE BOOK BLOCK INTO THE BOARDS, WITH THE BACKBONE FIRMLY AGAINST THE SPINE-BOARD. MARK THE BOARD AT THE FOREDGE OF THE BOOK BLOCK. ADD THE OVERHANG OF 1-1/2 THICKNESS OF BOOK BOARD. DRAW THIS LINE ON THE BOARD AND TRIM THE BOARDS TO THIS WIDTH.

QUARTER CLOTH

For a quarter-cloth or half-cloth binding, you will need to mark the side-covers for the width of the quarter cloth. This will make it easy to position the glued cloth to the boards. In marking the boards before cutting the cloth, you will be able to see an indication of the proportion or cloth to paper on the side-covers. See *Proportion on Boards,* page 43.

BUTTING PAPER TO CLOTH: Draw a pencil line down the middle of the spine-board. Measure across that board from the pencil line, over the gap to the front cover to however far you want the book cloth to show on the front cover. Draw a pencil line at this point, down the height of the front side-cover, parallel to the spine-edge. This is the location of the cloth, if you intend to butt the decorative paper on the side-cover against the quarter cloth.

Measure the same distance from the center line on the spine onto the back cover. Draw a line parallel to the spine-edge on the back board. This is where the paper will butt to the cloth, or where it will overlap the cloth.

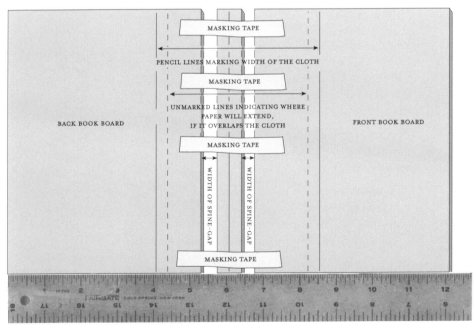

MARKING THE WIDTH OF THE CLOTH FOR A QUARTER CLOTH BINDING. USE THE PENCIL LINE MEASUREMENT TO MARK THE WIDTH ONTO THE CLOTH.

Measure from the pencil line on the front board to the line on the back board. This is the width to cut the spine-cloth. The decorative paper on the board will butt against the quarter cloth, or overlap it.

OVERLAPPING PAPER ONTO THE CLOTH: Some binders feel the cloth or leather may shrink in time, leaving a line of bare board between it and the paper. They overlap the paper onto the indented cloth or leather. Do not overlap unless you can indent the cloth, as the surfaces must be flush, so the paper will not snag when placed onto the bookshelf. See *Overlapping vs Butting Paper to the Spine-Cloth,* page 356.

INDENTING CLOTH: The procedure is the same as for leather. See page 275. You cannot dent all cloths. Heavy buckram with plastic will not indent as much as book cloth. Cotton will not indent.

If you are going to overlap the paper onto the cloth, measure from the front board to the line on the back board, mark your pencil line on each board 1/8" farther towards the foredge. This will give a total of 1/4" more width to the quarter cloth. The pencil lines will be visible as a guide for applying the glued cloth to the boards.

In the drawing on the previous page, the vertical dotted lines represent the location of the edge of the paper when it is pasted, overlapping the cloth. The dotted line is *not* drawn on the board, or the cloth.

DIMENSIONS OF THE QUARTER CLOTH: Cut a strip of book cloth for the spine with a straight edge. You must have a perfectly straight cut in order to butt the paper to the edge of the cloth.

Height of the quarter cloth is the height of the board, plus 2". Centered top to bottom, this will afford an 1" turn-in at the head and at the tail.

Width of the quarter cloth is obtained by measuring from the pencil line you drew on the back board to the line on the front board.

The quarter cloth must extend far enough onto the spine-edge of the board to securely attach the boards. It will bear tension, as it acts as a hinge, in conjunction with the inside hinge.

If you want an extremely thin amount of cloth, you must extend more onto the board to secure it. Then, overlap the cloth with paper to the amount of cloth desired. See *Proportion on the Boards,* page 43.

WHEAT PASTE vs PVA GLUE: The quarter cloth can be pasted, or some-times, it can be glued with PVA:

• *Wheat paste* can be used on most book cloth. The exception is extremely thick, plastic coated book cloth which needs the viscosity of PVA in order to stick. But this cloth is undesirable for its thickness, as well as its "tablecloth" appearance.

Wheat paste will not stain. Even unsized cotton can be used with cau-tion. In those instances, paste the board, not the unsized fabric. See *Making Your Own Book Cloth,* page 368.

• *PVA* has the advantage that it dries in about 10 minutes, whereas wheat paste requires about 45. PVA can creep slightly around the edges when pasting. This gives a border of stained book cloth. All things considered, wheat paste is a better choice, but I use PVA.

PASTING THE QUARTER CLOTH TO THE BOARDS: Lay the three boards on the table, with the masking tape connecting them facing the table. That side will now become the inside of the covers. The side of the boards facing up will be the outside of the covers.

Apply paste or glue to the back side of the book cloth. Place it on the boards, lining it up with the vertical pencil lines. You must also cen-ter it from head to tail.

Press lightly on the spine cloth at the gaps, being careful not to stretch the cloth. The cloth should not be pushed down against the table, in the area of the gap, but remain on a single plane.

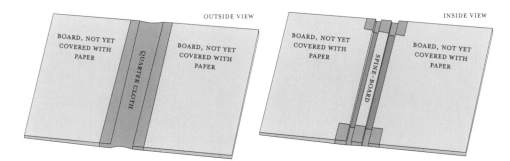

WIDTH OF THE CLOTH IS OBTAINED BY MEASURING THE LINES DRAWN ON THE BOARDS. IT IS THE CLOTH EXTENDS ONTO THE SIDE-COVERS, PLUS THE WIDTH OF THE SPINE-BOARD, PLUS THE GAPS BETWEEN THE BOARDS. IF THE PAPER IS TO OVERLAP THE CLOTH, ADD THE AMOUNT OF OVERLAP.

MAKING THE TURNS-IN: Turn the 3 connected boards over and lay on a clean, dry surface. Make sure the gaps have not slipped and the boards are parallel.

Remove only enough of the masking tape for the turn-in at the head. Make the turn-in at the head. Push the cloth firmly downward, so there is a tight fit of the cloth on the edge of the boards at the head.

Press the cloth into the gaps and along the thickness of the boards. It is easier using two bone folders, working from the left to the right:

· Crease the cloth turn-in firmly against the edge (depth) of the cover board on the left. Hold the bone folder in position. With a second bone folder, crease the cloth against the depth of the left side of the spine-board. The first bone folder will prevent the cloth from pulling away from the edge of that board.

· Hold the second bone folder in position along the left edge of the spine-board. With the first bone folder, press the cloth along the right edge of the spine-board. Hold this bone folder in position. Use the other bone folder to press the cloth against the depth of the side-cover on the right.

I refer to this process as *walking the bone folders.* It insures a crisp formation of the cloth to the surface and depth of the boards and cloth to cloth in the area of the gaps. For an illustration of *Walking the Bone Folders,* see page 156.

Rotate the boards 180°. Remove only the masking tape that would be in the way of the turn-in at the tail. Make the turn-in at the tail in the same manner as at the head.

Turn the boards over. Run the bone along the four board edges to crease. Use only one stroke per edge, as repeated stroking will make the cloth shiny. Do not push the cloth in the gap down against the table. This will stretch and distort the cloth.

Turn the boards over so the inside is facing up. Since the paste is still wet, be careful when you remove the remainder of the masking tape. I hold the board down with one hand, as I peel with the other. The boards will be secured in position once the adhesive dries.

FORMING THE I-BEAM: Once the cloth is totally dry, close the boards. This initial bending of the cloth at the gap is critical. Make sure there is a good straight crease with a bone folder as you close each board. Keeping the side-covers closed, press the spine board against the depth of the side-covers to form an *I*-beam.

Insert the book block, which still has a sleeve of wax paper around it, with the hinges on the outside. Push the back of the book tightly against the spine-board.

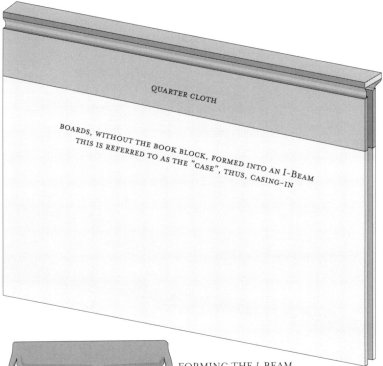

QUARTER CLOTH

BOARDS, WITHOUT THE BOOK BLOCK, FORMED INTO AN I-BEAM
THIS IS REFERRED TO AS THE "CASE", THUS, CASING-IN

CROSS-SECTION
DETAIL

FORMING THE *I*-BEAM

AFTER THE CLOTH DRIES, OPEN AND CLOSE THE BOARDS. FORM AN *I*-BEAM, BY PRESSING THE SIDE-COVERS TOGETHER AND PUSHING THE SPINE-BOARD DOWN ONTO THE EDGE OF THE SIDE-COVERS.

SPREAD THE SIDE-COVERS ONLY FAR ENOUGH TO INSERT THE BOOK BLOCK, WHICH IS IN A SLEEVE OF WAX PAPER.

PUSH THE BACKBONE TIGHT AGAINST THE SPINE-BOARD. IT IS READY TO CASE-IN.

CASING-IN THE BOOK BLOCK

Casing-In has far better results using a press. The press, described on page 39, has copper extending on the depth of the wooden boards. The copper extends 1½ board thickness beyond the wooden boards of the press. It clamps down on the gap between the spine-board and the side-covers, against the depth of the side-cover. This creates the *French groove*. See page 34.

The French groove insures the hinges which are attached to the book block are glued tightly against the edge of the side-covers.

The dowels and weight method of creating the French groove, described on page 38, is inferior to clamping in a press. The hinge is often not pasted onto the edge of the boards. The result does not look as well defined when you open the book.

Before attaching the book block to the boards, glue the loose tapes onto the hinges with PVA. Casing-In book cloth is one procedure where I prefer gluing with PVA over wheat pasting.

POSITIONING THE BOOK BLOCK INTO THE CASE: Form the I-Beam. Place the book block into the covers, centering top to bottom for equal overhang. *Make sure the back of the book block rests on the spine-board.* Gently lay the closed book on the table and open the front cover without disturbing the position of the book.

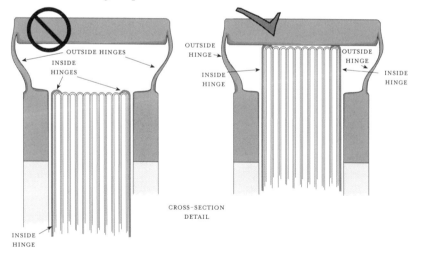

CROSS-SECTION
DETAIL

SET THE BACKBONE TIGHT AGAINST THE SPINE-BOARD. IN TEACHING WORK-SHOPS, NOT TAKING CARE IS THE MISTAKE MOST OFTEN MADE.

DRAWING IS SHOWN WITHOUT ROLLED CORE ENDBAND FOR CLARITY.

GLUING THE HINGE TO THE CASE: Cut four pieces of wax paper slightly larger than the book block. Lay two sheets aside. Slip two pieces of wax paper between the hinge of the book block, above the first page of the book block. Make sure the two sheets are tight against the spine-edge.

Press down on the wax paper with one hand to make sure the wax paper and the the book block do not shift while you glue.

Glue this hinge and the tapes, being careful not to glue the backbone. The book will not fully open to allow pages to lie flat. The back of the book block and the spine-board are never glued. The backbone must remain free to arc open as the pages are turned. Discard the top sheet of wax paper. The clean sheet will keep any glue from the sleeve of wax paper. A bead of glue can creep out under pressure.

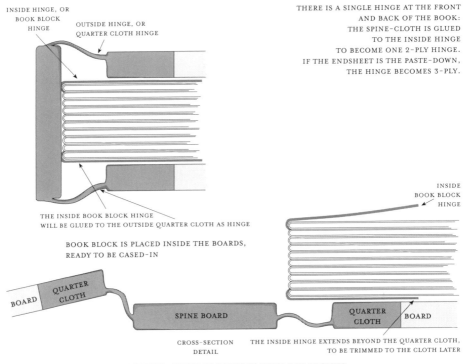

INSIDE HINGE, OR BOOK BLOCK HINGE

OUTSIDE HINGE, OR QUARTER CLOTH HINGE

THERE IS A SINGLE HINGE AT THE FRONT AND BACK OF THE BOOK: THE SPINE-CLOTH IS GLUED TO THE INSIDE HINGE TO BECOME ONE 2-PLY HINGE. IF THE ENDSHEET IS THE PASTE-DOWN, THE HINGE BECOMES 3-PLY.

THE INSIDE BOOK BLOCK HINGE WILL BE GLUED TO THE OUTSIDE QUARTER CLOTH AS HINGE

BOOK BLOCK IS PLACED INSIDE THE BOARDS, READY TO BE CASED-IN

INSIDE BOOK BLOCK HINGE

BOARD

QUARTER CLOTH

SPINE BOARD

QUARTER CLOTH

BOARD

CROSS-SECTION DETAIL

THE INSIDE HINGE EXTENDS BEYOND THE QUARTER CLOTH, TO BE TRIMMED TO THE CLOTH LATER

FRONT BOARD IS OPENED, SO THE BOOK BLOCK HINGE CAN BE GLUED

THE FRONT BOARD IS CAREFULLY OPENED. TWO SHEETS OF WAX PAPER ARE PUT UNDER THE INSIDE BOOK CLOTH HINGE. THE HINGE IS GLUED WITH PVA. REMOVE THE TOP SOILED WAX PAPER. THE FRONT BOARD IS CLOSED. TURN THE BOOK OVER, OPEN THE BACK BOARD AND GLUE THE OTHER HINGE.

Gently close the cover and press on top with your hand. *Do not open* to examine, or the cloth hinge will slip off the cover board.

Turn the book over. Open the back cover, insert two sheets of wax paper under the hinge. Glue this hinge, as before. Remove the top sheet of wax paper. Close the cover. The book may not be opened until it is pressed and the glue is dry.

PRESSING

The glued hinges must dry under weight before the book can be opened. By far the best way is to use a press which has copper edges extending to form the French groove. Three methods of drying will be described in order of their preference:

· *USING A PRESS:* Lay the press down. Insert the book into the press horizontally, with the spine board extending outside the press. Set the gap of the back side-cover onto the copper edge of the press. Lower the top board of the press, making sure the copper edge hits the gap between the boards. Tighten the press. Allow to dry at least two hours for PVA. If you use wheat paste to case—in, allow to dry overnight. See illustrations on pages 39, 40.

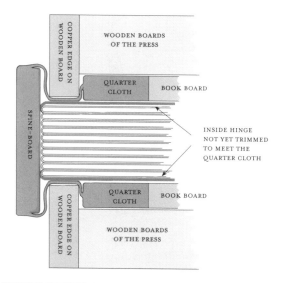

IN THE PREVIOUS DRAWING, THE SPINE-CLOTH CONNECTING THE BOARDS GAPS BETWEEN THE BOARDS. THE COPPER EDGE OF THE PRESS FITS THE CLOTH AGAINST THE GLUED INSIDE HINGE. THIS CREATES THE FRENCH GROOVE.

• *WITH WOODEN DOWELS AND WEIGHT:* Wooden dowels laid in the gap force some pressure against the glued hinges. However, it is not enough to make sure the hinge is tightly held against the edge of the side-cover while the glue is drying. The process is described and illustrated at the bottom of page 38.

• *UNDER WEIGHT:* The book can be laid on a table with the spine—board extending over the edge. A slight weight of three or four books can be put on the top, extending beyond the gap but not over the spine—board.

Be sure to leave the clean sheet of wax paper between cover and the sleeved book block. This will prevent moisture from the glue blistering the page next to the hinge.

Attaching the book block to the covers is referred to as *casing in,* thus, the term *cased—in codex.* In a fine binding, the tapes or cords used in sewing the book block are usually laced through the side-covers, adding additional strength to the hinging action.

TRIMMING THE INSIDE HINGE: After the glued hinges have dried, the book may be opened to be examined. Since the hinge was purposefully made too wide, it can now be trimmed easily to meet the turns-in of the spine-cloth:

Lay a support underneath the opened cover. Lay the straight edge on the good part of the hinge, not the area of the hinge to be trimmed. If the knife veers, it will cut into the scrap part of the hinge. Line up the ends of the straight edge with the quarter cloth coming around the board at the head and tail. Set an X-Acto™ knife blade against the straight edge at the head, then the tail, to make sure it lines up with the quarter cloth, prior to cutting. Trim. Peel off the excess before you remove the straight edge, just in case you have to make a second cut. Trim the hinge on the other board in the same manner. The board will be slightly scarred. See illustration on the bottom of page 159. An island paste-down will butt to the exposed hinge. If the endsheet is pasted down, the bulge of the hinge will be a straight line.

PASTING DOWN THE ENDSHEETS: Cover the outside of the boards. See page 279. The endsheets can be pasted down the same time as the hinges, if you use paste, not glue. See page 291.

EXPOSED HINGES: After the hinge is trimmed, covering the outside of the board and the inside island paste-down is done at the same time. See page 351.

COVERING THE BOARDS

SANDING THE BOARDS: Lightly sand the edge of the boards along the foredge, head and tail. Sand only enough to remove any ridge from hand cutting the board. It will also remove the blockish edge to the board. Also see illustration on page 244.

SPINE-EDGE   FOREDGE   SPINE-EDGE   FOREDGE

CROSS-SECTION OF BOARD   CROSS-SECTION OF BOARD
PRIOR TO SANDING   SLIGHTLY SANDING THE FOREDGE

I often take this a step further by using fine sand paper around a wooden block. I sand from the middle of the board, past the foredge. I taper the thickness of the foredge, on the outside, only. This gives a good feel holding the book, after the boards have been covered.

FRENCH GROOVE   INSIDE HINGE TRIMMED   OUTSIDE OF BOARD IS SANDED TO THE FOREDGE
                       TO QUARTER CLOTH

QUARTER CLOTH   BOOK BOARD

SPINE-BOARD

QUARTER CLOTH   BOOK BOARD

EXAGGERATED SANDING OF THE SIDE-BOARDS. THE OUTSIDE, ONLY, OF THE
BOARDS IS SANDED FROM THE CENTER TO THE FOREDGE. DEPTH OF THE BOARD ON
THE FOREDGE IS HALF THICKNESS. ANY LESS AND THE BOARD WOULD LOSE
STRENGTH.

OUTSIDE PAPERS: Select a paper to go with the cloth and endbands. Decide whether the outside paper will butt to the quarter cloth, or overlap. When overlapping, the cloth will have to be indented where the paper overlaps. See *Indenting Quarter Leather,* page 275. Indenting cloth is the same procedure, except there is no filler needed on the boards.

Width of the outside cover papers equals the width of the remaining uncovered board plus 1" to be pasted around the foredge of the board to the inside. Add 1/8" to the width of the paper if you will overlap the cloth.

Height of the papers equals the height of the board plus 2"; 1" extends around the bottom and 1" around the top to the inside. Cut two pieces of paper to size (both front and back should be the same size) making sure the grain runs parallel to the spine.

For the quarter cloth Flat Back with exposed cloth hinges, papers for the inside and outside of the boards are pre-cut.

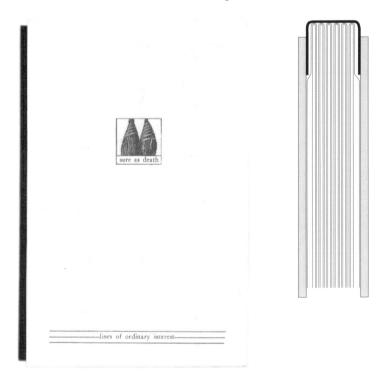

Left: Willyum Rowe, *sure as death*, published by Space heater Editions, 1986. Offset in an edition of 500. 18.5 x 12.5 x 1.2 cm.

Cased-In by Philip Zimmermann: Book was Smythe sewn, with foil stamped cloth glued to the backbone. Separate boards were covered on the outside. The front board was pasted to the cloth hinge, then to the first page. The back board was pasted to the hinge and the final page. A fuller explanation is on the facing page.

Right: Diagram cross-section of the head shows attachment of the separate boards.

INSIDE PAPERS

ISLAND PASTE-DOWN: For this binding, I always use exposed cloth hinges sewn to the book block. Since I want the hinges to show, I use an island paste-down on the inside of the board, not the endsheet.

On the inside of the boards the turns-in at the head, tail and foredge can show as narrow or as wide a border as desired, allowing far more possibilities of design than pasting sown the endsheet. See *Islands as Pastes-Down,* page 351.

ENDSHEET AS PASTE-DOWN: If your hinges are jaconette, you can paste down the first endsheet to the board, rather than using an island paste-down. For the procedure, see *Pasting Down the Endsheets for the Flat Back,* page 294.

CASE-IN WITHOUT SPINE-BOARD: On the facing page is a different approach to adding boards to the Flat Back. The book is cased-in with no spine board. The backbone is glued and a strip of cloth the height of the book block and 1½" wider is centered and placed onto the backbone. After it dries, trim along the head and tail, if necessary. No endbands are used in this binding. I devised this variation for quickly adding hard covers to a commercially Smythe sewn production book.

The two boards are covered on the outside, only. Wax paper is paced under the first page, which is blank. The page and the spine-cloth are glued with PVA, but not all the way to the spine-edge, since some of the cloth will show on the front and back boards.

The front board is laid on top, centered top to bottom and set in slightly from the spine-edge. It can overhang the foredge to give a square to the book, or be flush boards. The back board is attached to the final page in the same manner. The endsheet is the paste-down, reinforced by a hidden cloth hinge. Place under weight to dry.

PASTING THE PAPERS: For pasting procedures for the outside and inside papers, see *Covering the Boards,* page 279, *Paste-Down,* page 291 and *Exposed Hinge& Islands as Pastes-Down,* page 351.

OTHER METHODS OF SEWING FLAT SUPPORTS

18

OTHER METHODS OF SEWING FLAT SUPPORTS

Other methods of sewing flat supports (all along the spine, left to right, then right to left) are described here. The sewings in this chapter were learned from a workshop given by Betsy Palmer Eldridge, titled *Sewing Variations,* in Toronto at the Canadian Bookbinding and Book Artists Guild.[10]

Flat supports can be alum tawed split thongs, vellum or tapes. If you are going to leave the spine exposed, leather or vellum supports would be attractive.

Even if the spine is covered, such as in the Flat Back, locking the sewing is preferred by many binders.

FLAT-LAP-LOOP

The first method described for locking the sewing is called the *Flat-Lap-Loop.* The stations at the head and tail use the kettle stitch.

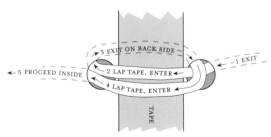

→ ODD-NUMBERED SIGNATURES →

← EVEN-NUMBERED SIGNATURES ←

THE FLAT-LAP-LOOP LAPS OVER THE SUPPORT, THEN LOOPS AROUND IT: TWO THREADS APPEAR ON THE BACKBONE, ACROSS THE TAPE, WITH ONE ON THE INSIDE.

FLAT-LOOP

The *Flat-Loop* is similar to the *Flat-Lap-Loop* on the previous page. The difference, is that here, the double thread is on the *inside* of the signature. It is accomplished by simply exiting on the forward side of the tape, rather than the hole on the back side of the tape.

The tape stations for all the odd-numbered signatures are sewn like the illustration at the top. The even-numbered are sewn as the drawing to the right.

The stations at the head and tail of the book block are sewn with a kettle stitch.

The *Flat-Lap-Loop* and the *Flat-Loop* are more secure than merely lapping the tape support. They are good to use at the beginning and ending tapes, if not across the entire book block.

→ ODD-NUMBERED SIGNATURES →

← EVEN-NUMBERED SIGNATURES ←

THE FLAT-LOOP SHOWS A SINGLE THREAD ACROSS THE TAPE ON THE OUTSIDE. INSIDE, THERE ARE TWO THREADS.

FLAT THROUGH THE SUPPORT

The *Flat, Through the Support* anchors by piercing the support. The thread exits on the back side of the support and enters by piercing through the middle of the support to the inside. Usually sewn on heavy cord rather than tapes, this sewing is used on heavy account ledgers.

There are 11 positions for piercing holes shown. However, no signature uses all 11 holes.

ODD-NUMBERED SIGNATURES: Pre-pierce holes 1, 2, 5, 8 and 11.

EVEN-NUMBERED SIGNATURES: Pre-pierce holes number 1, 4, 7, 10 and 11. The holes to enter through the tapes are not pre-pierced.

Most binders anchor north to south (head to tail), but not east to west. Tension must be good as you sew. You cannot compress the book block after it is sewn, as the pierced supports fix the compression of the book block.

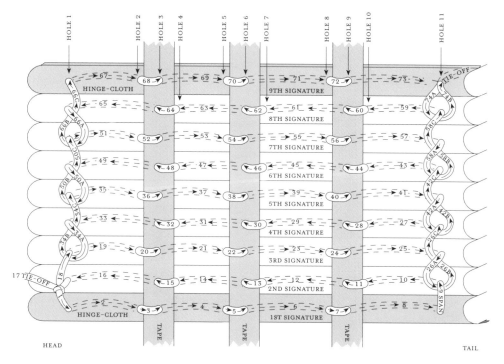

FLAT THROUGH THE SUPPORT LOCKS THE SEWING BY PIERCING THE TAPE IN THE CENTER, AS THE THREAD ENTERS.

GROUP GATHERED LAP-GROUP

A standard method of locking is referred to as *grouped gathered lap-group*. Betsy Palmer Eldridge says that over tightening will cause the spine to go concave. If you intend to round the book, she does not recommend locking, as rounding would be difficult.

Locking is shown in some English books; the Germans do not care for it. But on a Flat Back, it poses no problems and locks the signatures together. The bulkiness of the spine will not be a problem since it is covered by a spine-board.

1–18. The first two signatures are sewn in the normal manner, as described on pages 175–177. Locking takes place in sewing the third signature. The fourth and fifth are sewn without locking, like the first two. The sixth signature again locks. Every signature divisible by three is the locking procedure.

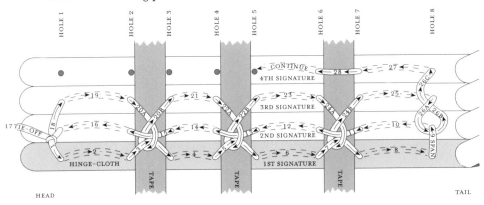

SEWING THE THIRD SIGNATURE BY LOCKING THE FIRST 3 TOGETHER. THE FOURTH AND FIFTH SIGNATURES ARE SEWN UNLOCKED, AS IN THE ILLUSTRATION ON THE FOLLOWING PAGE. THE SIXTH SIGNATURE LOCKS THE FOURTH AND FIFTH. THE LOCKING IS REFERRED TO AS *GROUPED GATHERED LAP-GROUP*[8].

SEWING THE THIRD SIGNATURE: The third signature and every signature divisible by three are sewn and locked with the previous two signatures:

19. Proceed on the inside towards the tail. Exit station (hole) 2.
Locking
20A. Drop down, lap over 2 previous stitches (steps 3 and 15), scoop under both.

20B. Come out on the back side and cross over. Climb and enter the third signature at hole 3.

21–24. Proceed to the next tape stations, exit and lock as before. Enter.

25. Proceed to the kettle station at the tail.

26A. Exit backward and link.

26B. Slip under to lock.

26C. Climb and enter the fourth signature.

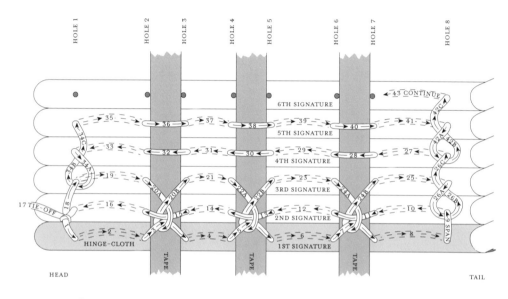

SEWING THE FOURTH AND FIFTH SIGNATURES: EXIT ON THE BACK SIDE OF THE TAPE, LAP AND ENTER ON THE FORWARD SIDE.

SEWING THE FOURTH AND FIFTH SIGNATURES:

27–41. Sew the fourth and fifth signatures without locking. Exit on the back side of the tape. Lap and enter on the forward side.

42. Form the kettle stitch: drop, link. Set on the sixth signature. Slip under to lock. Climb and enter the new signature.

REMAINING SIGNATURES: The sixth signature will be sewn locking the fourth and fifth with it. It is sewn in the manner of the third signature, except this time you are sewing from the tail to the head. If three more signatures are sewn, sew in the manner of the first three. See illustrations on the following page.

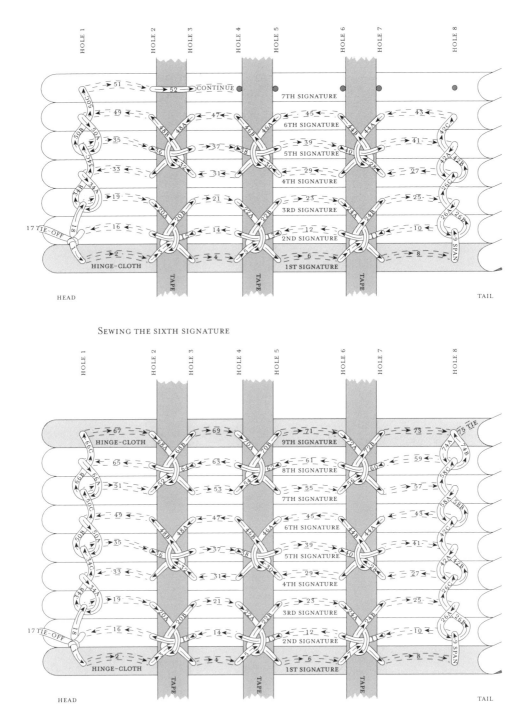

Sewing the sixth signature

GROUP GATHERED LAP-GROUP The sewing is completed, in incre-ments of 3 signatures.

Variation of the GROUP GATHERED LAP-GROUP

Fred suggests alternating which signature drops to lock with every
other tape. The odd-numbered tapes would be locked with the third,
sixth and ninth, as with the *Group Gathered Lap-Group* shown at the bottom of the facing page. The variation is on the even-numbered signatures. Here, the fourth, seventh and tenth signatures would be the
point to drop, gather lap and group, locking 3 signatures together.
Compare this, below, with the facing page.

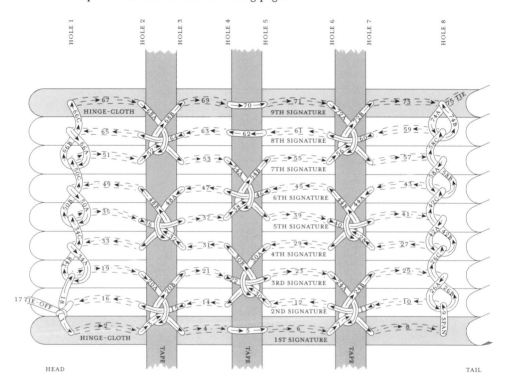

VARIATION OF THE GROUP GATHERED LAP-GROUP

FRED SUGGESTS STAGGERING THE LOCKING STITCHES. FOR THE THIRD, SIXTH AND
NINTH SIGNATURES, THE LOCKING TAKES PLACE ONLY ON THE ODD-NUMBERED
TAPES. THE EVEN-NUMBERED TAPES ARE LOCKED WHEN SEWING THE FOURTH AND
SEVENTH SIGNATURES.

COMPARE THIS SEWING WITH THE ONE ON THE PREVIOUS PAGE. IN THE PREVIOUS,
THERE IS A WEAK POINT BETWEEN THE THIRD AND FORTH SIGNATURES AND THE
SEVENTH AND EIGHTH.

FLAT FORWARD LOOP

The *Flat Forward Loop* can be sewn on a split flat support, such as a tape. It can be sewn on paired flat supports, such as vellum. Or, it can be sewn on split alum tawed thongs.

ODD-NUMBERED SIGNATURES

If you are splitting tapes or thongs, mark the height of the unsewn book block, centered on the back side of the support. Slit prior to sewing. When you exit hole 3, take the needle through the bottom of the slit. The part of the support that hangs below the first signature will show no slit.

EVEN-NUMBERED SIGNATURES

FLAT FORWARD LOOP DETAIL

Sew the book. Since the thread will swell the spine, the slit will not be quite long enough to sew the last one or two signatures. This is better than too long a slit. As needed, insert a thin bladed knife into the slit to extend the length of the slit just enough to sew the last signature. In this manner, the slit will not be visible on the support that extends above the final signature.

In sewing, exit the middle hole, wrap forward. Exit the hole back of the support. Enter the middle.

The sewing pattern at each support is the same as for a *3-Hole Pamphlet Sewing.*

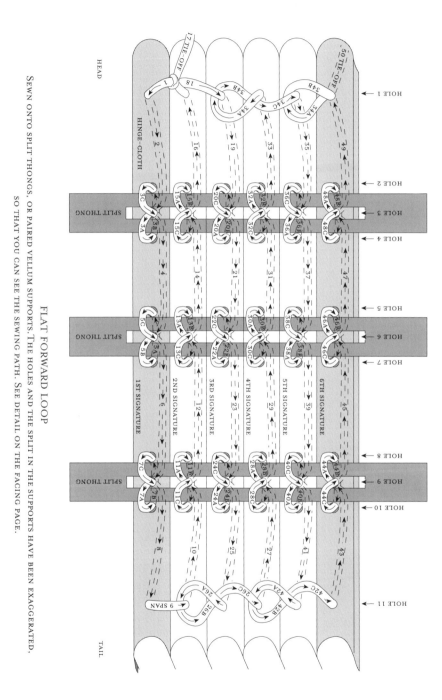

FLAT FORWARD LOOP

SEWN ONTO SPLIT THONGS, OR PAIRED VELLUM SUPPORTS. THE HOLES AND THE SPLIT IN THE SUPPORTS HAVE BEEN EXAGGERATED, SO THAT YOU CAN SEE THE SEWING PATH. SEE DETAIL ON THE FACING PAGE.

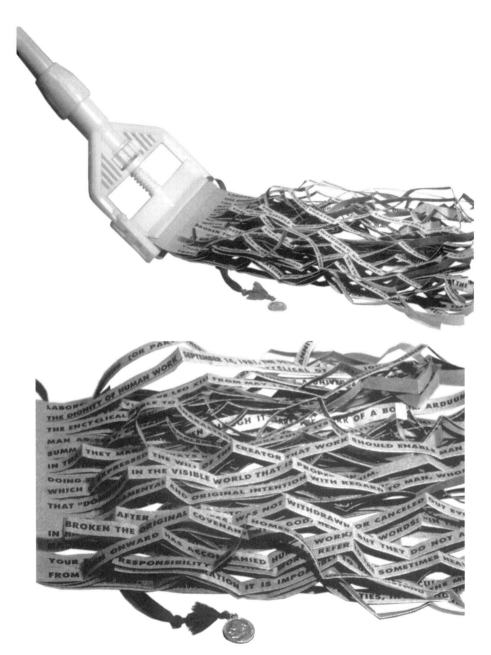

William Drendel, *Laborem Exercens-The Encyclical of John Paul II on Dignity of Human Work*, 1995. One-of-a-kind. 35.5 H (with handle 186 H) x 16.5 W x 9 cm. D. Collection of Judy A. Saslow.

WILLIAM DRENDEL, *JAPANESE FAN BOOK*, 1990. 19 X 19 X 6.5 CM. COLLECTION
OF RANDI RUBOVITS-SEITZ.

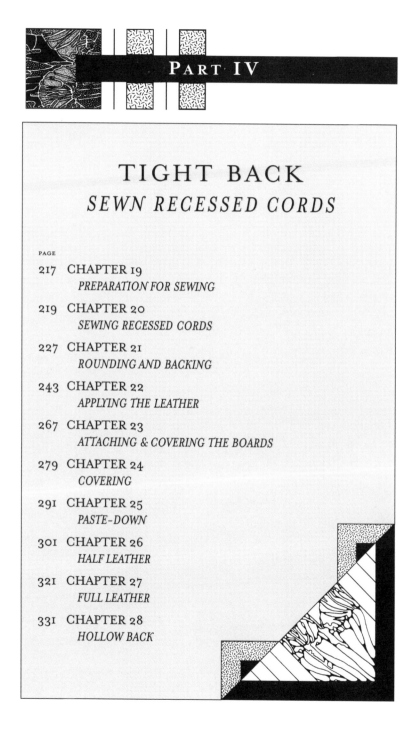

TIGHT BACK
SEWN RECESSED CORDS

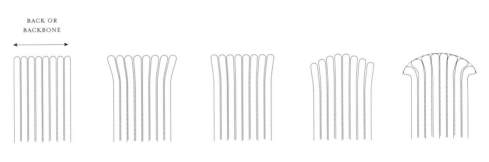

BACK OR
BACKBONE

FOLDED & GATHERED.
(F&G'S) JOGGED BUT
NOT YET SEWN.
SEE PAGE 77.

SEWN. SWELLING IS
CAUSED BY THICKNESS
OF THE THREAD.
SEE PAGE 220.

KNOCKED DOWN.
SIGNATURES WERE
COMPRESSED.
SEE PAGE 228.

ROUNDED. THE
BACKBONE WAS SHAPED
WITH A HAMMER.
SEE PAGE 230.

BACKED. A BONE
FOLDER WAS USED
FOR BACKING.
SEE PAGE 231.

PROGRESSION FROM ASSEMBLING THE BOOK BLOCK TO ROUNDING AND BACKING.
THE DEPTH OF THE BOOK BLOCK ON THE SPINE-EDGE IS REFERRED TO AS THE
BACK OR *BACKBONE*. AFTER THE BACK IS COVERED WITH LEATHER OR CLOTH, IT IS
REFERRED TO AS THE *SPINE*.

INTRODUCTION

The Tight Back is sewn Recessed Cords. The cords are then frayed. Super is wheat pasted across the *back* or *backbone,* extending approximately 1½" on each side of the back. The frayed cords are pasted to the super. The book block is then ready to be cased into boards.

In casing-in, the back of the book will be pasted to the spine-cloth which connects the two boards. The super, with cords attached will be pasted to the inside of the boards. Finally, the endsheets will be pasted to the inside of the boards.

A variation of the Tight Back is the Hollow Back, page 331. You might wish to read the description of both before beginning.

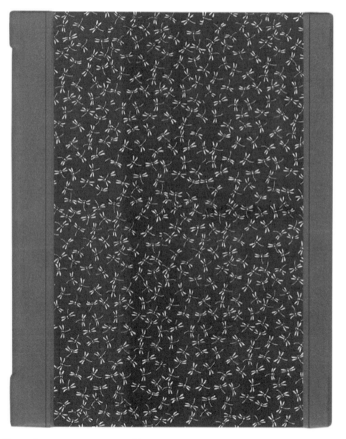

KEITH SMITH, HALF LEATHER TIGHT BACK BINDING SAMPLE. NOVEMBER 1997.
17.5 X 14 X 2.5 CM.

ORDER OF PROCEDURE FOR THE TIGHT BACK

Fred Jordan, quarter leather Tight Back binding sample. 1997.
20 X 14 X 2 CM.

19

PREPARATION FOR SEWING

Preparing the book entails folding the signatures, marking the stations, jogging, marking and sawing the sewing stations, setting up the sewing frame, if one is used and choosing the thread.

FOLDING THE SIGNATURES

The sheet must be folded down into signatures. Fred suggests the number of leaves be limited to an octavo. See *Folding Down a Sheet to a Signature,* pages 77 and 86.

Deckled paper must be folded in order to maintain the deckle on the foredge. If your paper has a deckled-edge, see *Deckled-Edge Signatures,* page 83.

JOGGING FOR MARKING THE STATIONS

Jog on the backbone, then on the head, not the tail. This makes for a smooth head to avoid plowing later on.

MARKING STATIONS ON THE BOOK BLOCK

Mark the stations. You might wish to review *Sewing Stations,* page 99 and *Marking the Stations,* page 102.

SAWING THE SEWING STATIONS

Jog, again, on the backbone, then on the head. Saw. See *Jogging for Sawing,* page 104, *Sawing for Recessed Cords,* page 106.

If you are re-sewing an old book, skip sawing and proceed to *Choosing the Thread.*

CHOOSING THE THREAD

Use an 18/3 Barbers 100% unbleached thread for sewing 8 to 10 signatures. For more elaborate information on thread and determining the amount of swell, see the Notes.[14]

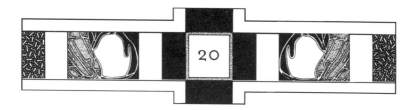

SEWING RECESSED CORDS

SEWING WITHOUT A FRAME: The Tight Back will be described as sewn with Recessed Cords. No sewing frame is necessary for sewing Recessed Cords.[15]

CORD SUPPORTS: For the Tight Back the cord supports are 6-ply flax or linen twine. A minimum of 5 cords across the backbone is used for strength in the book block and in attaching the boards.[16]

Length of the cords is determined by adding the thickness of the book block plus 4". This will allow 2" of cord to temporarily hang over towards the first and last page of the book block. *Example:* A book block which is 1/2" thick would need cords cut 41/2" long. Make the cords longer rather than shorter. You can always cut off the excess.

THREAD: Cut a length of linen thread that is easy to handle, about 4 feet in length. See *Thread,* page 107 and *Choosing the Thread,* page 217. You can add more thread with a *Weaver's Knot,* as described on page 111. Wax the thread by pulling it quickly across beeswax 2 or 3 times. Speed causes friction to melt the wax onto the thread.

Thread a dull needle so that one side of the thread is almost twice as long as the other. As you continue to sew, move the needle up, so you do not have to pull so much thread through the holes. This will save time.

FACE UP OR FACE DOWN: It makes no difference whether you sew from back to front, or front to back. See *Sewing on the Bench,* page 119 and *Back to Front, or Front to Back,* page 120.

In this manual, for uniformity, all sewings will be described sewing from the head to the tail. The head will always be on the left. The "first" signature refers to the *first to be sewn,* not whether it is the first in the book or the final signature.

SEWING

Tension must be correct in degree and uniform throughout. See
Tension in Sewing, page 121. Diagrams of this sewing will be shown using
5 cords. With the 2 kettle stations, there will be a total of 7 stations.

FIRST SIGNATURE: Place the first signature to be sewn on the table and
open to the center, keeping the bottom half on the table. This is
referred to as sewing *on the bench*. See page 119.

1. Start sewing from the outside of the signature to the inside,
through the sewing station at the head. Allow about 6" of thread to
remain on the outside.
Proceed on the inside along the fold towards the tail to the next station. Exit station 2 to the outside of the signature, on the back side
of the cord.
Since you are heading from left to right in sewing an odd-numbered
signature, the back side will be on the left.
2. Lap the cord, that is, pass over it. Re-enter station 2 on the forward side of the cord to the inside. Be careful not to pierce the cord.
3. Now that the needle has gone through two holes, you can adjust
the amount of thread dangling from the first station.
Pull in the direction of the backbone, towards the tail, until only
about 2" of thread remain hanging from the first station.
If you were to start with such a small amount extending, you might
accidentally pull the entire thread to the inside, when exiting the second station. This action will also pull the cord to the inside of the
signature, recessing it. Proceed to station 3.
4. Exit station 3 on the back side of the cord. Lap the cord and re-
enter station 3.
5. Pull the thread on the inside towards the tail and parallel with the
fold. This will pull the cord to the inside of the signature at station 3.
Proceed on the inside to station 4.
6. Exit station 4 on the back side of the cord. Lap the cord and re-
enter station 4.

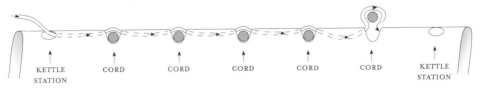

PATHWAY OF SEWING RECESSED CORDS: THE THREAD LAPS THE CORD AND RE-
ENTERS. TIGHTENING THE THREAD PULLS THE CORD INSIDE THE SIGNATURE.

7. Pull the thread on the inside towards the tail, pulling the cord to the inside of the signature at station 4. Proceed on the inside to station 5.

8. Exit station 5 on the back side of the cord. Lap the cord and re-enter station 5.

9. Pull the thread on the inside towards the tail, pulling the cord to the inside of the signature at station 5. Proceed on the inside to station 6.

10. Exit station 6 on the back side of the cord. Lap the cord and re-enter station 6.

11. Pull the thread on the inside towards the tail, pulling the cord to the inside of the signature at station 6. Proceed on the inside to station 7. Exit station 7. Close the first signature.

SECOND SIGNATURE: Place the second signature on top of the one just sewn and carefully align the two. Open the second signature to the middle.

12. Span (climb vertically). Enter station 7 of the second signature.

13. Proceed towards the head.

14. Exit station 6 on the *back side* of the cord. Since you are heading from right to left in sewing an even-numbered signature, the back side will be on the right. Lap the cord and re-enter station 6.

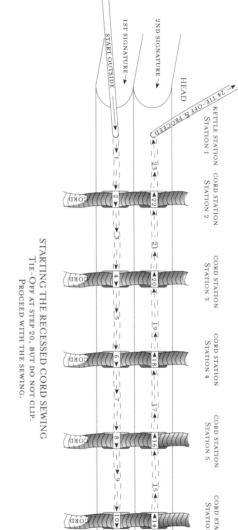

STARTING THE RECESSED CORD SEWING
TIE-OFF AT STEP 20, BUT DO NOT CLIP.
PROCEED WITH THE SEWING.

15–22. Proceed in this manner to sew the remainder of the cord stations for the second signature.

23. Proceed on the inside of the signature. Exit the first station at the head.

24A. Tie-off with the thread dangling from the first signature. See *Procedure for Tying a Square Knot,* page 109. After you have tied the square knot, do not clip the longer thread. Proceed with the sewing.

This is the only knot in the binding until either you run out of thread and must add more thread using a Weaver's Knot, or you complete sewing all signatures when a final knot is needed.

CAUTION: You may open the signature to check the tension on the inside, but only the top signature. Do not look through the remainder of the book until back has been pasted, or you will stretch the sewing.

In tightening the sewing, always pull the thread parallel with the backbone, in the same direction as you were sewing. Do not pull perpendicular to the back to avoid tearing the paper.

As each signature is sewn, press down on the top signature between the supports with your fingers, only. Do not use a bone folder. Gently tug on the cords, making sure there are no gaps in the cords. Be careful not to accidentally pull a cord completely from the sewing.

THIRD SIGNATURE: Set on the next signature. Open the new signature to the middle.

24B. Climb and enter the new signature at station 1.

25–35. Proceed on the inside towards the tail. Sew the cord stations in the same manner as the first signature. At the final cord, re-enter station 6. Proceed to the tail. Exit station 7 to form the first kettle stitch. See *Kettle Stitch,* pages 115–118.

36A. Drop to the inside. Link.

36B. Slip under to lock.

36C. Climb and enter the next signature.

REMAINING SIGNATURES: Sew the remaining signatures in the same manner. At the end of each row, form a kettle stitch. Link under the last two connected signatures. Slip under to lock, climb and enter the next signature.

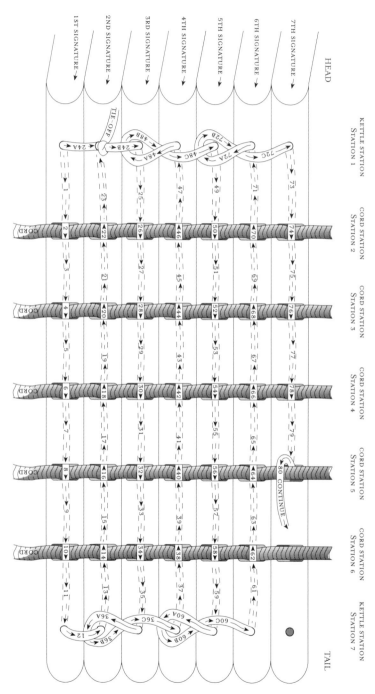

RECESSED CORD SEWING

Tie-Off at the end of the sewing with a half hitch. See page 114.
The diagram is the sewing path, not how the sewing will appear.
The cords will completely disappear, pulled inside the signatures.

FINAL TIE-OFF: If you have an odd number of signatures, the tie-off
will be at the tail. With an even number, the tie-off will be at the
head. After exiting the final station of the last signature, drop and
link. Re-enter the final kettle station to the inside of the signature.
This will form a partial kettle stitch, since you do not slip under to
lock, or climb to a new signature.

Tie-off the kettle stitch on the inside with a Half Hitch. This is
described on page 114. The sewing is complete.

NOTE: At the end of sewing every two or three signatures, pull up and
down on each cord, to check to see that they are free and have not
been snagged by the thread. Then, you will be sure that you can
tighten up the book block when *knocking down*, page 228, compressing
the signatures.

SLEEVE OF WAX PAPER: Wrap
the book block in an envelope of wax paper slightly
wider than the book block
and 2 1/2 times the height.
This is a moisture barrier
for attaching the boards. It
will also keep the book block
from getting soiled, or the
endsheets from getting
creased before they are protected with boards.

FRAYED CORDS

SUPER

SUPER AND
CORDS ARE ON
THE OUTSIDE
OF THE SLEEVE

MASKING TAPE

SLEEVE OF
WAX PAPER
TO PROTECT
BOOK BLOCK

Keep the cords on the outside of the wax paper sleeve.
After the super is added, it will also remain on the outside of the
sleeve of wax paper.

Start the wrapping on the front of the book block. Tape the wax
paper shut. The masking tape will be on the front. Lightly mark an
arrow pointing up on the masking tape. This is so when you case-in,
you will not attach the book block upside down.

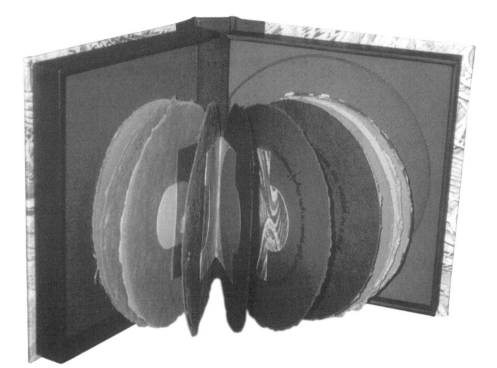

Elizabeth Steiner, *Moeraki Boulders*

"A circular book, in a clam box, designed and constructed by Elizabeth Steiner, in 1993. The book measures 140 mm. in diameter and the box 150 mm x 175mm. x 25 mm. The circular pages using commercial and hand made papers (banana, ginger and kniphofia) have torn edges and a binding structure which is a variation of one of Hedi Kyle's. The non-adhesive binding uses a variety of paste papers. The book may be extended to show all the pages and binding pieces in a continuous format. The box is also covered with paste paper. The text is hand written and photocopied. An edition of 5 signed and numbered."

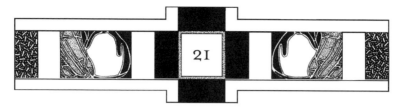

21

ROUNDING AND BACKING

FORWARDING: Forwarding is sewing, gluing the back, plowing, rounding and backing, forming the endbands and attaching and covering the boards. Forwarding is followed by finishing.

JOGGING

Jog the book on the back and the head. Carefully handle the book so that it does not go askew prior to pasting. Once it is pasted, no more jogging is necessary, as the back is fixed.

PASTING THE BACK

Extend the back 1/2" off the edge of the table. Lay a scrap of book board over the book block, about 1/2" *in from the edge* of the back. Boards cannot extend to the spine-edge because of swell in sewing. The weight would collapse the back to concave.

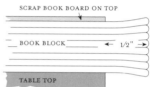

WEIGHTING THE BOOK BLOCK

Place a weight on top. The weight should extend to the edge of the cardboard, close to the spine-edge. The weight should not be so heavy as to distort the back to a concave or convex curve. The weight must be sufficient to keep the paste in the crevices from creeping onto the pages. A tight sewing is important.

Paste the back with wheat paste, applying a *thin* coat. The important thing is not to put on a thick coat, but to work the paste into the crevices between the signatures. This is the point at which you paste one signature to the next. Paste on the remainder of the back is not structural, only the paste in the crevices adheres one signature to the next. Allow the paste to dry.

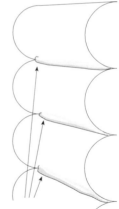

PASTE IN THE CREVICES
OF THE SIGNATURES

PASTE THE ENTIRE BACK. THE CRITICAL POINT IS TO SEAL THE CRACKS BETWEEN THE SIGNATURES. DO NOT LEAVE AN EXCESSIVE AMOUNT OF PASTE ON THE FOLDS.

Strokes are perpendicular to the surface, across the corrugated sur-face of the folds. This forces the paste into the cleavage, to the point where the signatures touch. This is the critical place for the adhesive, not the mountain peaks of the folds. In fact, many binders wipe off the paste on the folds, leaving it only in the cracks. Wipe with hori-zontal strokes to avoid removing paste from the cracks. Try to get as little paste on the cords as possible. Rounding is easier if the cords can slip. The book cannot be opened until the paste dries.

KNOCKING DOWN

Rather than compressing each signature with a bone folder as it is sewn, compression is done after the entire book block is sewn and pasted by *knocking down*. This is a bookbinding term for using a ham-mer on the book block. Knocking down gives an ideal amount of compression of the sewn signatures. Using a bone folder while sewing can result in excessive compression, making rounding and backing difficult, if not impossible.

The book block must be put in a press to knock down. If you do not have a press, place wooden boards on each side and tighten with *C*-clamps. Temporarily remove the sleeve of wax paper from the book block. It will be placed back on the book block after backing is com-pleted. Place the cords on the outside of the wooden boards, not between the top page and the board. If the cords were inside, they would indent the pages. Allow the spine-edge to extend 1" to 1½" from the top of the press.

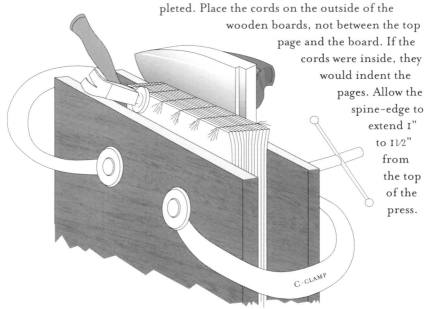

C-CLAMP

KNOCKING DOWN COMPRESSES THE AMOUNT OF SWELL ON THE BACK.

Place a flat stone or an old iron against the small amount of the final page of the book block. Rest the iron on the edge of the press. Tap the front of the book block with a hammer. Be careful not to kink the paper. Move the iron along the back of the book to support the area you are tapping on the front. This will compress the thickness of the back, reducing the swell from the added thread in sewing.

PLOWING THE FOREDGE: At this point, the foredge would be plowed prior to rounding and backing. Since no equipment is used in this manual, plowing the foredge has been eliminated.[17]

MEASURING BOARD THICKNESS

For this first book, use 4-ply rag mat board, *plus* the thickness of the leather.[18] The cover is the thickness of the book board, plus the thickness of the leather. See illustration at the right.

WHEN LEATHER IS PASTED, IT WILL SIT ON TOP OF THE BOARD.

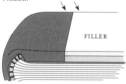

BOOK BOARD

Quarter leather on the spine will be turned in to the inside of the board. *Filler,* acid-free blotter, card or paper, which is the exact thickness of the leather will be pasted on the remainder of the inside of the board, butted to the leather turns-in. This is described on page 270.

FILLER WILL MAKE THE BOARD FLUSH WITH THE SURFACE OF THE LEATHER. THICKNESS OF THE COVER IS THE THICKNESS OF THE BOARD, PLUS THE FILLER.

FILLER

Mark the thickness of the cover, book board plus leather, on the outside of the first and last page of the book block with a sharpened #2 pencil. Lay the filler against the 4-ply mat board. Make one measurement of the combined thickness, using dividers or a pair of calipers. The thickness is marked along the spine-edge of the book. See illustration on the following page. The height and width of the boards will be measured later, page 243.

COVER IS THE THICKNESS OF THE BOARD, PLUS THE LEATHER.

Set one point of the divider on the spine near the head. Indent with the other point onto the first page. Do the same at the tail. Lay a straight edge on this front page, aligned with the two indentations.

DRAWING THE PENCIL LINE

Draw a thin pencil line completely across the height of the first page, determined by the indentation points. The line is parallel to the spine. Do the same for the last page of the book.

ROUNDING

Rounding is done with a hammer. If you round with a household hammer, the surface of the head is 1/4 the size of a binder's backing hammer. Care must be taken not to indent the shape of the hammer on the backbone.

With the book laying on a flat surface, place one hand on top of the book block with your thumb down the foredge to steady the book. Make striking glances with the hammer along the top of the back until it is at an oblique angle.

Turn the book block over. Keep pressure applied with the other hand on the foredge, maintaining the oblique angle. Strike the top of the back on this side, curving the back into an arch. This is referred to as *rounding*.

The purpose of rounding is to arc the backbone, setting the stage for backing, which will complete the shape of the arch and form the shoulders, the same size at the thickness of the boards. The boards will sit in the shoulder.

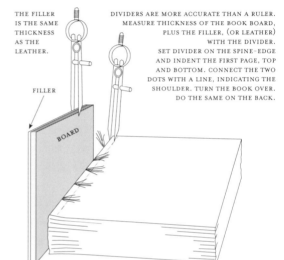

THE FILLER IS THE SAME THICKNESS AS THE LEATHER.

FILLER

BOARD

DIVIDERS ARE MORE ACCURATE THAN A RULER. MEASURE THICKNESS OF THE BOOK BOARD, PLUS THE FILLER, (OR LEATHER) WITH THE DIVIDER. SET DIVIDER ON THE SPINE-EDGE AND INDENT THE FIRST PAGE, TOP AND BOTTOM. CONNECT THE TWO DOTS WITH A LINE, INDICATING THE SHOULDER. TURN THE BOOK OVER. DO THE SAME ON THE BACK.

MARKING THE THICKNESS OF THE BOARD
ONTO THE BOOK BLOCK

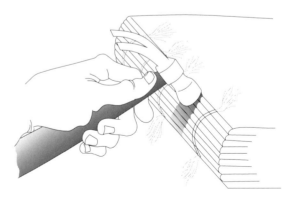

ROUNDING WITH A HAMMER

BACKING, CLAMPED BETWEEN BOARDS WITH *C*-CLAMPS

Traditionally, backing is done in a press with a backing hammer. The beginner will not have access to a backing hammer and a household hammer will not suffice because it has too small a head. It would tend to damaged papers on the back, or *backbone.*

Backing will be described using only a bone folder.[19] This is not a compromise. Recent attitudes are that a hammer unnecessarily damages the paper and the process can be done with a bone folder.[20]

Place backing boards on each side of the book block. If you make your own backing boards, they should be made of smooth, straight wood. The top edges of the boards are sawed to a 45° angle. The edge of the boards must be carefully lined up with the pencil lines, so that only the backbone and a board thickness of the book block extend above the backing boards.

CARE IN TIGHTENING THE PRESS: Extreme care must be taken as you clamp the press. You must be aware of two factors:

· Keep the edge of the beveled wooded boards on the pencil lines.

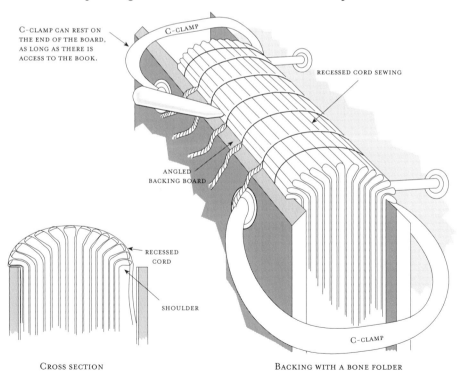

C-CLAMP CAN REST ON THE END OF THE BOARD, AS LONG AS THERE IS ACCESS TO THE BOOK.

C-CLAMP

RECESSED CORD SEWING

ANGLED BACKING BOARD

RECESSED CORD

SHOULDER

C-CLAMP

CROSS SECTION

BACKING WITH A BONE FOLDER

The book block may tend to pop up at one end or the other. As you tighten, make sure the edge of the wooden boards remains aligned with the pencil lines on both sides of the book block at the head and the tail.

· If you are using wooden boards with the *C*-clamps as a press, keep the top of the beveled edge boards even. Carefully tighten.

Paste the back with wheat paste and wipe off the excess to dampen and soften the paper. Do not get the paper too wet.

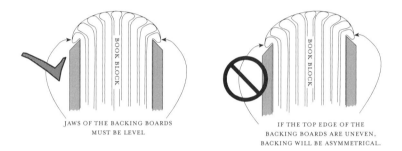

THE BEVELED WOODEN BOARDS MUST BE LEVEL. OTHERWISE, BACKING WILL RESULT IN AN ASYMMETRICAL ARC.

After wiping off the excess paste, wait a few minutes until the paste is tacky to proceed with the backing. If the backbone becomes too dry, re-paste.

USING A BONE FOLDER: Backing with a bone folder utilizes the same procedure as with the traditional hammer, but is accomplished more gently. The bone folder is pressed from the center of the backbone towards and beyond the spine-edge. Accomplish the backing in steps, or rows.

Begin by altering the first two signatures closest to the edge of the boards, on both sides of the back. Continue pressing along the next signature. Do the same on the other side of the back. Towards the center, lessen the pressure to almost none.

After backing creates the proper arc, backing is completed by creating a very smooth surface to the arched back. To do this, use the rounded edge of a rather thick bone folder. Rub back and forth across the arc of the backbone.

This will change the corduroy surface to almost completely smooth. This will be an ideal surface on which to apply the leather.[21]

PROPERLY
ROUNDED
AND BACKED

OVERLY
ROUNDED
AND BACKED

INSUFFICIENTLY
ROUNDED
AND BACKED

DENTED

ASYMMETRICALLY
ROUNDED
AND BACKED

ACHIEVING THE SHOULDER: Backing is not accomplished in a single attempt at altering the angle of the signatures. You must work from the outside in, then begin again. The extreme signatures at the spine-edge are difficult to form. With the first attempt, the end signatures will not lie flat against the acute angle of the thickness of the backing boards.

After more of the signatures are formed into the arch, go back and begin again. Now it will be easier to get the end signature to form against the backing boards. This creates an acute angle. That is, the angle from the sheet to the lip of the backbone is less than 90°. If the book does not back well, it may be due to forming the kettle stitches too tightly.

Once the book is removed from the press, this angle will spread to about 90° for a good fit against the depth of the book boards.[22]

 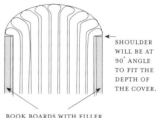

SIGNATURE
IS FORMED
TIGHTLY
AGAINST THE
BOARD.

SHOULDER
WILL BE AT
90° ANGLE
TO FIT THE
DEPTH OF
THE COVER.

BACKING BOARDS

BOOK BOARDS WITH FILLER
ON THE INSIDE OF THE BOARDS

ACHIEVING THE SHOULDER THE FIRST AND FINAL SIGNATURE ARE WORKED DOWN FLAT AGAINST THE BACKING BOARD. WHEN THE BOOK BLOCK IS REMOVED FROM THE PRESS, THE ANGLE OF THESE SIGNATURES WILL LESSEN TO APPROXIMATELY 90° TO FIT THE BOOK BOARDS.

FRAYING THE CORDS

Fraying the cords is done in the press. Since you are not going to lace-in the cords, cut each cord to 1" in length. Untwist each cord.

To untwist all the strands, run a bradawl through the cord many times. This will not only untwist strands, it will thin the cord by removing many strands. Fred speeds up the process using his short-toothed wire dog brush. This requires far fewer strokes to fray the cords. Clean out the brush periodically.

APPLYING THE SUPER

Place the sleeve of wax paper back onto the book block. Make sure it is slid back tight against the shoulder with the cords on the outside.

Super is a kind of stiffened gauze, sometimes referred to as *tarlatan, mull* or *crash.* It is applied to the back while the book is in the press. Super is used to reinforce the back and help attach the boards later.

Super will be pasted to the back now, but *not* pasted to the boards until later, on page 267, *Attaching the Boards.*

Width of the super is the width of the back plus 4". It will be centered on the back with 2" overhang on each side to attach the boards.

Height of the super does not run the full length of the back. With Fred's modifications, the super fills in the middle of the back.

For your first book, Fred suggests the following proportions of turns-in to height of the spine:
• For a 10" tall book block, leave 3⁄4" at the head without super and 11⁄4" at the tail without super. Cut the super to 8" tall.
• For an 8" tall book block leave 5⁄8" at the head and 11⁄8" at the tail without super. Cut the super to 61⁄4" high.

These will be the points where the leather will be turned in at the head and the tail. It is a matter of proportion and design, not structure. On your second book, you may want to experiment with the size of the turns-in, as they create a bulge on the spine. For proportion of the bulges to the height of the spine, see the drawings on page 46. The size of the bulges of the leather turns-in on the spine are determined at this point, as they are the same locations as the super. Lightly mark the point down from the head and up from the tail where the super will be positioned.

WIDTH OF THE SUPER IS THE WIDTH OF THE BOOK BLOCK
PLUS 4". THIS GIVES AN OVERHANG OF 2" ON EACH SIDE.

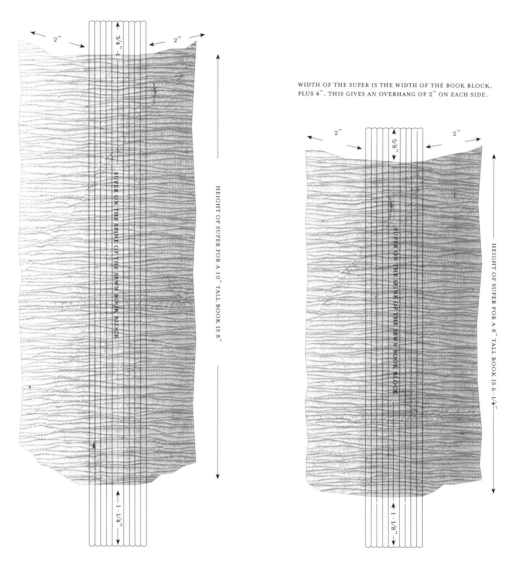

WIDTH OF THE SUPER IS THE WIDTH OF THE BOOK BLOCK,
PLUS 4". THIS GIVES AN OVERHANG OF 2" ON EACH SIDE.

2"   3/4"   2"   SUPER ON THE SPINE OF THE SEWN BOOK BLOCK   HEIGHT OF SUPER FOR A 10" TALL BOOK IS 8"   1-1/4"

2"   5/8"   2"   SUPER ON THE SPINE OF THE SEWN BOOK BLOCK   HEIGHT OF SUPER FOR A 8" TALL BOOK IS 6-1/4"   1-1/8"

MEASURING THE SUPER. WIDTH IS THE WIDTH OF THE BACK, PLUS 4". THIS GIVES
2" OVERHANG FOR EACH BOARD FOR ATTACHMENT. HEIGHT OF THE SUPER COV-
ERS ONLY PART OF THE BACK. IT DOES NOT COVER THE AREA OF THE TURNS-IN AT
THE HEAD AND TAIL. FOR A 10" BOOK, LEAVE 3⁄4" AT THE HEAD AND 1 1⁄4" AT THE
TAIL WITHOUT SUPER. FOR AN 8" BOOK, LEAVE 5⁄8" AT THE HEAD AND 1 1⁄8" AT THE
TAIL WITHOUT SUPER.

PASTING THE BACK: Do not paste the super. Apply paste to the back. Place the super on the back, lining up vertically with the marks near the head and tail and centering the super from left to right.

After one minute, apply a second coat of paste to the super, but only the part of the super which covers the back. Brush with your hand to adhere the super.

Allow the super to dry totally before proceeding.

WILLIAM DRENDEL, *CLAIRE'S BOW*, 1993. ONE-OF-A-KIND COPTIC SEWING. 15.2 X 27.2 CM. DIAMETER.

PLOWING

Old books *should never be plowed!* Plowing is a form of cropping the book. You do not have the authority to crop an old book and it reduces the value of the object.

Working on a new book, you might decide to plow the foredge and the tail, but the head of the book *should be plowed.* This prevents dust and grime from working down into the book and causing trouble. This is particularly a problem with soft paper.

PLOWING A NEW BOOK WITH A DECKLED EDGE: Usually, deckled edges are left on the foredge and the tail. Unless folios were compiled, the paper has been folded down into signatures with a fold at the head. The head is plowed. Fred believes that the head should always be plowed, even if it contains a natural deckle. This is to avoid dust creeping into the book.[23]

To fold down a deckled edge sheet into signatures, see *Deckled Edge Signatures,* page 83.

PLOWING THE HEAD AND THE TAIL: If you have a bookbinder's plow and a lying press, traditionally, you would plow the head and tail at this point. The foredge can be plowed prior to rounding. See page 229.

If you are not plowing, the surface of the head and tail will remain slightly uneven, rather than mirror smooth, as when plowed. The critical edge to be smoothed is the head. That is why you should always jog on the head, not on the tail. If you cut the signatures the same height and jog properly, your book will not need to be plowed.

However, if you wish to do edge decoration, it may be necessary to plow so that you can work on a smooth surface. Edge decoration should be done before the boards are attached. It would be the final step prior to attaching the boards. See *Finishing,* page 335.

ENDBANDS

"Headbands" is often used to refer to the sewing not only at the head, but also at the tail. The former is the *headband,* the latter, technically, is the *tailband.* In referring to both sewings, the proper term is *endbands.* A good book to examine on sewing endbands is titled *Headbands, How To Work Them.*[3] In this manual, we will not go into sewing endbands.

FAUX BANDS: Commercially manufactured faux endbands can be purchased in rolls from a binder's supply. They are generally available in red and white or black and white. They are cut to size and pasted at the head and tail.

Faux-sewn endbands are available by the roll. Two colors of thread are machine-stitched along the edge of 1/4" wide linen.

ROLLED CORE ENDBANDS: For the beginner, Fred prefers making rolled core endbands as a substitute for the more elaborate hand-sewn endbands. We prefer them over the commercially sewn faux endbands:

The rolled core endband is a common 19th century production shortcut. Instead of sewing endbands around a core, the core is merely covered with fabric.

FORMING THE CORE: The core is generally cord which has had wheat paste worked into it, then tightened and rolled on a hard surface and allowed to dry. Choose the diameter of cord in proportion to the size of your book.

Length of the core is a minimum of 2 1/2 times the thickness of the book block. This will be enough to make one headband and one tailband. After it is covered, it will be cut in half and trimmed to fit the round. One part will be use on the spine-edge at the head; the other half is for the tail.

However, you could cover a long length of cord. You could cut off the width needed for the endbands for each additional book.

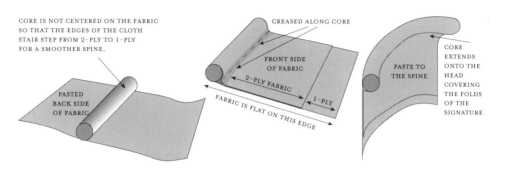

CORE IS NOT CENTERED ON THE FABRIC SO THAT THE EDGES OF THE CLOTH STAIR STEP FROM 2-PLY TO 1-PLY FOR A SMOOTHER SPINE.

PASTED BACK SIDE OF FABRIC

CREASED ALONG CORE

FRONT SIDE OF FABRIC

2-PLY FABRIC

1-PLY

FABRIC IS FLAT ON THIS EDGE

PASTE TO THE SPINE

CORE EXTENDS ONTO THE HEAD COVERING THE FOLDS OF THE SIGNATURE

ROLLED CORE ENDBANDS THE CORE IS COVERED WITH CLOTH. CREASE THE CLOTH AT THE BOTTOM EDGE OF ONE SIDE OF THE CORE ONLY. THIS ALLOWS THE CORE TO PROTRUDE ONTO THE HEAD.

Do not use rolled paper as a core. It will quickly crack and break in the center from flexing.

Do not use vellum as a core. It does not flex well and can easily rip the endband right off the book.

COVERING THE CORE: The core can be covered with a thin plain or patterned cloth.

Width of the fabric is the width of the core.

Height is approximately 2".

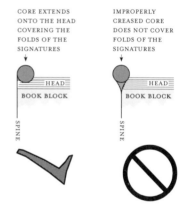

CORE EXTENDS ONTO THE HEAD COVERING THE FOLDS OF THE SIGNATURES

IMPROPERLY CREASED CORE DOES NOT COVER FOLDS OF THE SIGNATURES

HEAD

BOOK BLOCK

SPINE

HEAD

BOOK BLOCK

SPINE

Apply a coat of wheat paste to the fabric. Place the core off-center on the fabric, with the width of the core parallel to the width of the fabric. Fold the fabric over the core. Press firmly along the bottom edge of the core on one side only. This creased side will be pasted to the backbone, allowing the core to protrude over the book block.

GAIL FERRIS, TRADITIONALLY SEWN HEADBANDS. TITLES OF THESE BOOKS ARE
LISTED ON PAGE 418. GAIL FERRIS IS A BOOK BINDER AND BOOK COLLECTOR.

TOP OF FACING PAGE: JENNY HILLE, *LEXINGTON, MA*, 1992, *CLAREMONT, CA*,
1993. ALL AROUND HEADBAND BASED ON GREEK HISTORICAL STRUCTURES, SEWN
ON A COPTIC BINDING WITH WALNUT BOARDS. 16 X 10 X 3.5 CM. "INSTEAD OF
BEING LIMITED TO ITS TRADITIONAL LOCATION ON THE HEAD AND TAIL, THE
GREEK-TYPE HEADBAND IS CARRIED ALL AROUND THE EDGES IN A TOTALLY
CLOSED LOOP WHICH ENDS WHERE IT BEGAN. TIES-DOWN FORM A DESIGN ON THE
WALNUT BOARDS." GBW NEW ENGLAND EXHIBIT CATALOG, 1992.

JENNY HILLE IS A CONSERVATOR, AUTHOR AND BINDER. SHE IS THE AUTHOR,
ALONG WITH JANE GREENFIELD, OF *HEADBANDS, HOW TO WORK THEM*.

BOTTOM OF FACING PAGE: JENNY HILLE, GRECO-BYZANTINE MODELS BASED ON
MANUSCRIPTS AT THE BEINECKE, YALE UNIVERSITY.
BOUND 1989. 20.7 X 15 X 7 CM.

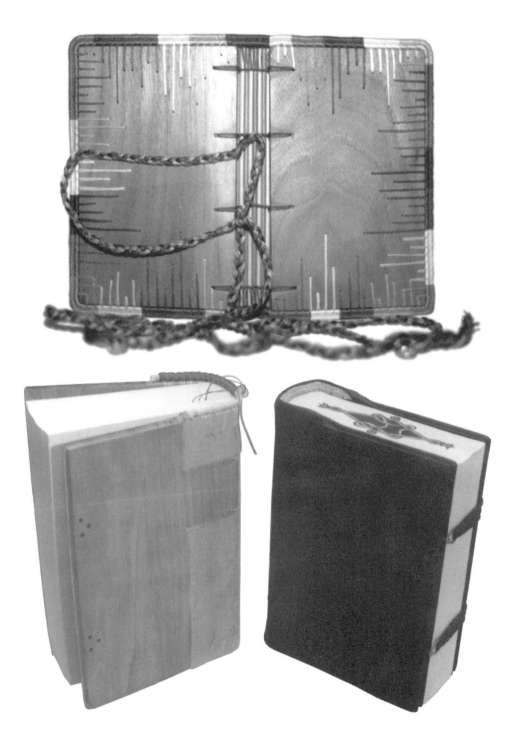

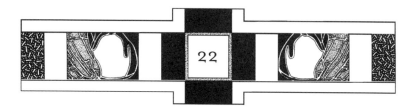
APPLYING THE LEATHER

MEASURING AND CUTTING THE BOARDS

Forwarding continues with covering and attaching the boards.
Measure and cut the boards in the traditional manner:

Height of the boards is measured after the endbands are attached to the
back of the book. To obtain the height of the boards, measure from
the bottom of the tailband to the top of the headband. Add 2 thicknesses of leather.

With the boards centered vertically, this will give an overhang
(square) of approximately 1⁄8" at the head and the tail. The *square* is
the distance the board extends beyond the book block. Traditionally,
the square is three thicknesses of board you are using as the covers.
The square should be the same on the foredge, head and the tail. It is
approximately 1⁄8".

The height of the board if no endbands are used is the height of the
book block plus 1⁄4". This will give an overhang of 1⁄8" at both the
head and the tail. However, I would strongly recommend using endbands; it dresses up the binding with very little effort.

For this first book, a 9" tall book block is suggested. That would
require boards approximately 93⁄8" high, depending on the diameter
of the endbands.

Width of the board is the distance from the shoulder to the foredge of the
book block, plus the overhang of about 1⁄8" to 3⁄16".

Measure the height of the boards first. Make sure the overhang on
the foredge is the same or slightly more than that for the head and
the tail.

The foredge overhang is traditionally 11⁄2 thicknesses of board. This
equal amount of protrusion along the head, foredge and tail is
referred to as the *square of the book*.

Fred often increases the amount of overhang, based on what proportion is pleasing to the eye. A larger overhang gives a border on the inside of the boards when the book is opened. This can be decorated. See pages 354, 355.

Set the board securely against the shoulder of the book block. Center the board by looking at the board with the book block in front of it. That way, you can see the overhang at the head and tail as well as the foredge.

Mark the board where the super ends at the head and tail.

SANDING THE BOARDS: Cut and sand the boards. The boards are sanded on the outside only. Sand only enough to remove the sharp edge from the head, tail and foredge.

Cut the filler which will go on the inside of each board. It must be the exact thickness of the leather and the same measurements as the boards. Like the boards, the grain must be parallel with the spine. Set aside filler until needed, page 270.

CUTTING AND PASTING PAPER ACROSS THE BACK

Set aside the two separate and notched cover boards. Place book block in standing press with the backbone facing up. Allow 1/2" of the book block to be above the edge of the press. If you do not have a press, use 2 wooden boards with C-clamps.

Paper will be pasted to the backbone and sanded. Cut 80 lb. Superfine or other smooth acid-free paper, to fit on the back. Grain of the paper should be parallel with the spine.

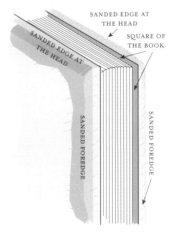

Height of the paper extends from the core of the headband to that of the tailband.

Width of the paper is the width of the back.

Paste the paper and apply to the back over the super. Lightly rock a bone folder across the spine paper to make a smooth surface. Smash any ridges on the back, if necessary, by rubbing with a bone folder. Allow to dry totally overnight.

SANDING THE HEAD, TAIL AND FOREDGE OF THE BOARDS

SANDING THE SPINE-PAPER

Cut the sand paper less than the height of the backbone. This is so that you are not constantly sanding over the endbands, as you sand up and down the backbone, as well as across, in a shoeshine manner. Use fine grit sandpaper.

The purpose of sanding is to lightly remove the ridges of the paper. The light sanding will leave one half sheet thickness or less of the paper on the mountain peaks. Most of the thickness of the pasted on paper goes into the crevices.

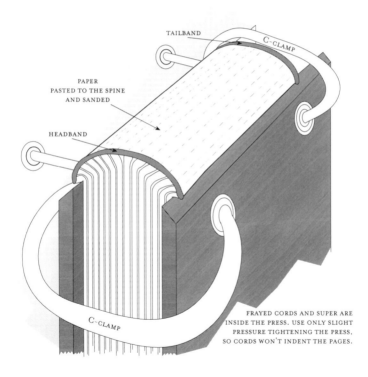

TAILBAND

C-CLAMP

PAPER
PASTED TO THE SPINE
AND SANDED

HEADBAND

C-CLAMP

FRAYED CORDS AND SUPER ARE
INSIDE THE PRESS. USE ONLY SLIGHT
PRESSURE TIGHTENING THE PRESS,
SO CORDS WON'T INDENT THE PAGES.

PAPER IS PASTED ON THE BACK AND ALLOWED TO COMPLETELY DRY. IT IS SANDED UNTIL MOST OF THE PAPER IS REMOVED, EXCEPT IN THE CREVICES. IT ACTS AS A FILLER, MAKING A VERY SMOOTH BACK. THIS MAKES AN IDEAL SURFACE FOR THE LEATHER.

CAUTION: Be careful not to sand through the super or the cords. Sand only enough to make a smooth backbone.

If the back is not smooth, even though you have sanded off most of the paper, you will have to add a second piece of paper. Cut the paper. Paste it and apply over the first paper. Allow to dry thoroughly. If you try to sand paper which is only dry on the surface, it will roll off when you attempt to sand.

Once the corrugation disappears, the back will be smooth and a proper foundation for the leather. Even if two layers of paper are required, the end result is only a half thickness of paper on the mountain peaks of the signatures. More than that would affect the opening of the book. Layers of paper across the back would stiffen the action of opening the book.

KEITH SMITH, *STRUCTURE OF THE VISUAL BOOK*, BOOK NUMBER 95, BOUND QUARTER LEATHER TIGHT BACK, DECEMBER 1997. DECORATIVE PAPER ONLAY ON LEATHER, WITH PRINTED PAPER INLAID WITH MARBLED PAPER ON THE BOARD. 23.2 X 16 X 2.5 CM.

NOTCHING THE BOARDS

Since the leather will not be pared, it is necessary to notch the boards to allow the leather to fit flush with the edge of the boards.

HORIZONTAL NOTCHES FOR QUARTER LEATHER: Notches along the head and tail at the spine-edge will allow quarter leather to be flush with the boards when the leather is pulled around to the inside of the board when making the turns-in.

For this first quarter leather binding, we suggest the leather extend onto the board 1½". On your second or third binding, you might play with the proportion of leather to decorative paper on the side-covers. See *Proportion on the Board,* page 43.

Width of the horizontal notches for this first book will measure 1½"in from the spine-edge on each board. Mark the depth on the board, in from the spine-edge towards the foredge at the head and tail. Mark the back board in the same manner. See diagrams pages 248 and 249.

Depth of the notch is the same as the thickness of the leather. Use calipers to measure the leather. Mark the other board in the same manner. See illustration on the following page.

VERTICAL NOTCHES: Notches along the spine-edge will keep the leather between the boards flush with the spine-edges of the boards. This will allow the board to sit tight against the shoulder, even at the point of the leather turns-in at the head and the tail.

Height of the vertical notches lines up with the super on the book block. Lay the sewn book block on the front board. Line up the spine-edges of the book and board. Mark on the board where the super begins down from the head and where it ends up from the tail. Remove the book block. Mark the depth of the notches on the board in from the spine-edge.

For quarter leather, neither the horizontal nor vertical notches will solve the problem of the edge of the leather which is on on the board, the full height on the outside of the boards. The outside of the board will be built up with a filler to *almost* the level of the leather. See illustrations on pages 271, 272 and 275.

Half leather is discussed beginning on page 301. The chapter on full leather begins on page 321.

MARKING AND CUTTING THE NOTCHES: Mark all the notches to be cut prior to cutting any. That way you will be sure to make the vertical notches measured from the head or tail, rather than from the cut of the horizontal notches. Check the grain of the board to make sure it runs up and down, that is, parallel to the spine.

1. Mark the boards 1½" in from the spine-edge at the head and tail. Draw a pencil line connecting the dots. This will be the position the leather extends onto the boards.

2A, 2B. At the head, measure down on the board the thickness of the leather. Draw a horizontal line 1½" long, from the spine-edge to the vertical pencil line. Do the same at the tail for this board as well as the other board.

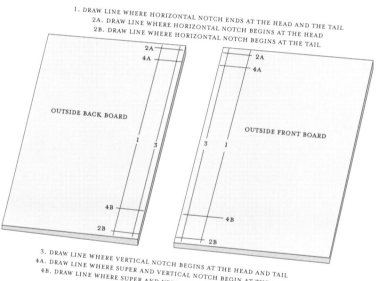

DRAWING THE NOTCHES FOR QUARTER LEATHER, HORIZONTAL NOTCHES ARE MADE AT THE HEAD AND THE TAIL, SINCE THE LEATHER WILL NOT BE PARED.

WIDTH: (LINE 1) OF NOTCH EXTENDS ON THE BOARD THE SAME DISTANCE AS THE TRIMMED LEATHER. IN THIS DESCRIPTION, THE NOTCH EXTENDS 1½" ON THE BOARD.

DEPTH: (LINES 2A AND 2B) NOTCH IS THE THICKNESS OF THE LEATHER.

VERTICAL NOTCHES ARE CUT ALONG THE SPINE-EDGE. LINE 4A EXTENDS DOWN FROM THE HEAD, TO WHERE THE SUPER BEGINS ON THE SPINE. THE OTHER LINE, 4B, UP FROM THE TAIL TO THE SUPER.

DEPTH: (LINE 3) OF THE VERTICAL NOTCHES IS THE THICKNESS OF THE LEATHER.

3. Mark the boards in from the spine-edge at the head and tail the thickness of the leather. Draw a pencil line connecting the dots. This is for the vertical notch, permitting the turns-in to fit flush with the boards.

4A. Draw a horizontal line, down from the head the thickness of the leather. The line is 1⁄2" long from the spine-edge to pencil line 3.

4B. Do the same at the tail for this board as well as the other board. Mark the boards lightly with a pencil, with an arrow pointing up. This may help prevent placing them on upside down. The notches must line up with the super.

Cut out the notches using a sharp knife and a straight edge. Set the book block and boards aside.

NOTCHES FOR QUARTER LEATHER

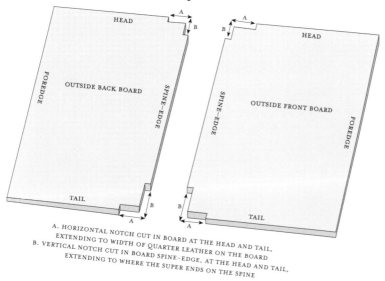

A. HORIZONTAL NOTCH CUT IN BOARD AT THE HEAD AND TAIL, EXTENDING TO WIDTH OF QUARTER LEATHER ON THE BOARD
B. VERTICAL NOTCH CUT IN BOARD SPINE-EDGE, AT THE HEAD AND TAIL, EXTENDING TO WHERE THE SUPER ENDS ON THE SPINE

CUTTING THE NOTCHES: USE A STRAIGHT EDGE AND THIN BLADED KNIFE TO CUT THE NOTCHES.

A. THE HORIZONTAL NOTCHES ELIMINATE THE NEED TO PARE THE SHORTER SIDE OF THE LEATHER, WHICH TURNS-IN AT THE HEAD AND THE TAIL. IT WILL ALLOW THE TURNS-IN TO BE FLUSH WITH THE BOARDS, ON THE EDGE OF THE BOARD.

B. THE VERTICAL NOTCHES KEEP THE LEATHER FROM BULGING INTO THE GAP BETWEEN THE BOARDS. THE LEATHER TURNS-IN ARE FLUSH WITH THE SPINE-EDGE OF THE BOARDS.

CUTTING FILLER FOR INSIDE OF THE BOARDS: Thickness of the board plus the filler was measured earlier, page 229, in order to determine the shoulder in rounding and backing. At that time, scrap filler was used. With the boards cut to size, you can now measure and cut the filler. The filler must be in place, between the book board and the book block, in order to measure the quarter leather.

Height of the filler is the exact height of the boards. It cannot be trimmed later, as you would risk cutting the leather.

Width of the filler is the width of the boards or slightly wider. The width can be trimmed off later if it extends beyond the board.

Cut the filler, but do not notch. Set them on the inside of the boards. The filler will be trimmed and pasted to the board later, described on page 270.

All the Tight Back and Hollow Back bindings described in this manual have filler pasted to the inside of the book block.

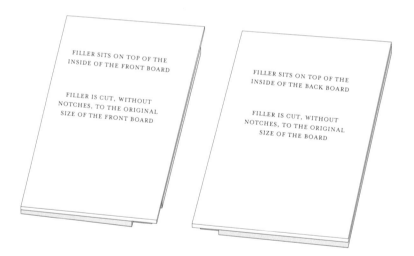

CARD, PAPER OR BLOTTER IS CHOSEN AS FILLER. ON THE INSIDE OF THE BOARDS, FILLER MUST BE THE SAME THICKNESS AS THE LEATHER. GRAIN OF THE FILLER MUST BE PARALLEL WITH THE SPINE. CUT FILLER TO THE SIZE OF THE BOARDS, BUT DO NOT CUT NOTCHES IN THE FILLER AT THIS TIME. LAY FILLER ON TOP OF EACH BOARD.

THE FILLER WILL GO BETWEEN THE BOARD AND THE BOOK BLOCK. THEY WILL NOT BE PASTED TO THE BOARD UNTIL LATER, INCREASING THE FINAL DEPTH OF THE BOARD. SEE PAGE 275.

PREPARATION AND PASTING THE LEATHER

Pasting the leather will be described for quarter leather.[24]

Height of the leather is measured with a string, a scrap of paper or a cloth measuring tape. It is set *into the horizontal notches*:

Hold the scrap paper above the board at the spine-edge. Set the end of the paper at the bottom of the vertical notch on the spine-edge. Proceed up the board, around the horizontal notch as you go around the head. The scrap paper proceeds down the board along the spine-edge to the tail. Wrap the paper around, in the horizontal notch. Proceed up the board to the end of the vertical notch at the tail. Mark the ending point on the scrap paper. Lay the paper flat and measure. This will give you the height of the leather.

If your book block is 9" tall and the turn-in at the head is 3⁄4" and the turn-in at the tail is 11⁄4", the leather should be about 11⁵⁄8" in length.

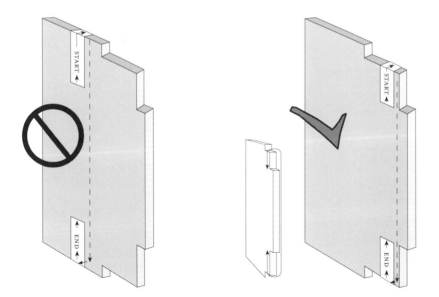

HEIGHT OF THE LEATHER IS MEASURED WITH STRING OR SCRAP PAPER. START AT BOTTOM OF THE VERTICAL NOTCH AT THE HEAD, GO OVER THE HORIZONTAL NOTCH AT THE HEAD. PROCEED TO THE TAIL. GO AROUND HORIZONTAL NOTCH. PROCEED TO TOP OF THE VERTICAL NOTCH AT THE TAIL.

WIDTH OF QUARTER LEATHER: Width of the leather for this first bind-ing is suggested to extend 1½" onto both boards. The leather will be cut slightly wider so that it can be trimmed.

Width of your leather will be the width of the back, plus 3¼". This will give slightly more than 1½" of leather extending onto the boards.

For your next binding, you might try using less, or more leather extending onto the board. The horizontal notches will be adjusted accordingly. See *Proportion on the Board,* page 43.

NOTE: Height of leather *cannot be trimmed.* It must be cut to fit the ver-tical notches exactly.

Width of the leather must be cut wider than needed. It is important that the leather extend beyond the horizontal notches along the head and tail. The width *must be trimmed* to the precise end of the horizontal notches.

MARKING THE LEATHER: Mark the leather on the inside with a pencil and straight edge. Grain of the leather should be parallel with the spine of the book. Try to economically position the strip to be cut, keeping in mind possible use for the remainder of the hide.

Cut the leather with a thin bladed knife on a sheet of zinc or a self-seal mat.

MARKING THE GUIDE POINT ON THE LEATHER: On the outside of the leather, a pencil dot will be placed as a guide to aid in positioning the pasted leather onto the backbone and boards. See drawing on the facing page.

Along the length of the leather, measure 1¼", plus 1⁄16", in from the tail. Place a pencil dot on the edge of the outside of the leather for a guide. This will help to fit the turn-in precisely in the vertical notch at the tail.

MARKING THE PENCIL LINES ON THE BOARDS: Set the filler aside. Set both boards into the hinge. The spine-edge of the boards sits against the shoulder of the book block, except for the vertical notches. The book block is protected by a sleeve of wax paper. The super and cords are on the outside of the sleeve.

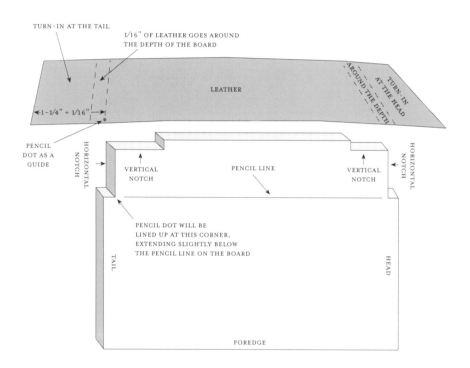

MARK THE GUIDE POINT WITH A PENCIL ON THE LONGER EDGE OF THE LEATHER, IN FROM THE TAIL.

THE BOOK WILL BE IN THE PRESS AS SHOWN IN THE ILLUSTRATIONS ON PAGES 255 AND 256. ONLY ONE BOARD AND THE LEATHER IS SHOWN ABOVE AND ON THE FOLLOWING PAGE FOR DESCRIPTIVE PURPOSES.

IN ADDITION, THE LEATHER WILL BE FOLDED, BUT NOT CREASED, IN HALF DOWN THE LENGTH.

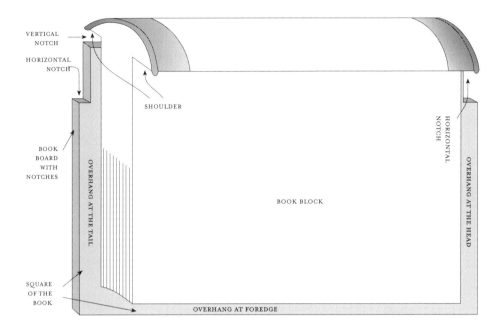

CENTER THE BOOK BLOCK ONTO THE TWO BOARDS. VIEW IS FROM THE BOOK TOWARDS THE BOARD. THIS WILL SHOW YOU SIMULTANEOUSLY THE OVERHANG AT THE TAIL, FOREDGE AND HEAD. THE SPINE-EDGE OF THE BOARD RESTS ON THE SHOULDER, EXCEPT AT THE VERTICAL NOTCHES.

OVERHANG: The overhang of the board at the head and tail should be equal.

Place the book in the press or in wooden boards with *C*-clamps.

Be careful not to move the position of the boards. Allow the spine-edge of the book to protrude above the jaws of the press farther than the leather will extend. This will give space to place the leather onto the boards. Tighten the press.

Center the unpasted leather on the spine laterally. Mark the boards vertically with a pencil line where the leather extends onto the boards. Set the leather aside.

PASTING THE LEATHER: Paste the leather. For a reminder of how to paste, see Chapter 4, *Paste,* page 54. It is important to read *Pasting Leather,* page 59. For light leather, mist the good side of the leather with water to prevent capillary action from going through.

Lay the leather on your pasting surface with the inside up. Apply a generous amount of wheat paste. Hold the leather in the center and brush outward. Continue pasting. The leather will cling in position without further holding. Paste again. Periodically, pick up the edge of the leather to examine the other side. When the outside of the leather is totally wet, paste has saturated the leather and it is ready to apply to the spine and the boards.

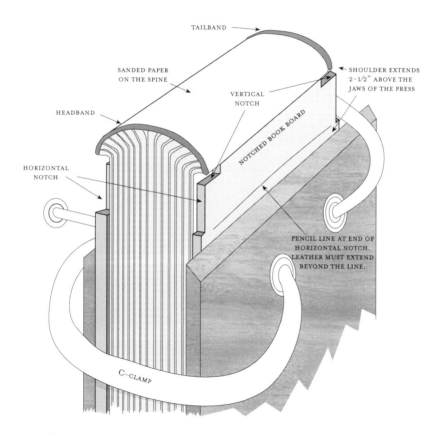

THE BOOK BLOCK WITH BOARDS IS PLACED IN THE PRESS. QUARTER LEATHER IS POSITIONED AND THE BOARDS ARE MARKED WITH A PENCIL LINE WHERE THE LEATHER EXTENDS ON THE BOARD. THE LEATHER IS REMOVED TO BE PASTED.

APPLYING THE LEATHER: Pick up the leather; fold it in half along the length, but do not crease. Open the leather and position the soft crease above the center of the spine. Before lowering it, align the pencil dot with the edge of the board at the tail. See *Marking the Guide Point on the Leather,* page 252. Set the leather on the spine.

CRITICAL: Make sure the leather *extends beyond the pencil lines* on the boards. Otherwise, the leather will not fill the notch along the head and tail. It must extend beyond, so that you can trim it later.

With just a little pressure, press from the spine to the boards with both hands. This will stretch and tighten the leather onto the spine and the boards for good contact. Press the leather along the boards to make sure it adheres in all areas.

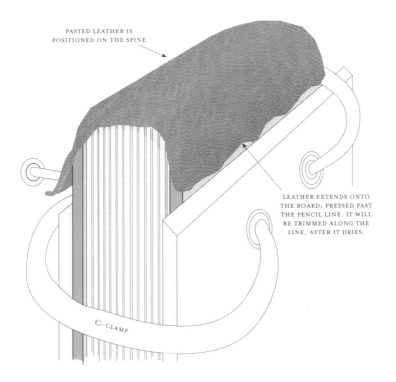

PASTED LEATHER IS
POSITIONED ON THE SPINE

LEATHER EXTENDS ONTO
THE BOARD, PRESSED PAST
THE PENCIL LINE. IT WILL
BE TRIMMED ALONG THE
LINE, AFTER IT DRIES.

C–CLAMP

THE PASTED LEATHER IS CENTERED ON THE SPINE. PRESS ON THE SPINE WITH THE
PALMS OF YOUR HANDS IN A DOWNWARD MOTION ONTO THE BOARDS. THIS WILL
PULL THE LEATHER TAUT ACROSS THE SPINE AND ONTO THE BOARDS.

When pressing, always use the heel of your hands. Fingers place extreme pressure in local areas and can stretch the leather unevenly. Lack of pressure between the fingers causes the leather to distort.

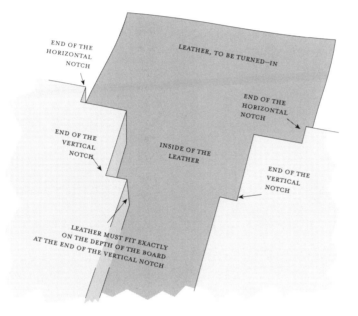

REMOVE THE BOOK BLOCK. TURN IN THE LEATHER AT THE HEAD. MAKE SURE THE LEATHER COMES EXACTLY TO THE END OF THE VERTICAL NOTCH ON THE EDGE OF THE BOARD. IF IT IS TOO LONG, TRIM THE LEATHER TO FIT.

AFTER MAKING THE TURN-IN AT THE HEAD, DO THE SAME AT THE TAIL.

MAKING THE TURNS-IN AT THE HEAD AND TAIL: Remove the book from the press and lay it on the table. Work fairly quickly since the paste will be drying out, but do not rush. Open the front cover so that both boards and spine are flat on the table. Remove the book block.

Make the turn-in at the head. Make sure the leather extends *exactly* to the end, but not beyond, the vertical notch on the *edge* of the board. If it extends beyond, open the leather and trim it to fit precisely. The leather can and should extend beyond the pencil line on the surface of the board. Leather can easily be trimmed on the surface, but not on the depth, of the board. See illustration above and page 264.

Use a table knife or a sharp bone folder to press the leather against the edge of the board. It is important that the leather crisply stair steps from the plane of the spine, up the depth of the board, onto the plateau of the board. I find it easier to use two, rather than one bone folder. After I form the crease along the edge of one board, I hold it in place while I crease the edge of the remaining board. Otherwise, the leather has a tendency to pull away from the edge of the first. See *Walking the Bone Folder,* page 156.

Make the turn-in at the tail in the same manner.

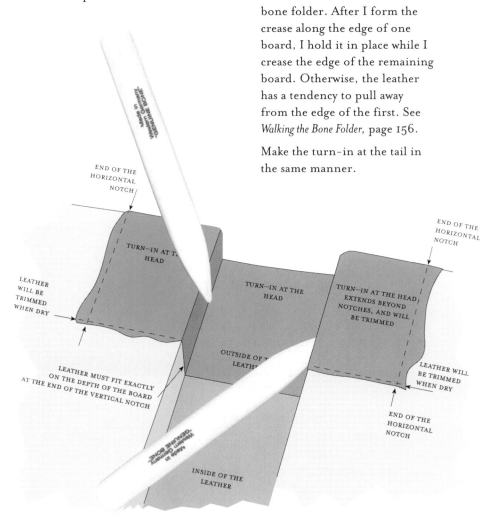

END OF THE HORIZONTAL NOTCH

TURN-IN AT THE HEAD

LEATHER WILL BE TRIMMED WHEN DRY

END OF THE HORIZONTAL NOTCH

TURN-IN AT THE HEAD

TURN-IN AT THE HEAD EXTENDS BEYOND NOTCHES, AND WILL BE TRIMMED

OUTSIDE OF THE LEATHER

LEATHER MUST FIT EXACTLY ON THE DEPTH OF THE BOARD AT THE END OF THE VERTICAL NOTCH

LEATHER WILL BE TRIMMED WHEN DRY

END OF THE HORIZONTAL NOTCH

INSIDE OF THE LEATHER

THE TURNS-IN MUST BE PRESSED SHARPLY AGAINST THE DEPTH OF THE BOARDS. USE A TABLE KNIFE OR SHARP BONE FOLDER TO PRESS THE LEATHER ALONG THE SPINE-EDGE OF THE BOARD. HOLD THAT IN PLACE WITH ONE BONE FOLDER, WHILE YOU FORM THE OTHER EDGE. THIS WILL KEEP THE FIRST FROM PULLING OFF THE DEPTH OF THE BOARD.

THE TURN-IN AT THE HEAD AND TAIL MUST FIT EXACTLY INTO THE VERTICAL NOTCHES ON THE EDGE OF THE BOARD. ONLY THE SURFACE OF THE BOARD CAN BE TRIMMED.

PLACING BOARDS BACK ON THE BOOK BLOCK: Re-paste the leather between the boards that will touch the spine. Paste that portion of the turn-in of the leather which will sit against the book block.

1. With the boards open, place the book block onto the back board.

2. Make sure the shoulder fits snugly against the edge of the board, not on top of the board. Center the book block so that the overhang at the head and tail are equal.

3. Close the front board, making sure the board goes over and fits into, the shoulder. The edge of the bare board, as well as the edge of the leather turn-in, must sit against the shoulder. Place a sheet of wax paper between the board and the sleeved book block.

1. SIT BOOK BLOCK CENTERED ON BACK BOARD.

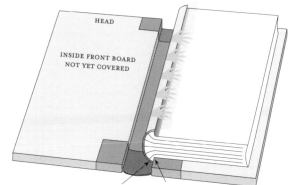

HEAD

INSIDE FRONT BOARD NOT YET COVERED

2. SHOULDER RESTS ON THE DEPTH OF THE BOARD, WHICH HAS BEEN EXAGGERATED FOR ILLUSTRATION.

2. BOARD FITS INTO SHOULDER.

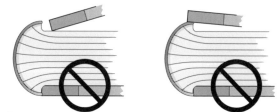

3. INCORRECT POSITIONING OF TOP BOARD, IN CLOSING THE COVER.

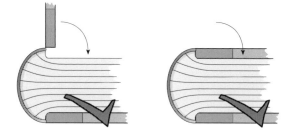

3. BRING TOP BOARD UP TO BEGINNING OF SHOULDER. CLOSE THE COVER. MAKE SURE THE DEPTH OF THE BOARD FITS INTO THE SHOULDER.

Looking along the edge of the boards at the head and the tail, the leather should extend beyond the notches. Part of the leather is trimmed now and part after it is dry:

• The leather is trimmed on the edges of the boards while it is wet. This is a *T*-shaped cut on the edge of each board, at the head and the tail.

• The leather is trimmed along the pencil line on the front and back boards after the leather is totally dry.

MAKING THE T-SHAPED SLITS ON THE EDGE OF THE BOARDS: The *T*-shaped cut relieves pressure. This will permit pressing the leather on the edges of the boards, along the full extent of the horizontal notch. This must be done while the paste is still wet:

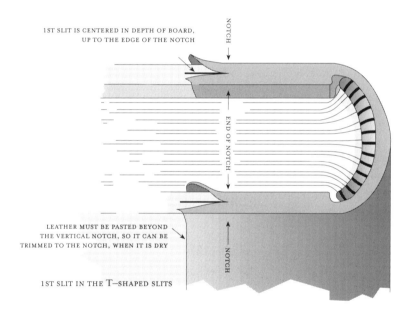

WHILE THE LEATHER IS WET, SLITS ARE MADE ON THE DEPTH OF THE BOARD:

1. THE LEATHER EXTENDING BEYOND THE HORIZONTAL NOTCHES IS SLIT TO THE NOTCH. THE FIRST SLIT IS PARALLEL WITH THE BOARD, CENTERED ON THE DEPTH OF THE BOARD.

2. THE SECOND SLIT IS AT RIGHT ANGLE TO THE FIRST, ALONG THE ENDING OF THE HORIZONTAL NOTCH. THE SLITS ARE *T*-SHAPED.

THIS RELEASES PRESSURE, SO THE TURN-IN AROUND THE BOARD CAN BE PRESSED INTO THE NOTCH, FLUSH WITH THE BOARD.

FIRST SLIT: Stand the book upright. With a sharp, thin bladed knife, slit the leather *on the edge* of the board. Start on the bare board where the leather ends. Place the knife centered on the edge of the board. Carefully slit the leather up to where the notch begins. Do this on both boards, at the head and the tail. See illustration on the facing page.

SECOND SLIT: The second part of the *T*-shaped slit will be perpendicular to the first. It is cut along the exact edge of the end of the horizontal notch. See illustration below.

With a bone folder, press the leather flush with the board, along the notch, to the ends.

The leather *must* extend the full length of the horizontal notch. Do this on both boards at the head and the tail. When the leather is dry, it will be trimmed along the pencil line to the depth of the board, where the notch ends.

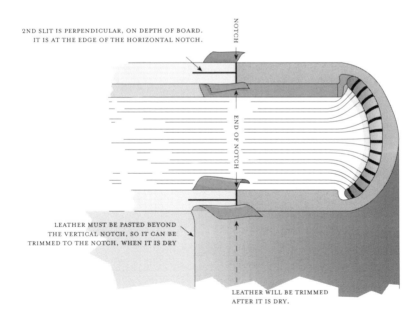

MAKING THE SECOND SLIT OF THE *T*-SHAPED SLITS. THIS IS DONE WHILE THE LEATHER IS WET. NOW A BONE FOLDER CAN PRESS THE LEATHER TURNS-IN FLUSH WITH THE EDGE OF THE BOARD,

SHAPING THE LEATHER: Place the book back in the press with the leather above the jaws of the press.

Roll the flat surface of a dull stainless steel table knife or bone folder along the spine. Use the back edge of the knife, at an angle tightly against the turn-in, to make a crease on the spine at the depth of the turn-in. This crease will be only on the spine. It will not extend onto the boards. Do this at both turns-in. It gives a finished look. The turns-in are no longer a bulge, but now design. *Form follows function.*

Remove the book from the press. Cut two scrap sheets of Davey book board larger than your book. Sandwich the book between the two sheets of book board and place it on a table. Set a weight on top. It can be several books or something that weighs about two pounds. Leave the book under the weight to dry overnight.

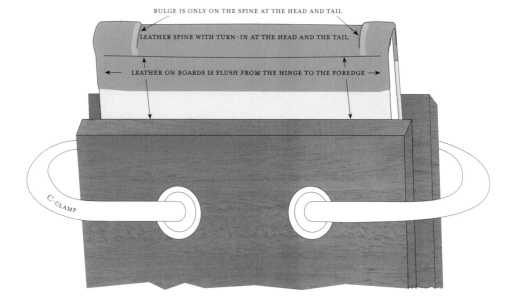

WHILE THE BOOK IS IN THE JAWS OF THE PRESS, THE SPINE IS SHAPED WITH A BONE FOLDER. A CREASE IS MADE AT THE EDGES OF THE TURNS-IN TO GIVE DEFINITION TO THE LEATHER.

FIRST OPENING: The next day, open the front board with your fingers holding the super against the book block. Fan the board open and closed a few times. Do the same with the back board. This creases the leather at the hinging point between the spine and the board.

TRIMMING THE LEATHER ON THE OUTSIDE OF THE BOARDS: On the front board, lay a straight edge on top of the good leather, not on top of that to be trimmed off. Line up the straight edge with the horizontal notch, under the *T*-shaped cuts at the head and tail. This will position the straight edge at the end of the horizontal notches on the boards and directly above the pencil line, which has been covered by the leather. The cut will be from the end of the notch at the head to the end of the notch at the tail. See illustration on page 264.

Before making the cut, test the position of the straight edge by setting the blade into the slit at the head and then at the tail, to make sure the straight edge is precisely lined up.

If the knife wanders, it will veer into the excess leather rather than into the good leather. Trim off the excess leather on this board.

Cut only deep enough to sever the leather. Hold the straight edge in place while you peel off the trimmed leather from the surface of the board. In that way, if any part of the leather has not been cut completely through, you can make a second cut over the first.

When the excess leather has been peeled away, turn the book over. Trim the leather on the other board in the same manner.

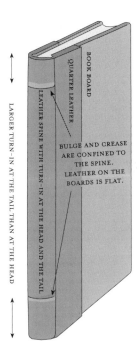

THE TURNS-IN CREATE A BULGE ON THE SPINE, DOWN FROM THE HEAD AND UP FROM THE TAIL. THE BULGE AND THE CREASE BOTH END AT THE HINGE. THEY DO NOT EXTEND ONTO THE BOARDS, WHICH ARE TOTALLY FLAT.

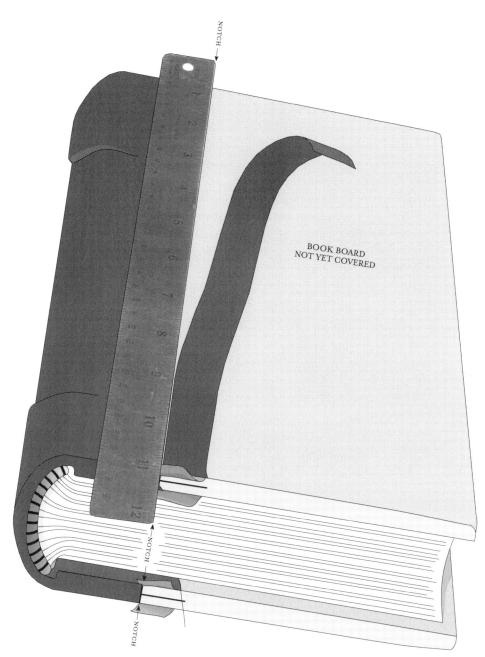

NOTCH

BOOK BOARD
NOT YET COVERED

NOTCH

NOTCH

TRIM THE LEATHER ON THE OUTSIDE OF THE BOARDS AFTER THE LEATHER IS
TOTALLY DRY. LAY A STRAIGHT EDGE ON THE GOOD PART OF THE LEATHER. SET
THE BLADE IN THE SECOND PART OF THE *T*-SHAPED SLIT AT THE HEAD TO CHECK
ALIGNMENT OF THE STRAIGHT EDGE. SET THE BLADE IN THE SLIT AT THE TAIL.
ONLY THEN TRIM AWAY THE EXCESS LEATHER, WHICH WILL BE ALONG THE PENCIL
LINE ON THE BOARD. HOLD STRAIGHT EDGE IN PLACE WHILE YOU PEEL OFF THE
EXCESS LEATHER, IN CASE YOU HAVE TO MAKE A SECOND CUT.

TRIMMING THE LEATHER ON THE INSIDE OF THE BOARDS:

The turns-in will have to be cut square, so that you can easily fill in the remainder of the board with filler to bring the surface up to the height of the leather.

1. Open the front board. Place a support under the board so that it is level and firm for cutting. Line up a straight edge with the end of the notch at the head and the tail.

2. Trim away the excess. Leave straight edge in place until you peel away the excess leather.

3. Since leather stretches, you may have to make horizontal cuts on the surface of the board to trim the leather along the end of the vertical notches, parallel with the top edge of the board.

Trim the turns-in on the back board.

CAUTION: Do not try to cut leather on the depth of the board, or you will risk cutting through the leather to the outside of the spine. That is why the turns-in were cut to fit exactly to the end of the vertical notches, as explained in the last paragraph on page 261.

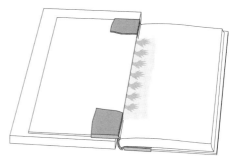

1. PLACE A SUPPORT UNDER THE OPENED BOARD TO GIVE SUPPORT FOR CUTTING.

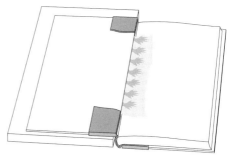

2. LINE UP STRAIGHT EDGE WITH EDGE OF HORIZONTAL NOTCH. MAKE A VERTICAL CUT TO TRIM OFF THE EXCESS OF THE TURNS-IN AT THE HEAD AND TAIL.

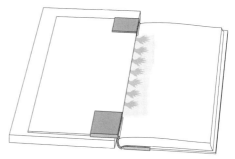

3. MAKE HORIZONTAL CUTS TO TRIM OFF THE EXCESS OF THE TURNS-IN AT THE HEAD AND TAIL.

TRIM THE VERTICAL AND HORIZONTAL EDGES OF THE LEATHER ON THE INSIDE SURFACE OF THE BOARDS. LEATHER ON THE DEPTH OF THE BOARD CANNOT BE TRIMMED.

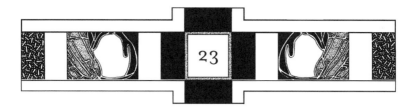

ATTACHING THE BOARDS

Before adding the boards, you may wish to color the edges of the book block. See *Edge Decoration,* page 369.

The leather and the cords and super secure the book block to the boards. They act as hinge, permitting the covers to open and close.

CUTTING A NOTCHED PIECE OF CARD: Prior to pasting, a scrap piece of card must be notched. This will be used to insure the boards will remain open while drying. Take a scrap of card. Cut two notches the thickness of the book board, 3" apart.

TESTING THE NOTCHED PIECE OF CARD PRIOR TO PASTING: Test the notched card by opening the covers until they are behind the book block. Set the scrap of card on the top edges of the boards. Set the scrap of card aside.

The super and cords will be pasted to the boards with both boards opened and turned back. If leather hinges had been pared, the boards would be turned back until parallel. Since you are not paring leather, the boards will be turned back until the foredges of the boards are approximately 3" apart.

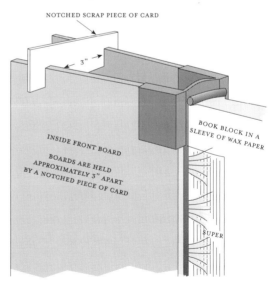

TEST THE NOTCHED SCRAP OF CARD TO MAKE SURE IT WILL HOLD THE BOARDS OPEN, PRIOR TO PASTING DOWN THE SUPER AND THE CORDS.

PASTING DOWN THE SUPER AND CORDS

The hinges are set, attaching the boards by pasting down the super
and cords, rather than lacing-in the cords. This is done prior to
adding the filler, so the filler can absorb some of the bulge of the
pasted down cords and super.

1. Open both the front and back covers. Slip one or two books, or
scrap book board under the front cover as a foundation while pasting.

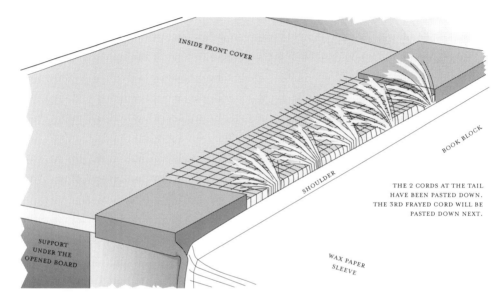

INSIDE FRONT COVER

BOOK BLOCK

SHOULDER

THE 2 CORDS AT THE TAIL
HAVE BEEN PASTED DOWN.
THE 3RD FRAYED CORD WILL BE
PASTED DOWN NEXT.

SUPPORT
UNDER THE
OPENED BOARD

WAX PAPER
SLEEVE

SUPER AND CORDS ARE PASTED TO THE FULLY EXTENDED BOARDS.

2. Paste the edge of the book boards between the turns-in. Do not
paste the edges of the turns-in on the edge of the board, which is
referred to as the *joint* or *hinge*.

Paste the area of the inside book board at the spine-edge between the
turns-in. Pull the super up the edge of the board, onto the pasted
surface. Paste the super again, up the edge of the board and with
strokes from the spine-edge towards the center of the board. This
will pull the super taut onto the board.

Run a bone folder along the edge of the board to make sure the super
is tight in the hinge. Take care not to get paste on the leather turns-
in. If you do, immediately wipe off the leather with a paper towel.

3. Put down all cords with wheat paste. Paste over the top of each. Flatten with a bone folder and flair them out. This is to avoid bulk. Check hinge again to make certain the cords and super are tight against the edge of the board.

4. Place a sheet of wax paper on the pasted board. Place

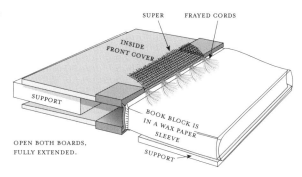

OPENING THE BOARDS FULLY IN PREPARATION FOR PASTING THE CORDS AND SUPER TO THE BOARD.

A BOOK OR SCRAP BOOK BOARDS ARE PLACED BETWEEN THE COVERS AS A FOUNDATION FOR PASTING.

two scrap book boards on the table. Carefully turn the book over, keeping the front board fully open. Lay the book block on the two book boards as a support to protect the hinge. Place a support on top of the opened front board. Open the back board so it rests on the support as shown above.

Paste down the super and cords on this board in the same manner.

Remove the support between the boards, careful to keep the boards fully open at all times. Insert the notched scrap of card onto the two boards to maintain their open position. Check the hinge to make certain the super and cords are adhered to the edge of the board.

Stand the book up to dry with the notched scrap of card on the boards. Place a scrap card under the foredge of the book block to steady it. Allow the boards to air dry thoroughly.

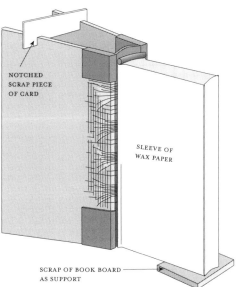

AFTER PASTING BOTH SIDES, STAND UPRIGHT WITHOUT CLOSING THE BOARDS. LOCK THE BOARDS WITH THE NOTCHED CARD. PLACE A SUPPORT UNDER FRONT EDGE OF BOOK BLOCK TO STEADY IT. ALLOW TO DRY OVERNIGHT.

ADDING FILLER TO THE BOARDS

Filler is paper, card or blotter used to fill in the board so that it is level with the leather.

MARKING AND CUTTING THE SHAPE OF THE INSIDE FILLERS: Both inside and outside fillers must be pre-cut before any pasting.

Open the boards and remove the loose sheets of wax paper. Place the filler you have cut the same size as the boards on the inside of the board.

Height of the filler should be the height of the board and the grain of the filler must be parallel to the spine.

Width is the width of the board or wider. It can be trimmed after it is pasted to the board.

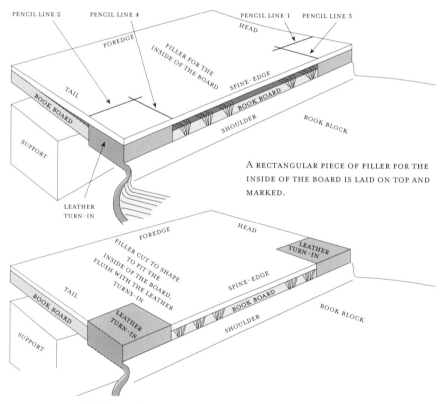

A RECTANGULAR PIECE OF FILLER FOR THE INSIDE OF THE BOARD IS LAID ON TOP AND MARKED.

THE FILLER IS LAID ON A CUTTING SURFACE AND THE CORNERS AT THE SPINE-EDGE ARE CUT OUT SO THE FILLER FITS THE REMAINDER OF THE BOARD AND IS FLUSH WITH THE LEATHER TURNS-IN. ON THE INSIDE OF THE BOARD, THE FILLER IS PRECISELY THE SAME THICKNESS AS THE LEATHER.

1. Square up the filler with the top edge and the spine-edge of the board. Place a pencil dot on the filler at the head where the leather meets the board. Do the same at the tail. Place a straight edge at the two dots. Draw a line down from the head just past where the turn-in ends.

2. Draw up from the tail just past where the turn-in at the tail ends.

3. Place a dot on the filler along the spine-edge near the head, where the turn-in ends. Measure the distance from the head to that dot. At the foredge, measure down from the head the same distance. Place a straight edge at the two dots. Draw across, from the spine-edge just past the turn-in, intersecting the vertical pencil line number 1.

4. Place a dot on the filler along the spine-edge near the tail, where the turn-in ends. Measure the distance from the tail to that dot. At the foredge, measure up from the tail the same distance. Place a straight edge at the two dots. Draw across, from the spine-edge just past the turn-in, intersecting the vertical pencil line 2. See page 270.

Set the other filler on the inside of the other board. Mark it in the same fashion. Keep track of which filler goes with which board.

Cut out the corners of the filler at the pencil lines using a straight edge and a sharp knife.

MARKING AND CUTTING THE OUTSIDE FILLERS FOR QUARTER LEATHER: On the *outside* of the board, for quarter leather, the filler should be 1/2 to 2/3 the depth of the leather. The reason the filler must be thinner than the leather on the outside of the board is that the edge of the leather will be indented. If the filler were the same thickness as the leather, you would have to indent the entire filler, as well as the small part of the leather. This would be almost impossible.

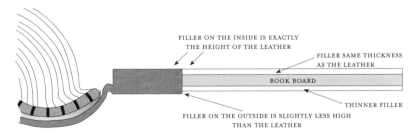

FILLER ON THE INSIDE IS EXACTLY
THE HEIGHT OF THE LEATHER

FILLER SAME THICKNESS
AS THE LEATHER

BOOK BOARD

THINNER FILLER

FILLER ON THE OUTSIDE IS SLIGHTLY LESS HIGH
THAN THE LEATHER

CROSS-SECTION ILLUSTRATES THE THICKNESS OF *THE FILLER FOR THE OUTSIDE OF THE* BOARD FOR QUARTER OR HALF LEATHER BINDINGS. ON THE OUTSIDE OF THE BOARD, THE FILLER IS SLIGHTLY *LESS* THAN THE THICKNESS OF THE LEATHER. TO TEST, RUN YOUR FINGER ACROSS THE FILLER ONTO THE LEATHER.

Lay a scrap filler on the outside of the board, butted against the leather. Run your fingers from the filler across the adjoining leather to test the depth. You should have a slight step up to the leather.

This is so the decorative paper which will be pasted over the filler and the indented leather will be slightly less than the remainder of the leather.

This will keep the edge of the paper from being scraped when the book is pulled from the bookshelf. See the illustration: *Indenting Quarter Leather*, page 275.

Height of the filler for the outside of the board should be cut the height of the board or slightly taller and trimmed after it is pasted to the board. Grain is parallel to the spine.

Width of the filler extends from the vertical edge of the quarter leather to the foredge. Cut the filler slightly wider than necessary. It can be trimmed to the exact width after it is pasted to the board.

LEATHER SITS ON TOP OF BOOK BOARD.

LATER, FILLER WILL BE PASTED ON THE BOARD, TO BRING SURFACE ALMOST TO THE LEVEL OF THE LEATHER.

BOOK BOARD NOT YET COVERED

FILLER WILL BE PASTED ON THE BOARD TO BRING IT UP TO ALMOST, BUT NOT QUITE, THE LEVEL OF THE LEATHER.

FILLER ON THE OUTSIDE OF THE BOARD IS USED ONLY WITH QUARTER OR HALF LEATHER.

FILLER

FILLER

FILLER IS CUT FOR THE OUTSIDE OF THE BOARDS, PAGE 271.

IT IS PASTED ON THE BOOK BOARD TO BRING THE SURFACE ALMOST TO THE LEVEL OF THE QUARTER LEATHER. THIS ELIMINATES THE NEED FOR PARING LEATHER, TO FEATHER IT OUT ONTO THE SURFACE OF THE BOARD.

FRED ALSO USES THIS PROCEDURE FOR MAKING CLAMSHELLS, PARING ONLY THE LEATHER TURNS-IN AT THE HEAD AND THE TAIL.

PASTING DOWN THE INSIDE AND OUTSIDE FILLERS ONTO ONE BOARD:
Open the front board. Place a support under the board so that it is
level and firm for pasting and attaching the filler. This is so you can
press down firmly.

Only one board is pasted at a time. Paste the board, not the filler.
Take care not to get paste on the leather turns-in. If you do, immediately wipe it off with a paper towel. Be generous with the paste. Wait
a moment and give a second, even coat.

Set the filler onto the inside of the board. Take care to make the filler
fit tightly against the leather turns-in, for as tight a seam as possible
and so it lines up with the spine-edge of the board. Add a sheet of
wax paper between the board and the sleeved book block. Close the
board. Lay a scrap book board on top of the book and allow to sit for
5 minutes, until the inside filler is securely adhered. This will keep it
from shifting.

Remove the scrap board. Turn the book over with the outside of this
board facing up. Place the book block on a scrap board to protect the
shoulder. Trim the inside filler along the head, foredge and tail.
This must be done before pasting the filler on the outside of the
board. It would be difficult to trim both fillers at once. Add a sheet
of wax paper between the board and the sleeved book block. Close the
board. Paste filler onto the outside of this same board.

In applying the paste, stroke
from the leather out, over the
edges of the board out, over
the corners. Never stroke from
the head, tail or foredge
inward. That would cause paste
to go under the board onto the
book block. The wax paper
sheet is a precaution. Be generous with the paste. Wait a
couple minutes and apply a
second, even coat of paste.

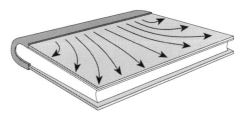

DIRECTION OF PASTING IS FROM THE LEATHER,
OUT. NEVER PASTE FROM THE FOREDGE, IN.

Set the filler onto the board. Take care to butt the filler tightly
against the leather for as tight a seam as possible. Hold the filler at
the seam. With the other hand, stroke outward to flatten the filler
and to remove any excess paste towards the head, tail and foredge.

Lay a scrap book board on top of the outside filler on the closed book. The scrap board should extend just to the quarter leather. Allow to sit for 5 minutes, until the outside filler is securely adhered. Open the board and trim away any excess filler. Close the board.

PASTING DOWN THE FILLERS ONTO THE REMAINING BOARD: Turn the book over. Lay the book on a scrap book board which extends just to the quarter leather.

Paste the filler for the inside, then the outside of the second board in the same manner as the first.

When completed, set the book on heavy book board which extends to the leather. Place another scrap board on top, butted against the leather, covering the filler. Add a weight which covers the scrap board. The weight should not extend over the leather. Allow to dry overnight, or indent quarter leather, then dry overnight.

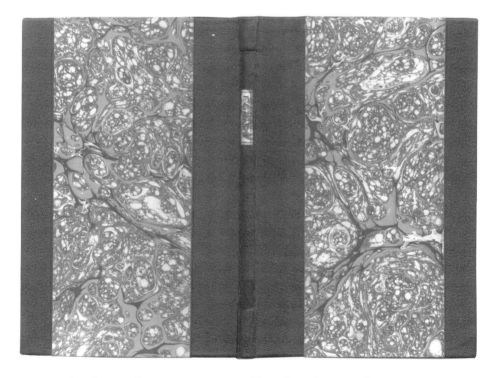

FRED JORDAN, *EXAMPLE 4*, HALF LEATHER TIGHT BACK. JUNE 1998. LASER PRINTED PAPER LABEL ON THE SPINE. ANOTHER VIEW OF THIS BOOK IS ON PAGE 16. 23.6 X 16.2 X 1.4 CM.

INDENTING QUARTER LEATHER

Indenting keeps the boards flat while the pasted fillers are drying, as well as indenting the leather.

Decorative paper on the outside of the board must overlap quarter or half leather. The leather is indented the amount of the overlap. The compressed area of the leather permits the overlapping paper to sit flush with the leather.

Keeping all surfaces of the outside of the boards flush is important. Pulling the book off the shelf could snag the edge of the paper, if it sits higher than the leather.

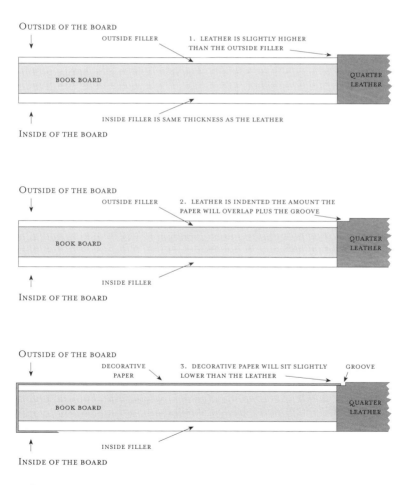

INDENTING QUARTER LEATHER, SO THE DECORATIVE PAPER WILL SIT FLUSH.

INDENTING A LINE: The leather should be indented 1/8" in from the filler to allow room for the decorative paper and groove, as illustrated on the previous page.

Before the 1/8" surface of the leather is indented with boards and a press, a line is drawn on the leather with a dull table knife to line up the indenting board. This is not a cut, but an indentation.

With a straight edge and stainless steel table knife that is not sharp, indent the edge of leather on the outside of the board from head to tail. The indentation is 1/8" in from the filler.

INDENTING THE SURFACE: Cut two pieces of book board for indenting the leather. Masonite or wood can be used also. The indenting will be done on the outside of both covers at once.

INDENTING A LINE ON THE LEATHER, 1/8" IN FROM THE FILLER WITH A STRAIGHT EDGE AND A STAINLESS STEEL TABLE KNIFE

Wood should not be used as an indenting board on white leather. It may stain the leather.

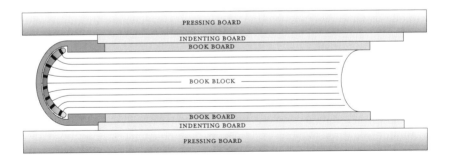

INDENTING THE SURFACE OF THE LEATHER: THE PRESS MUST NOT TOUCH THE BOOK, BUT APPLIES PRESSURE ONTO THE BOARDS USED FOR INDENTING. LEAVE THE BOOK IN THE PRESS FOR 2 OR 3 HOURS.

IF YOU DO NOT HAVE A PRESS, USE A HEAVY WEIGHT ON TOP OF THE PRESSING BOARD, OR C-CLAMPS, AS SHOWN ON THE FACING PAGE.

Height of the indenting boards is the height of the cover plus 1/2". This will insure the leather will be indented from head to tail. The board must have a straight clean cut edge.

Width of the indenting board extends beyond the outside filler plus 1/8" onto the leather which will be indented.

If the leather is not damp from pasting, dampen with a cotton ball and water. Get as little water on the board as possible. Do not dampen the leather on the inside of the board.

1. Lay one pressing board on the table. Lay one indenting board in place on top of the book. Make sure the board is even with the line drawn on the leather. Flip over the book with the indenting board in place and set it on the pressing board. Position the spine of the book extending beyond the pressing board, so that the indenting board is close to the edge of the pressing board. This will permit the use of *C*-clamps for indenting.

2. Add the other indenting board on top the book, lined up.

3. Place a pressing board on top.

Indent the boards either with a press, using *C*-clamps, or place a heavy weight on top the pressing boards. Leave the book under pressure for 2 or 3 hours.

1. PUT INDENTING BOARD IN PLACE ON TOP OF BOOK. FLIP. SET ONTO PRESSING BOARD WITH INDENTING BOARD CLOSE TO THE EDGE.

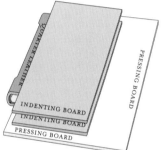

2. POSITION SECOND INDENTING BOARD ON THE BOOK.

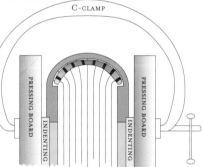

3. PLACE PRESSURE WITH *C*-CLAMPS WITH THE FEET OF THE CLAMPS AT THE END OF THE INDENTING BOARD FOR MAXIMUM PRESSURE.

LEATHER CAN BE INDENTED WITH BOARDS AND *C*-CLAMPS AS ABOVE, WITH A WEIGHT, OR WITH A PRESS AS SHOWN ON THE FACING PAGE.

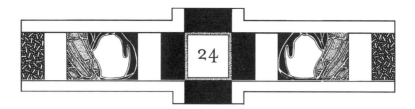

24

COVERING THE BOARDS

Covering is adding the decorative paper to the outside of the boards, on the area not covered by leather or cloth.[25] Then the endsheet will be pasted on the inside of the board, page 296. Papers for quarter leather or cloth will be described first. Paper for half leather or cloth is described on page 318.

The procedure for covering the outside of the boards is the same for the Tight Back, Flat Back, as well as for the Pamphlet Binding with Boards, with this exception:
• Outside paper must overlap leather, but can butt to cloth. See *Overlapping vs Butting the Paper to the Spine–Covering,* page 356.

FLUSH OUTSIDE PAPERS: If more than one paper is used on the outside of the boards, they must be inlaid to avoid snagging. See *Inlaid Papers,* page 359.

MEASURING PAPER FOR THE OUTSIDE OF THE BOARDS
Width for overlapping leather or cloth is the distance from the indented line on the leather, page 276, to the foredge of the board, plus 1" overhang at the foredge to be turned-in. Grain of the paper should be parallel to the spine.

Width for butting the outside paper to quarter cloth is the distance from the quarter cloth to the foredge, plus 1" to be turned-in.

Height out the outside paper for all bindings is the height of the board, plus 2", to be centered from top to bottom. The paper will extend approximately 1" beyond the head and the same distance beyond the tail.[26] Overhang of paper on these three sides is referred to as the *turns-in.*

The pasted turns-in will be brought around to the inside of the board. See *Steps 3–6,* pages 282–285.

PREPARATION FOR PASTING: You might want to review the chapter on pasting, page 54.

Cased-In Quarter Cloth Binding   (flat back or pamphlet binding with boards)

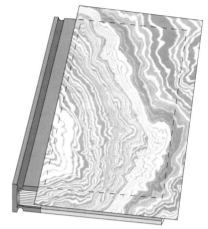

FLAT BACK
THE MEASURED AND CUT PAPER FOR THE OUTSIDE
OF THE BOARD HAS BEEN SLIPPED UNDER THE COVER,
OVERLAPPING THE EDGE OF THE QUARTER CLOTH
TO CHECK THE 1" OVERHANG AT THE HEAD, FOREDGE
AND THE TAIL, PRIOR TO PASTING.

PAPER FOR THE OUTSIDE OF THE BOARD WILL OVERLAP
THE QUARTER CLOTH BY ABOUT 1/8". OR, THE OUTSIDE
PAPER CAN BUTT UP AGAINST QUARTER CLOTH.

Rounded and Backed Quarter Leather Binding

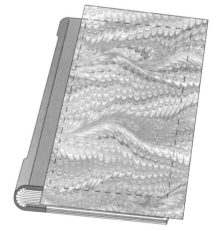

TIGHT BACK
THE MEASURED AND CUT PAPER FOR THE OUTSIDE
OF THE BOARD HAS BEEN SLIPPED UNDER THE COVER,
OVERLAPPING THE EDGE OF THE QUARTER LEATHER
TO CHECK THE 1" OVERHANG, PRIOR TO PASTING.

PAPER FOR THE OUTSIDE
OF THE BOARD WILL OVERLAP QUARTER LEATHER
TO MIDDLE OF THE INDENTED LINE DESCRIBED ON PAGE 275.

PRE-CUTTING PAPER FOR THE OUTSIDE OF THE BOARD:

HEIGHT OF THE PAPER IS THE HEIGHT OF THE BOARD, PLUS 2". THIS GIVES AN
OVERHANG OF 1" AT THE HEAD AND TAIL.

WIDTH IS THE DISTANCE 1/8" IN ON THE LEATHER OR CLOTH TO THE FOREDGE,
PLUS 1". MEASUREMENTS FOR THE OUTSIDE PAPER FOR THE FLAT BACK AND THE
PAMPHLET BINDING WITH BOARDS IS MEASURED THE SAME AS FOR THE TIGHT
BACK, IF THE PAPER IS TO OVERLAP, RATHER THAN BUTT TO THE CLOTH.

PASTING THE PAPERS

Cut two scrap sheets of wax paper about 2" larger than the dimensions of the book. Place one sheet between the front board and the book block, which is in a sleeve of wax paper. Place the second between the back board and the book block. Close the book.

STEP 1: Paste one decorative paper for the outside of one board.

Once the paper lays flat on the pasting surface, it is ready to apply to the board. Brush the entire surface of the outside paper once more to remove excessive paste, leaving a thin layer of paste on the paper.

Position the pasted paper on the outside of the board.

Make sure overhang top and bottom is nearly equal.

PAPER PASTED AND APPLIED TO OUTSIDE OF FRONT BOARD

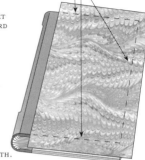

BOOK IS CLOSED.
BOOK BLOCK HAS A SCRAP SHEET OF WAX PAPER UNDER THE BOARD TO KEEP PASTE FROM TOUCHING THE BOOK BLOCK.

OVERLAPPING:
POSITION THE PAPER SO THAT IT COVERS HALF THE INDENTED LINE ON THE LEATHER. SEE PAGE 275, 276.

BUTTING:
SET THE PAPER CLOSE TO THE CLOTH AND SLIDE IT UNTIL IT BUTTS AGAINST THE SPINE-CLOTH.

OPEN THE BOARD TO CLIP CORNERS OF THE PAPER

WET PASTE ON THE OVERHANG OF THE PAPER, REFERRED TO AS THE TURN-IN.

FILLER ON THE INSIDE THE FRONT BOOK BOARD

REMOVE THE SCRAP SHEET OF WAX PAPER

1" OVERHANG

CLIP THE CORNERS OFF THE PAPER

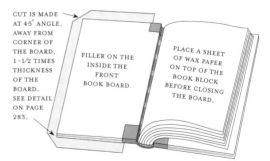

CUT IS MADE AT 45° ANGLE, AWAY FROM CORNER OF THE BOARD, 1-1/2 TIMES THICKNESS OF THE BOARD. SEE DETAIL ON PAGE 283.

FILLER ON THE INSIDE THE FRONT BOOK BOARD

PLACE A SHEET OF WAX PAPER ON TOP OF THE BOOK BLOCK BEFORE CLOSING THE BOARD.

FIRST STEPS IN PASTING: A SCRAP SHEET OF WAX PAPER IS PLACED BETWEEN THE BOARD AND THE BOOK BLOCK, WHICH IS ENVELOPED IN A SLEEVE WAX PAPER. AFTER THE BOOK IS OPENED, *STEP 2*, DISCARD THE SCRAP WAX PAPER. DO NOT CLIP THE CORNERS OFF THE OUTSIDE PAPER UNTIL *STEP 3*, PAGE 282, ILLUSTRATED ON PAGE 283.

POSITIONING THE OUTSIDE PAPER OVERLAPPING LEATHER OR CLOTH:
Set the paper down covering half the indented line on the leather or cloth, which is approximately 1/8" from the edge of the material. See page 275, 276. Proceed to *Step* 2 below.

POSITIONING THE OUTSIDE PAPER BUTTING TO CLOTH: Set the paper down on the board very close to the edge of the cloth. Slide it into position, so it is butted against the cloth. Proceed to Step 2 below.

POSITIONING AN OUTSIDE CLOTH OVERLAPPING QUARTER LEATHER: If you are using cloth, set it on the board with the edge of the cloth covering half the indented line on the leather.[27] See page 275, 276. Do not be concerned if there are wrinkles in the cloth, as long as the edge is lined up with and tacked to, the indented line. Lift the cloth at the foredge until most of the cloth is above the board, except the edge which is attached along the indented line. Lay the rest of the cloth down onto the board, pushing lightly with the palm of your hand from the spine-edge of the cloth towards the foredge. Proceed to Step 2 below.

STEP 2: For either overlapping or butting, the next procedure is to lightly press along the edge of the pasted material. Lightly hold it in place while you use the palm of your hand to brush from the center to the top, bottom and foredge to work out any air bubbles. Watch that the paper or pasted cloth does not slip from the position where it is aligned with the leather or spine-cloth.

Do not press hard, as it is not necessary. It will dry with a smoother surface if you do not have random areas of extreme pressure caused by finger tips. Paper will shrink as it dries.

Open the board and discard the scrap of wax paper, which is wet from touching the outside paper. The position of the cut made in Step 3 is critical:

STEP 3 CUTTING OFF THE PAPERS AT THE CORNERS: An overhang of the outside paper is about 1" all way around. The excess of paper at the corners must be removed. *Do not attempt* cutting the corners off prior to pasting. Alignment must be exact. You will never position the paper precisely to the board. Cutting the corners off prior to pasting only complicates a simple procedure.

With the board fully open, cut the corners off the paper at the head and tail with a 45° angle. Amount of paper removed must be exact.

The cut should be out from the board, leaving paper which is 1½ times the thickness of the board. See illustration below and on the following page.

If your diagonal cut is too close to the board, the bare board will be exposed at the corner when making the turn-in. If the cut leaves too much paper at the corner, you will have an excess of folded paper in folding the outside paper around to the inside of the board.

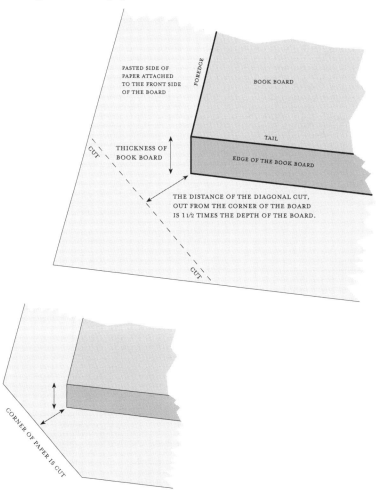

STEP 3: CUT THE CORNERS OFF THE PAPER AT THE HEAD AND THE TAIL WITH A 45° ANGLE. THE CUT SHOULD BE OUT FROM THE BOARD, LEAVING PAPER WHICH IS 1½ TIMES THE THICKNESS OF THE BOARD.

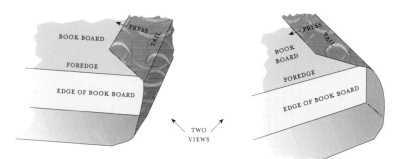

STEP 4: TURN-IN AT THE HEAD AND THE TAIL

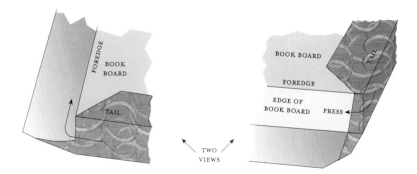

STEP 5: CREASE PAPER WITH BONE FOLDER ALONG THE EDGE OF THE BOARD, FROM THE
TAIL, AROUND THE CORNER, ONTO THE FOREDGE. DO THE SAME AT THE HEAD.

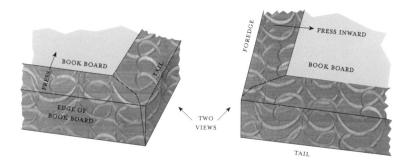

STEP 6: TURN-IN AT THE FOREDGE

MAKING THE TURNS-IN, STEPS 4–6

STEP 4: Fold the paper around the tail, tight against the edge of the board, onto the inside surface of the book board. Push with your thumb on the paper in the direction towards the head. This will tighten the paper on the edge of the board, as well as on the inside.

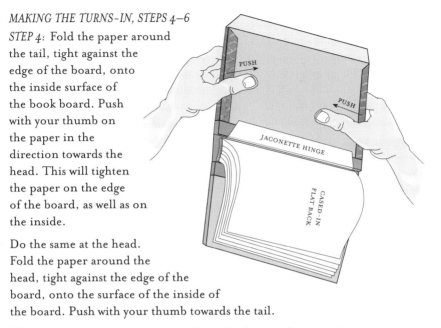

Do the same at the head. Fold the paper around the head, tight against the edge of the board, onto the surface of the inside of the board. Push with your thumb towards the tail.

The turn-in at the head and the tail can be done at the same time, holding the board cupped in your hands, making the turn-in at the tail with one thumb, while simultaneously using the other thumb at the head. This will assure the position of the paper does not slip on the outside of the board and will tighten the paper to the board.

STEP 5: Place the board on the table with the inside of the board facing up. Place the bone folder flat against the edge of the board at the tail, close to the foredge. Take the bone folder tightly around the corner onto the foredge, with the bone folder flat against the edge of the board. This creases the paper at the corner. Do the same at the head.

STEP 6: Turn-In the paper along the foredge. Press it tightly up the edge of the board, onto the inside of the board. Press in a stroking manner towards the spine-edge to tighten the paper.

Check the outside of the board to see that you have not pulled the paper away from its position at the leather or cloth.

STEP 7: Tap the foredge of the board lightly on the table. Or, use a bone folder to tap the foredge at the head and the tail. This will crease and flatten the folded paper at the corners.

STEP 8: Lay the bone folder over the seam at the corners on the inside of the board. Press downward to crease and flatten the folded over paper.

Place a scrap sheet of wax paper on top of the book block. Close the board.

STEP 9: The amount of turn-in on the inside of the board is equal along the head and tail, because you centered the paper top to bottom when applying it.

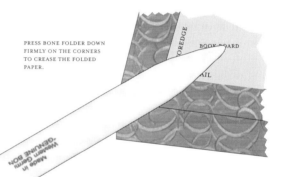

TAP THE BONE FOLDER AGAINST THE EDGE OF THE BOARD AT THE HEAD AND THE TAIL.

FOREDGE

BOOK BOARD

TAIL

STEP 7 TAPPING THE EDGE OF THE BOARD TO CREASE THE FOLDED PAPER

PRESS BONE FOLDER DOWN FIRMLY ON THE CORNERS TO CREASE THE FOLDED PAPER.

FOREDGE

BOOK BOARD

TAIL

STEP 8 CREASING THE FOLD ON THE SURFACE OF THE INSIDE OF THE BOARD

However, you may find the turn-in along the foredge is larger than planned. Wet paper expands in one direction, perpendicular to the grain. With certain papers, the expansion is excessive. You may wish to trim the turn-in along the foredge while it is on the book and still wet, to keep an equal amount on all three sides.[28] When the endsheet is pasted down, the shape of the bulge from the turns-in will show. Or, you can prevent the bulge from being seen by pasting down a center island filler flush with and butted to, the turns-in. This would be added just prior to pasting down the endsheet.

STEP 10: Wash up the pasting area and dry the surface in preparation for pasting the outside paper for the remaining board.

Paste and cover the second board.

Place a scrap sheet of wax paper on top of the book block. Close the board.

STEP 11: Place scrap book board on each side of the book which extends to, but does not cover the leather or cloth. The scrap boards should end at the indenting line on the leather to maintain pressure on the edge of the paper, since the main surface of the quarter leather is higher than the indented area.

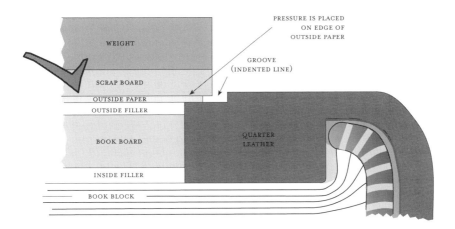

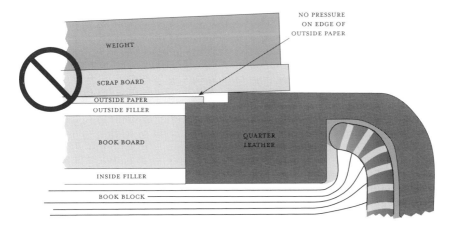

STEP 11: WEIGHTING DOWN THE PAPERS TO DRY

The book sandwiched between the scrap boards is weighted down with a slight weight of two or three books extending beyond the top scrap book board in all directions . Dry overnight. The sleeve of wax paper will keep moisture from the boards from touching the book block.

A NICE PASTED PAPER WAS APPLIED TO THE OUTSIDE OF THE BOARDS OF THIS EXAMPLE. HOWEVER, I FORGOT TO DRY IT UNDER WEIGHT TO AVOID THE PULL FACTOR.

THE GRAIN OF THE PAPER DISTORTED THE BOARDS, MAKING IT IMPOSSIBLE NOW TO PASTE DOWN THE ENDSHEETS. FRED CALLS THIS MISTAKE A *GULL WING*.

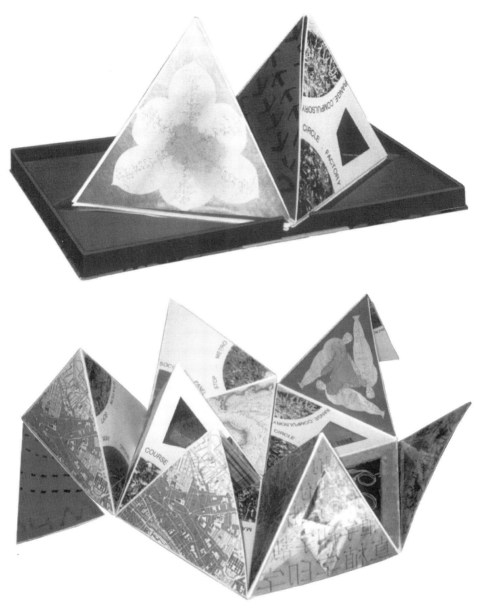

Elizabeth Steiner, *Which Way?*

"A triangular book in a clam box, 192 mm. x 170 mm. x 23 mm. Designed and constructed by Elizabeth Steiner, New Zealand. 1997. The structure is based on Scott McCarney's *In Case of Emergency:*, using two intersecting fold books, that allow the pages to be arranged in many different ways. The diagrams, illustrations and text relate to instructions for crafts, road signs that are confusing to travellers, ancient diagrams as well as those using new technology. The thirty two triangular pages are laminated on either side of Tyvek, to withstand frequent folding and unfolding. The coloured pages have been reproduced by laser printing and coated with an acrylic varnish. An edition of 25 signed and numbered."

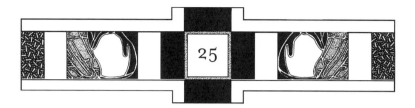

25

PASTE-DOWN

The inside of the board is completed by pasting down the first end-sheet onto the front board and the last sheet onto the back board. The paste-down covers the filler on the Tight Back and the jaconette hinge on the Flat Back and the Pamphlet Binding with Boards.

The turn-in of the paper on the outside of the board will show as a border along the head, foredge and tail on the inside of the board.

NOTE: Any decoration of the leather which entails thread or paper pressed into the leather must be done prior to pasting down the end-sheet. To keep the thread from raveling, the ends must extend around the head and tail onto the leather turns-in. The ends of the thread will be secured, covered by the pasted down endsheet. See pages 365–367.

DIFFERENT PASTE-DOWN PROCEDURE FOR EACH BINDING: The end-sheets are pasted down differently for each of the three bindings. The description of how to paste down the endsheets are on the following pages:

· The Pamphlet Binding with Boards is on the following page.
· The Flat Back is on page 294.
· The Tight Back is on page 296.

PREPARATION FOR PASTING: For all the bindings, first remove the sleeve of wax paper and discard it. Cut four scrap sheets of wax paper, each slightly larger than the boards. Two sheets of wax paper will go between the first endsheet and the book block. Make sure they extend all the way to the spine-edge. Place the other two sheets between the final endsheet and the book block. After pasting and applying the endsheet to the board, the top, wet sheet of wax paper will be discarded. The second sheet remains in place to protect the book block from moisture or dirt.

PASTING DOWN THE ENDSHEETS
FOR THE PAMPHLET BINDING

1.   Open both boards flat on the table. Insert two sheets of wax paper under the first and two under the last endsheet. Lay the book block on the front board.

Paste the endsheet, stroking from the spine, past the foredge, head and tail. Do not paste from the edge of the sheet inward, or you will push paste under the endsheet to the other side.

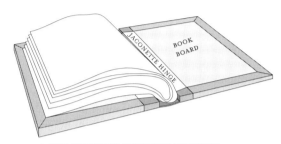

1. LAY 2 SCRAP SHEETS OF WAX PAPER UNDER FINAL ENDSHEET. PASTE THE ENDSHEET.

2.   Lift the endsheet and discard the scrap sheet of wax paper. Press the endsheet against the edge of the back board without pulling, which will stretch it. Lay the endsheet on the back board. Press lightly with the palm of your hand from the spine towards the foredge, head and tail.

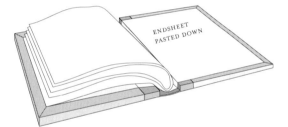

2. ATTACH THE ENDSHEET TO THE BACK BOARD. PLACE A SHEET OF WAX PAPER ON TOP OF THE PASTED ENDSHEET.

This will remove any air bubbles. Run a bone folder along the spine-edge of the board for a tight fit at the hinge.

Lay a fresh sheet of wax paper on top of the wet endsheet.

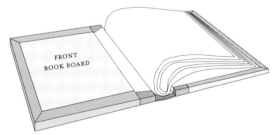

3. REST BOOK BLOCK ON BACK BOARD. INSERT A SHEET OF WAX PAPER UNDER FIRST ENDSHEET TO PASTE THE FRONT ENDSHEET.

PASTING DOWN THE ENDSHEETS FOR THE PAMPHLET BINDING WITH BOARDS IS DONE WITH THE COVERS OPENED FLAT ON THE TABLE.

3. Rest the book block on the back board. Place two sheets of wax paper are between the top endsheet and the book block, ready for pasting. Paste the first endsheet.

4. Prop the book block vertically, slightly leaning to the back board by standing an object on the back board. Remove the wet scrap of wax paper. Attach the pasted endsheet to the front board, in the same manner as the other.

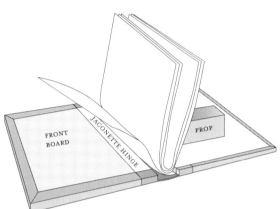

4. PLACE A PROP ON THE BACK BOARD TO SUPPORT THE BOOK BLOCK. PASTE THE OTHER ENDSHEET AND ATTACH TO THE FRONT BOARD.

5. Leave the book block propped vertically, adding a prop to the front board, as well. Use small props to allow air to get to most of the wet endsheets.

After an hour, move the position of the props to allow air to get to the area of the endsheets where the props were located. Allow the endsheets to air dry overnight before closing the boards.

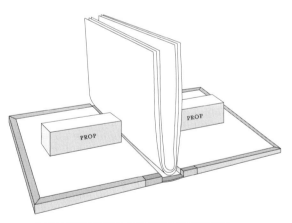

5. USE 2 SMALL PROPS TO HOLD THE BOOK VERTICALLY. MOVE PROPS AFTER AN HOUR SO AIR CAN GET TO THE BOARD WHERE THE PROPS HAVE BEEN. ALLOW TO DRY OVERNIGHT.

THE SECOND ENDSHEET FOR THE PAMPHLET BINDING WITH BOARDS IS PASTED WITH THE BOOK BLOCK PROPPED VERTICALLY. PLACE A SECOND PROP TO HOLD THE BOOK BLOCK. ALLOW TO DRY OVERNIGHT.

PASTING DOWN THE ENDSHEETS FOR THE FLAT BACK

Casing-in the Flat Back is the easiest of the three bindings. The end-sheets could be pasted the same time as the hinges if you wish, but the outside of the boards already would be covered, weighted and dried. Attaching the hinges to the board is described on page 191. If you decide to paste the endsheet down the same time as the hinge, we suggest wheat paste, not PVA. *Gluing the Hinge,* page 192, uses PVA, but that is for books that the endsheet is pasted down separately, as well as for exposed hinges, where the island paste-down must be a separate step. See *Islands as Pastes-Down,* page 351.

The following procedure is for wheat pasting down the endsheets, whether done at the same time as the hinges, or later. If you have already attached the hinges, simply omit *Step 4*:

1. Form the case in the shape of an I-Beam, as described on page 190. Discard the sleeve of wax paper. Place the book block into the covers, centering top to bottom for equal overhang. Make sure the spine of the book block rests on the spine-board. Gently lay the closed book on the table and open the front cover without disturbing the position of the book.

2. Cut four pieces of wax paper slightly larger than the book block. Lay two sheets aside. Slip two pieces of wax paper between the hinge of the book block, above the first page of the book block. Make sure the two sheets are tight against the spine-edge.

Press down on the wax paper with one hand to make sure the wax paper and the the book block do not shift while you paste.

3. Paste the entire endsheet.

4. Paste the hinge to the endsheet. Paste the tapes to the hinge. Do not paste the spine, or else the book will not open to allow pages to lie flat. The spine must remain free to arc open as the pages are turned.

5. After pasting the hinge, remove the top sheet of wax paper which has paste on it and discard. Gently close the cover and press on top with your hand. Do not open to examine, or the cloth hinge will slip off the cover board.

Turn the book over. Open the back cover, insert two sheets of wax paper between the hinge and the book block. Paste as before in Steps 3 and 4. Remove the top sheet of wax paper. Close the cover. The book may not be opened until it is pressed and the paste is dry.

Press the book as described on page 193.

Penny Carey-Wells, *Not Flowing, Draining*, one-of-a-kind book with audio tape, 1994.

A papermaker in Hobart, Tasmania, Penny also has an interest in books. This formidable piece is quite delightful. The book sits on a lectern, not shown, about waist high.

Raise the heavy metal cover and bring it over to rest on the padded leather cushion and the pressure activates a sound track.

Original soundtrack by Michael Fortescue and friends, handmade paper, etched copper, wood, leather, cassette player. 1994, 40 cm. x 30 cm. x 15 cm.

PASTING DOWN THE ENDSHEETS FOR A TIGHT BACK

Before you start pasting you will need to
locate the notched scrap piece of card
used in *Attaching the Boards,* page 267. It will
be needed to hold the boards opened after
the endsheets are pasted down.

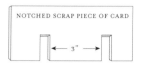

NOTCHED SCRAP PIECE OF CARD

←— 3" —→

1. Open the top board and rest it on a support of one or two books
or scrap book boards as a firm support for pasting. The frayed cords
can be seen at the hinge, covered by the inside filler.

Slip a sheet of wax paper under the top endsheet. Make sure it
extends all the way to the spine-edge.

2. Paste the endsheet, stroking from the spine, past the foredge,
head and tail. Do not
paste from the edge
of the sheet inward,
or you will push paste
under the endsheet
to the other side.

3. Lift the endsheet
and discard the scrap
sheet of wax paper.
Press the endsheet
against the edge of
the board without
pulling, which will
stretch it. Lay the
endsheet on the
board. Press lightly
with the palm of your
hand from the spine
towards the foredge,
head and tail to
remove air bubbles.

Run a bone folder
along the edge of the
board for a tight fit
at the hinge. Board
must remain open
until totally dry.

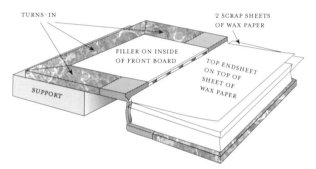

TURNS-IN

2 SCRAP SHEETS
OF WAX PAPER

FILLER ON INSIDE
OF FRONT BOARD

TOP ENDSHEET
ON TOP OF
SHEET OF
WAX PAPER

SUPPORT

OPEN THE BOARD READY TO PASTE THE TOP END-
SHEET FOR A TIGHT BACK OR HOLLOW BACK.

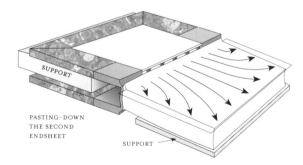

SUPPORT

PASTING-DOWN
THE SECOND
ENDSHEET

SUPPORT

PASTE THE ENDSHEET FROM THE SPINE TOWARDS
THE EDGES, NEVER FROM THE EDGE INWARD.

4. Carefully turn the book over, keeping the wet board open. Set the book block onto a scrap piece of book board to protect the shoulder. The wet endsheet on the board will rest on the clean, dry surface. Open the board and place a support between them as shown at the bottom of the facing page.

5. Slip a scrap sheet of wax paper under the top endsheet. Paste this endsheet and adhere it to the board.

6. Stand the book on its tail with the support between the boards in place to keep the boards open. Remove the support between the boards and set the notched scrap piece of card onto the boards at the head to maintain their open position of the boards. Watch that the notches do not press against the wet paste-down, wrinkling the pasted paper.

Place a thin scrap of book board under the foredge of the book block as a support to steady it. Allow the endsheets to air dry overnight before closing the boards.

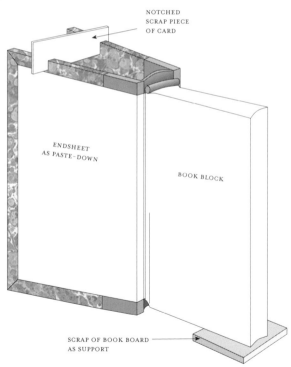

NOTCHED
SCRAP PIECE
OF CARD

ENDSHEET
AS PASTE-DOWN

BOOK BLOCK

SCRAP OF BOOK BOARD
AS SUPPORT

THE BOOK IS STOOD UP TO AIR DRY AFTER THE ENDSHEETS AS PASTES-DOWN HAVE BEEN ATTACHED TO BOTH BOARDS.

When the pastes-down are dry, your Pamphlet Binding with Boards, Flat Back or Tight Back is ready to be completed with perhaps a label for the spine or front cover. You may wish to add decoration. These are described in the Part V, *Finishing,* page 335.

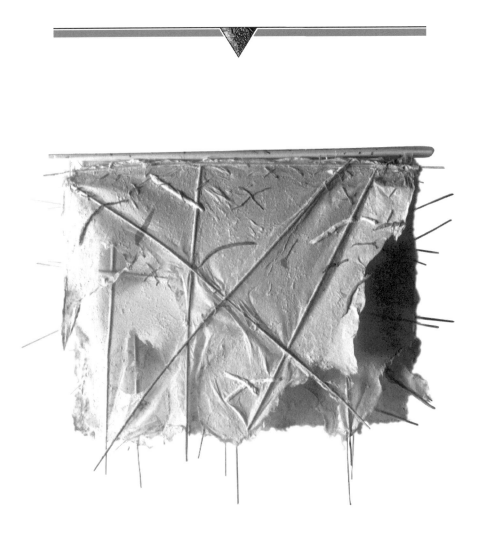

PENNY CAREY WELLS, *LAST YEAR'S CALENDER,* ONE-OF-A-KIND, HANDMADE PAPER, WOOD, STRING, 1989. 50 CM. X 40 CM. X 8 CM.

PENNY CAREY WELLS, *EXPANDING FILE OF INDUSTRIAL RELATIONS, WORK PLACE SAFETY AND EQUAL PAY FOR WOMEN*, ONE-OF-A-KIND, HANDMADE PAPER, WOOD, METAL, 1994. 1.5 M. X 60 CM. X 70 CM.

Tᴉɢʜᴛ Bᴀᴄᴋ ʜᴀʟғ ʟᴇᴀᴛʜᴇʀ ʙʟᴀɴᴋ ʙɪɴᴅɪɴɢ, ᴏɴᴇ-ᴏғ-ᴀ-ᴋɪɴᴅ.
Kᴇɪᴛʜ Sᴍɪᴛʜ, Dᴇᴄᴇᴍʙᴇʀ 1997. Pʜᴏᴛᴏ ɪɴʟᴀʏ ᴏɴ ᴄᴏᴠᴇʀ ᴏғ ᴋᴇɪᴛʜ sᴛᴀɴᴅɪɴɢ ɪɴ
ᴀ sᴛʀᴇᴀᴍ ᴡɪᴛʜ Sᴄᴏᴛᴛ McCᴀʀɴᴇʏ ʙᴏᴏᴋ sᴄᴜʟᴘᴛᴜʀᴇ ɪɴ ᴛʜᴇ ʙᴀᴄᴋɢʀᴏᴜɴᴅ.
21.5 x 13.3 x 1.5 cᴍ. Gɪᴠᴇɴ ᴛᴏ Aᴀᴛɪs Lɪʟʟsᴛʀᴏᴍ.

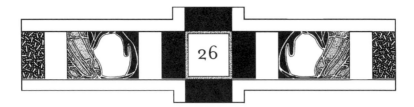
HALF LEATHER

Half or full leather are started in the same manner as for quarter leather, with a few differences. The differences for half leather will be discussed first. Full leather will be described beginning on page 321.

HALF LEATHER BINDING: To make a half leather binding, make a quarter leather binding, up through notching the boards, but stop at that point. Follow the procedures from page 217–246, except for the width of the boards. Do not add the leather to the spine at this time.

HALF LEATHER
THE LEATHER ON THE FOREDGE WILL BE RECTANGULAR, RATHER THAN TRIANGLES AT THE CORNERS.

BOARDS FOR HALF LEATHER
MEASURING AND CUTTING THE BOARDS:
Height of the boards is the same as described on page 243.

Width of the board is the same as described on page 243, minus the thickness of the leather.

NOTCHING THE BOARDS FOR HALF LEATHER: The horizontal notch, *A,* along the head and tail of the board and the vertical notch, *B,* are the same as described on page 247. In addition, half leather has a horizontal notch, *C,* along the head and tail at the foredge. Notch *C* is the width of the half leather along the foredge.

NOTCHING THE BOARDS FOR HALF LEATHER

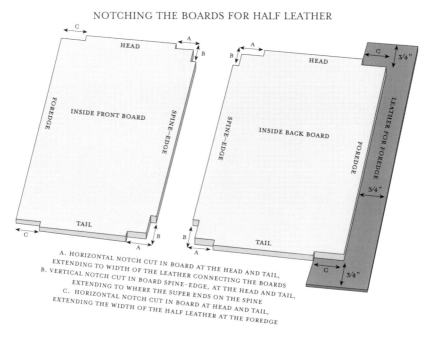

A. HORIZONTAL NOTCH CUT IN BOARD AT THE HEAD AND TAIL,
EXTENDING TO WIDTH OF THE LEATHER CONNECTING THE BOARDS
B. VERTICAL NOTCH CUT IN BOARD SPINE-EDGE, AT THE HEAD AND TAIL,
EXTENDING TO WHERE THE SUPER ENDS ON THE SPINE
C. HORIZONTAL NOTCH CUT IN BOARD AT HEAD AND TAIL,
EXTENDING THE WIDTH OF THE HALF LEATHER AT THE FOREDGE

CUTTING THE NOTCHES: Use a straight edge and thin bladed knife
to cut the notches. Notches *A* and *B* accommodate the leather on the
spine. Notch *C* is for the leather on the foredge.

A. The horizontal notches eliminate the need to pare the shorter side
of the leather, which turns-in at the head and the tail. It will allow
the turns-in to be flush with the boards, on the edge of the board.

B. The vertical notches keep the leather from bulging into the gap
between the boards. The leather turns-in are flush with the spine-edge
of the boards.

C. The notch at the foredge is cut. The leather will be applied to the
foredge, prior to that on the spine.

The turns-in on the foredge are the same width at the head, foredge
and tail, unlike the spine, which has a bigger turn-in at the tail.

Leather will be applied to the foredge of the boards prior to that at
the spine. This is because it will be easier handling individual boards
than if they have been attached by leather between the boards on the
spine.

The board thickness is important in measuring the turn-in of leather
which is not pared. The thick leather rolled around the board takes
more width than pared leather.

LEATHER FOR THE FOREDGE

Two pieces of leather will be needed, one for each board, on the foredge.

WIDTH OF HALF LEATHER AT THE FOREDGE: Width of the leather on the outside of the board at the foredge can vary: Sometimes, it is very small, with only 1/8" *showing,* since most of the foredge leather has been overlapped by the decorative paper as shown at the right. In no case should the leather be less than 1/2" wide on the outside of the board.

Often, the same amount of leather shows at the foredge, as is seen on the outside of the board at the spine-edge. See page 301.

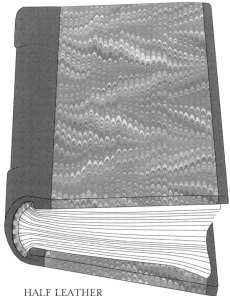

Width is 3/4" for the turn-in on the inside of the board, plus the amount you wish to show on the outside of the board, plus 1/8" extending towards the spine. The 1/8" will be covered by decorative paper.

Example: If you wish 11/2" of leather showing on the board at the foredge, as well as the spine, the width of the leather for the foredge will be cut to 23/8".

HALF LEATHER

THE LEATHER ON THE FOREDGE MAY BE A NARROW STRIP, JUST ENOUGH TO STRUC-TURALLY REINFORCE AND PROTECT THE EDGE OF THE BOARD. AESTHETICALLY, IT CAN BE STRIKING. COMPARE IT WITH THAT ON PAGE 301.

Height of the foredge leather is the distance from Notch *C* on the board at the head, to Notch *C* at the tail, plus 11/2". This will allow 3/4" turn-in at the head and tail.

EQUAL AMOUNT OF TURNS-IN: The turn-in at the head and the tail on the foredge leather will be the same, not more at the tail as with the spine leather. See illustration on page 309.

Cut the two pieces of leather for the foredge of each board and you are ready to paste.

APPLYING FOREDGE LEATHER: Draw a pencil line on the outside of the boards, from the edge of Notch *C* at the head to that at the tail.

Paste the leather for the foredge of one board at a time. Refer to pasting procedures in Chapter 4, page 54.

Apply the leather to the outside of the board. Line up with the edge of the leather so it just covers the pencil line. Allow an equal amount extending from the head and tail.

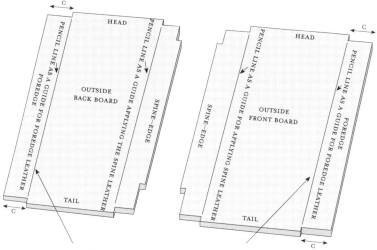

PENCIL LINES AS GUIDE IN APPLYING FOREDGE LEATHER

PASTE THE LEATHER FOR ONE FOREDGE AT A TIME. LINE IT UPON THE PENCIL LINE. TURN THE BOARD OVER TO MAKE THE TURNS-IN.

INSIDE VIEW OF BOARD: The leather will overhang the board ¾" along the foredge and, ¾" along the head and tail to the end of and slightly beyond notch *C*. It is important that the leather *extend beyond* notch *C,* so that it can be trimmed to the edge of the notch, after the leather is dry.

MITERING THE CORNERS: The corners of the leather will be trimmed off. A single cut will be made at the head and the tail, across the leather at a 45° angle. It is represented by the dotted line in the drawing at the top of the facing page.

The amount trimmed must be measured exactly. Measure out from the corner of the board the same distance as the depth of the board.

The middle drawing on this page shows how to cut the leather. Use a tool that holds a single edge razor blade. Use a new blade to make these cuts.

SMALL CUTS: Hold the tool at a 45° angle to the surface of the table. This will give a bevel cut, which is important.

Slice through the leather at a 30–45° angle.[28] If you have a ¾" overhang of leather, probably all you will need to do is press down, in a single action.

LARGER CUTS: If you have a large overhang, you will have to pull the blade across, as you are pressing down at an angle, in order to make the complete cut. Hold the leading edge of the blade slightly higher. This will make it easier to proceed across the leather.

Trim the leather at the head in the same manner as this cut at the tail.

PASTE THE BEVEL: Before making the turns-in, apply paste to the thickness of the leather on the mitered cut.

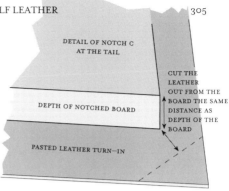

DETAIL OF NOTCH C
AT THE TAIL

CUT THE LEATHER OUT FROM THE BOARD THE SAME DISTANCE AS DEPTH OF THE BOARD

DEPTH OF NOTCHED BOARD

PASTED LEATHER TURN–IN

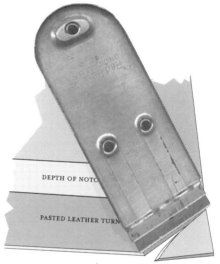

DEPTH OF NOTC

PASTED LEATHER TURN

CUT THE LEATHER AT A 45° ANGLE

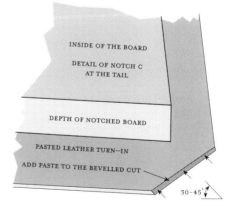

INSIDE OF THE BOARD

DETAIL OF NOTCH C
AT THE TAIL

DEPTH OF NOTCHED BOARD

PASTED LEATHER TURN–IN

ADD PASTE TO THE BEVELLED CUT

30–45°

MITER THE LEATHER AT 45° ANGLE, OUT FROM THE BOARD SAME DISTANCE AS THE DEPTH OF THE BOARD.

MAKING THE TURNS-IN:

1. Turn-in the leather at the head and tail into notch *C*. The leather should completely fill, if not extend slight beyond, notch *C*. Use only moderate pressure; you do not want to stretch the leather.

2. Make the turn-in along the foredge, starting at the head. The leather should meet the turn-in at the head on the surface of the board. Work the leather from the foredge and the head at the corner, so that the seam of beveled leather comes together and is flat onto the surface of the board.

3. In turning in the leather at the head, as well as the foredge, you will have a small loop of leather protruding at the depth of the board, right at the corner. Push it up the depth of the board with a bone folder and then onto the surface of the board.

4. Work the corner at the tail and foredge in the same manner.

Paste the remaining piece of leather for the other foredge. Apply, trim and make the turns-in.

Lay the covers out flat on a sheet of book board.

MAKING THE TURNS-IN

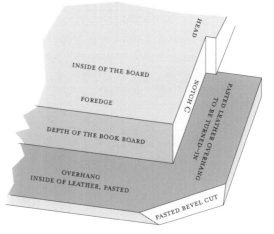

AFTER PASTING AND APPLYING THE LEATHER TO THE OUTSIDE OF THE BOARD, TURN THE BOARD OVER. FOREDGE LEATHER MUST EXTEND TO, OR SLIGHTLY BEYOND, THE END OF NOTCH C. MAKE THE BEVELED CUT AND PASTE IT.

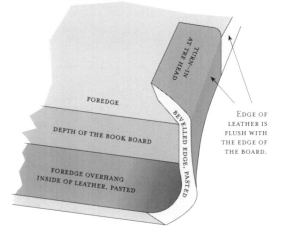

EDGE OF LEATHER IS FLUSH WITH THE EDGE OF THE BOARD.

1. MAKE THE TURNS-IN AT THE HEAD AND THE TAIL.

Place another book board on top, which completely covers the boards. Place a small amount of weight on top and allow to dry for 15 minutes.

The leather covered boards are sandwiched between book boards, because they will absorb some of the moisture from the leather as it is drying.

APPLYING THE LEATHER TO THE SPINE

Paste the leather for the spine.

Follow the directions for *Applying Leather to the Spine,* beginning on page 251.

TRIMMING THE LEATHER ON THE SPINE: Follow the instructions for trimming the leather on the outside and inside of the boards, pages 260–265. Do not cut or paste the filler to the boards at this time. *Filler for the Boards* will be discussed on page 310.

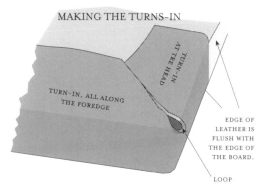

MAKING THE TURNS-IN

2. TURN-IN THE LEATHER ALL ALONG THE FOREDGE. WORK THE SEAM CLOSED ON THE SURFACE OF THE BOARD. A SMALL LOOP WILL GAPE OPEN ON THE DEPTH OF THE BOARD AT THE CORNER.

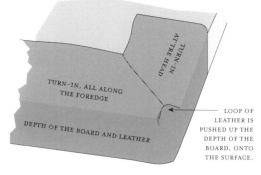

3. USE THE POINT OF THE BONE FOLDER TO PUSH THE LOOP UP THE DEPTH OF THE BOARD AND ONTO THE SURFACE.

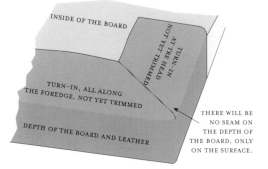

4. PRESS DOWN ON THE SURFACE OF THE LEATHER WITH THE FLAT SIDE OF THE BONE FOLDER TO MAKE THE LEATHER ALL THE SAME LEVEL.

TRIMMING THE FOREDGE LEATHER
TRIMMING THE FOREDGE LEATHER ON THE OUTSIDE OF THE BOARD:
Lay the outside of the board face up. Line up a straight edge with the
end of notch *C* at the head and tail. The straight edge will be on top
of the good leather. If it is too narrow to hold the straight edge,
build up a support to the same level as the foredge leather. The
straight edge will be directly above the pencil line. Trim away any
excess.

Continue the trimming by making a straight cut *down the depth of the
board* at the head and tail, at the end of notch *C*. There will be no
need for the *T*-shaped cuts used on the spine leather. Turn the board
over and trim the inside.

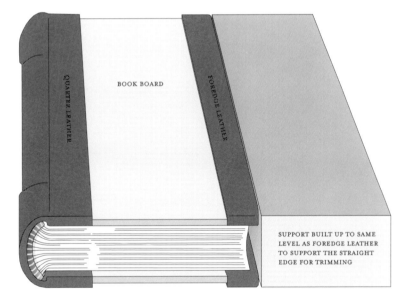

TRIMMING THE FOREDGE LEATHER ON THE OUTSIDE OF THE BOARD: BUILD UP A
SUPPORT TO THE HEIGHT OF THE FOREDGE LEATHER. THIS WILL SUPPORT THE
STRAIGHT EDGE, WHICH IS LAID ON THE GOOD PART OF THE LEATHER.

HOLD THE STRAIGHT EDGE DOWN, AS YOU PEEL AWAY THE EXCESS NEXT TO THE
BOOK BOARD. IF YOU HAVE NOT CUT COMPLETELY THROUGH THE LEATHER, YOU
CAN MAKE A SECOND CUT IN THE SAME GROOVE AS THE FIRST.

TRIMMING THE FOREDGE LEATHER ON THE INSIDE OF THE BOARD: The leather at the foredge probably stretched when it was turned in. It must be trimmed evenly on all three sides and, at right angles.

Use a pencil to mark the position of the leather to be trimmed, the same distance in from the head, foredge and tail.

Since the straight edge will be placed on top of the narrow, good leather while trimming, butt a scrap of book board against the board to help support the straight edge. When trimmed, the leather on the inside of the board will appear as in the drawing below.

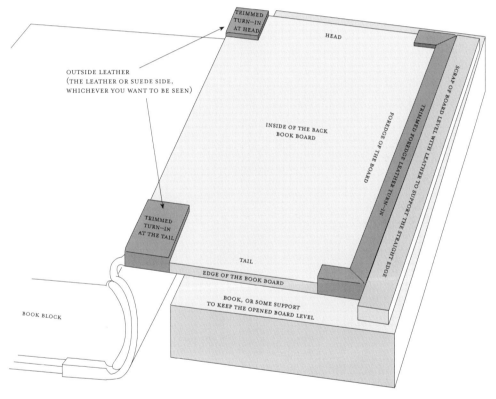

TRIMMED TURN–IN AT HEAD

HEAD

OUTSIDE LEATHER
(THE LEATHER OR SUEDE SIDE,
WHICHEVER YOU WANT TO BE SEEN)

INSIDE OF THE BACK BOOK BOARD

FOREDGE OF THE BOARD

TRIMMED FOREDGE LEATHER TURN–IN

SCRAP OF BOARD LEVEL WITH LEATHER TO SUPPORT THE STRAIGHT EDGE

TRIMMED TURN–IN AT THE TAIL

TAIL

EDGE OF THE BOOK BOARD

BOOK, OR SOME SUPPORT TO KEEP THE OPENED BOARD LEVEL

BOOK BLOCK

TRIMMING THE FOREDGE LEATHER ON THE INSIDE OF THE BOARD: THE FOREDGE LEATHER IS TRIMMED AT THE HEAD, ALONG THE FOREDGE AND AT THE TAIL, WITH AN EQUAL WIDTH. IF THE LEATHER IS NARROW, LAY A SCRAP OF BOOK BOARD NEXT TO THE FOREDGE LEATHER TO SUPPORT THE STRAIGHT EDGE FOR TRIMMING.

THE SUPER AND CORDS HAVE NOT YET BEEN ATTACHED TO THE BOARDS.

THE LEATHER ON THE SPINE IS TRIMMED THE SAME AS QUARTER LEATHER. SEE PAGES 260–265.

ATTACHING THE BOARDS: Attach the boards in the same manner as for quarter leather. See pages 267–269.

SHAPING THE LEATHER: Place the book back in the press and shape the leather, as described on page 262. Follow the *First Opening* procedure on page 263.

INSIDE FILLER FOR THE BOARDS

The filler for the inside of the boards will be added first. The foredge leather in the inside must first be trimmed square to allow easy fitting of the filler, which must fit snugly. Filler will bring the level of the board up to the exact level of the leather at the spine and foredge.

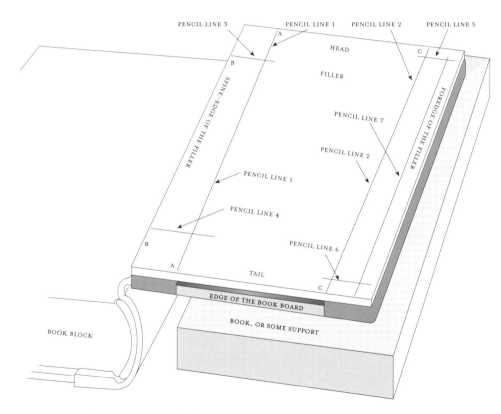

MARKING THE FILLER: WITH THE FILLER LINED UP ON TOP OF THE BOARD, PEN-CIL LINES 1–4 CAN BE MARKED. MOVE THE FILLER TO THE LEFT, UNTIL THE FOREDGE OF THE FILLER LINES UP WITH NOTCH *C*. LINES 5 AND 6 CAN THEN BE MARKED, USING THE LEATHER AS A GUIDE. LINE 7 MUST BE MEASURED.

CUTTING FILLER FOR INSIDE OF THE BOARDS: Thickness of the filler
on the inside of the boards is the exact thickness of the leather.

MARKING THE CUTS-OUT FOR THE INSIDE FILLER: Line up the filler
with the spine-edge of the board. Mark the position of notches *A, B*
and *C* on the spine-edge, head and tail of the filler.

1. Draw a pencil line connecting notch *A* at the head to A at the tail.
2. Draw another line, connecting notch *C* at the head and tail.
3. Measure down from the head to the position of the pencil dot
marking the end of notch *B.* Place a straight edge at a right angle to
the head of the board, at the end of notch *A.* Place a pencil dot at the
measurement of the distance of notch *B* from the head. Draw a horizontal pencil line from the end of notch B, past pencil line 1. This
will give the shape to cut out around the spine turn-in at the head.
4. Along pencil line 1, measure up from the tail to the position of
the pencil dot marking the end of notch *B.* Draw a horizontal pencil
line from the end of notch B, past pencil line 1. This will give the
shape to cut out around the spine turn-in at the tail.
5. Move the filler laterally, off the spine-edge, until all the leather at
the foredge is visible. The foredge of the filler will be lined up with
the end of notch *C.* Keep the head and tail of the filler lined up with
the head and tail of the board.

Dimensions of the filler must be cut to fit precisely, as it can only be
trimmed at the head and tail, between the leather, after it is pasted to
the board. Thickness of filler is the exact thickness of the leather.

First, cut the filler to the exact height and approximate width of the
boards. Then, the notches will be made.

Make a pencil dot on the edge of the filler, down from the head, at
the end of the trimmed foredge turn-in. Draw a horizontal line, at a
right angle to the foredge of the filler, in on the filler, past pencil
line 2.

6. Mark a dot on the edge of the filler, up from the tail, at the end of
the foredge turn-in. Draw a horizontal line in past pencil line 2.
7. Measure from the foredge of the board, in, to the end of the
turn-in of leather along the foredge. Mark this measurement on the
filler at pencil lines 5 and 6. Connect the dots with a vertical line.

CUTTING-OUT THE SHAPES : Cut out the shapes on the filler. Lay it on the board to check that it fits snugly, butting up to all edges of the leather. In pencil, lightly mark this filler is for the inside back board. Mark and cut out the filler for the inside of the front board.

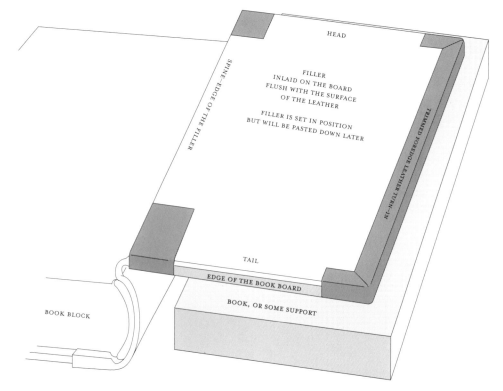

FILLER IS CUT TO FIT THE BOARD. IT IS SET INTO POSITION TO CHECK THAT IT FITS SNUGLY. CUT BOTH INSIDE FILLERS. PASTE THE BOARD AND SET ONE FILLER IN PLACE. INSERT A SHEET OF WAX PAPER. CLOSE THE BOARD. OPEN OTHER BOARD AND PASTE. SET FILLER IN PLACE. SLIP WAX PAPER BETWEEN FILLER AND THE BOOK BLOCK. CLOSE BOOK. WEIGHT DOWN WITH SLIGHT PRESSURE. ALLOW TO SIT OVERNIGHT.

PASTING DOWN THE INSIDE FILLER: After both inside fillers are cut, they are pasted down. Paste the board, not the blotter/filler. After it is in position, place a sheet of wax paper between the filler and the book block. Close the board.

Open the other board and paste. Fit the filler into position. Place a sheet of wax paper between the filler and the book block.

Sandwich the book between two scrap sheets of book board, which are slightly larger than the book. Place a weight of two or three large books on top. Allow to sit overnight.

TRIMMING THE INSIDE FILLER: Remove the weight. Open the cover with the inside of the cover face up. Place a support that is a cutting surface under the open board, similar to the illustration on the facing page. Trim any filler that protrudes along the head and tail. Do not trim across the turns-in, or you may cut the leather. It is easier to trim the inside filler now, before the outside filler is added. If any outside filler also extends, it is very difficult to trim at the same time.

OUTSIDE FILLER FOR THE BOARDS

MEASUREMENTS FOR THE OUTSIDE FILLER: Cut the filler for the outside of each board:

Height of the outside filler is the height of the board, or slightly larger. It can be trimmed after it is pasted.

Width of the outside filler must be cut precisely the distance between the trimmed leather extending in from the spine-edge, to the trimmed foredge turn-in.

Thickness of the outside filler is not the same as the leather. It must be slightly less. This is so the leather can be indented. See *Marking and Cutting the Outside Filler*, page 271.

WIDTH OF THE OUTSIDE FILLER MUST BE CUT PRECISELY.

PASTING DOWN THE OUTSIDE FILLER: After both outside fillers are cut, they are pasted down. Paste the board, not the blotter/filler. Be careful not to get paste on the leather. If you do, immediately wipe it off. Carefully turn over the board and paste. Add the outside filler to the second board.

Sandwich the book between two scrap sheets of book board, which are slightly larger than the book. Place a light weight of two or three books on top. Allow to sit for an hour before trimming the outside filler.

TRIMMING THE OUTSIDE FILLER: Remove the weight. Open the cover and turn the book over with the outside of the open cover facing up. Place a support under the book block to protect the shoulder. Trim any filler that protrudes along the head and tail. Do not trim across the edge of the leather, or you might cut it.

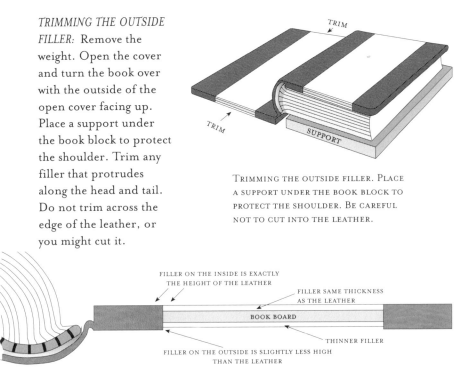

Trimming the outside filler. Place a support under the book block to protect the shoulder. Be careful not to cut into the leather.

Cross section shows the filler on the outside of the board is not as thick as that on the inside, which is exactly the thickness of the leather.

INDENTING THE LEATHER

INDENTING THE LINES: The spine leather and foredge leather will be indented at the same time. In order to position the indenting board, a line must be drawn on both leathers. The line on the spine leather is 1/8" in from the filler. The process is described on page 275, *Indenting Quarter Leather* and *Indenting a Line*, page 276.

Indent the line on the spine leather, but do not indent the surface at this time.

A line is indented 1/8" in on the spine leather, as well as the foredge leather.

The line on the foredge leather is 1/8" in from the filler. Indent the line on the foredge leather in the same manner as the spine leather.

Turn the book over. Indent the line on the spine leather and on the foredge leather.

INDENTING THE SURFACE: Remove the sleeve of wax paper and discard. The folds and masking tape might indent onto the book block.

Cut two pieces of book board for indenting the leather. Masonite or wood can be used also. The indenting will be done on the outside of both covers at once.

Wood should not be used as an indenting board on white leather. It may stain the leather.

The pressing boards must not be much larger than the book, if you are using C-clamps.

Height of the indenting boards is the height of the cover plus 1/2". This will insure the leather will be indented from head to tail. The board must have a straight clean cut edges.

Width of the indenting board must be precise. It extends from the center of the indented line on the spine leather to the center of the indented line on the foredge leather.

If the leathers are not damp from pasting, dampen with a cotton ball and water. Get as little water on the board as possible. Do not dampen the leather on the inside of the board.

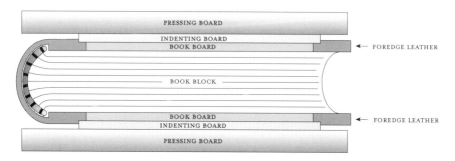

INDENTING THE SURFACE OF THE LEATHER: THE PRESSING BOARDS MUST NOT TOUCH THE LEATHER, BUT APPLY PRESSURE ONTO THE BOARDS USED FOR INDENTING. LEAVE THE BOOK IN THE PRESS FOR 2 OR 3 HOURS.

IF YOU DO NOT HAVE A PRESS, USE A HEAVY WEIGHT ON TOP OF THE PRESSING BOARD, OR *C*-CLAMPS, AS SHOWN ON PAGE 317.

1. Lay one pressing board on the table. Lay one indenting board in place on top of the book. Make sure one edge of the board is even with the line drawn on the spine leather and the opposite edge even with the line on the foredge leather. Flip over the book with the indenting board in place and set it on the pressing board. Position the spine of the book close to the edge, or extending beyond the pressing board, so that the indenting board is close to the edge of the pressing board. This will permit the use of C-clamps for indenting. Likewise, the pressing board cannot protrude beyond the foredge of the book, if you are using C-clamps, because the throat of the C-clamps will not permit pressure at the edge of the indenting board, where it is needed.

Size of the pressing boards is not that critical when using a press. See illustrations on the previous and next page, as well as on this.

2. Add the other indenting board on top the book, lined up.

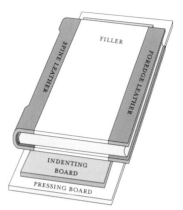

1. PUT INDENTING BOARD IN PLACE ON TOP OF BOOK.
FLIP. SET ONTO THE PRESSING BOARD WITH
INDENTING BOARD CLOSE TO THE EDGE.

2. POSITION SECOND INDENTING BOARD ON THE BOOK.

3. PLACE ON THE TOP PRESSING BOARD.

3. Place a pressing board on top. Make sure the pressing boards do not touch the leather.

4. Indent the boards either with a press, using *C*-clamps, or place a heavy weight on top the pressing boards. Leave the book under pressure for 2 or 3 hours.

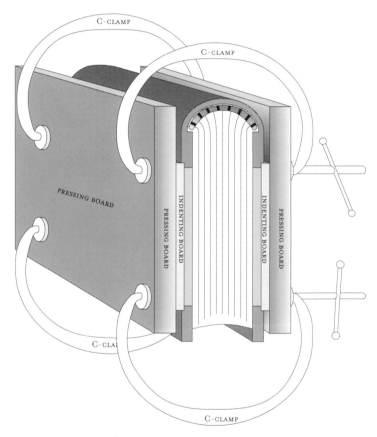

4. PLACE PRESSURE WITH 4 C-CLAMPS, WITH THE FEET OF THE CLAMPS
AT THE 4 CORNERS OF THE INDENTING BOARDS FOR MAXIMUM PRESSURE.

STEP 4 INDENTING WITH A PRESS OR *C*-CLAMPS: LEATHER CAN BE INDENTED WITH BOARDS AND 4 *C*-CLAMPS. IF YOU HAVE A PRESS, THE BOOK WITH INDENTING AND PRESSING BOARDS CAN BE PLACED IN A PRESS, AS ILLUSTRATED ON PAGE 315.

OUTSIDE PAPERS FOR HALF LEATHER OR CLOTH

Covering the Boards is similar to the description for quarter leather, page 279. The following is specific to covering the boards when half leather is used:

Height of the outside paper is the height of the board, plus 2", centered top to bottom. The only turns-in are at the head and the tail.

Width for overlapping leather or cloth is measured from the indented line on the spine leather to the indented line on the foredge leather. Width must be cut exactly.

If the paper swells in width, run your thumb nail along the edge of the cloth or leather at the foredge to know where to trim. Remove to a cutting surface with the pasted side up. Trim with a straight edge and rotary bladed knife while still wet. Immediately paste again and apply to the board before cleaning paste from the straight edge and blade. Make the turns-in at the head and the tail.

Width for butting paper to half cloth is measured from the edge of the spine-cloth to the edge of the cloth at the foredge. Grain is parallel with the height of the paper and board. The only turns-in will be at the head and the tail. Width must be cut exactly.

Fred suggests you make a test to find the exact width for the particular paper you are using: Cut a scrap of the same paper 1/4" wide, with the grain in the correct direction. It should be cut to the precise width between the two leathers. Wet the scrap paper and wait a moment. Lay it down with one end butted to the spine leather and allow the other to extend slightly over the foredge leather. This will show you how much that particular paper stretches with the grain. Cut the paper to be pasted the the width of the dry paper, minus the amount it has stretched when wet.

Every paper expands differently, depending on the amount of grain.

Paste and apply the paper and make the turns-in. If you have measured incorrectly, you can remove the pasted paper to a cutting surface and trim. Paste again and apply to the board. However, cutting wet paper is tricky. Fred's approach is easier.

NO FILLER UNDER CLOTH: No filler is used on the board when covering with cloth. You can indent the cloth and overlap, or you can butt the paper to the cloth. It is important that the paper be the same thickness as the cloth, so that both are level, that is, *inlaid.* This will prevent either from being pulled away from the edge when placing the book on, or removing it from, the bookshelf.

Paste the paper and apply to the board. Place a scrap sheet of wax paper under the board. Close the board. Paste and apply paper to the other board.

PLACING UNDER PRESSURE The book is dried under pressure. The procedure is a variation to *Step 11,* page 287: Place scrap book board on each side of the book which extends to, but does not cover the leather or cloth on the spine or the foredge. The scrap boards should end at the indenting lines on the leathers to maintain pressure on the edge of the paper, since the main surface of the leathers are higher than the indented areas. This is the same concept as the drawings on page 287.

The book sandwiched between the scrap boards is weighted down with a weight of two or three heavy books extending beyond the top scrap book board in all directions. Dry overnight. The sheet of wax paper between the book block and the cover will keep moisture from the boards from touching the book block.

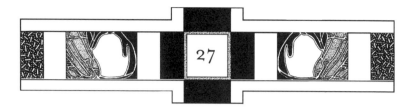
FULL LEATHER

A full leather binding is something special. Fred prefers them for the most important work. Not only does it have the beauty of the leather, but it is also more substantial. It does the best job of protecting the book, which is the purpose of all binding. There are many ways in which full leather can be decorated. See *Finishing,* page 335.

I usually shy away from them because they are so flamboyant and because paring leather is not something to which I look forward. With the approach Fred is showing, making a full leather binding technically is not so difficult.

To make a full leather binding, follow the steps for making a quarter leather Tight Back, with the following differences:

FULL LEATHER BINDING

BOARDS FOR FULL LEATHER

MEASURING AND CUTTING THE BOARDS: Width of the board is the distance from the shoulder to the foredge of the book block, plus the overhang, of about 1/8" to 3/16", minus the thickness of the leather.

Height of the boards is measured after the endbands are attached to the spine of the book. Measure from the bottom of the tailband to the top of the headband. Unlike for quarter leather, do not add 2 thicknesses of leather.

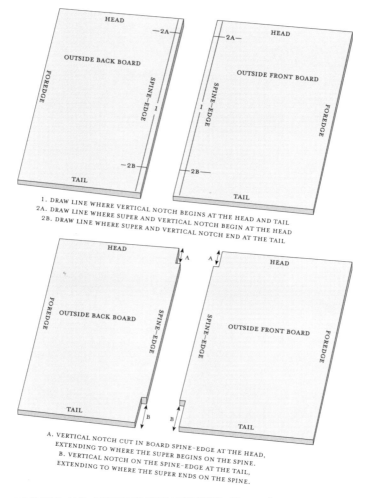

1. DRAW LINE WHERE VERTICAL NOTCH BEGINS AT THE HEAD AND TAIL.
2A. DRAW LINE WHERE SUPER AND VERTICAL NOTCH BEGIN AT THE HEAD
2B. DRAW LINE WHERE SUPER AND VERTICAL NOTCH END AT THE TAIL

A. VERTICAL NOTCH CUT IN BOARD SPINE-EDGE AT THE HEAD, EXTENDING TO WHERE THE SUPER BEGINS ON THE SPINE.
B. VERTICAL NOTCH ON THE SPINE-EDGE AT THE TAIL, EXTENDING TO WHERE THE SUPER ENDS ON THE SPINE.

DRAWING AND CUTTING THE NOTCHES: NOTCH *B* WILL BE TALLER ON THE SPINE THAN *A*. THIS WILL GIVE A SENSE OF A BASE, WITH A LARGER BULGE OF LEATHER AT THE TAIL THAN AT THE HEAD. SEE ILLUSTRATION ON PAGES 46 AND 367.

Cut, but do not notch, filler which is the same thickness as the
leather and same dimensions as the boards. Set on the inside of the
board in order to determine the shoulder in rounding and backing.

SPINE-PAPER: Cut and paste paper across the spine as described on
page 244. Sand the spine-paper. Refer to page 245.

NOTCHING THE BOARDS: There are no horizontal notches along the
head and tail of the boards. The vertical notches, page 247, still must
be made along the spine-edge of the boards. This allows the turns-in
of leather to be flush with the spine-edge of the board. Draw and cut
the notches.

LEATHER

Height of full leather is measured
with a string or scrap paper or
cloth measuring tape. Hold the
end of the scrap paper at the
bottom of the vertical notch *A*
at the head. Proceed up to the
head of the board. Wrap the
scrap paper around the edge of
the board to the other side.
Proceed all the way to the tail.
Wrap around the tail and up to
the end of the vertical notch *B*
at the tail.

Mark the ending point on the
scrap paper. Lay the paper flat
and measure. This will give you
the height needed for full
leather.

NOTE: Height of leather *cannot
be trimmed.* It must be cut to fit
the vertical notches exactly.

Width of full leather is the width of
both boards, the spine, plus the
two foredge turns-in. Fred
suggests leaving a 1" turn-in on
each foredge, which will be
trimmed to ¾".

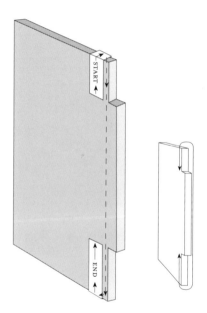

HEIGHT OF THE LEATHER:
USE A SCRAP OF PAPER OR
STRING. START AT THE BOTTOM
OF THE VERTICAL NOTCH AT THE
HEAD. GO OVER THE HEAD OF
THE BOARD. PROCEED TO THE
TAIL. GO AROUND AND UP TO
THE END OF THE VERTICAL
NOTCH AT THE TAIL.

This will give an equal size turn-in at the head and the foredge of each board. There will be a larger turn-in at the tail. See illustrations on page 327.

To measure the width needed for full leather, set the boards and the inside fillers on the book block. Use a scrap of paper, string or tape measure. Measure from 1" in from the foredge on the inside of the front board to the foredge of the board. Wrap around to the outside. Continue to the spine. Wrap snugly around the spine and proceed to the foredge of the back board. Proceed around the board to the inside, to 1" in on the board.

This is the width to cut the leather. The turns-in will be trimmed to ¾" after they are pasted and have dried.

The board thickness is important in measuring the turn-in of leather which is not pared. The thick leather rolled around the board takes more width than pared leather.

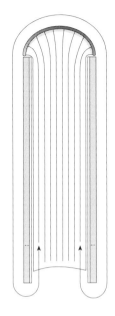

WIDTH OF FULL LEATHER:
USE A SCRAP OF PAPER. START ON THE INSIDE OF THE BOARD AT THE END OF THE TURN-IN. PROCEED AROUND THE FOREDGE OF THE BOARD TO THE SPINE. CONTINUE AROUND THE SPINE TO THE FOREDGE AND INSIDE TO THE END OF THE TURN-IN.

CUTTING THE LEATHER: On the inside of the skin, mark the leather the dimensions with a pencil and straight edge. Grain of the leather should be parallel with the spine of the book. Try to economically position the area to be cut, keeping in mind possible use for the remainder of the hide.

Cut the leather with a thin bladed knife on a sheet of zinc or on a self-seal mat.

PASTING AND APPLYING THE LEATHER: The book block is in a sleeve of wax paper. The boards are placed on the book block, tight against the shoulder. The fillers are set aside for now. The book with boards is placed in the press, as high up as possible and still hold the book in the press. Follow pasting procedures on page 255.

To apply the leather, pick up the leather and hold it above the spine, centering it from side to side. At the head, extend the leather beyond the board the distance of the top notch.

Lay it on the spine with the ends draping over. Press with the palms of your hands to stretch the leather over the spine. *Do not stretch towards head and tail.* The leather must fit the notches. Take the book out of the press without pressing the leather onto the boards.

Lay the book on the back cover. Grasp the leather on the front board at the foredge and lift the leather gently until it is attached to only about 1" of the board at the spine-edge. lay the leather down on the board. Gently pat the leather on the board without stretching.

Turn the book over. Lift the leather on this board, close to the spine. Lay it back on the board and pat.

Open and remove the book block from the boards and set aside. Both boards are open on the table with the inside of the boards and leather facing up. Check to see if the leather is in the proper position for the notches. Roll the turn-in over at the head to see if it covers the cut notches. Unroll. Do the same at the tail.

TRIMMING AND TURNING-IN THE CORNERS: Trim leather at the corners the same as for half leather. See *Mitering the Corners,* page 304. Save the corners to fill in the turn-in. See *Step 3,* page 327.

Turn-in the leather along the head and tail and then the foredge. This is the same as with half leather. See *Making the Turns-In,* page 306.

PLACE BOARDS BACK ON THE BOOK BLOCK: Re-paste the leather between the boards. Set the book back into the boards. Follow procedures and illustrations the same as for quarter leather, on page 259.

SHAPING THE LEATHER: The book *cannot* be put back in the press to shape the leather on the spine, as with quarter leather. Wet leather would get indented with press marks.

To shape the spine on full leather, stand the book on the foredge. Use a bone folder to make the creases across the spine at the end of the bulge made by the turns-in.

Close the book. Place the book on a piece of book board. Place another on top. Lay one or two good size books on top for weight. Allow to dry overnight.

Follow the procedure for *First Opening*, page 263.

TRIMMING THE LEATHER ON THE INSIDE OF THE BOARDS: The turns-will be cut square, so that you can easily fill in the remainder of the board with filler to bring the surface up to the height of the leather. This is done only after the leather is totally dry.

1. Open the front board. Place a support under the board so that it is level and firm for cutting. Measure from the head to the end of the vertical notch at the head along the spine-edge.

Place pencil dot *A* the same distance down from the head and in from the foredge, about 2".

Measure the same distance in from the foredge. Place pencil dot *B* near the head, down about 2". Mark the same measurement with pencil dot *B* on the foredge, up from the tail about 2".

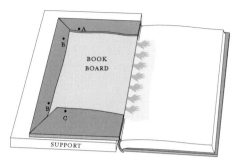

1. PLACE A SUPPORT UNDER THE OPENED BOARD TO GIVE SUPPORT FOR CUTTING. MARK THE PENCIL DOTS.

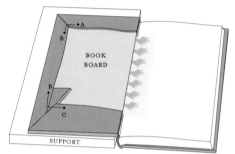

2. INDENT THE LEATHER AT THE CORNERS, LINED UP WITH THE VERTICAL NOTCHES AND THE PENCIL DOTS.

3. PASTE THE TRIANGULAR SCRAP OF LEATHER CUT FROM THE CORNER TO FILL IN THE TURN-IN AT POINT "B" AND "C". THE BEVEL OF EACH PIECE OF LEATHER WILL FIT TOGETHER.

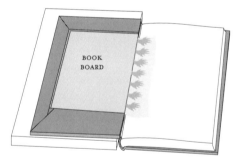

4. TRIM OFF THE EXCESS OF THE TURNS-IN AT THE HEAD, FOREDGE AND TAIL. THE PIECE OF LEATHER ADDED WILL FILL IN THE LINE OF THE BORDER AT THE TAIL AND FOREDGE.

TRIMMING THE TURNS-IN ON THE INSIDE OF THE BOARDS.

Measure from the tail to the end of the vertical notch at the tail along the spine-edge. Place pencil dot C the same distance up from the tail and in from the foredge, about 2". This will give you the location to trim the turns-in along the head, foredge and tail of the inside of the board.

2. In cutting off the excess at the head, try to avoid cutting too far into the border of leather at the foredge. Use your thumb nail to mark when to end the cut. Do the same at the tail and the foredge. This will give L-shaped indentations as a guide in trimming.

3. Use the scrap of leather cut off from the corner to piece the turn-in at the foredge and tail. The bevel of the triangular scrap will fit into the bevel of the turn-in at the tail.

4. Line up a straight edge with the L-shaped indentation and the notch at the head. Trim away the excess. Do the same at the tail and the foredge.

Trim the leather turns-in on the back board in the same manner.

CAUTION: Do not try to cut leather on the depth of the board, or you will risk cutting through the leather to the outside of the spine. That is why the turns-in were cut to fit exactly to the end of the vertical notches, as explained on page 323.

ATTACHING THE BOARDS: Attach the boards in the same manner as described for quarter leather. See page 267–269. The notches on the scrap piece of card described on that page will have to be cut wider to fit over the leather covered boards.

CUTTING FILLER FOR THE INSIDE OF THE BOARDS: On page 323, filler the same thickness as the leather was cut the dimensions of the board. It will now be trimmed to fit. Measure the area of the bare board on the inside of the front cover. Cut the filler to these dimensions. Set the filler in as a test. It must fit snugly along the edges of the turns-in. Run your finger from the filler onto the leather and back onto the filler. There should be a smooth transition if the filler is the exact thickness of the leather. If not, replace the filler with a proper thickness of filler.

Try this same filler on the inside of the back board. If it is a precise fit, cut the filler for the inside of the back board the same.

PASTING THE FILLER TO THE BOARDS: Open the front board. Place a support under the board so that it is level and firm for pasting and attaching the filler so you can press down firmly.

Only one board is pasted at a time. Paste the board, not the filler. Take care not to get paste on the leather turns-in. If you do, immediately wipe it off with a paper towel. Be generous with the paste. Wait a moment and give a second, even coat.

Set the filler onto the inside of the board. Take care to make the filler fit tightly against the leather turns-in, for as tight a seam as possible and so it lines up with the spine-edge of the board. Add a sheet of wax paper between the board and the sleeved book block. Close the board.

Turn the book over. Open the back board and place a support under it. Paste this board in the same manner. Set the filler onto the board. Place a sheet of wax paper between the board and the sleeved book block. Close the board. Place a scrap board on top which cover the entire book. Place a weight of two or three books on top. Allow to dry overnight.

NOTE: Any decoration of the leather which entails thread or paper pressed into the leather must be done at this time, prior to pasting down the endsheet. To keep the thread from raveling, the ends must extend around the head, foredge and/or tail onto the leather turns-in. They will be covered by the pasted down endsheet. See page 365. For various ideas for decorating, see *Finishing,* page 335.

PASTE-DOWN: Remove the sleeve of wax paper and discard it. The endsheets are now pasted down to the inside of the boards. The procedure is the same, whether quarter, half or full leather. Follow instructions on page 296.

Fred Jordan, sewn Raised Cords, bound in full leather with blind tooling. The book is *Gothic & Renaissance Bookbindings*, by E. Ph.
Goldschmidt, Ernest Benn, Ltd., London, 1928. 29.4 x 22.5 x 4.5 cm.

Neither Raised Cord sewing nor blind tooling of leather is described
in this manual.

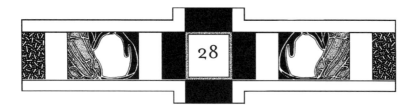
HOLLOW BACK

The Hollow Back, or sometimes referred to as the *Spring Back,* is sewn, rounded and backed the same as the Tight Back. The quarter, half or full leather is applied the same, with the exception of adding of a tube on the spine under the leather. Attaching the boards, covering, paste-down and finishing are the same as for the Tight Back.

ACTION OF OPENING THE BOOK: The tube is made the same dimensions as the spine. It is pasted to the spine before the leather is applied.

The tube allows the leather to pop from the spine as the book is opened. The backbone being free of the leather can arc open, allowing the book to open flatter than a Tight Back, where the leather is pasted to the backbone. Closing the book, the leather is pulled tight against the spine as the tube compresses.

THE SINGLE SIDE OF THE TUBE GOES NEXT TO THE BOOK BLOCK.

THIS SIDE IS PASTED ONTO THE BACKBONE OF THE BOOK

THE TUBE FOR THE HOLLOW BACK

HOLLOW BACK
PERMITS THE BACKBONE TO ARCH OPEN, ALLOWING THE PAGES TO LIE FLATTER

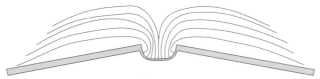

TIGHT BACK
HAS AS BACKBONE PASTED TO THE LEATHER. PAGES BLOSSOM OPEN.

DETAIL of the head at the spine-edge of a found Hollow Back with full cloth covering. The boards are opened to show how the cloth pops from the spine to permit the text block to flex.

The Hollow Back opens better on a thicker book, 1½" to 2" thick, rather than on a thinner book. And, it is the thicker book which needs the wider backbone to have the ability to arc in an extreme concave shape as the pages are turned. Examine at a large unabridged dictionary and you will see the structure.

Facing page:

Scott McCarney, found Hollow Back book, altered. Valentine's Day, 1995. Scott quartered the book with a band saw. He used the quarter at the spine and head. 12 x 11 x 3 cm.

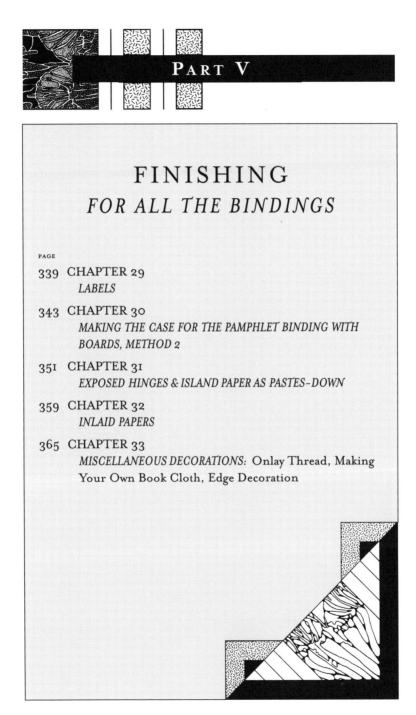

PART V

FINISHING
FOR ALL THE BINDINGS

INTRODUCTION

Finishing is the final step in binding, which is decoration. Decoration can be on the boards, spine, edge of the book block, or the inside of the boards. I often include altering the endsheets.

TOOLING: Titles are often stamped into the leather or cloth. This is referred to as *tooling*. The tool is like a branding iron, but not heated to burn in an impression, but simply make one. If the tool is used with heat only, the indented line or text is referred to as *blind* stamping. Often a sheet of color, gold or silver foil is placed on the surface. The heated tool then makes an impression, transferring the foil into the indented leather or cloth.

Traditionally, tooling has been done in many ways. We will be discussing methods that can be done without special tools.

As a substitute for tooled lines, Fred has devised onlaying color thread. See *Onlay Thread,* page 365. For a substitute for text, we will have to rely upon printed labels, page 339.

All decoration is approached the same for the Pamphlet Binding with Boards, The Flat Back, Tight Back or Hollow Back. In Chapter 31, exposed hinges will be described. See page 351. That must be limited to the Pamphlet Binding with Boards, The Flat Back, since book cloth hinges will be used. The approach would be the same for the Tight Back, but you would have to have the skill to pare leather and, to pare it paper thin. Therefore, exposed hinges for that binding will not be discussed.

Finishing spans such a large area, that we will only describe a few and suggest others. A deeper exploration of the subject promises to be the next collaborative book by Fred and me. Stay tuned.

QUARTER CLOTH CASED-IN FLAT BACK WITH PHOTOGRAPHIC PAPER ON OUTSIDE OF BOARDS. THE SAME BOOK-IN-PROGRESS IS ON PAGES 159, 160 AND 340.

29

LABELS

COMPUTER LABELS: Labels are best inlaid. Level with the decorative paper, the label will not catch, sliding in and out of the book shelf. See *Inlaid Papers,* page 359. If the book is small, some cut the paper for the outside of the boards to fit the computer printer. The title is printed on the paper prior to covering the boards.

Text, with title and author, can be designed on the computer and printed out onto a nice color of laid paper, rather than the usual white bond.

If you have a laser printer, computer supply stores offer various shapes of labels on metallic or color papers which can be used with your printer.

FUSING: If you make laser printed labels on a laid paper, it is a good idea to place the print into a 400° oven for 30 seconds, in order to fuse the carbon to the irregular surface. Otherwise, the text may rub off. Make a test and run your finger across the text to make sure it is fixed before you paste it to your cover.

I make my labels using Quark XPress. This allows me to add a border, as well as to use different size of type, leading and kerning, often not possible with lesser programs. If a tone in a border is needed, rather than obtaining it via the printer, you can water color the laser printout. This adds hand work, softens the look of the label.

CALLIGRAPHIC: The title can be script, hand lettered, drawn or painted. The letters of the words can be cut out and individually applied, or inlaid. Perhaps one large single letter would be a less ambitious undertaking. The text might appear within this single shape.

A paper or cloth drawing, collage or water color, with title incorporated, can be used to cover the boards.

SILK SCREENING: A small silk screen can be made up. The title can be screened onto the quarter cloth, prior to, or after the cloth is attached to the boards. Any stencilling method can be used.

FABRIC: Text can be silk screened onto cloth used to cover the boards. Line etching prints surprisingly well on many different kinds of fabrics, including fuzzy ones.

PHOTO COVERINGS: Photographers can use pre-sensitized photo linen to print an image, as well as the title. After processing, the linen can be pasted to the boards without cracking the emulsion. The image could be oil painted after it is on the board.

Certain photographic papers will accept a fold. You can print an image for the cover. Next to, or superimposed upon, you can photographically print the title.

Instead of a full range of tones, the printing could be purposefully very light. This would permit applied color to the photo. Preferably the color would be added after the photo is wheat pasted to the board. Follow the procedure for *Covering the Boards,* page 279.

PHOTOGRAPHIC ISLAND PASTE-DOWN ON THE INSIDE OF THE BOARD COMPLETES THIS VIRTUAL BOOK. THIS SAME BOOK-IN-PROGRESS APPEARS ON PAGES 159, 160 AND 337. FROM A 1980 PHOTOGRAPH OF DEBORAH FLYNN POST.

A title can be collage onto an image. This can be placed in a color copier. The photo copy can be used as part of the covering for the board, or the entire board, butting to the quarter cloth.

Gary Frost sometimes uses economy in adding a laser label to his booklets. He prints one label which extends from the spine onto the front board. The information presented on the spine is duplicated and often expanded, on that area of the label which shows on the front. See page 137.

This label could also extend to the back board to include a colophon.

Influenced by Gary, I have used a label which starts on the outside of the board at the foredge and continues around to the inside of the board. The title on the outside is parallel with the foredge, so that only a small amount of label shows on the front board. The paper might be a light marbled paper or a lightly printed digital image, with the text in black, or in white.

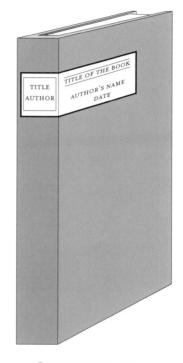

ONE LABEL PASTED ON THE SPINE, EXTEND-ING TO THE FRONT BOARD.

FOREDGE TITLES: Rather than labeling the spine, you can place the title on the foredge. Prior to casing-in, place the book block in the press, sandwiched between scrap boards. Write, water color or draw the title on the foredge.

The title can be silk screened onto the foredge.

The title and/or drawing can start on the front cover, extend onto the foredge and be completed either on the back cover, or inside the book block on the title page.

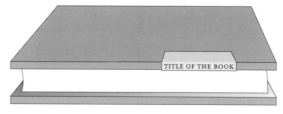

LABEL WITH MOST OF THE INFORMATION ON THE INSIDE OF THE BOARD.

30

CASE FOR THE PAMPHLET BINDING, METHOD 2

Method I for making the case for the Pamphlet Binding with Boards is described on page 143. Compare it with the following, taught to me by Gary Frost, to see which you prefer.

Method 2 requires measuring the gap between the boards, marking the boards and pasting the quarter cloth to the boards. The quarter cloth attached to the boards is referred to as the *case*.

I prefer this method for the exposed hinge which permits decorating the inside of the board. Method I has nothing but the white of the endsheet as paste-down. Here, there is the texture of the exposed hinge plus a simple or elaborate island paste-down. For examples see pages 340, 351, 352, 354, 355 and 363.

EXPOSED HINGES FOR THE PAMPHLET BINDING

If you wish to trim the hinge even with the turns-in on the boards, it is far less complicated, if you will make the hinges extra wide, so they will extend on the inside of the board past the turns-in of the quarter cloth. When the hinge is pasted to the inside of the board and has dried, it can be trimmed easily to the exact width of the quarter cloth. If your hinge was shorter than the quarter cloth, you would have to trim the cloth on the front of the board, on the depth and on the inside. This would be more complicated.

For exposed cloth hinges on the Pamphlet Binding with Boards, follow the description for the binding, which begins on page 125. Instead of using a jaconette hinge use the same color book cloth which you will use on the outside of the boards for the quarter cloth.

In folding the hinge, the good side of the cloth goes on the valley of the fold. While sewing the single signature book block, the mountain peak of the hinge will be seen. That is the side of the fabric which will be pasted to the boards.

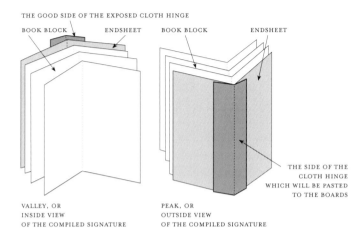

THE GOOD SIDE OF THE EXPOSED CLOTH HINGE

BOOK BLOCK   ENDSHEET   BOOK BLOCK   ENDSHEET

THE SIDE OF THE
CLOTH HINGE
WHICH WILL BE PASTED
TO THE BOARDS

VALLEY, OR   PEAK, OR
INSIDE VIEW   OUTSIDE VIEW
OF THE COMPILED SIGNATURE   OF THE COMPILED SIGNATURE

EXPOSED CLOTH HINGE OF THE PAMPHLET BINDING WITH BOARDS IS MEA-
SURED AND SEWN THE SAME AS THE HIDDEN JACONETTE HINGE DESCRIBED ON
PAGE 130.

IT IS IMPORTANT IN THE EXPOSED HINGE TO FOLD THE GOOD SIDE OF THE CLOTH
IN ON ITSELF, SO THE CORRECT SIDE WILL SHOW WHEN IT IS PASTED DOWN.

STEPS IN MAKING THE CASE, METHOD 2:

1. Place a scrap piece of card temporarily on each side of the book
block. Place the cut and sanded boards on the outside of the card.
The card is to increase the space between the closed boards and the
book block. This will allow plenty of room for the thickness of the
papers which will be pasted down on the inside of the boards.
Sometimes I increase this measurement by a half thickness of a book
board, as in the illustration to the right.

Jog on the tail and spine-edge, so that the boards, card and book
block are flush on these two edges.

2. Place three strips of masking tape from the back board, across the
spine, onto the front board.

The masking tape will insure the proper spine-gap between the
boards until the quarter cloth is added.

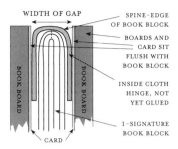

STEP 1: ASSEMBLE THE BOOK BLOCK AND BOARDS, WITH CARD BETWEEN AS TEMPORARY SPACERS.

THIS IS THE GAP BETWEEN THE BOARDS.

STEP 1: HERE THE BOOK BLOCK IS THE SAME WIDTH AS ABOVE, BUT THE GAP BETWEEN THE BOARDS HAS BEEN MADE SLIGHTLY WIDER.

STEP 2: PLACE MASKING TAPE AROUND THE BOARDS TO FIX THE GAP BETWEEN THE BOARDS.

3. Lay the assembled book on the table on the back cover. Carefully open the front board so that the inside of both boards facing up. The masking tape side will be against the table. See illustration below. Remove the book block and set it aside. Throw away the two pieces of card.

Lay a straight edge down along the bottom of the two boards to make sure they are square to each other. The side of the boards facing you now will become the outside.

Width of the quarter cloth is in proportion to the boards. Sometimes I cut a scrap of paper to fit on e board in the area where the quarter cloth will be. Then, I can see the proportion of cloth to board.

Mark the width for the quarter cloth with the pencil lines on the boards. These will be used as a guide for positioning the pasted quarter cloth.

Height of the cloth is height of the boards plus 2". Cut the cloth.

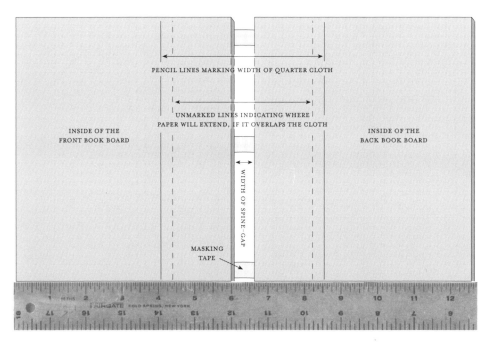

STEP 3, BELOW: ALIGN THE BOARDS WITH A STRAIGHT EDGE. MARK THE BOARDS WITH PENCIL LINES AS A GUIDE TO LAY DOWN THE PASTED QUARTER CLOTH. THIS IS THE WIDTH OF THE QUARTER CLOTH, ONLY IF THE PAPER BUTTS UP. IF THE PAPER OVERLAPS, THE AMOUNT OF CLOTH YOU SEE WILL BE LESS.

BOARDS

For quickness, use PVA glue. Glue the quarter cloth and lay in position on the pencil lines, on the outside of the boards, centered top to bottom. Pat to adhere, but do not push between the boards or you will stretch the cloth.

Turn the boards over. Hold the boards in place while removing the masking tape. Make the turns-in. Paste paper on the inside of the spine as described on page 147.

Attach the book block to the case as described on pages 149–154 and *Walking the Bone Folders*, page 156. Trim the excess off the hinge, only after the hinge is dry.

Since you used PVA on the boards, the case is ready to add the outside papers and the island pastes-down immediately. We both recommend wheat paste for attaching the papers, especially if you are butting or inlaying papers. You can slide the paper around, whereas with PVA, it sticks immediately.

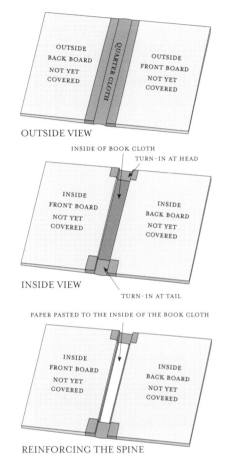

OUTSIDE VIEW

INSIDE VIEW

REINFORCING THE SPINE

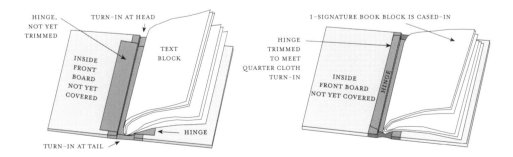

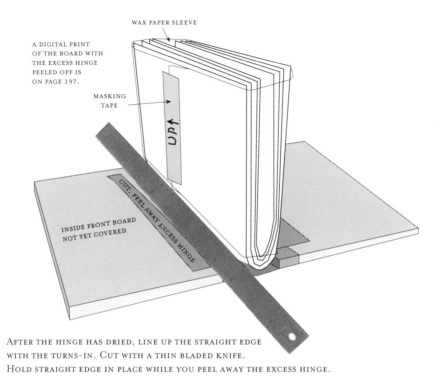

WAX PAPER SLEEVE

A DIGITAL PRINT
OF THE BOARD WITH
THE EXCESS HINGE
PEELED OFF IS
ON PAGE 197.

MASKING
TAPE

UP

CUT. PEEL AWAY EXCESS HINGE

INSIDE FRONT BOARD
NOT YET COVERED

AFTER THE HINGE HAS DRIED, LINE UP THE STRAIGHT EDGE
WITH THE TURNS-IN. CUT WITH A THIN BLADED KNIFE.
HOLD STRAIGHT EDGE IN PLACE WHILE YOU PEEL AWAY THE EXCESS HINGE.

COVERING THE BOARDS WITH ISLAND PASTES-DOWN

The Pamphlet Binding with Boards, as well as the Flat Back, may be
sewn with exposed cloth hinges. Covering the outside and the inside
of the boards can be done at once. This is because the boards are
dried in the closed position.

Follow the procedure for covering the boards and using an island
paste-down on page 359.

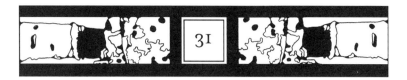

31

EXPOSED HINGES & ISLANDS AS PASTES-DOWN

The Pamphlet Binding with Boards, page 125 and the Flat Back, page 157, were described with a jaconette hinge sewn with the signatures. When the book block was cased-in with the hinge, the endsheet was pasted to the board to cover the inside of the boards. The endsheet covered over the jaconette hinge. This is the way such books are usually made.

I learned the two bindings from Gary Frost. He taught me to use book cloth as the hinge. The endsheet is not pasted down, so that the hinge is exposed. To complete the inside of the board, an *island of paper* is pasted down.

BOTH SIDES OF 1 BOARD ARE COVERED TO PREVENT BOARD WARPAGE.
DON'T COVER BOTH OUTSIDE BOARDS, THEN BOTH ISLAND PASTES-DOWN.

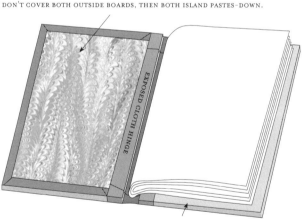

EXPOSED CLOTH HINGE

COVER BACK BOARD NEXT

ISLAND PASTE-DOWN *on a Pamphlet Binding with Boards*

THE ISLAND PASTE-DOWN IS A VARIATION FOR QUARTER CLOTH PAMPHLET BINDING WITH BOARDS, AND THE FLAT BACK. A SEPARATE PRE-CUT PAPER IS THE INSIDE PASTE-DOWN, BUTTED TO THE EXPOSED HINGE.

BOTH SIDES OF THE BOARDS CAN BE COVERED AT ONCE, RATHER THAN WAITING FOR THE OUTSIDE PAPERS TO DRY. THE BOARDS ARE DRIED CLOSED WITH A SHEET OF WAX PAPER BETWEEN THE BOARD AND BOOK BLOCK.

ISLAND PASTE-DOWN: The *Pamphlet Binding with Boards* and the *Cased-In Flat Back* can be sewn with book cloth hinges attached to the book block. With this method an island paste-down is used on the inside of the board, rather than pasting down the endsheet of the book block, to permit the cloth hinge to show. The inside of the board becomes a decorative element, not just a white sheet of paper.

An island paste-down on the inside of the board has these benefits:

· It is easier to paste a hinge of book cloth up the edge and onto the surface of the board than it is to paste down the first sheet of paper. The endsheet often wrinkles going onto the board.

· It is quicker. Paste the outside paper onto one board, then the inside island paste-down to the same board. Insert a sheet of wax paper and close the board. The other board is then covered, all at once, requiring less than 5 minutes. This is possible, since the boards will dry closed. Refer to *Covering the Boards in a Single Session,* page 62 and *Preventing Board Warpage,* page 60.

· The exposed cloth hinge looks good on the inside of the board.

· An island paste-down is not limited in dimensions, as is the case in pasting down the endsheet. This offers possibilities of design.

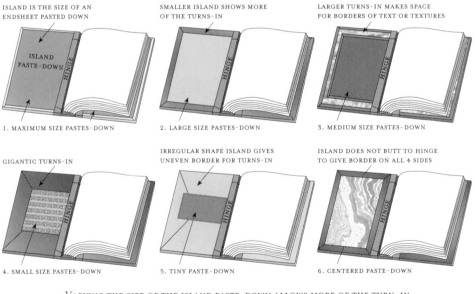

ISLAND IS THE SIZE OF AN ENDSHEET PASTED DOWN

SMALLER ISLAND SHOWS MORE OF THE TURNS-IN

LARGER TURNS-IN MAKES SPACE FOR BORDERS OF TEXT OR TEXTURES

1. MAXIMUM SIZE PASTES-DOWN

2. LARGE SIZE PASTES-DOWN

3. MEDIUM SIZE PASTES-DOWN

GIGANTIC TURNS-IN

IRREGULAR SHAPE ISLAND GIVES UNEVEN BORDER FOR TURNS-IN

ISLAND DOES NOT BUTT TO HINGE TO GIVE BORDER ON ALL 4 SIDES

4. SMALL SIZE PASTES-DOWN

5. TINY PASTE-DOWN

6. CENTERED PASTE-DOWN

VARYING THE SIZE OF THE ISLAND PASTE-DOWN ALLOWS MORE OF THE TURN-IN FROM THE OUTSIDE OF THE BOARD TO BE SEEN INSIDE.

UNLIKE PASTING DOWN THE ENDSHEET, THE INSIDE OF THE BOARD BECOMES A DECORATIVE ELEMENT, NOT JUST A WHITE SHEET OF PAPER.

HINGES: The exposed cloth hinge for the Pamphlet Binding is described on page 343. The exposed hinge for the Flat Back is simply substituting book cloth for the jaconette hinge described on pages 161–169. The exposed cloth hinge is illustrated sewn on page 160.

The following should be repeated: If you wish to trim the hinge even with the turns-in, it is far less complicated, if you make the hinges extra wide, so they will extend on the inside of the board past the turns-in of the quarter cloth. When the hinge is pasted to the inside of the board and has dried, it can be trimmed easily to the exact width of the quarter cloth. If your hinge was shorter than the quarter cloth, you would have to trim the cloth on the front of the board, on the depth and on the inside. This would be more complicated. For the Flat Back, sew and case-in as described on page 157.

COVERING THE BOARDS

If you are going to use an island paste-down on the inside of the board, covering the boards for the Pamphlet Binding and Flat Back is similar to the description on pages 279. However, the remainder of this chapter will discuss the differences when not using the endsheet as paste-down.

MEASURING PAPERS FOR THE OUTSIDE OF THE BOARDS: It is essential to pre-cut both outside and inside papers before beginning to paste. The grain is parallel to the spine.[25]

FLUSH SURFACE FOR THE OUTSIDE OF THE BOARDS: Width of the quarter-cloth also is dependent upon whether you will butt the paper or overlap it onto the cloth. Butting paper to cloth can be done, if both are the same thickness, to maintain a flush surface.

It is imperative to have a flush surface on the outside of the boards, but not the inside. Taking a book off a bookshelf causes wear, but not as much as placing the book onto a crowded shelf. If the quarter cloth is thicker than the paper, it is less apt to catch removing the book from the shelf than pushing the book back into place. See *Inlaid Papers,* page 359.

MEASUREMENTS FOR AN ISLAND PASTE-DOWN: The island of paper on the inside of the board is cut to butt to the trimmed hinge, but over-lap the turns-in at the head, tail and foredge. See illustrations on pages 340, 351, 352, 354, 355 and 363. On page 357, the hinge is not exposed, but probably jaconette. The endsheet is pasted onto the board, but barely so. The island paste-down is elaborately inlaid with 13 pieces of paper.

BOARDS WITH LARGE OVERHANGS, SUCH AS THIS PAMPHLET BINDING WITH BOARDS, ALLOW FOR AN EVER–PRESENT BORDER OF TEXT ON THE INSIDE OF THE BOARDS.

TEXT IS LASER PRINTED ONTO LAID PAPER, CUT IN STRIPS AND PASTED TO THE BOARDS, REMINISCENT OF GOLD TOOLING.

KEITH SMITH, BOOK 183, *A MAKE-BELIEVE BOOK OF POETRY,* 25 DECEMBER, 1997. EDITION OF 3, TIMES THE NUMBER OF COPIES THIS TEXTBOOK MAY EVER SELL. MARBLED PAPERS COURTESY OF DIANE MAURER. BINDING BY THE AUTHOR. REPRODUCED ACTUAL SIZE.

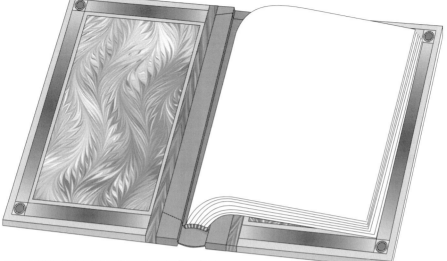

BOARDS WITH LARGE OVERHANGS, SUCH AS THIS FLAT BACK,
ALLOW FOR EVER–PRESENT BORDERS ON THE INSIDE OF THE BOARDS.

THIS BOOK, AND THAT ON THE FACING PAGE, WERE BOUND QUARTER LEATHER.
AS I OFTEN DO, A THIN VERTICAL STRIP OF MARBLED PAPER IS INLAID ON THE OUTSIDE AND INSIDE BOARDS,
AGAINST THE LEATHER. THIS GIVES A LINE OF DECORATION BETWEEN THE LEATHER AND DECORATIVE PAPER/S,
REMINISCENT OF GOLD TOOLING IN TRADITIONAL BINDINGS.

INCREASING THE SQUARE OF THE BOOK OFFERS OPPORTUNITY FOR DESIGN FOR
THE OPENED BOOK. HERE, VARIOUS DECORATIVE PAPERS ARE INLAID.

COMPARE THE OVERSIZE BOARDS WITH EVER-PRESENT BORDER WITH THE BORDER
OF INLAID MARBLED PAPERS ON PAGE 173.

OVERLAPPING VS BUTTING THE PAPER TO THE SPINE-COVERING: If you are using leather, the paper *must* overlap the indented leather. Refer to: *Indenting Quarter Leather,* page 275. If you are using book cloth on the spine, the papers for the outside of the boards can overlap the cloth, or can butt up tangent. This must be taken into consideration when measuring the width of the paper.

Fred always overlaps the quarter cloth with the outside paper. The edge of the cloth could ravel over time, even though book cloth is heavily sized. But the primary reason Fred overlaps is to avoid damage placing the book on and removing it from, the shelf.

Sliding the book onto the shelf, the leather would be pulled from the board, if it sits higher on the board than the paper. With the paper overlapping the edge of the leather is protected.

Pulling the book from the shelf, the paper could be snagged. That is why the edge of the leather has been indented to keep the overlapped paper below the surface of the leather.

I always butt the outside paper to quarter or half cloth bindings. If you butt the paper, two things are critical:
· use sized book cloth so the edge will not unravel.
· paper must be the same thickness as the cloth, so neither will snag sliding the book onto, or pulling it from, the shelf. If the book cloth is thicker, paste down a filler paper on the uncovered area of the outside of the board prior to pasting down the outside decorative paper. This is to bring the decorative paper to the same level as the book cloth. See *Indenting Cloth,* page 187.

PASTING THE PAPERS: Follow Steps 1–9 for applying one outside paper to one board, pages 281–286. While you are pasting one outside paper, also paste one island paste-down, so that there will be no waiting between adding moisture to the front and back of the same board. This counter-balance of tension will avoid board warpage.

Immediately attach the inside island paste-down after covering the outside of that board. Place a sheet of wax paper between the board and book block. Close the board. Paste the outside and inside papers for the remaining board. After both boards are covered, I stand the book up to dry with the covers slightly open to allow air on both side of the boards. Since both sides of the boards are covered at once, the boards will not warp and do not need to dry under weight.[25]

Refer to *Preventing Board Warpage,* page 60.

Remove the sleeve of wax paper. When the boards are dry, if there is a slight curve to the boards, you can carefully bend the board back to flat. Take extreme caution; too much pressure will crease the board. The binding is complete.

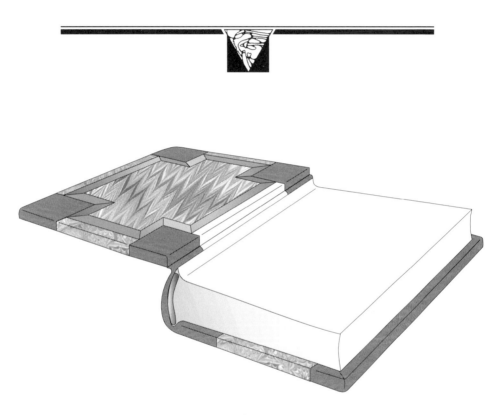

INLAYS of ISLANDS as PASTES-DOWN:

THIS HALF LEATHER VIRTUAL BINDING HAS A FRAGMENT OF THE ENDSHEET PASTED DOWN, EXTENDING ONLY OVER THE HINGE AND SLIGHTLY OVERLAPPING THE LEATHER TURNS-IN ALONG THE SPINE-EDGE.

THE REMAINDER OF THE INSIDE OF THE BOARD IS AN ELABORATE ISLAND PASTE-DOWN, WHICH SLIGHTLY OVERLAPS THE LEATHER TURNS-IN ALONG THE FOREDGE.

TWELVE LINEAR PIECES ARE INLAID AS A BORDER. IN THE CENTER IS A MARBLED PAPER. I CHOSE THIS DESIGN TO SHOW OFF AS MUCH OF THE LEATHER TURNS-IN ON THE INSIDE OF THE BOARD AS POSSIBLE. I ALSO MADE THIS BINDING AS AN INTRODUCTION TO INLAYS, WHICH IS THE NEXT CHAPTER.

1. Inlaid papers pasted to outside of board.

2. Turns-In made on inside of board.

3. Island paste-down is added on the inside of the board. It butts against the exposed satin book cloth hinge and overlaps the turns-in.

4. Completed Flat Back is in quarter cloth, a satin book cloth. For how to cut inlays of paper, see page 360.

32

INLAID PAPERS

COLLAGE: Several papers can be a collage for the boards. If they are to be pasted to the outside of the boards, they must not overlap. Otherwise, when the book is placed into and removed from the shelf, edges will tend to catch and peel back or tear. The papers must be *inlaid,* all on the same surface, all the same thickness . The collage is not fixed prior to pasting. The pasted pieces are slid and butted together on the board.

IMPROMPTU: The design is almost always pre-planned, but can be improvised, contingent pasted pieces, placed side by side until the board is covered.

EVEN OVERHANG: If you are improvising the design on the outside of the board, the touching papers must overhang at the head, foredge and tail to be used as the turns-in.

PASTING INLAYS: Paste all papers for the outside and inside of one board, only.

1. Butt the paper/s against the quarter cloth, centered top to bottom. There must be an even overhang at the head, foredge and tail. See figure 1 on the facing page.

After all are papers are attached to the outside of the board, you might trim any excessive overhang, but the final trim occurs after the turns-in are made.

2. Cut the corners, as described on page 282, *Cutting Off the Paper at the Corners.* Make the turns-in. Make sure the turns-in butt against each other so no board is seen between the cracks. Now use a small straight edge and trim the turns-in so they are precisely even at the head, foredge and tail. See figure 2.

3. Add the island paste-down as described on page 351. See figure 3 on the facing page. Place a sheet of wax paper and close the board.

4. This board is complete. Cover the remaining board in the same manner.

PRE-CONCEIVED DESIGN

A line drawing can be ruled off. Each shape is assigned a tone, color and/or pattern of paper. Notes can be made on the line drawing.

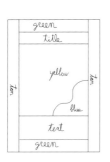

1. LINE DRAWING FOR COVER

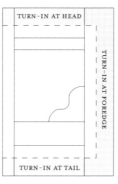

2. DRAWING WITH TURNS-IN

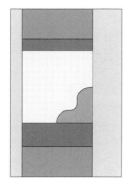

3. ASSEMBLED PIECES OF CUT PAPERS.

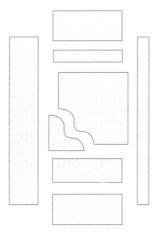

4. PIECES FLIPPED OVER AND SEPARATED TO BE PASTED.

5. FLAT BACK WITH INLAID PAPERS ON THE FRONT BOARD

1. THE DESIGN IS PLANNED.

2. SPACE IS CONSIDERED FOR THE TURNS-IN.

3. THE PAPERS ARE CUT AND PUSHED ADJACENT TO SEE IF THEY FIT.

4. ALL THE PIECES ARE FLIPPED OVER IN ORDER, READY TO PASTE. KEEP A DISTANCE BETWEEN EACH PIECE FOR PASTING. APPLY TO THE COVER, STARTING WITH THE PIECE THAT BUTTS TO THE SPINE CLOTH.

5. MAKE THE TURNS-IN. APPLY THE INSIDE ISLAND PASTE-DOWN. PLACE A SHEET OF WAX PAPER BETWEEN BOARD AND BOOK BLOCK. COVER THE BACK BOARD. STAND THE BOOK ON THE TAIL WITH COVERS SLIGHTLY OPEN TO DRY.

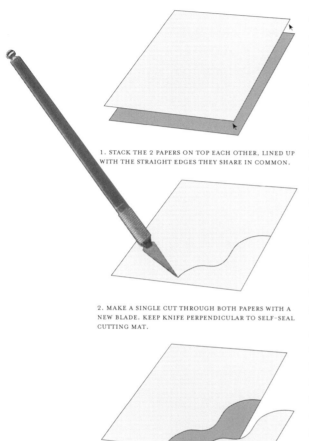

1. STACK THE 2 PAPERS ON TOP EACH OTHER, LINED UP WITH THE STRAIGHT EDGES THEY SHARE IN COMMON.

2. MAKE A SINGLE CUT THROUGH BOTH PAPERS WITH A NEW BLADE. KEEP KNIFE PERPENDICULAR TO SELF-SEAL CUTTING MAT.

3. USE THE LARGER PIECE OF THE LIGHTER COLOR WITH THE SMALLER PIECE OF THE DARKER. THE BACK COVER COULD USE THE LEFTOVERS, WITH THE DESIGN IN REVERSE COLORS.

STRAIGHT CUTS: Use a straight edge and X-Acto™ knife with #11 blades to cut pieces. When all the cuts are made, arrange the design to check for fit. Make sure you allow for the turns-in on the head, tail and foredge.

INLAY CUTS: If curves are involved, pieces cannot be cut individually. The seams would not consistently butt.

Step 1: Lay the adjacent curved pieces on top of each other making sure the bottom piece is large enough for the shape.

Step 2: Cut the curve of both papers, the concave and the convex , in a single action.

TOOLS: A thin bladed knife is needed. I use an X-Acto™ knife with #11 blades. Use a new blade for every inlay cut. The once-used blades can be used later for less critical cutting.

A self-seal cutting mat is an ideal surface to cut the inlays. Using book board is perilous. When the blade crosses a previous cut, the diverging blade will cause a disaster.

CUTTING PROCEDURE: Keep the blade perpendicular to the cutting surface, or the bottom paper will be a different size.

Angle of the blade is important to prevent rough edges. I hold mine rather steep for better results. The angle is no more than that shown above. Start at the head, *beyond* the papers, cut through to beyond the tail, making the curve, as well as insuring severing both sheets.

EVEN OVERHANG: If your pre-conceived design is for the outside of the board, place the pasted papers on the board, butting them. After all are in place, check to see that the overhang at the head, foredge and tail are even. If not, there are two approaches to trimming:

· Trim any pieces that need it with scissors before making the turns-in. Cut the corners. See page 282, *Cutting Off the Paper at the Corners.*

Make the turns-in carefully to maintain all the seams butted on the edge and the inside of the board.

· Sometimes I wait until the turns-in of all the pieces are completed before trimming the overhang. I can make a more even turn-in by trimming the wet paper on the inside of the board with a rotary knife and straight edge than I can by trimming the dangling papers with scissors before making the turns-in. Of course, I run the risk of ripping the wet paper.

SETTING UP DESIGN FOR PASTING: Whether individually cut pieces, or inlay cuts, all the items making up the design are collected and arranged on the table, face down. They should be spread out with an inch of space between each piece. This is so they can be individually pasted without permitting the brush to accidentally slide under a piece which has not yet been pasted. See *Step 4,* page 360.

Try to paste all items of the design at once, including paper/s for the other side of the same board. This is so you can apply all the papers to both sides of the board at once.

If the design is too complicated, paste as much as you can handle and apply them to the board. Weight the board and allow to dry before proceeding with that side of the board and the other side.

PASTE, NOT GLUE: Wheat paste lends itself to inlaying because the pasted paper can be slid into place, butting up precisely to the tangent paper. PVA would not permit this, as it is so tacky it will not slide once it touches the surface of the board.

KEITH SMITH, *KEITH SMITH AT HOME*, BOOK NUMBER 82, 1982. A ONE-OF-A-KIND WITH PHOTOGRAPHS WITH APPLIED COLOR AND INLAYS. THE BINDING IS A FLAT BACK BINDING IN QUARTER CLOTH WITH A MATT ON FRONT COVER FOR A RECESSED PHOTOGRAPH. BOARDS ARE ELABORATELY INLAID WITH A VARIETY OF DECORATIVE BOOK PAPERS. 35 X 30.5 X 2.4 CM.

33

MISCELLANEOUS DECORATIONS

A few more items of decoration will be discussed. First is *Onlay Thread*. Next is *Making Your Own Book Cloth,* page 368. Finally, various means of *Edge Decoration,* page 369.

ONLAY THREAD

In place of tooling leather, other means of decoration can be done without equipment. One of my favorites was devised by Fred. Lines, that is *straight* lines, are difficult to achieve in leather. I have messed up many bindings during the final stage, *Finishing*.

Thread-as-lines is fairly fool proof. Fred uses silk buttonhole twist.

WHEN TO APPLY: There are two factors to keep in mind:

· Any decoration of the leather which entails thread or paper pressed into the leather must be done *prior to pasting down* the endsheet. To keep the thread from raveling, the ends must extend around the head and tail onto the leather turns-in. The ends of the thread will be secured, covered by the pasted down endsheet.

· Thread can be applied when the leather is totally dry or wet. For your first book, Fred recommends thread only be added when the leather is dry. If you do it when the leather is wet, you run the risk of shifting the boards. The stage to apply the thread is prior to attaching the boards. Fred suggests just after *Trimming the Leather on the Inside of the Boards,* page 265. The hinge is more flexible before super is pasted to the boards, but you could add the threads after pasting the super.

PROCEDURE:

1. Make indentation for the thread with a dull kitchen knife or thin bone folder and straight edge on the front of the board. Lines are indented, not cut.

Lay the bone folder in the line at the head and stroke down the edge of the board. Do the same at the tail. This is important so that the thread/s will be flush with the boards to prevent wear and snagging while sliding the book onto and off the shelf.

On the inside of the board, line up the straight edge with the indentations. Indent the leather turns-in at the head and tail.

2. Cut the lengths of thread 2" longer than the height of the boards.

3. Place paste on your fingers and run the lengths of thread through it. Dry your hands.

4. Hold both ends of a single thread. Lay it on the line with an equal amount of overhang at the head and tail. Run your finger down the leather over the thread to tack it down and to remove any excess paste. Pull the overhanging thread at the head around the edge of the board, within the groove. Set in in the groove on the turn-in. Push downward to remove any slack or excess paste. Pull the thread around the tail, pushing toward the head. Place a sheet of wax paper between the book block and board.

5. Close the board. Set in the press or under weight for 5 minutes.

6. Remove the book from the press. Apply the thread/s to the other board. Insert wax paper and close the board. Set in the press for 5 minutes. Remove from the press. Throw away the sheets of wax paper. Stand the book on the tail with boards slightly open. Allow to air dry.

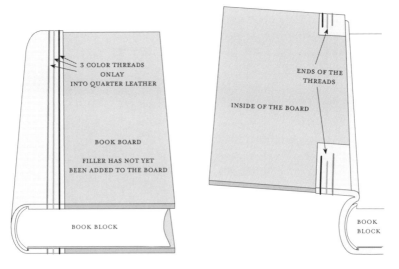

THREAD CAN BE ONLAID INTO THE LEATHER ON THE OUTSIDE OF THE BOARD TO GIVE LINES OF COLOR, FLUSH WITH THE SURFACE OF THE LEATHER. THE PROCESS MUST BE DONE PRIOR TO PASTING DOWN THE ENDSHEET. ENDS OF THE THREAD MUST EXTEND TO THE INSIDE OF THE BOARD TO BE COVERED BY THE PASTE-DOWN TO INSURE THEY DO NOT RAVEL. AN EXAMPLE IS SEEN ON THE FACING PAGE.

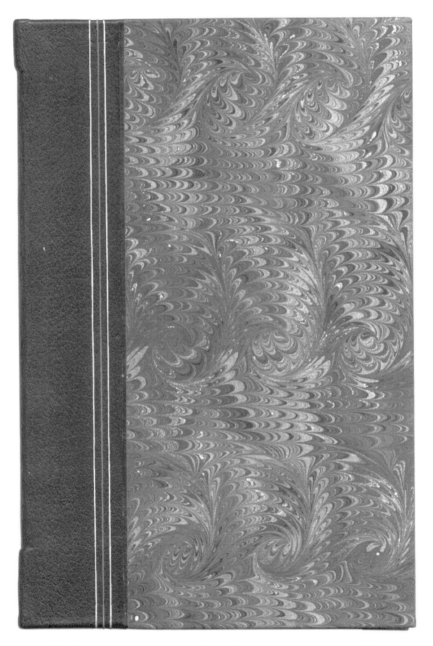

Fred Jordan, quarter leather Tight Back binding sample. 1997. Three onlay color threads were pressed into the leather as line decoration. 24.3 x 16.4 x 1.4 cm.

MAKING YOUR OWN BOOK CLOTH

At times, I have a particularly nice cotton fabric that I wish to use on a cover. Perhaps I have printed an etching on the cloth, or printed a title. I have tried PVA and it was a disaster. If PVA seeps through to the outside of the cloth, it will stain; paste will not.

I tried wheat paste onto the cloth, but it was a mess, stretching the fabric. I tried pasting the board and applying the fabric to it. That was less a mess, but the fabric did not adhere in areas, where the paste had soaked into the board. In addition, the fabric stretched as I applied pressure. I could not get it flat or remove wrinkles I made in applying it to the board. The woof and weft were no longer straight and at right angles to each other.

Fred Jordan came to the rescue: The cotton cloth was steam ironed to remove wrinkles. We wheat pasted a sheet of light text weight white archival paper. When the paper was saturated, the cloth was laid over the paper. A clean blotter was laid on top. A brayer or rolling pin was gently rolled across the blotter to adhere the cloth to the pasted paper.

Some paste may seep through the cloth, if your application was too thick. It almost always will not stain. The blotter may have to be changed during the process of rolling out, so that it does not adhere to the cloth, if seepage occurs.

The advantage of the cloth being paper-backed is so that it will be easy to upholster the book boards. The woof and weft will not stretch out of shape. Upholstering will be as easy as handling paper. The paste applied to the paper backing will not seep through to the cloth.

The ability to make your own paper-backed book cloth opens possibilities of design:
· wider selection of cloth
· pieced and sewn quilt squares
· pieced and sewn cloth and paper combinations
· cloth you have imaged.

EDGE DECORATION

Edge decoration is generally done before the boards are added to the book block. It would be difficult to draw on the edge of the book block with boards in the way. It also keeps the pigment off the covers.

The book block of the The Pamphlet Binding with Boards is too thin to work with edge decoration. Bindings with several signatures offer a blank canvas.

WATER COLOR: Place a scrap board on each side of the book block, flush with the edge with which you are going to work. Place the book block with the scrap boards in the press. The edge of the working surface should be slightly above the jaws of the press. There must be good compression if you are using water colors so that they do not bleed into the pages,

1. The head, foredge and tail can be water colored with a single hue.

2. The color can have a transition in value or hue.

3. Brush strokes can leave some of the edge uncolored, or transparent and/or opaque colors can overlap.

4. The color can be applied in speckles either with the use of an air brush, or wire screen and tooth brush. If the latter, practice first. Start beyond the surface and approach. If any large spots drip, they should happen prior to approaching the surface of the edge.

5. All odd-numbered signatures can be placed in the press and colored with any of the four preceding approaches. Even-numbered signatures can be left blank or colored. See examples on page 370.

SPECKLING WITH A TOOTH BRUSH ACROSS A WIRE SCREEN IS CRUDER THAN AIR BRUSHING, BUT RANDOM SIZE DOTS ARE ENJOYABLE. START BRUSHING TO THE SIDE, SO ANY HUGE SPOTS WILL NOT FALL ON THE SURFACE YOU ARE SPECKLING.

BLEEDS: Bleeds can be attractive. Use little pressure on the press and allow the edge to extend way above the jaws. Test a blank binding and take notes. After a couple attempts you may find a way of brushing on the pigment that gives the amount of bleeding you prefer.

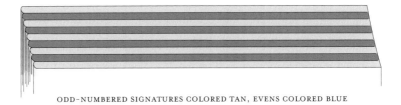

ODD-NUMBERED SIGNATURES COLORED TAN, EVENS COLORED BLUE

ODD IN A TAN WASH TO BLANK WHITE OF THE PAPER, EVENS BLANK WHITE TO BLUE

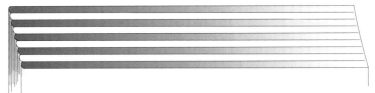

ODD IN A TAN WASH TO BLANK WHITE, EVEN SIGNATURES LEFT BLANK WHITE

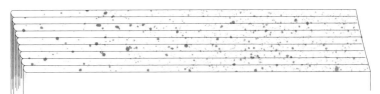

EDGES HAVE BEEN SPECKLED WITH INK AND TOOTH BRUSH ACROSS A WIRE SCREEN

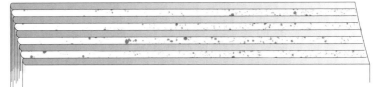

ODD SIGNATURES TAN TO BLANK WHITE, EVEN-NUMBERED HAVE BEEN SPECKLED

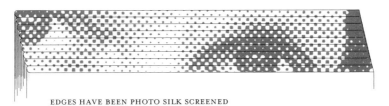

EDGES HAVE BEEN PHOTO SILK SCREENED

LINE DRAWING: Lines can be drawn on the edge with an ink pen. I use a Rapidograph™. However, the best results are working on an edge that has been plowed, as they are mirror smooth. Since you may not have access to such equipment, fine line work will not be possible. When I draw lines on the edges, I prefer to use diagonals.

STEP 1: LINE DRAWING ON THE EDGE OF A BOOK BLOCK OF COMPILED SIGNATURES, PRIOR TO IMAGING OR SEWING. THE SHAPES ARE WATER COLORED.

I draw the lines on compiled signatures, not those which have been folded down. The drawing is done on blank signatures, prior to sewing. I may water color the resulting triangles formed by the zigzag lines.

After I have completed the drawing on the head, tail and foredge, I rearrange the folios in the signature.I alternate every other one. The signatures are then compiled in this new order. The result is the lines in the drawing now undulate. This is caused by the *creep* in compiling signatures.

The blank book is then imaged, sewn and bound. For a more traditional approach, see the edge drawing by Jenny Hille, reproduced on page 241.

STEP 2: EACH SIGNATURE IS COMPRISED OF 4 COMPILED FOLIOS. AFTER THE DRAWING IS COMPLETED, EACH SIGNATURE IS RE ORGANIZED AS FOLIO 1,3, 2, 4. THIS ALTERNATES THE ORDER. THE RESULTING CREEP CAUSES A ZIGZAG IN THE LINE DRAWINGS. THE NEWLY ORDERED BOOK BLOCK IS IMAGED AND SEWN, OR SEWN AND THEN IMAGED.

Another level of manipulating alternate signatures can be done after the edges are at the state of the book shown on the previous page:

CUT FOREDGE OF ODD-NUMBERED SIGNATURES AT 45 DEGREES

CUT FOREDGE OF EVEN-NUMBERED SIGNATURES AT 135 DEGREES

Place all the odd-numbered signatures in order in one pile with all the evens in another. Jog the stack of odd-numbered signatures and trim the foredge at a 45° angle. Jog the even-numbered signatures. Trim the foredge at a 135° angle.

THE REASSEMBLED BOOK BLOCK HAS A ZIGZAG FOREDGE

Place the odd and even-numbered signatures back together in order. The resulting foredge will zigzag—like a picket fence.

Todd Pattison, full leather binding
of *With It, Book 134* by Keith Smith,
1997. Edition of 10. View of the tail
with speckled edges. 20 x 14 x 2.5 cm.

CONCLUSION

Drawings and/or text of only a few sheets can have a substantial hard cover binding with the Pamphlet Binding with Boards. The Flat Back is the workhorse for the artist, offering several dozen pages sewn and cased-in with boards. For the longer projects of 8 or more signatures, the book can be sewn recessed cords, rounded and backed. The cover for the Tight Back might be leather. The description of these three will serve most of the binding needs for the artist.

Fred and I hope that this manual opens many possibilities for those who are not book binders to create lovely, functional and archival hard cover books in cloth or leather.

For the book binder, the method described beginning on page 243 of not paring leather has its advantages and can be adapted to their use: Quarter leather for books and clam shells can have paring limited to the turns-in. The cut leather on the outside of the boards can be butted with filler, which is slightly thinner than the leather. The edge of the leather is indented, prior to finishing. This will permit the decorative paper in finishing to sit flush with the leather. Limited paring of leather quickens the process, without compromise.

For Fred and me, this book has been a learning experience as well. Collaborations are not only a compromise for each participant, but a growing experience. I learned far more than Fred, because he had so much more to give.

PART VI

REFERENCE

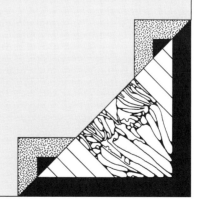

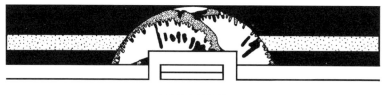

NOTES

1   Page 19, 137, 400

        Book Binding by Hand, for Students and Craftsmen, Laurence Town, Faber and Faber, 24 Russell Square, London. Second Edition, 1963.

        Bookbinding and the Care of Books, Douglas Cockerell, Lyons & Burford, publishers. ©1901, Reprinted 1991. ISBN 1-55821-104-7.

        The Craft of Bookbinding, A Practical Handbook, Eric Burdett, published by David & Charles, Newton Abbot, London, Vancouver. Second Impression 1978. ISBN 0 7153 6656 4.

        Der Bucheimband, Fritz Wiese, published, ISBN 3877063020. *The Thames and Hudson Manual of Bookbinding,* Arthur W. Johnson, Thames and Hudson, Ltd., London. Second Printing 1981. Library of Congress Catalog Card Number 81-50759.

        Gary Frost: Explorer of Book Structure & Action, Gary Frost, published by Dry Frio Bindery, P. O. Box 86, Utopia, Texas, 78884-0086. 1997.

        A History of English Craft Bookbinding Technique, Bernard Middleton, The Holland Press, London. Second Supplemented Edition 1978. ISBN 0 900 470 83 6.

        Marbling, A Complete Guide to Creating Beautiful Patterned Papers and Fabrics, Diane Maurer with Paul Maurer, A Friedman Book, 1991. ISBN 0-517-02019-X.

        Student Guide To Book Conservation, Gary Frost, published by Dry Frio Bindery, P. O. Box 86, Utopia, Texas, 78884-0086, Spring 1998.

        Three Bookbindings, Gary Frost, published by Dry Frio Bindery, P. O. Box 86, Utopia, Texas, 78884-0086, 1993.

2   Page 19

        Signature is used in this manual, instead of *section,* in deference to Fred Jordan's terminology.

3   Page 20, 238

        Jane Greenfield & Jenny Hille, *Headbands, How To Work Them,* Oak Knoll Books, Second Revised Edition, reprinted 1996. ISBN 0-938768-18-2 hard back ISBN 0-938768-51-4 paperback

        Oak Knoll Books, 414 Delaware Street, New Castle, DE 19720. Telephone: 302 328 7232. Fax: 302 328 7274. Email: oakknoll@oakknoll.com

4   Page 22, 41, 43, 44, 45, 47, 280, 281, 284, 285, 286, 288, 296, 297, 301, 303, 351, 352, 354, 355 and 357

        All marbled and paste papers photo–reproduced in the diagrams are from Diane Maurer, P. O. Box 78, Water Street, Spring Mills, PA 16875 Telephone: 814 422 8651. Fax: 814 422 7858

5   Page 45

        Betsy Palmer Eldridge, binder, conservator, teacher, from Toronto, Canada. The *millimeter binding* was demonstrated by John Hyltoft at the Guild of Book Workers Standards Seminar annual in Tuscaloosa, Alabama.

6   Page 49

        Abbey pH Pen available from any binders' supply, or, directly from *Abbey Newsletter,* 7105 Geneva Drive, Austin, TX 78723. Telephone: 512 929 3992.

7   Page 50

Cynthia Mowery, Bookmakers, Inc. 6601 66th Avenue, Suite 101, Riverdale, MD 20737. Telephone: 301 459 3384. Fax: 301 459 7629

8   Page 99

The statement is not technically correct. The holes through which you sew are indeed the sewing stations, if you are sewing an unsupported sewing, such as the Coptic, or, if you are sewing raised or Recessed Cords.

However, in supported sewings, the cords, thongs or tapes are the sewing station, not the pierced hole/s which allow access to them. This only causes a problem in the definition for sewing tapes: Each tape is the station, but each tape requires a hole on either side. The two holes per tape are not the sewing station, but merely the holes. The tape is the sewing station.

9   Page 107

keith smith *BOOKS* email: ksbooks@netacc.net
web site: http://net2.netacc.net/~ksbooks

10   Pages 115, 199

My thanks to Betsy Palmer Eldridge, Toronto, ONT Canada, for her personal critiques on stitches, as well as her lecture on *Sewing Structures* at the Canadian Bookbinders and Book Artists Guild.

11   Page 127

Paper cover pamphlet sewings are described in *Books without Paste or Glue*, Volume I, *Non–Adhesive Binding*, Keith A. Smith, published by keith smith *BOOKS*. Third Edition 1993, ISBN 0-9637682-0-4.

There are 13 other single section sewings, all with paper covers, which are described in *1–2– & 3–Section Sewings*, Volume II, *Non–Adhesive Binding*, Keith A. Smith, published by keith smith *BOOKS*. First Edition 1995, ISBN 0-9637682-2-0.

12   Page 127

PORTFOLIO BOOK: The Portfolio Book is similar to the Pamphlet Binding with Boards, page 125. Both consist of a single signature. The Portfolio Book differs in that it is oversize. It is usually at least 17" tall, containing large prints. It is ideal for the book artist.

SEWING: Read Part II, beginning on page 125. Place a cloth hinge on the back of the signature, as described on page 130. For such a large book, you may wish to have a 2–ply hinge. The first layer, for strength, is jaconette. See page 130. The top layer hinge, for looks, is book cloth.

Sew the signature, endsheets and hinge/s with a Pamphlet Sewing. See pages 131–139.

MAKING THE CASE: The case is made similar to Method 2, page 343.

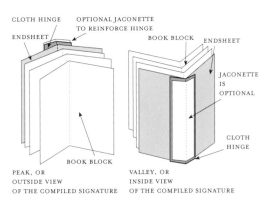

CLOTH HINGE   OPTIONAL JACONETTE TO REINFORCE HINGE
ENDSHEET
BOOK BLOCK   ENDSHEET
JACONETTE IS OPTIONAL
CLOTH HINGE
BOOK BLOCK

PEAK, OR OUTSIDE VIEW OF THE COMPILED SIGNATURE

VALLEY, OR INSIDE VIEW OF THE COMPILED SIGNATURE

A 2-PLY HINGE IS RECOMMENDED. THE FIRST TO BE GLUED IS JACONETTE FOR STRENGTH. IT IS COVERED BY THE BOOK CLOTH HINGE.

The difference is the boards will not be flush with the book block, as in Method 2. Since the Portfolio Book is so large, it requires a different spine than the smaller Pamphlet Binding with Boards.

BOARD DIMENSIONS: The boards are set in 1/2" from the spine. Overhang at the head, foredge and tail is considerably larger than for the Pamphlet Binding with Boards, as a matter of proportion. Use medium to heavy weight book board.

Cut the boards and set them on the book block, with the spine-edge of the boards 3/8" to 1/2" in from the spine of the book block.

Use masking tape to connect the boards around the spine. Open the boards.

Measure the space between. It is the spine-gap. Refer to the illustrations on pages 143, 144, as well as 346 and 347.

Cut the spine-cloth and paste it to the boards, as described on pages 143. Reinforce the spine, as shown on page 147. It is now ready to case-in.

ATTACHING THE BOOK BLOCK TO THE CASE: Follow the instructions for casing-in, page 149.

COVERING THE BOARDS: Follow instructions on page 279.

FINISHING: Ideas for decoration are suggested beginning on page 335.

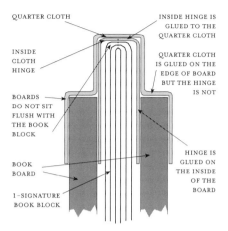

QUARTER CLOTH

INSIDE HINGE IS GLUED TO THE QUARTER CLOTH

INSIDE CLOTH HINGE

QUARTER CLOTH IS GLUED ON THE EDGE OF BOARD BUT THE HINGE IS NOT

BOARDS DO NOT SIT FLUSH WITH THE BOOK BLOCK

HINGE IS GLUED ON THE INSIDE OF THE BOARD

BOOK BOARD

1-SIGNATURE BOOK BLOCK

CROSS-SECTION OF THE ROUND SPINE
WHEN THE BOARDS ARE OPEN, A LARGE GAP BETWEEN THE BOARDS CONSISTS ONLY OF INSIDE HINGE GLUED TO THE QUARTER CLOTH.

THE BOARDS START WELL IN FROM THE SPINE-EDGE, AT LEAST 3/8" FROM THE BACKBONE. THE SPINE IS LESS WIDE THAN FOR THE SAME BOOK CASED-IN WITH A FLAT SPINE.

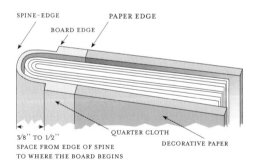

SPINE-EDGE

PAPER EDGE

BOARD EDGE

3/8" TO 1/2" SPACE FROM EDGE OF SPINE TO WHERE THE BOARD BEGINS

QUARTER CLOTH

DECORATIVE PAPER

THE GAP ON EACH SIDE OF THE BOARD WILL ALLOW THE BOARDS TO SIT IN FROM THE SPINE-EDGE, WHEN THE BOARDS ARE CLOSED.

13 Page 130
Cynthia Mowery, Bookmakers, Inc.

14 Page 173, 217
CHOOSING THE THREAD: Thread largely determines the amount of swell. These are some of the factors that can alter the amount of swell:
 · Number of signatures in the book block

- Number of leaves in the signature
- The hardness or softness of paper
- Sewing each signature separately, 2-on, or more.
- Sewing too loose or too tight

Normal thickness of the paper is not a factor in the resulting swell. Thread inside the signature swells the spine. It is not the pages or the paper, but the signature and the thread which determine swell.

Thickness of paper determines only the width of the spine, not the swell, which is a result of sewing. Using 70 lb. text weight paper, instead of 80 lb. can reduce the width of a spine of a 250 page book, easily by 1/4". But this is not related to swelling or rounding.

1. Number of signatures in the book

Unless you are creating the book, the first three factors determining the swell are beyond your control. If you are starting from scratch, you can decide on the number of pages in the signatures and thus, the number of signatures used. This will determine how many rows of thread will be needed to sew the book. With fewer signatures to be sewn, fewer rows of thread exist to swell the spine.

Conversely, if you use folios, you will double or triple the rows of thread, greatly increasing the swell.

The number of signatures must be considered in determining swell. A book of ten signatures needs thicker thread than the same book imposed as a twenty signature book. The more signatures, the thinner the thread, keeps the ideal amount of swell. Of course, the thread used has a limit on how thin it can be before it is too fragile. The thread must have strength. If you cannot reduce the weight of the thread any further, then reduce the number of rows of thread. This is done by sewing 2-on, or 3-on, or more. This will be discussed later.

2. Number of leaves in the signature

Thread inside the signature expands each signature.

A book of a great number of pages not only should use a thinner weight paper, but be laid out at least as octavos (8vo), that is, as 16 a page signature (signature). If possible, the thin paper should be folded down as a sextodecimo (16mo), that is, as 32 pages with 16 leaves. The more pages contained within a signature, the less rows of thread will be used.

A book of a few number of pages not only should use a thicker weight paper, but also increase the swell by sewing by the number of signatures to be sewn. By laying out the book not as octavos (8vo), but as quartos (4to), twice the amount of thread will be layered in the spine. Laying the book out as folios would, again, double the amount of thread used.

Control over the layout into signatures, from the sextodecimo, down to the folio, results in a great range of swelling that will occur.

3. The hardness or softness of paper

Density of paper is a factor. If a softer paper is used, such as Rives, it will absorb the thread more than a hard paper, such as Mohawk Superfine. Two different book blocks may have the same number of pages, the signatures in each are octavos and both have the same weight of paper. But if the paper in one book block is Superfine and the other is Rives, they will require a different weight of thread to sew, to obtain the same, correct amount of swelling. A thicker thread will be required for the softer paper and a thinner thread for the more dense.

Choice of thread is determined by a number of signatures and how soft or hard the paper. Binders rarely have control over the number of signatures, or, how soft or hard the paper. Therefore, they must control the amount of swelling by the choice of thread and whether to to sew I–on, or more.

The thicker the thread, the more the spine will swell. With thinner thread, less swelling will occur.

Sewing a book of 70lb. text weigh paper, with ten signatures, laid out as octavos, should probably be sewn with a #18 linen thread.

4. Sewing each signature I–on, 2-on or more

After considering the first three factors, the amount of swelling may still be too great, especially in a book of a large number of pages. The final factor in reducing the amount of swell is to reduce the amount of thread used in sewing. This is done by sewing two, three or more signatures at a time, rather than each individually. This is referred to as sewing 2-on, 3-on, or more.

When books have more than fifteen or twenty signatures, you should consider sewing 2 or more on. Sewing 2-on allows you to maintain the same thickness of thread as a book with half as many signatures. This maintains the strength of a thicker thread. Sewing 2-on is not described in this manual.

SWELL: The difference between the thickness of the spine of an unsewn book block and a sewn book block is referred to as *swell*.

DETERMINING THE SWELL: Gauging the swell which will occur on the spine as a result of sewing is not easy. It comes with practice. The proper thickness of the spine can be tested after a book is sewn, pasted and knocked down: Lay on the back board, in from the spine-edge about ⅜". Set the book on a table and lay the front board on the sewn book block. Make sure the board is in from the spine-edge ⅜". Using a board or straight edge on end, set it on the top book board and press down. It should be the same height as the spine. This will allow the proper amount of extra thickness at the spine-edge to create a round, yet leave the boards flat against the book block and parallel.

ADJUSTING THE AMOUNT OF SWELL: If you are not sure which thickness of thread to use, this is another approach: Sew a third of the book and while it is still on the frame, measure the amount of swell. If you find you have too little swelling, change to a thicker thread. Sew the middle third of the book with the thicker thread. Sew the final third with the same thread as the beginning third of the book. It is critical that the number of signatures sewn with the thinner beginning signatures is the precise number of signatures at the other end of the book sewn with the same thread for a proper round.

SWELLING THE BACK: Size of thread depends on several factors. If the binding contains many sections, generally a thinner #18/3 thread would be used, rather than a thicker #12. Use an 18/3 Barbers 100% unbleached thread for sewing 8 to 10 signatures.

However, if the book has a number of tipped–in prints, or will eventually contain collage or photographs, the foredge will bulge open. The book will be wedge–shaped. The backbone must be increased in depth. Sewing with a heavier gauge thread will swell the back to approach the depth of the foredge, permitting the covers to remain parallel.

15　Page 219

SEWING FRAME: No sewing frame is necessary for sewing Recessed Cords or Sewing Onto Tapes. If you were sewing Raised Cords, you would need a sewing frame. None of the bindings in this manual need to be sewn on a frame. Since we are eliminating the need for equipment in this manual, no sewing frame is described.

If you wish to know how to use one, or wish to have plans for an easy-to-build frame, they are described and illustrated in *Exposed Spine Sewings*, Volume III, *Non—Adhesive Binding*, on pages 18–23.

PRESSING SIGNATURES: If you are re-sewing an old book, signatures to be sewn should be pressed to form a tight crease. A bone folder is useful only on new paper being folded down into signatures.

Alternate each signature, with the fold to the left, the next to the right. Place the signatures in the press with smooth sides of boards facing the signatures. Press overnight.

16   Page 219

NUMBER OF CORDS FOR BOOKS: In sewing Recessed Cords, a minimum of 5 cords across the spine are used for average height books. Small books may use only 4 or 3 cords, for books about 3 to 4" in height. For larger books, you may wish to use more cords.

17   Page 229

PLOWING: Plowing with equipment is not described in this manual, as the process is explained without equipment. Plowing is not necessary, except on the head of the book. This will result in a smooth surface, helping the closed book to resist dust from filtering down into the pages, while the book is stored on a shelf.

Fred suggests you trim the head, rather than plow it. This is better done signature by signature, prior to sewing, or by carefully cutting the height, as each signature is made. If the signatures were accurately cut prior to sewing, that should suffice. If the head is uneven, you should trim it now, in lieu of plowing. However, this is risky and can only be successfully done on thin books:

Determine how much is to be trimmed from the head. Using a right angle, lightly mark with a pencil line across the first page.

Check the height at the spine-edge by measuring down the tail to your pencil line. Do the same at the foredge. If the measurements are identical, your pencil trim-line is at 90° from the spine-edge and foredge and parallel with the tail.

To trim the head, place a straight-edge along your pencil line. Use a sharp, thin-bladed knife. Cut in as many strokes as necessary until you cut through the entire book block. Make sure each stroke along the straight-edge is perpendicular to the cutting surface and falls in the groove of the previous cutting.

18   Page 229

CHOOSING BOARD THICKNESS: The general thickness of board is chosen by the proportion to the size of the text block.

The precise thickness of board is not chosen directly, but is the result of the thickness of the thread.

In choosing the thread, you determine the thickness of board required. Before sewing the book. However, the thickness of the board is only a guess for the beginner.

If the thread is a little too thick, an excessive amount of swell will occur. Using a thicker board will compensate for the larger round.

Obviously, it is better to have the proper amount of swell and not have to compound one mistake with another.

However, compensating with the larger board salvages that binding attempt.

Keep in mind that a soft paper, such as Rives absorbs the thread. Using 70 lb. Rives will require a thinner board than sewing with the same thickness thread using 70 lb. Superfine. It is a hard paper; it will not absorb the thread, resulting in more swell. It will result in a bigger round.

19   Page 231

In creating the shape of the arch in backing, you are altering the angle of the spine in rows, from the edge to the center of the spine. This depends on the number of signatures in the book block:

BACKING A BOOK OF 8 TO 12 SIGNATURES: In creating the shape of the arch in backing, you are altering the angle of the spine in rows, from the edge to the center of the spine. For an average size book, this should take 3 to 4 steps, or rows, in from each edge of the spine. Each row is altered a little less than the previous. The center of the spine, which is the height of the arch, is hardly touched.

Here, only the arch of the fold of the signature is flattened. The signature is not struck to one side or the other, but the corrugation is lessened for a smooth surface to the spine.

The center of the spine is not flattened, as much as it is smoothed. Remember, it is part of the overall arch of the spine, which is a continuous curve. The corrugation of the edges of the folded signatures is eliminated in the process of backing. A smooth spine is required, so that when the leather or spine-cover is applied, there will be no bumps or ridges.

Keep working back and forth until you are satisfied with the shape of the arch and make sure the arc is uniform all along the spine.

BACKING A THIN BOOK: A book of 6 or fewer signatures is difficult to shape the spine into an arch, since there are so few signatures. In backing, the end signature on one side of the book is worked. It is shaped with a bone folder. Then, on the other side of the spine, that end signature is worked. The second signature in, is worked on one side of the book. Then, on the other side, the second signature in, is shaped. The center signature/s is slightly flattened to complete the shape of the arch in backing the book.

BACKING A THICK BOOK: A very large book will entail more steps in backing. Working from side to side, always towards the center may require 15 or 20 signatures on each side to be shaped to form the arch in backing the book.

20   Page231

Backing with a bone folder is easier for the sewings devised for *Exposed Spine Sewings.* Since all the bindings have exposed spines, the backbone cannot appear dented. The folds of the sections have to be pristine.

21   Page 233

It is very difficult to round and back books with only a few number of pages and few signatures:

· There must be at least 20 pages. If you have a book of less than 20 pages, the spine will not be thick enough to achieve a round.

· It is easier if there are at least 10 signatures to round. Small books of 40 to 100 pages should be made up of signatures which are laid out as folios or quartos. Do not use octavos or larger on a thin book. Even though the book would contain the minimum of 40 pages, there would not be enough signatures to achieve a round.

22   Page 233

TESTING THE BOARD THICKNESS: Fred feels the most important thing is to get the reader to go through the entire process first, without being entangled in all the subtleties. Therefore, for the thickness of the board, the text simply says to use 4-ply rag mat board. Thickness of the cover will be the thickness of the 4-ply mat board, plus the thickness of the leather/filler on the inside of the board.

With your second binding attempt, you can refine the proper thickness of the board you should use for the covers. Binder's supply outlets offer book board in at least five thicknesses. You might invest in a few sheets of each.

Thickness of the board is decided before the book is sewn, relying upon experience of how much round you are going to add to the book. See *Measuring Board Thickness*, page 229.

Test a possible thickness of board after knocking down: Place a piece of book board on each side of the book, but not all the way to the spine-edge. Allow about 1" of the book at the spine-edge not to be covered. Press on the top board. If it depresses to about the height of the sewn spine-edge, it is probably the proper thickness of the book board.

By *adding round* means how much the depth of the book is increased by the sewing. *Swell* is discussed in Note 14, page 382.

Until experience teaches how much swell to add when you sew, you will have to rely upon working backwards. That is, sew the book, then compensate with a thinner or thicker board, depending upon how much swell you happen to acquire. After the book is sewn, pasted and knocked down, lay it on the table. Take a piece of book board and lay it on the top of the book block, in from the spine-edge about ⅜". Press on the board, running your finger over the board and across the top edge of the spine. This will help you see how thick the spine is compared to the foredge, plus the thickness of one board. Two thickness of board, plus the thickness of the book block at the foredge should equal the thickness of the spine-edge. This would be the ideal amount of swelling to achieve a proper round.

Aesthetically, the thickness of the board is in proportion to the thickness of the book block and the dimensions of the page. Small books would look stubby with thick board side-covers. An oversize book would look flimsy and the covers would not provide protection if the board is extremely thin.

With experience, you can choose the thickness of the board before you start to sew.

Without experience, you may have other problems with thickness of the board, besides the amount of swell. You might use the dividers to mark the book for rounding with the proper thickness of board and your sewing may achieve the proper amount of swelling. However, you may make a mistake in rounding and backing. If the book is placed too high in the press, the result will be a shoulder larger than the thickness of your board.

You can solve this problem by substituting a thicker board.

23   Page 237

PLOWING A NEW BOOK WITH A DECKLE EDGE: I disagree with Fred about plowing off a deckle from the head. To me, it makes the head look bald. If I had to plow the head, I would also plow the tail, leaving a deckle only on the foredge. A book looks lovely with a deckled edge confined to the foredge.

If you should decide to leave a deckled edge on all sides, including the head, the book *must* be designed to be stored in a clam shell. This will prevent dust from settling into the edges of the paper, at least until the clam shell is discarded by some future owner of the book.

24   Page 251

GRAIN vs SUEDE SIDE OF THE LEATHER: Generally, the grain side of the leather shows, while the suede side is pasted to the board. Once in a while the suede is chosen to be seen and the grain side is pasted down. To avoid confusion, the side of the leather to be seen will be referred to as the *outside leather.* The side which will not show on the finished book will be referred to as the *inside leather.*

Select leather with color and texture proper in psychological tone to the subject matter and date of the book. The leather must be coordinated with the color of the book block, decorative papers, endbands and use of gold, color foil or blind stamping, if any.

25   Page 279, 353, 356

BALANCING THE GRAIN OF PAPERS: Some papers stretch more than others. Certain papers have lots of grain. If you were to use one of these papers on the outside of the board, then paste down an endsheet with less grain, the board would warp. It would take two layers of the second to equal the pull of the grain of one sheet of the former. The solution is to line the board: First, paste down a sheet of the paper used as the endsheet, cut to fit the entire surface of the inside of the board. Then cover the outside board with the paper with lots of grain. Finally, make your endsheet paste-down.

Obviously, you need to make a test covering a scrap board with the papers you are using, if you are not sure if the outside and inside papers are balanced in the pull of the grain.

26   Page 279

A larger turn-in with a smaller paste-down on the inside of the board can be an element of design. The paste-down might be the endsheet cut smaller, or in an irregular shape. An island paste-down might be used. See the examples in the chapter beginning on page 351.

27   Page 282

GRAIN OF BOOK CLOTH: Some cloth will shrink when it dries. If it shrinks from where it was put down, try cutting the cloth at 90° to the original cut.

28   Page 286

TRIMMING WET PAPER: Trimming wet paper is difficult. Lay a small straight edge into position on top of the area of the turn-in which will remain. Trim off the excess with a thin bladed sharp knife, keeping the blade at a low angle. The handle should be very close to the paper. This will help avoid ripping the paper.

Hold the straight edge in place, as you try to peel off the trimmed paper. This serves two purposes: You may have to make a second incision in the precise groove of the first cut. Secondly, the straight edge will keep the turn-in from lifting, when you pull up the trimmed paper.

It is tricky cutting paper that is wet, as it is apt to tear. Better than an X-Acto™ knife for this purpose is a rotary blade knife. If you do a lot of pasting, it will be a good investment. They may be cheaper purchased from a fabric store, than at an art supply store.

GLOSSARY

Each term is defined with its first usage in the text of this manual. In the *Index of Terms*, page numbers are listed for important uses of key terms. The definitions below are used in this manual, as well as in other books on binding by Keith Smith.

accordion pleat 1. Several parallel, alternating and closely placed folds. Pleats are usually not pages, but an additional hinging device between the backbone and the attached folios or sections. Very often the pleat is the backbone, with separate side-covers, rather than a flat back. Pleats also expand the depth of the backbone to accommodate additions to the book block. 2. Also known as *the concertina fold*.

across (also referred to as *all across*) 1. Perpendicular to the folds, cover to cover.† 2. Sewing which proceeds from section to section, generally in two or more separate sewings, using paired stations. Examples are *Blanket Stitch with Slit Strap, 2—Needle Coptic Sewing* and the *Celtic Weave*. Sewing across the spine is always more secure than sewing along the spine. If a thread breaks, only the sewing at those paired stations is affected. If the thread breaks sewing along the spine, the entire binding is compromised.

adhesive Generic for glue and paste. Glues used for binding remain pliable and are used on the backs over the sewing of most bindings. Glue on the backbone may be a heat glue, made from animals. It is archival, in that it may be easily removed, but not in the sense it attracts insects which eat it. Another pliable glue is a poly-vinyl-acetate. Plastic based, PVA does not attract animals, but is not archival, inasmuch as it is not removable and thwarts attempts at book restoration. Pastes are used to adhere leather to spines, paper to paper and paper to boards. Wheat or rice paste are commonly used. See: *wheat paste*.

adhesive binding single leaf binding without sewing using a synthetic adhesive consolidation on the back.* Referred to as *perfect binding*.

against the grain Folding paper at right angles to the grain.

along (also referred to as *all along*) Parallel to the folds, head to tail.†

angle To move diagonally.†

Asa-No-Ha Toji Japanese name for the stab binding also known as the *Hemp-Leaf Binding*. There are four traditional Japanese stab bindings. The others are the *Yotsume Toji*, or *Japanese 4—Hole Binding*; the *Kikko Toji*, or *Tortoise-Shell*; and the *Koki Toji*, or *Noble*. The *Noble Binding* is also referred to as the *Kangxi Binding*, after its reputed originator. These stab sewing are described in *Books without Paste or Glue*, Volume I, *Non-Adhesive Binding*.

back or **backbone** 1. The binding edge of a text prior to sewing or adhesive consolidation.*

NOTE: The back differs from the spine, which is part of the cover which overlays this.

back saw Moulding saw or tenon saw used to cut the sewing stations when the book block is held in a finishing press.

---

* *A VOCABULARY of TERMS for BOOK CONSERVATION PRACTICE*, by Gary Frost

† "GLOSSARY of TERMS, based on the work of Pamela Spitzmueller and Gary Frost," a handout in a workshop by Betsy Palmer Eldridge.

backward (reverse) Counter to the direction of the sewing.†

bead 1. Top edge of the book (when viewing the book upright). 2. The little roll formed by the knot of an endband. See: *spine-bead* and *inside bead.*

beeswax Cake of wax usually purchased in a small block from a binder's supply. It is used for waxing all unwaxed thread, prior to sewing.

blind A type of book. See: *Venetian blind.*

blind embossing Stamping type into leather, without gold or foil.

board or **book board** A layered stock specifically for side-covers.

bodkin A sewing tool which is a type of awl. Unlike an awl which has a shaft which graduates in thickness, a bodkin has a thin metal shaft which remains constant in diameter except for narrowing at the point. It is similar to a *bradawl*, which is a carpenter's tool. An awl is inferior for piercing sewing stations, as it is difficult to obtain proper size of the opening in the paper. Choose a bradawl or bodkin which will give a hole slightly less than the diameter of the needle which will be used in the sewing.

bone or **bone folder** A flat, polished tool, made of bone or plastic. Paper is folded by hand to a temporary fold. The bone is used to score the fold to a permanent position and to flatten the fold. This is done in a single stroke, as burnishing the paper will scar or make it shiny. A substitute is a dull stainless steel table knife, which will not mar the paper.

book block or **text block** Total of the collated sections (signatures), folios, or sheets, constituting the body of a book.

book block pleat See: *concertina guard.*

booklet 1. A one-section binding. 2. A pamphlet. 3. A magazine.

bostrophedon A Germanic term meaning as the ox plows. In a single word, it graphically describes moving across a field, back and forth in a continuing S fashion. It is as if a page of text were read, the first line from left to right, the second from right to left and continued in this alternating manner. This movement and thus his term, describes the Scott McCarney binding. He also calls this the *snake format.*

bradawl A straight shafted awl with chisel edge used to make holes for brads or screws. Like the bodkin, a bradawl is ideal for piercing sewing stations in paper in bookbinding. Either tool is superior to an awl for piercing sewing stations.

butterfly sewing An across the spine sewing which utilizes paired stations. Each needle spans, enters the next section, then cross inside to exit the other station. The *Butterfly* is also known as the *Yamato Toji,* or *Japanese 4–Needle Sewing.* It is a 12th century binding. The *Butterfly* is described on page 220, *Exposed Spine Sewings,* Volume III of *Non-Adhesive Binding.*

The *Butterfly,* or *Japanese 4–Needle Sewing,* is not to be confused with the *Japanese 4–Hole Stab Binding,* which is described on page 75, in Volume I of *Non-Adhesive Binding, Books without Paste or Glue.*

case The two side-covers connected by the spine-cloth or leather.

catch-word In early printed books, the last word on a page was positioned at the foot. The same word was repeated at the top of the next page. Perhaps this served as a bridge in reading from page to page, but its purpose was a guide in collating signatures.

chain stitch "Chain stitch" is an embroidery term, not actually a stitch in bookbinding. In binding, the chain is a result of a succession of link stitches. *Link* is a stitch; *chain* is the resulting pattern.

to change over To continue sewing in the different section.†

clamshell A box for storing a book with a lid, hinged to open like covers.

climb To move upward.†

codex (plural: **codices**) A book, bound along one edge. One of the four types of books, the others being the fan, blind and the fold book.

NOTE: Many binders do not agree with this definition.

compiled signature A signature, or section, constructed by assembling two or more folios, rather than folding down a sheet.

compound binding A hybrid book structure of two of the same or differing types of books. There are 4 types of books: the fan, the blind, oriental fold book and the western codex. Creating a structure of two or more of these types of books is a compound binding. Examples: 1. Sewing sections onto an accordion pleat for a concertina binding. 2. Including a fold book as a unit, along with sewing sections into a single spine.

concertina 1. A type of binding, utilizing the concertina fold. 2. The concertina fold is also called an accordion pleat.

concertina guard A form of construction securing sections to folded stubs with a pamphlet sewing and, in turn, sewing the stubs together to form a text block.*

content Statement within the book of text and/or pictures. In a no-picture book, it is the cast shadows, cut shapes, holes, et cetera.

continuous support sewing Use of a single support, as opposed to sewing onto cords or tapes. The paperback sewings in Volume II of *Non-Adhesive Binding, 1– 2– & 3– Section Sewings,* are examples. It is important to reinforce the spine on the cover. Folding or pasting a second ply of paper in this area strengthens the sewing.

to continue on To continue sewing in the same section.†

core A support. It might be a cord, or rolled material to form a cylindrical support, generally out of leather. The endband is formed on a core.

cover stock or **cover weight** Heavy paper used for covers as opposed to text weight used for book blocks. Commercial printing papers generally come in both cover weight and text weight.

covering Forwarding is followed by Covering and Finishing. If the outside of the boards are not full leather or cloth, the area of the board that is not covered with cloth or leather is covered with decorative paper. The paste-down is made on the inside of the boards.

crease A fold induced by pressure marking or die debossing, not cutting. * Some binders refer to this procedure as a *score.*

creep The successive protrusion from the outermost folio to the innermost within a section or signature.

crossbar The wooden dowel held above and parallel to the base of the sewing frame by threaded posts. The crossbar is often slotted to accept threaded hooks.

curl The distortion of a sheet due to differences in structure, coatings, or moisture from one side to the other.

deckle In papermaking, the width of the wet sheet as it comes off the wire of a paper machine.

deckled-edge The untrimmed feathery edges of paper formed where the pulp flows against the deckle.

digital scan Half-tone photographic images created on a computer scanner. I do not use the term photograph, reserving that dear term for silver prints.

display Presentation of the object, generally through turning pages. Books with one-sided display, the fan, blind and fold book might be displayed fully extended on a table, or wall displayed. Books with unusual formatting may be presented in the round as sculpture, the pages not meant to be turned.

dos-à-dos A specific traditional format of two connected codices which have a back cover in common.

drop To move downward.†

duodecimo aka **12to** 1. A sheet folded down to yield a section of 12 leaves or 24 pages. 2. Four folios, each slipped inside the other, to form a unit of sewing. See: *folio, quarto, sexto, octavo, sextodecimo* and *z-fold*. In folding down a sheet to form a duodecimo, the first fold is against the grain, so that the final fold is with the grain.

endband Wrapping and beading decorative thread, usually of colored silk or cotton, at the head and tail of codices. Thread is wrapped around a core and periodically stitched into the book block. "Imitation" machine-made head bands are sold by the yard and pasted onto the backbone of commercial hard cover books.

NOTE: The term *headband* is often erroneously used, if the band described includes, or is specifically at the tail. Therefore, I use the term *endband*, rather than *headband*, as it includes the bands sewn at both the head and tail.

end paper In traditional binding, the sheet which is glued down on the inside of the cover board, extending across the gutter as the first page.

endsheets The first (and last) folio or section of a book may be blank and perhaps a nice laid paper in a particular color different from the bulk of the book block. Endsheets function as a mat surrounding a drawing. It is blank space to clear the mind before the introduction of the content of the opus.

enter To pass from the spine side to the fold side.†

exit To pass from the fold side to the spine side.†

F&G's (Folded and Gathered) The *F&G's* are the assembled signatures ready for sewing.

false kettle The (true) kettle stitch is the proper sewing procedure for ending one section, changing direction of movement in adding the next. The (true) kettle drops and links, slips and climbs. A *false kettle* would fail in one of these steps, usually failing to slip under in order to lock. True and false kettle stitches and link stitches in general are described on pages 25–31 in *Exposed Spine Sewings*, Volume III of *Non-Adhesive Binding*, and on pages 107–118 in *Bookbinding for Book Artists*.

fan A book, bound at one point. One of the four types of books, the others being the blind, codex and the fold book. Fans and blinds are used by South Sea Island cultures.

finishing Finishing is decoration of the book after forwarding and covering.

first section In the sewing procedures, the term first does not necessarily mean the beginning of the book. On the bench, you may very well start sewing from the back, towards the front of the book. In that instance, the "first" section to be sewn is the final section of the book. See *Face Up* and *Face Down*, page 119, in *Bookbinding for Book Artists*.

flap An single extension on each side of the spine at the hinge-fold. The flap is usually one piece, crossing the spine and included in the sewing. Covers are attach to the flap.

flat back Sewing without rounding the spine.

flat back cover Paper cover with two folds which delineate the spine from the side-covers. These folds create the hinging action of the cover and are called *hinge-folds*.

flush cover 1. A cover whose front and back panels are the same dimensions as the pages. 2. In commercial binding, a cover that has been trimmed with the text block, so that cover and text block are the same size. See: *overhang cover*.

fold See: *accordion, hinge-fold, fold-out, gate fold* and *thrown-out*.

fold book A book, whose binding is mechanical; the sheet is folded back and forth upon itself to create pages. One of the four types of books, the others being the fan, blind and the codex.

fold-out See: *throw-out*.

folio aka **fo** A folio is a sheet folded in half to yield four pages and two leaves. The fold is with the grain. The resulting folio will have the grain parallel with the spine.

Folios can be units in binding, sewing through the fold-as-hinge. A folio can be slipped inside another folio to construct a quarto, rather than folding down a sheet to form a quarto. See: *quarto, sexto, octavo, duodecimo and z-fold.*

foredge 1. The front edge of a book. (pronounced forrej). 2. The edge of the side-cover and book block opposite the spine.

format The size, style, type page, margins, page set-up, et cetera.

forward In the direction on the sewing.†

forwarding After the book is sewn, forwarding is gluing the back, plowing, rounding and backing, sewing the endbands and attaching the boards. Forwarding is followed by covering and finishing.

gate fold Two facing fold-outs in a codex. Each fold-out is hinged on the foredges of an opened folio. When the gate fold is opened, or thrown-out, there are four facing pages, the two at each extreme extend beyond the book block.

gathering Assembling the folded signatures into the proper order for binding. See: *F&G's.*

grain The direction in which most fibers lie which corresponds with the direction the paper is made in commercial production machinery.

gutter 1. The blank space or inner margin, from printing area to binding.

half hitch A type of knot for tying-off, when there is only one loose end of thread: The needle slips under a stitch and is pulled until there is a small loop. The needle proceeds through the loop, before the thread is pulled tight. *Half hitch* is diagrammed on page 114.

head and **tail** The top and bottom of a book when stood upright. They are at right angles to the backbone or spine-edge and foredge.

head band/tail band Wrapping and beading decorative thread, usually of colored silk or cotton, at the head and tail of codices. Thread is wrapped around a core and periodically stitched into the book block. "Imitation" machine-made head bands are sold by the yard and pasted onto the backbone of commercial hard cover books.

NOTE: The term *headband* is often erroneously used, if the band described includes, or is specifically at the tail. Therefore, I use the term *endband,* rather than *headband,* as it includes the bands sewn at both the head and tail.

Hemp-Leaf Binding The stab binding also known as *Asa-No-Ha Toji.* There are four traditional Japanese stab bindings. The others are the *Yotsume Toji,* or *Japanese 4—Hole Binding;* the *Kikko Toji,* or *Tortoise-Shell;* and the *Koki Toji,* or *Noble Binding,* which is also referred to as the *Kangxi Binding,* after its reputed originator.

Stab sewings are described in *Books without Paste or Glue,* Volume I of *Non-Adhesive Binding.*

hinge-fold The folds on either side of the spine, delineating the side-covers from the spine-cover. See: *flat back cover.*

horizontal wrapper See: *wrapper.*

implied compound binding A inventive folding of pages or itinerary through a book that suggests a hybrid book structure of two of the same or differing types of books.

imposition The laying out of pages on a sheet, so that they will be in numerical order after the sheet is folded down as a folio or section or signature.

inner Between paired sewing stations. The approach to a station which is towards the center of the spine, rather than to the outer, which is near the spine-hinge. *Inner* should not be confused with the term *inside.*

inside The position on the valley side of a section, as opposed to the mountain peak, which is called the *outside.*

to the inside Toward the head or tail.†

inside bead In sewing *Endbands as Change-Over*, the sewing procedure results in beads on both sides of the packing. The bead on the spine side is referred to as the *spine-bead*. The bead facing the foredge is called the *inside bead*. See: *Two-Sided Beading*, page 139, *Exposed Spine Sewings*, Volume III *Non-Adhesive Binding*.

I suggest you look at the following book: *Headbands, How To Work Them*, by Jane Greenfield & Jenny Hille, published by Oak Knoll Books.

jaconette A thin coated fabric used to reinforce a spine or joint in a book box.

Japanese 4–Needle Sewing The Japanese name for this sewing is *Yamato Toji*. It is a 12th century binding, also referred to as the *Butterfly Sewing*. Sewing is across the spine, utilizing paired stations. Each needle spans, enters the next section, then cross inside to exit the other station. The *Japanese 4–Needle Sewing* is not to be confused with the stab binding called the *Japanese 4–Hole Binding*. The *Japanese 4–Needle Sewing* sewing is described on page 220, *Exposed Spine Sewings*, Volume III of *Non-Adhesive Binding*.

Japanese 4–Hole Binding Japanese stab binding also known as the *Yotsume Toji*. There are four traditional Japanese stab bindings. The others are the *Asa-No-Ha Toji*, or *Hemp-Leaf Binding*; the *Kikko Toji*, or *Tortoise-Shell*; and the *Koki Toji*, or *Noble Binding*, which is also referred to as the *Kangxi Binding*, after its reputed originator. Stab sewings are decribed in *Books without Paste or Glue*, Volume I, *Non-Adhesive Binding*. The *Japanese 4–Hole Stab Binding* is not to be confused with the sewing across the spine, called the *Japanese 4–Needle Sewing*.

jog To knock down and level to an edge, preferably at the head to keep text in registration.

Kangxi Binding Japanese name for the stab binding, named after its reputed originator. It is also known as the *Noble*, or the *Koki Toji*. There are four traditional Japanese stab bindings. The others are the *Yotsume Toji*, or *Japanese 4–Hole Binding*; the *Kikko Toji*, or *Tortoise-Shell*; the *Asa-No-Ha Toji*, or *Hemp-Leaf Binding*.

Stab sewings are decribed in *Books without Paste or Glue*, Volume I, *Non-Adhesive Binding*.

kerf or **kerf stations** Cuts made with a back saw across the section folds of an unsewn text. * See: *sewing stations*.

kettle or **kettle stitch** Sewing procedure of ending one section, changing direction of movement in adding the next. The sewing drops backwards and links, slips and climbs. True and false kettle stitches and link stitches in general are described on pages 25–31 in *Exposed Spine Sewings*, Volume III of *Non-Adhesive Binding*.

key a 2–pronged metal unit, about the size of a key. A key for each cord rests under the slot in the base of a sewing frame temporarily tying the cord while the sewing proceeds.

Kikko Toji Japanese name for the stab binding known as the *Tortoise-Shell Binding*. There are four traditional Japanese stab bindings. The others are the *Yotsume Toji*, or *Japanese 4–Hole Binding*; the *Asa-No-Ha Toji*, or *Hemp-Leaf Binding* and the *Koki Toji*, or the *Noble*, or the *Kangxi Binding*, after its reputed originator.

Stab sewings are decribed in *Books without Paste or Glue*, Volume I of *Non-Adhesive Binding*.

Koki Toji Japanese name for the stab binding known as the *Noble*, or the *Kangxi Binding*, after its reputed originator. There are four traditional Japanese stab bindings. The others are the *Yotsume Toji*, or *Japanese 4–Hole Binding*; the *Kikko Toji*, or *Tortoise-Shell*; the *Asa-No-Ha Toji*, or *Hemp-Leaf Binding*. Stab sewings are decribed in *Books without Paste or Glue*, Volume I of *Non-Adhesive Binding*.

lap To pass over a support or sewing thread.†

leaf 1. A sheet. 2. Two pages, back to back; a recto/verso.

link To pass under another thread.†

loop To circle around a support or sewing thread.†

moulding saw Backsaw or tenon saw used to cut the sewing stations when the book block is held in a finishing press.

Noble Binding Name of the Japanese stab binding known as the *Koki Toji,* or the *Kangxi Binding,* after its reputed originator. There are four traditional Japanese stab bindings. The others are the *Yotsume Toji,* or *Japanese 4—Hole Binding;* the *Kikko Toji,* or *Tortoise-Shell;* and the *Asa-No-Ha Toji,* or *Hemp-Leaf Binding.* Stab sewings are decribed in *Books without Paste or Glue,* Volume I of *Non-Adhesive Binding.*

octavo aka **8vo** 1. A sheet folded in half three times, to yield a section of 16 pages with 8 leaves. 2. Three folios, each slipped inside the other, to form a unit of sewing. A sextodecimo, or 16mo, has 32 pages with 16 leaves. See: *folio, quarto, sexto, octavo, duodecimo, sextodecimo* and *z-fold.* In folding down a sheet to form an octavo, the first fold is with the grain; the second is against and the third is with the grain. The resulting section will have the grain parallel with the spine.

one-of-a-kind A book conceived and executed as a single copy. The word *unique,* meaning "special" should not be used to define a single copy item, as the term *unique* applies to production work as well.

NOTE: Some librarians define a book as an item which must have more than one copy by definition. Consequently, they do not recognize or purchase ones-of-a-kind. On one occasion I was dismayed at this reasoning of a librarian who could not consider purchasing a one-of-a-kind. The librarian said it was the wrong department and said take it to the museum on campus to the sculpture curator! —What would happen if this librarian should happen to run across an ancient book, of which only that single copy survived? Would they say it no longer a "book", but now, sculpture?

1—on Sewing 1—on applies to sewing multi-section (multi-signature) sewings along the spine: In addition to using the kettle stations at the head and tail, every sewing station is used. The middle stations lap or loop the supports.

open ended Open ended stations refer to the use of the head and the tail as sewing stations. The support is not pierced. It is a passive station, that is, the thread wraps around the head or tail, marking the change-over.

opened folio The two facing pages at any point to which the codex is opened.

Oriental fold book See: *fold book.*

outer Towards the outside of paired sewing stations, rather than centrally, between. *Outer* should not be confused with the term *outside.*

outside The position on the mountain peak of a section, as opposed to the valley, which is called the inside.

to the outside Away from the head or tail.†

overhand knot Half a square knot. For instructions how to tie, see: *Knots,* page 50, *Books without Paste or Glue,* Volume I, *Non-Adhesive Binding;* and *Knots,* page 108, *Bookbinding for Book Artists.*

overhang cover A cover larger in size than the pages it encloses. The amount of the side-cover that extends beyond the book block, bordering the head, foredge and tail is called the *square.* See: *flush cover.*

pack To loop several times around.†

page 1. One side of an unfolded sheet. 2. That portion of a folio or section or signature bordered by folds and/or the edge of the sheet.

paired stations Sewing directly across the spine employs two sewing stations. Other paired stations along the spine are sewn independently. Each paired station uses one thread and two needles.

pamphlet 1. A one-section text. 2. A booklet. 3. Type of sewing for a booklet.

pamphlet sewing Type of sewing used to bind a booklet. See: page 57, *Books without Paste or Glue,* Volume I, *Non-Adhesive Binding* and page 16, *1—2—& 3—Section Sewings,* Volume II, *Non-Adhesive Binding.* and pages 134—139, *Bookbinding for Book Artists.*

The term "pamphlet ſtitch" should be avoided, as it is a sewing, not a ſtitching. *Pamphlet ſtitch sewing* is correct, but awkward. The pamphlet sewing uses a "*B*" ſtitch, as opposed to a *figure 8* ſtitch, described on pages 132–135, *1– 2– & 3–Section Sewings*, Volume II, *Non-Adhesive Binding*. See pages 133–139 in *Bookbinding for Book Artists*.

paſte See: *adhesive* and *wheat paste*.

perfect bound 1. Adhesive binding without sewing or ſtitching. 2. Binding of a book which has no sewing and no folds on the backbone. The book therefore has no sections, signatures or folios, only a ſtack of sheets. The back is glued. Commercial paperbacks are generally (imperfectly) perfect bound. Thus, unfortunately there is a general low eſteem for any book with paper covers. In the paſt, the main difference between trade books which were paperback and hard cover, was the latter was sewn. Now, many publishers are reducing the quality of their hard covers and are using perfect binding, rather than sewing them.

pleat An Oriental fold used to attach sections, rather than as a complete book in itself. Attachment is usually with a pamphlet sewing. *Pleat* is also known as a *concertina, concertina guard,* or *accordion fold.* See: *accordion pleat.*

ply In this text, the term is used as one piece of paper, rather than the process of making paper in layers. Two-ply is only used in this text to mean a sheet folded back upon itself for reinforcement, or two surfaces glued together. The term is never used to mean *duplex,* a type of commercially made paper with a different color on each side of the sheet.

production books Books made in an edition, whether by hand, or published (printed).

pull factor The characteriſtic of leather, some papers and fabrics to ſtretch when wet and to shrink or pull when they dry. In paſting these items to boards, it is not using a press, but the counter-balancing of the pull factor which prevents board warpage. See: *Warpage,* page 61, *Bookbinding for Book Artists.*

punch Metal cylindrical tool with sharpened hollow shaped end for cutting and solid head for ſtriking with a hammer to cut through paper. Shapes are usually various diameters of circles and, rarely, squares, diamonds, oblongs.

quarto aka **4to** 1. A sheet folded in half twice, to yield a section of four leaves or eight pages. 2. Two folios, one slipped inside the other, to form a unit of sewing. See: *folio, sexto, octavo, duodecimo, sextodecimo* and *z-fold.*
In folding down a sheet to form a quarto, the firſt fold is againſt the grain; the second is with the grain. The resulting section will have the grain parallel with the ſpine.

ream Five hundred sheets of paper.

recto/verso Two pages, back to back; a leaf. Recto is a right hand page. Verso is the back of that leaf, not the page facing the recto in the opened folio.
NOTE: Recto does not mean *front;* verso does not mean *back.* A recto or a verso is a front side when it is viewed. Each becomes a back when the page is turned and it is not in view. Recto/verso is convenient terminology for folding and collating signatures.

saddle wire or s**addle ſtitch** In commercial binding, to faſten a booklet by wiring it through the fold or the side of the single section. The machine is adjuſted to the thickness of the opened section and uses a ſpool of wire. It is looped through the section, cut and crimped, similar to ſtapling.

score 1. To indent with a bone folder, but not cutting. 2. A light surface cut made to facilitate folding or flexing in card or board. See: *crease.*

section 1. A sheet folded down to yield eight or more pages, such as a quarto, sexto or duodecimo. 2. Two or more loose folios compiled to form a quarto, sexto or duodecimo, et cetera. A section can be blank paper, or printed. If printed, then it is ſpecifically a *signature.*
NOTE: To avoid confusion of terms in this book, *section* is never used to mean a *portion,* or a *chapter* of the book.

NOTE 2: If the sheet has been printed, then folded down, it is referred to in printers' terminology as a *signature*. Any signature can be called a section, but only a section which has been printed is technically a signature. See: *signature*.

self cover A cover of the same paper as the text block.

sew a set To sew one more than one section on at a time.†

sewing 1—on See: *1—on*.

sewing path The journey of the needle and thread, in and out of the sewing stations, in constructing a sewing.

sewing stations 1. The mark, or the pierce along the spine-fold of the cover and the backbone of the section, or folio showing the positions of the sewing. The supports are the stations, rather than the holes. Each tape requires a hole on either side. The two holes per tape are not the sewing station, but merely the holes. The tape is the sewing station. 2. Path of the needle through paper to create the sewing on the spine. If made with a saw, they are called *kerf stations*. See: *sewn vs stitched*.

sewing 2—on See: *2—on*.

sewn vs **stitched** Sewing refers to the thread path along the valley and mountain peak, as opposed to set in from the fold. That is *stabbing*. Stabbing is stitching, not sewing. Path of the needle limited to the gutter is not "stitching", but sewing. Sewing is done with *stitches*. Therefore, "stitches" is appropriate when referring to sewing in the fold, but *stitching* equals stabbing.

sexto aka **6to** A sheet folded down to create a section of 6 leaves, or 12 pages. The sheet is first folded against the grain with a *Z*-fold, dividing the sheet into thirds. That is then folded in half with the grain. See: *folio, quarto, octavo, duodecimo, sextodecimo* and *z-fold*.

sextodecimo aka **16mo** A sheet folded down to create a section of 32 pages with 16 leaves. See: *folio, quarto, sexto, octavo, duodecimo and z-fold*.

sheet 1. An unfolded piece of paper. 2. A leaf. 3. The full size of the paper before being folded down into a folio or section. 4. In single sheet bindings, a sheet is two pages back to back; a recto/verso. A sheet is one piece of paper, consisting of two pages. It is not a section, since it has no fold as a hinge. Sheets can be folded down as folios or sections. Without being folded down, a sheet can still be a unit of sewing. However, a sheet is limited as a book element: The full sheet, without a fold, can only be used in a stab binding, a single sheet pamphlet sewing, or an album binding. All of these are described in *Books without Paste or Glue*, Volume I, *Non-Adhesive Binding*.

side-cover Front and back cover, as opposed to the spine.

signature A specific type of section, differing from the general term of *section*, in that a signature is a sheet that first has been printed, then folded down. A signature is a section, but a section is not necessarily a signature. Signature is a printer's term; section is a binder's term.

simple/compound Terms used only to differentiate basic bindings from hybrids constructed by combining two or more basic types of books.

slip (v.) To pass under itself.†

slips (n.) The ends of tapes, cords, or supporting straps attached to the covers.

slit Slit is a severing with a knife. It has length, but no width. See: *slot*.

slot A slot is an opening, constructed by two slits, parallel and no more than about 1/8" apart. Slots, rather than slits, are needed to accommodate the thickness of the inserted photographs, or weaving a strap or flap, to help prevent buckling of the sheet.

Smythe-sewn Commercial method of machine-stitching a book. See: *sewn vs stitched* in the Glossary.

spacers..A stub added to the mountain peak to be sewn with the folio. It expands the spine the same amount as the (photo) insert for that page. After the inserts are added, the foredge of the album will not bulge wider than the spine.

span To climb and change over to another section.†

spine or **spine-cover** 1. The depth of a bound book, connecting the two side-covers. The spine-covers the back, or backbone. 2. That part of the book that is visible when it is on the shelf. It is sometimes referred to as the *backstrip*.

spine-bead In sewing *Endbands as Change-Over*, the sewing procedure results in beads on both sides of the packing. The bead on the spine side is referred to as the *spine-bead*. The bead facing the foredge is called the *inside bead*. See: *Two-Sided Beading*, page 139, *Exposed Spine Sewings*, Volume III of *Non-Adhesive Binding*.

spine tab A strip woven onto the spine.

square or **square of the book** 1. The projection of the side-cover beyond the book block. 2. Only the part of the cover that extends beyond the book block and borders the head, foredge and tail. The total surface of the cover is referred to as an *overhang cover*.

square knot Reef knot See: *Knots*, page 108, *Bookbinding for Book Artists*, or *Knots*, page 60, *Books without Paste or Glue*, Volume I, *Non-Adhesive Binding*, for instructions how to tie.

station 1. A place where the sewing stops to attach a section to other sections or to a common support or to both.† 2. Passive sewing stations is the use of the head and tail as change-over. This is referred to as *open ended*. In diagramming sewings with endbands as change-cover, I assign the support, usually cords, at the head and the tail a sewing station number. They are not pierced sewing stations, but passive, that is, open ended. This makes for easy reference in the drawn illustrations. See: *paired stations*.

stitching See: *sewn vs stitched* in the Glossary.

strap Horizontal supports across the spine onto which supported sewings are made. The strap is usually separate from the cover and attached after the sewing. In the *Buttonhole Binding*, the straps are sections of the spine.

stub Cutting out a page/s from a Tight Back, close to the spine-edge, after it is bound to make space for an insert which will not bulge the spine. For a Flat Back, *spacers* are used.

suminagashi "The original and easiest method of marbling, inks flowing freely on water, producing meandering lines of color." —Diane Vogel Maurer with Paul Maurer, *Marbling, A Complete Guide to Creating Beautiful Patterned Papers and Fabrics.*[1]

super Super is a kind of stiffened gauze, sometimes referred to as *tarlatan*, *crash*, or *mull*.

supported sewings Sections sewn together around common straps, tapes or cords, which go across the back, perpendicular to it. The supports are generally attached to side-covers.

swell Thickness added to the backbone by the accumulation of sewing threads or any guards. See: *Choosing the Thread*, page 217 and 382, *Bookbinding for Book Artists*. Also, see: *Swelling the Backbone*, page 47, *Books without Paste or Glue*, Volume I, *Non-Adhesive Binding* and *expanding the spine pleat*, page 226 and 272, also in *Books without Paste or Glue*.

tab A narrow strip woven as means of attachment.

tail 1. The bottom edge of a book when standing upright. 2. The edge opposite the head and perpendicular to the spine and foredge.

tail band See: *headband* and *endband*.

NOTE: The term *headband* is often erroneously used, if the band described includes, or is specifically at the tail. Therefore, I use the term *endband*, rather than *headband*, as it includes the bands sewn at both the head and tail.

tapes Woven fabric supports, usually linen, onto which the sewing occurs. They are usually 1/4" wide and always are non-adhesive.

tenon saw Moulding saw or backsaw used to cut the sewing stations when the book block is held in a finishing press.

tension Regulation of tautness. Uniform shape and tautness is desired. Betsy Palmer Eldridge says that the tension varies with each sewer. It varies even if one person stops for a break. It is best to start and sew the entire book at once. The operative word is *snug*. Tension should not be loose, but neither should it be tight. I find that men tend to sew too tightly. Link stitches lose their teardrop shape when pulled tightly.

text block See: **book block.**

tie-off Joining two threads with a knot at the beginning or end of a sewing.

ties-down The threads which extend from the endband, in on the spine to the next station to anchor the endband. The tie-off may enter a station on the section, or link under a support at that station.

throw-out A fold-out. The action of unfolding of a fold-out or throw-out is referred to as *thrown-out*. A throw-out might be a single fold, gate fold, or any other page which is larger than the book block and folded down for storage. Traditionally refers to a fold-out at the end of a book containing a map. The map is thrown-out, so that it remains visible while any other page in the book can be read and turned.

A *throw-out* has the fold at the foredge. A *throw-down* has the fold at the tail. A *throw-up* has the fold at the head.

Tortoise-Shell Binding The Japanese stab binding, also known as the *Kikko Toji*. There are four traditional Japanese stab bindings. The others are the *Yotsume Toji*, or *Japanese 4—Hole Binding*; the *Asa-No-Ha Toji*, or *Hemp-Leaf Binding* and the *Koki Toji*, or *Noble Binding*. The *Noble Binding* is also referred to as the *Kangxi Binding*, after its reputed originator. Stab sewings are decribed in *Books without Paste or Glue*, Volume I, *Non-Adhesive Binding*.

2—on Sewing 2-on applies to sewing multi-section (multi-signature) sewings along the spine: With the exception of the first two and final two, sections (signatures) the remaining sections (signatures) do not use all the sewing stations, except for the kettle stations at the head and tail. The sewing alternates back and forth between two sections being sewn on at once. Therefore, not all the middle stations are used.

types of books There are four basic types of books, determined by how they are bound:

1. at one point is called a *fan*.
2. at two points is the *Venetian blind*. The fan and blind are used by South Sea Island cultures.
3. across one edge, is the western *codex*.
4. alternate folds back and forth upon itself is the *Oriental fold book*. The other three types of books are sewn. The fold book's binding is mechanical.

unsupported sewings Sections sewn directly together, without common straps, tapes or cords.

Venetian blind A book, bound at two points. One of the four types of books, the others being the fan, codex and the fold book. Fans and blinds are used by South Sea Island cultures.

verso See: *recto/verso.*

vertical wrapper See: **wrapper.**

wheat paste An adhesive, like rice paste, used to adhere leather to the spine and decorative papers to the board. For formulas of making wheat paste, see: *Wheat Paste*, page 54, in *Bookbinding for Book Artists.*

with the grain Folding paper parallel to the grain of the paper.

wrapped stations Head and tail of the sections used as sewing stations. Passive, as opposed to a pierced or slit stations. Open ended.

wrapper Paper covering board covers without the use of adhesives. See: *Flat Back with Boards*, page 244, *Books without Paste or Glue*, Volume I, *Non-Adhesive Binding and Separately Wrapped Boards*, page 246, *Books without Paste or Glue*.

Yamato Toji Japanese name for the 4–needle sewing, across the spine. It is also referred to as the *Japanese 4–Needle Sewing*, as well as the *Butterfly Sewing*. It is sewn across the spine, utilizing paired stations. Each needle spans, enters the next section, then cross inside to exit the other station. *Yamato Toji* is described on page 220, *Exposed Spine Sewings*, Volume III, *Non-Adhesive Binding*.

Yamato Toji, or *Japanese 4–Needle Sewing* is not to be confused with the the *Japanese 4–Hole Stab Binding*, which is described on page 75, in Volume I of *Non-Adhesive Binding, Books without Paste or Glue*.

Yotsume Toji Japanese name for the stab binding also known as the *Japanese 4–Hole Stab Binding*. There are four traditional Japanese stab bindings. The others are the *Asa-No-Ha Toji*, or *Hemp-Leaf Binding*; the *Kikko Toji*, or *Tortoise-Shell*; and the *Koki Toji*, or *Noble Binding*, which is also referred to as the *Kangxi Binding*, after its reputed originator.

Stab sewings are decribed in *Books without Paste or Glue*, Volume I, *Non-Adhesive Binding*.

Z-Fold Procedure to create a 12 and a 24 page section. The sheet is first folded in thirds, against the grain (the *Z*-fold). Folding the *Z*-fold in half once, with the grain, gives a sexto. Folding the sexto in half with the grain gives 12 leaves, or 24 pages. It is called a *duodecimo*. See: *folio, quarto,sexto, octavo, duodecimo* and *sextodecimo*.

INDEX of TERMS

CENTIMETERS TO INCHES

All the photo reproductions list the dimensions metrically, since most countries use the metric system. I have had complaints from some from the States that dimensions of the captions are listed in centimeters, not inches. One person even sent a chart for me to place in the index, so people like she can convert the listed dimensions to inches. This is the chart:

Icm =	0.39"	26	10.24	51	20.08	76	29.92
2	0.79	27	10.63	52	20.47	77	30.31
3	1.18	28	11.02	53	20.87	78	30.71
4	1.57	29	11.42	54	21.26	79	31.10
5	1.97	30	11.81	55	21.65	80	31.50
6	2.36	31	12.20	56	22.05	81	31.89
7	2.76	32	12.60	57	22.44	82	32.28
8	3.15	33	12.99	58	22.83	83	32.68
9	3.54	34	13.39	59	23.23	84	33.07
10	3.94	35	13.78	60	23.62	85	33.46
11	4.33	36	14.17	61	24.02	86	33.86
12	4.72	37	14.57	62	24.41	87	34.25
13	5.12	38	14.96	63	24.80	88	34.65
14	5.51	39	15.35	64	25.20	89	35.04
15	5.91	40	15.75	65	25.59	90	35.43
16	6.30	41	16.14	66	25.98	91	35.83
17	6.69	42	16.54	67	26.38	92	36.22
18	7.09	43	16.93	68	26.77	93	36.61
19	7.48	44	17.32	69	27.17	94	37.01
20	7.87	45	17.72	70	27.56	95	37.40
21	8.27	46	18.11	71	27.95	96	37.80
22	8.66	47	18.50	72	28.35	97	38.19
23	9.06	48	18.90	73	28.74	98	38.58
24	9.45	49	19.29	74	29.13	99	38.98
25	9.84	50	19.69	75	29.53	100	39.37

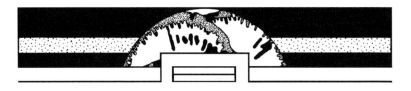

INDEX of ILLUSTRATIONS

INDEX OF NAMES

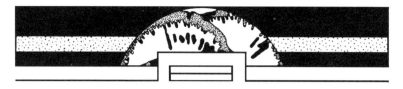

REFERENCE OF PHOTOGRAPHIC
ILLUSTRATIONS

All digital scans are by Keith Smith. All photographs scanned are by Keith Smith, unless, otherwise stated.

Page 14, Fred Jordan, June 1998. Sample full leather Tight Back with blind tooling.

Page 16 and 274, Fred Jordan, June 1998. *Example 4*, half leather Tight Back.

Page 23, Fred Jordan, *Binding Tools*, 1979. Quarter leather Pamphlet Binding with Boards.

Page 24, Todd Pattison, *The Little Library*, 1995. A found half leather Raised Cord binding, altered.

Page 25, Fred Jordan, full leather Tight Back, June 1997. The book is *The Perfect Tribute*, by Mary Raymond Shipman Andrews, 1908.

Page 26, Keith Smith, *Bobby*, Book Number 100, Offset in 3 colors in an edition of 50. Hand bound by the artist, Flat Back, half leather with leather hinges. Published by Nexus Press, Atlanta, 1985. Digital scan by Brad Pease.

Page 27, Scott McCarney, *Art: Search and Self Discovery*. Full cloth, found Hollow Back binding, altered. 1993. Digital scan by Brad Pease.

Page 28, Philip Zimmermann, *Civil Defense*, Space heater Multiples, 1983, 1984. Pamphlet sewing, paper cover.

Page 42, Keith Smith, Book 81, 1981. Quarter cloth Flat Back. Digital scan by Brad Pease.

Page 47, Keith Smith, quarter leather blank Tight Back album with paste papers. 1998.

Page 53, Fred Jordan, *Hatches*, 1983. Bound Raised Cords, full leather, with gold tooling. Digital scan by Brad Pease.

Page 57, Adéle Outteridge, Helen Sanderson and Charlotte Drake-Brockman, untitled, 1997. Photographed by Adéle Outteridge.

Page 65, Adéle Outteridge, *Tea Bag Book II*, one-of-a-kind, 1994–95. Photographed by Adéle Outteridge.

Page 85, Judith Haswell, *Sing Weaving*, 1996. Constructed and photographed by Elizabeth Steiner.

Page 92, Cropped photograph of Scott McCarney, Photographed by Judy Natal, 1994.

Page 108, Adéle Outteridge, *Threaded Sphere*, one-of-a-kind, 1995. Photographed by Adéle Outteridge.

Page 122, 123, Adéle Outteridge, *Gaia*, one-of-a-kind, 1997. Photographed by Adéle Outteridge.

Pages 126, 127, 128, Keith Smith, *Back and Forth*, Book Number 108. 1985. Self published, offset in an edition of 200, hand bound by the artist. Pamphlet Binding with Boards with quarter leather spine and leather hinges.

Page 132, Fred Jordan, full leather Pamphlet Binding with Boards, 1979. *The Edward and catherine O'Donnell Collection of Modern Literature.*

Page 137, Gary Frost, *Three Bookbindings*, 1993. Sewn Boards Binding, self published. See *Note 1*, page 379.

Page 173, Keith Smith, Book 53, 1974. One-of-a-kind quarter cloth Flat Back. Digital scan by Brad Pease.

Page 174, Barbara Mauriello, *Laced Book/Box*, 1997. Barbara Mauriello, *Amen, The Thirteenth Day*, 1997. Photographed by Barbara Mauriello.

Page 196, Willyum Rowe, *sure as death*, offset edition of 500, published by Space Heater Editions, 1986. Cased-In by Philip Zimmermann.

Page 208, William Drendel, *Laborem Exercens–The Encyclical of John Paul II on Dignity of Human Work*, 1995. One-of-a-kind. Photographed by William Drendel. Digital scan by Brad Pease.

Page 209, William Drendel, *Japanese Fan Book*, 1990. Photographed by William Drendel. Digital scan by Brad Pease.

Page 215, Fred Jordan, quarter leather prototype for Tight Back as described in this manual with no paring of leather, 1997.

Page 225, Elizabeth Steiner, *Moeraki Boulders*, 1993. Photographed by Elizabeth Steiner.

Page 236, William Drendel, *Claire's Beau*, 1993. Digital scan by Brad Pease.

Page 240, Gail Ferris, traditionally sewn headbands. Digital scans by Brad Pease.
Top: The half leather Tight Back is *Coaching Days and Coaching Ways*, W. Outram Tristram, London Macmillan and Co. and New York, 1888. Rebound 1995.
Middle: *An Anthology of Revolutionary Poetry*, Compiled and Edited by Marcus Graham, First Limited Edition, 1929. The Active press, Inc. New York, NY. Full leather.
Bottom: *The Innocents Abroad*, or *The New Pilgrims' Progress*, Mark Twain, A. Roman & Company, San Francisco, Cal. 1873. Quarter leather.

Page 241, Jenny Hille, All around Greek headband, 1991, Jenny Hille, Greco-Byzantine models, 1989. Photographed by Jenny Hille.

Page 246, Keith Smith, *Structure of the Visual Book*, Book Number 95. Bound December 1997 in quarter leather Tight Back, with onlay on leather and inlaid papers on the board.

Page 289, Elizabeth Steiner, *Which Way?* 1997. Photographed by Elizabeth Steiner.

Page 295, Penny Carey-Wells, *Not Flowing, Draining*, 1994. Photographed by Penny Carey-Wells.

Page 298, Penny Carey-Wells, *Last Year's Calendar*, 1989. Photographed by Penny Carey-Wells.

Page 299, Penny Carey-Wells, *Expanding File of Industrial Relations*, *Work Place Safety and Equal Pay for Women*, 1994. Photographed by Penny Carey-Wells.

Page 300, Keith Smith, half leather Tight Back binding with photo inlay on cover, 1997.

Page 329, Fred Jordan, *Gothic & Renaissance Bookbindings*, 1929. Bound Raised Cords, full leather, with blind tooling.

Page 333, Scott McCarney, found Hollow Back, altered. 1995. Digital scan by Brad Pease.

Page 354, Keith Smith, Book 183, *A Make-Believe Book of Poetry*, 1997. Quarter cloth Pamphlet Binding with Boards.

Page 363, Keith Smith, *Keith Smith at Home*, Book Number 82, 1982. Quarter cloth Flat Back binding with photo and book paper inlays.

Page 367, Fred Jordan, prototype for Tight Back as described in this manual with no paring of leather, 1997.

Page 373, Todd Pattison, full leather binding of *With It, Book 134* by Keith Smith, 1997.

ABBREVIATED LIST OF PAPER AND LEATHER SOURCES

Aiko's Import Art Materials Attn Charles Izui 3347 N Clark St Chicago IL 60657. 773/404-5600
Tues-Sat 10-5 & mail order. Large variety of Japanese papers.

Archival Quality Materials University Products Inc 517 Main St Box 101 Holyoke MA 01041-0101. 1-800/628-1912 FAX 1-800/532-9281. Customer service & questions 1-800/762-1165.
Binding equipment, tools, display cases & supplies for conservation, restoration, preservation. Catalogue available.

Archivart Archival Products for Conservation & Restoration 7 Caesar Place Box 428 Moonachie NJ 07074. 201-804-8986 & 1-800/804-8428. FAX 201/935-5964.
Acid-free matboard, lining papers, endleaf, tissues, corrugated, folder stock.

Art Outfitters Attn Kerry Kemp 1201 Main St Box 97 Little Rock AR 72203. 501/374-4323 FAX 501/374-4380 PenCraft@aol.com
Supplies & one-day workshops in bookbinding & calligraphy.

Art Supply 2711 Main St Houston TX 77002 Attn Vikki Trammell

713/652-5028 FAX 713/552-5773 artsupply@swbell.net

Artexte 460 St Catherine St W Ste 508 Montréal QUE H3B 1A7 Canada 514/874-0049 FAX 514/874-0316
Contemporary visual arts documentation centre. Distribution service of exhibition catalogues & Artextes Editions.

Artist & Craftsman Supply 540 Deering St Portland ME 04103. 1-800/876-8076. 207/772-7272 FAX 207/772-0001.
Cotton pulp, glues, exotic papers & boards. Catalogue available.

Ashe Artist Materials 1316 Pacific Ave Venice CA 90291-3608. 213/821-4720
Printmaking & art papers.

Bookcraft Supplies Attn Mrs D M Tomlinson 273 Longhurst Ln Mellor Cheshire England SK6 5PW 061/427-7348
Bookcloth, leather, marble papers.

Bookmakers 6001 66th Ave Ste 101 Riverdale MD 20737. 301/459-3384
Supplies & equipment for hand bookbinding, book & paper conservation. A selection of papers & leathers.

Buch und Papierrestaurung Attn Martin Strebel Bahnhofstrasse 15

CH-5502 Hunzenschwil Switzerland 062 897 39 70 FAX 062 897 00 46
Bücher graphiken karten pergamente.

Buntin Reid Paper 1330 Courtney Pk Dr E Mississauga ONT L5T 1K5 Canada 905/670-1351. *Machine made paper.*

The Calligraphy Shoppe Attn David Betts 7296 Coolidge Rd Ft Myers FL 33912. 1-800/592-3887 FAX 941/267-7854.
Bookbinding & calligraphy supplies. Mail order. Books on binding. Workshops. Full catalogue available $3.

Carriage House Paper Donna & Elaine Koretsky 79 Guernsey St Brooklyn NY 11222-3111. 1-800/669-8781 718/599-7857 FAX 718/599-7857
Molds & deckles, fibers & pulp, equipment, supplies, books, handmade paper, studio rental & workshops.

Catherine's Rare Papers The Arizona Center 455 N 3rd St Ste 239 Phoenix AZ 85004 602/252-6960.
Rare & exotic handmade papers from around the world. Production paper mill specializing in papers handmade from desert plant fibers. Price list & swatch books available.

Colophon Book Arts
Supply Inc
Attn Nancy Altus Morains
3611 Ryan Rd SE
Lacey WA 98503-3860
360/459-2940
FAX 360/459/2945
www.thegrid.net/colophon

Commanchero Traders
Paul & Bonnie Range
Rt2 Box 511 Burnet TX
78611. 512/756-8844
*Source for brain-tanned elk,
vegetable-tanned deer & other
cured game skins.*

Conservation Materials
1395 Coreg St Ste 110
Box 2884 Sparks NV
89431. 1-800/733-
5283. 702/331-0582
*Materials, supplies, tools for the
professional conservator &
archivist.*

Curry's Art Store Ltd
756 Yonge St Toronto
ONT M4Y 2B9 Canada
416/967-6666.

Davey Company
164 Laidlaw Ave
Box 8128 Jersey City NJ
07306. 201/653-0606.
Book board.

Dieu Donné Papermill Inc
433 Broome St New
York NY 10013-2622.
212/226-0573
FAX 212/226-6088.
ddpaper@yorick.nycy-
bernex.net
*Handmade paper, custom pulp
& papermaking supplies, class-
es/workshops, studio rental,
internships, exhibitions of
paperworks & artist books, lec-
tures/demos & kids' programs.*

Elica's Paper 1801 Fourth
St Berkeley CA 94710
510/845-9530
FAX 510/845/-5619
Selection of Japanese papers.

Essence Du papier
4160 rue St Denis

Montreal QUE
H2W 2M5 Canada
514/288-9691
Marbled paper.

Falkiner Fine Papers Ltd
76 Southampton Row
London England WC1B
4AR. 01-831 1151.
*Fine selection of papers with sets
of swatches available. Also mail
order.*

Harcourt Bindery
51 Melcher St Boston
MA 02210.
617/542-5858
FAX 617/451-9058
*Imported cloth, leather, tools,
supplies & non-acidic marbled
papers. Catalogue available.*

Harmatan Leather Ltd
Westfield Ave,
Higham Ferrers
Northamptonshire
NN9 8Ax England
0933 312471
FAX 0933 412242

Hollander's at Kerrytown
407 N Fifth Ave
Ann Arbor MI 48104
313/741-7531.
*Over 500 decorative papers,
bookcloth, miscellaneous bookbinding supplies (pva glue, awls,
thread, needles board, etc).
Workshops in binding, origami.*

Hollinger Corp
Box 8360
4410 Overview Dr
Fredericksburg VA
22404. 703/898-7300.
1-800/634-0491
FAX 703/898-8073 & 1-
800/947-8814
*Archival cases, sleeves, board,
labels, boxes, folders.
Preservation/Encap-sulation
equipment & supplies.*

The Japanese Paper Place
Attn Nancy Jacobi
887 Queen St W
Toronto ONT M6J 1G5
Canada 416/703-0089

FAX 416/703-0163
Fine papers, brushes & paste.

Kate's Paperie 8 W 13th St
New York NY 10011.
212/633-0570
FAX 212/366-6532
*Papers, gift wrap & ribbon,
photo albums, stationery. Paper
swatch program $1.75 to 2.75.*

Kelly Paper 1441 E 16th St
Los Angeles CA 90021
213/749-1311
www.kellypaper.com
Commercial paper in small lots.

Los Angeles Art Supply
2130 S Sawtelle Blvd #210
Los Angeles CA 90025.
213/312-6880
Printmaking & art papers.

Lee Scott McDonald Inc
523 Medford Box 264
Charlestown MA 02129.
617/242-2505
FAX 617/242-8825
*"For all your handmade paper
needs" including marbling supplies. Catalogue available.*

Diane Maurer Hand
Marbled Papers Box 78
Water St Spring Mills PA
16875. 814/422-8651
FAX 814/422-7858
*Hand marbled papers. Supplies
for marbling & paste papers. 1
day workshops.*

Moore & Pearsall Leathers
Ltd 47 Front St E
Toronto ONT M5E 1B3
Canada 416/363-5881
Binding supplies & leathers.

Iris Nevins P O Box 429
Johnsonburg NJ 07846
908/813-8617
FAX 908/813-3431
*Hand marbled papers custom
retail & wholesale. Include
postage stamp when requesting
ordering information.*

Oregon Art Supply 720 E
13th Ave Eugene OR
97401. 541/683-2787

Beautiful papers & book art supplies from around the world.

Ott's Discount Art Supply
714 Greenville Blvd
Greenville NC 27858
1-800/356-3289
Art & graphic supplies at the best prices anywhere. Save up to 75% off everyday. Catalogue.

Paper Arts Mill & Studio
Attn C. Grey 930 W
23rd St Ste 16 Tempe
Industrial Pk II Tempe
AZ 85282-1820.
602/966-1988
FAX 602/966-2628
paperart@primenet.com
http://www.paperarts.co
m/rotall/
Exotic handmade decorative acid-free commercial fine art papers, bookbinding, paper-making, casting, supplies, paper mill, made to order pulp, work-shops, tools, custom embossers, chops, wax & seals, creative invitations, stationery, gifts, books, retail, mail order cata-logue $2 shipping.

Paper Routes Fine Art
Materials 3333 Elm St
Dallas TX 75226
214/748-9322
Papers & unique inventory of fine art materials.

Paper Trails
48006 St Andrew's Rd
Pendleton OR 97801
541/278-9322
paper@oregontrail.net
Handmade paper from the foothills of the Blue Mountains of Eastern Oregon.
www.papertrails.com

Papers!
3019 Central Ave W
Albuquerque NM 87106.
505/254-1434
FAX 505/260-1133

la Papeterie Saint Gilles
304 rue Felix Antoine
Savard CP112 St Joseph
De La Rive QUE G0A
3Y0 Canada
Handmade paper.

Papierladen
Attn Jonathan Osthoff
Schellingstrasse 71
80799 München
Germany
089/288 1030
FAX 089 288 10321
Papers including hand-made & marbled. Binding supplies & lit-erature pertaining to paper & bookbinding.

Royalwood Ltd
517 Woodville Rd
Mansfield OH 44907
419/526-1630
1-800/526-1630
FAX 419/526-1618
Waxed, colored Irish linen thread, 2, 3, 4 & 7-ply, in 30 colors. Color chart available $2.

Vicki Schober Co
2363 North Mayfair Rd
Milwaukee WI 53226.
414/476-8000
FAX 414/476-8041
1-800-541-7699
Specialty papers & boards to serve the graphic arts, fine arts, photography & picture frame industries. Catalogue available of papers & books.

Daniel Smith Inc
4130 First Ave S Seattle
WA 98134-2302
206/223-9599 Customer
service 1-800/426-6740
US & Canada
Mail order variety of supplies & tools.

Talas 568 Broadway Ste 107
New York NY 10012
212/219-0770
FAX 212/219-0735
Binding supplies, papers, leather, tools & equipment. Catalogue $5.

Twinrocker Handmade
Paper
Kathyrn & Howard Clark
100 E Third St Box 413
Brookston IN 47923
317/563-3119 & 3210
Professional hand mill making a large selection of papers custom made to order & on hand retail by the sheet. Individuals & groups can receive quantity dis-counts & monthly mailings of current inventory with sample book or swatch set by joining Twinrocker Studio Services. (Free brochure.) Papers for let-terpress, binding, drawing & pastel, printmaking, calligraphy, watercolor, stationery & invita-tions.

The Two Rivers Paper Co
Attn Jim Patterson
Pitt Mill Roadwater,
Watchet, Somerset
TA23 0QS England
Watchet (0984) 41028
FAX Watchet (0984)
40282. *Handmade water-colour paper "Tub Sized-Loft Dried".*

BOOKS-on-BOOKS

CONCEPT

Structure of the Visual Book, keith a smith *BOOKS,* Third Edition 1994, discusses concepts of ordering a book of pictures by means of a group, series, or sequence. Pacing is stressed by composing the pages as well as the individual pictures. Utilizing the space between pictures is part of the awareness of time in books. 240 pages with 198 photographic illustrations by 53 book artists. $25
ISBN 0-9637682-1-2

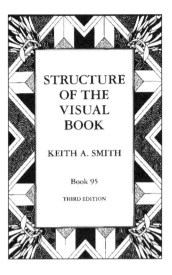

CONCEPT

Text in the Book Format, Second Edition, 1995, is a concern for conceiving text as a book experience. This differs from writing a running manuscript or the single sheet format. A book experience cannot be fully revealed in a recitation but demands holding the physical object and turning pages conceived as part of the content. This approach does not treat the book format as a vessel, but allows writing to emanate from the inherent properties of the book—the opposite of sticking words into the object. 128 pages. $17.50
ISBN 0-9637682-3-9

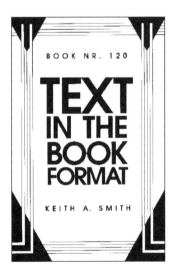

All the books are printed on archival paper. Available either as Smythe sewn paperback, or, in sheets, folded and gathered sections, if you wish to hand bind your own copy.

How To Bind
Non—Adhesive Binding, Volume I:
Books without Paste or Glue, keîth a smîth
BOOKS, Third Edîtion, 1994.
Introdučtion covers binding, paper,
sewing, knots and tools. This is followed by detailed wrîtten
inštručtions for 32 simple to com-
plex sewings. The procedures are
also presented in 250 drawings, diagrammed štep by štep. 50 photographic reprodučtions of bindings
by 22 binders. Source sečtion contains addresses of suppliers of
papers, tools and equîpment; workshops; guilds; dealers, book štores
and periodicals. 320 pages.
$30
ISBN 0-9637682-0-4

How To Bind
Non—Adhesive Binding, Volume II:
1— 2— & 3—Sečtion Sewings, keîth a smîth
BOOKS, Firšt Edîtion, 1995. Wrîtten
and drawn inštručtions for 122
sewings which yield four, to perhaps
a hundred pages imposed as one,
two or three sečtions. Almošt all of
these sewings on continuous limp
paper supports were devised by
Smîth, as the book was wrîtten.
Photos of bindings by 28 contemporary binders and artîšts. 320 pages.
$30
ISBN 0-9637682-2-0

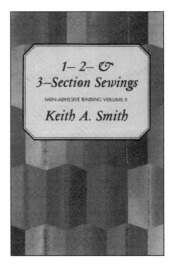

HOW TO BIND
Non—Adhesive Binding, Volume III:
Exposed Spine Sewings, keíth a smíth
BOOKS, Firſt Edítion, 1995.
Variations on raised support sewings
wíth pack cords, or endbands as
change—over, rather than using
kettle ſtítches. Descríptions of
sewing across the ſpine include
2—Needle Coptic, Greek Binding,
Celtic Weave and Caterpillar. Moſt
of the sewings were devised by Smíth
as the book was wrítten. Nine various Coptic sewings are described.
Photographic illuſtrations by contemporary binders are shown.
320 pages.
$30
ISBN 0-9637682-4-7

Individuals or stores can order directly from keith a smith *BOOKS.*
Group Discounts available for people ordering 6 or more assorted titles.
Email for information, or check the web site.

To order, or for a free brochure on all titles, contact:
Keith Smith, 22 Cayuga Street, Rochester, NY 14620-2153
Telephone or FAX: 716 473 6776
or Email: ksbooks@netacc.net

Web Site: http://net2.netacc.net/~ksbooks

COLOPHON

BOOK NUMBER 181
is a collaboration between Fred Jordan and Keith Smith. This book was begun in November 1996 on a Power Computer PowerTower Pro 225 and completed on a Power Macintosh G3. There was no running manuscript. Text was formatted as it was written, using Quark XPress 3.3. Drawn illustrations were imported from Macromedia Freehand 5.5 and Adobe Photoshop 4.0. Books and photographs were scanned on a Nikon Scantouch, using Adobe PhotoShop 4.0.

BOOKBINDING for BOOK ARTISTS
was periodically proofed on a Hewlett Packard LaserJet 4MV. The book was sent to the printer on-disk, postscript, using Iomega Jaz 1GB removable cartridges, for direct platemaking: 1200 dots per inch for the type and 150 line screen for the drawings and digital scans.

Typeface is Mrs. Eaves from Emigré. Drawn and photographic illustrations are by the author, except for the photographs listed on page 415. Headers and dingbats are from *Art Deco Spot Illustrations and Motifs* by Willyum Rowe, Dover Publications, 1985.

BOOK NUMBER 181
cover design and title page is by Scott McCarney.

This first printing of the First Edition is offset in 3000 copies on Finch Vellum 80 lb. text and cover with matte film lamination. The book is Smythe sewn, paperback.

An additional 200 copies are available unbound in sheets, folded and gathered, for those who might wish to hand bind their own copy of this book.

Keith A. Smith & Fred A. Jordan
June 1998

KE◉TH